The Kinds of Poetry I Want

T0367136

The Kinds of
Poetry I Want

Essays & Comedies

Charles Bernstein

THE UNIVERSITY OF CHICAGO PRESS, CHICAGO & LONDON

The University of Chicago Press, Chicago 60637
The University of Chicago Press, Ltd., London
© 2024 by Charles Bernstein
All rights reserved. No part of this book may be used or reproduced
in any manner whatsoever without written permission, except in
the case of brief quotations in critical articles and reviews. For more
information, contact the University of Chicago Press, 1427 East
60th Street, Chicago, IL 60637.
Published 2024
Printed in the United States of America

33 32 31 30 29 28 27 26 25 24   1 2 3 4 5

ISBN-13: 978-0-226-83608-9 (cloth)
ISBN-13: 978-0-226-83609-6 (paper)
ISBN-13: 978-0-226-83610-2 (e-book)
DOI: https://doi.org/10.7208/chicago/9780226836102.001.0001

Page 347: Charles Bernstein and David Antin (May 15, 2011).
Photograph: © Alan Thomas.

Library of Congress Cataloging-in-Publication Data

Names: Bernstein, Charles, 1950– author.
Title: The kinds of poetry I want : essays & comedies / Charles Bernstein.
Description: Chicago : The University of Chicago Press, 2024. | Includes
    bibliographical references and index.
Identifiers: LCCN 2024014451 | ISBN 9780226836089 (cloth) | ISBN 9780226836096
    (paperback) | ISBN 9780226836102 (ebook)
Subjects: LCSH: Poetry—History and criticism. | Criticism.
Classification: LCC PN1136 .B426 2024 | DDC 811/.54—dc23/eng/20240402
LC record available at https://lccn.loc.gov/2024014451

♾ This paper meets the requirements of ANSI/NISO Z39.48-1992
(Permanence of Paper).

You'd never know it, but buddy I'm a kind of poet
And I've got a lot of things to say.

Johnny Mercer

CONTENTS

FOREWORD

Twenty-Five Sentences Containing the Words "Charles Bernstein"

Paul Auster

Charles Bernstein is a poet. Charles Bernstein is a critic. Charles Bernstein is a man who talks. And whether he is writing or talking, Charles Bernstein is a trouble-maker. Being fond of trouble-makers myself, I am particularly fond of the trouble-maker designated by the words Charles Bernstein.

Charles Bernstein has reintroduced a spirit of polemic into the world of American poetry. In the exhausted atmosphere in which so much of our writing takes place, Charles Bernstein has battled long and hard to make both writers and readers aware of the implications embedded in each and every language act we partake of as citizens of this vast, troubled country. Whether or not you agree with what Charles Bernstein has to say is less important than the fact that it has become more and more important to listen to what he is saying.

At times, Charles Bernstein reminds me of a Talmudic rabbi. At times, Charles Bernstein reminds me of a stand-up comic performing for the late-night crowd at a Borscht Belt hotel—booked in for a two-week run and never using the same material twice. At times, Charles Bernstein reminds me of the city slicker who walks into a Wild West saloon and orders a glass of milk, and then proceeds to outpunch, outshoot, and outwit all the roughnecks who laugh at him.

What I mean to say is that Charles Bernstein is unpredictable. Charles Bernstein is everywhere. Charles Bernstein is relentless and wholly committed to speaking and writing the truth as he sees it and hears it and lives it.

For a long time not many people were interested in what Charles Bernstein was thinking. Now people are paying good money to allow their children to listen to Charles Bernstein's thoughts. For the moment, Charles Bernstein is dispensing those thoughts here at Princeton, but next year he will begin to do so on a more permanent basis in Buffalo, New York, where he has been named to the Gray Chair of Poetry and Literature. I think this is very good for Charles Bernstein. I also think it will be very good for Charles Bernstein's students—who, one hopes, will grow up to become trouble-makers themselves.

I should add that Charles Bernstein has published numerous books, including *The Sophist, Resistance, Islets/Irritations, Content's Dream, Stigma, Controlling Interests, Senses of Responsibility,* and *Poetic Justice.* I believe it was poetic justice when Charles Bernstein was awarded a Guggenheim Fellowship a number of years ago. I also believe it is poetic justice that Charles Bernstein should be here to read his poetry to us today. Because Charles Bernstein is one of the few poets who knows that there is far more poetry in the world than justice.

Now that we have settled into our seats and are ready to begin, I will repeat the words Charles Bernstein only once more. But this last time is the best time of all, for it allows me to experience the pleasure of saying: Here is Charles Bernstein.

[1990: Introduction to a reading at Princeton University on March 14; first published in *Why Write?*, Burning Deck Press, 1996. Thanks to Paul Auster for permission to reprint here.]

ACT ONE

Pixellation

(*moderato*)

In fayth Euphues thou hast told a long tale, the beginning I have forgotten,
the middle I understand not, and the end hangeth not together.

John Lyly, *Euphues: The Anatomy of Wit* (1579)

Ocular Truth and the Irreparable [Veil]

Nature is too much with us, ███ or ███,
Little we see in culture that is ███

"Deficit" is always the given, ███ fate, ████████ acknowledgement of limitations or blindness ██████.

████████ I don't know ██ prerequisite ██████████

██████ certain of that, █████ sure ███

Every touch ██████ the history of touch.

"Ocular proof," ██ undisputable ████, ████ metaphysical pea inside ██ ██ in a shell's game, █████████████ shellacking.

████████████ (bluster) ████████████
████████████████████
self-reflection.

█████████████████████████████████ irreparable ████████████████████
████████████████████████████
████████████████████████████
████████████████████ socially debilitating transfers █████████████████████

Liberalism is capitalism with a █████ face.

████████████████████████████████
██████████ I want to be protected from it.

███

██████████ Recovery is no more possible than is redemption. ███

████████████.

███ furious revanchist cultural politics ███████████████

███

██████████

███

███

███

economic slavery ██████████████████ claims of culture, high and low.

███

█████████████████████████

Lying is not necessarily a means of hiding ████████; ██████████████

of overturning it.

██████ Philo-Puritan.

███

███████████████████████████████████ contradictory

impulses and dark sides.

███████████████████████████████ pierces the narrative

███

█████████████ *schawtzes* ██████████

███

███████████ psychiatrically, the pierced ████████

███

████ create variant psychic ████████████████

███

███

███

█████████ Each, in turn, is *worse* than the other, ████████

██████████.

██████████████████ harrowing, but hardly unique, ████████

███

████████████████

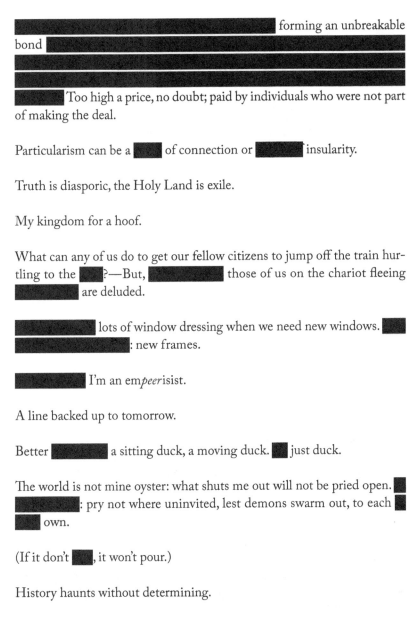

███████████████████████████████████ forming an unbreakable bond ██
██
██

███████ Too high a price, no doubt; paid by individuals who were not part of making the deal.

Particularism can be a ████ of connection or ██████ insularity.

Truth is diasporic, the Holy Land is exile.

My kingdom for a hoof.

What can any of us do to get our fellow citizens to jump off the train hurtling to the ███?—But, ███████████ those of us on the chariot fleeing ████████ are deluded.

████████████ lots of window dressing when we need new windows. ████ ████████████: new frames.

████████████ I'm an em*peer*isist.

A line backed up to tomorrow.

Better █████████ a sitting duck, a moving duck. ███ just duck.

The world is not mine oyster: what shuts me out will not be pried open. ███ ████████████: pry not where uninvited, lest demons swarm out, to each ███ ████ own.

(If it don't ████, it won't pour.)

History haunts without determining.

For as long as I can remember.

██████████████████ specter of the unhinged, unthought flash of the newly occurring—████████████ invariably dismissed as fantasy, bulldozed by █████████ and █████████ alike. ████████████ flickering utopian moment, ████ hope and despair ███ singed together in song, █ our aesthetic horizon.

█████ is in crisis. That is its opportunity.

<u>Alfred Lord, from *The Singer of*</u> ███ (via Al █████):
Our real difficulty arises from the fact that . . . we are not accustomed to thinking in terms of fluidity. ████████ difficult to grasp something that is multiform. █████████ necessary to construct an ideal text or to seek an original, ████████ dissatisfied with an ever-changing phenome-non████████ cease trying to find an original███████████
████ each performance is an original.

████████ Meshugana yogi: If you are aware of it, it's not perfection.

The kind of █████ I want: In order to form a more perfect disunion.

████████ chickens are coming home to goose even as we find our noose is coked. ██████████, the geese are chicken but drugs only make matters worse.

One oxymoron said to the other oxymoron: *Jew will not replace us*. It's a ████████.

████████ Yogi to Baby Blue: It's all over even when it's not.

<u>Louis ███ Neice, *Modern* █████ (19█):</u>
The pure music poet is hardly ever found in practice, ██████████
██████████████████████████████████████ puts words together merely for the sound they make. As all the denotations and con-notations █████ are to be discounted, █████████████
████ conventions of language. ███████████████████████ a poem entirely consisting of █████████ of invented nonsense █████.
████████ phonetic cyphers. The ████ meeting such a ████ need be nothing more than an ear. █████████████████████████
████████ almost impossible ███████████████████
████████████████ would not be worth doing. How long can any of us listen to █████ a language █████ do not understand? ████ how differentiated ████████ to such █████?

To say a █████ is put together only for the sounds it makes is to say the █████ finds its own meaning rather than ████████. How long can any of us listen to █████ a language we ████████, before we suffocate?

How differentiated are our reactions ██████████? Poems that may have been impossible ██████ have transformed what it is possible to ███.

Sometimes you gotta do what you can't do and so you ██.

██

██████████

The ██████ in Interpretation
    "During his speech, █████████████████████████████
██
██he said."
[██████July 5, 2020]
    —Thank God!

A price of being marked as ████████ is to imagine you are ██████████.

██████ Koestenbaum, ██████████:
The tragedy of Oscar Wilde is not that he was ruined; the tragedy is that he did not live long enough to enjoy his ruin. █████████████████████
██████ repeated and contradictory ████████████

████████████████████. ████████ of fools.

██ one thing to die; █ can live with ███. But this getting old . . .

I think you're pronouncing the name wrong. It's ██████████ Nabokov not Nabokov.

████████████████████████████

██ so proudly hailed, ██
██ omertà or blood oath. ██
████████████████████████████████ the precarious ██████████
██
██████████████ demographic shifts ████████████████████
██
██
██

█████ iconized by ████████████████████████████
████████████ reason-resistant ██████████████████.

Rossellini has Socrates saying in almost every scene that the most import-
ant thing is to acknowledge what you don't know, which means to contin-
ually question what you do; that the "truth" is not knowing. We need, in
other words, to find the ███████████ in ourselves. Otherwise we become
██ hooded █████████████████████.

There are no absolutes is also an absolute. The trap of relativism: all beliefs are
equal since there is no one, overriding truth. This is not the same as saying:
All truths are social and historical, while all the while hopping on one foot,
exclaiming that aesthetic and ethical judgment is a different kind, dances to
a different drummer, than scientific knowledge. In the sphere of aesthetics
and ethics, there are conflicting, incommensurable truths. Still, that does
not diminish the urgent task of finding, and making, truth: Finding by
making, making by finding, finding by founding, making by foundering.
Speak truth to truth. (For F██)

Peter Schjeldahl, in the *New Yorker* (October 19, 2020), on those who sup-
port showing the work of Philip Guston: "Suddenly silhouetted, the fac-
tion is made up of a scant minority of citizens who take an active interest
in art and espouse cosmopolitan values—the culturally privileged, whom
museums represent and serve while, these days, laudably trying to extend
their appeal to neglected audiences."

    Is art only to be shown that depicts ████████████ in frame-locked
form; and if only one interpretation is possible, then that is saying only
what aspires to kitsch, or the didactic. Schjeldahl says that only "cosmopol-
itan" audiences would override the ██████████████ idea of the mu-
seum as a safe space. Does he and ██ *New Yorker* ████ really want to use
a word that has long been associated with rootless ████, in an article about
one of them and his attempts to make art about anti-███████ and racism.

    Surely the problem is that Guston's █████ figures are too legible—
especially when coming from rootless cosmopolitans and cultural
Bolshevists.

Outside the Blake show at the Tate in London ██████████████████
████████████████████████████████████ challenging
imagery, █████████████████████████████████████
██████████████████████████."

███
██████████████████████████ aesthetic liberty, ██████████
██
██████████████████████████████

Did you mean Eliotic or idiotic?

David Bergman (in correspondence):

Last summer I went to the ████████████ museum. I wish ███████
███
██ If an
artist gives ██
███
███
███
███
██████████████████████. My oldest friend's grandmother
had an expression, "If you like it, good luck to you." █████████
██████████

██████ and ████████ form the double consciousness, the bookends, of
███ishness.

I want █████████ totters on the verge of ████████, never losing the
sigh of precarity.

Oymen.

for Paul Bové

[2021: *Critical Inquiry, In the Moment*]

The Body of the Poem

"Oh, prefer? oh yes—queer word."

Melville, "Bartleby, the Scrivener: A Story of Wall Street"

American poetry has been plagued from the start by an irreconcilable conflict between aesthetic illiberalism and aesthetic justice. Aesthetic justice is the resistance to morality in pursuit of the aesthetic, where the aesthetic is understood as a temporary, flickering zone of counterfactuals that allow for possibility, reflection, intensified sensation, and speculation—what I call the *pataquerical*.

Aesthetic justice occurs when intuitive preferences outfox rationalized principles.

Judging as "elitist" poetry that challenges the status quo of anhedonic rationalization and expressive normalization is a right-wing stink bomb in leftish clothing. Using contagious accessibility as a test of poetry delegitimizes nonconforming aesthetic exploration. The atavistic message, to the washed and unwashed alike, is that nonconforming thought or experience is unavailable to them and a threat to their nativist identities. The repression of the aesthetic by moral expressionism is a nullification of the possibilities of identity, privileging the expressive or autobiographical in name only, while actively negating unregulated identifications, desires, fears, and confusions. Such moral regulation is an affront to the "calling" of poetry in and as miscegenation in favor of purity and the cant of authenticity and "spirituality."

The "ancient enmity" of which I speak here, echoing Bei Dao's echoing Rilke, is not between great poetry and an uneventful life but rather, more starkly, between poetry and everyday life. Poets who have lived, on the surface, the most ordinary lives have made extraordinary poetry. And, painful as it is to acknowledge, people who live turbulent lives often do not have the inclination or opportunity to write poetry, or, when they do, their poetry may be scarred by experience as much as spiked by it. Bad poetry is as likely to come from those who seem to suffer as from those who seem not to (and there is an art to both seeming to and seeming not to).

Art's not fair.

People we'd like to be the best, who deserve to be, are, often as not, not. The worst produce some of the best, nor is their cruelty compensated for by their great art, which exacerbates the quandary, casting a thrilling, demonic light on their achievements.

In Dante's world, as heretic, I would suffer for eternity (maybe I am). The beauty of Dante's terzina wouldn't offer me much relief from the heat of damnation. (I'd take my copy of Cavalcanti into the fires.) I abhor Dante's monarchist and sectarian Christian supremacism but love the music he makes of it.

Poetry is not a compensation for an otherwise uncompensated life, which is what allows a poem to be such a powerful balm for poet and reader. But poetry can rankle everyday life by being itself troubled, turbulent, aggrieved, ecstatic, forlorn, bereaved, despairing—bathetic or comic, extreme and precarious.

The painful, but also liberating, fancy I am proposing, against all odds, is that the poem is rent from the life experience of its composer. The poem, in this tenuous view, embodies not the life experience of the composer but the aesthetic experience that is the work, no matter how much we resist this symbolic imperative, compelled by our heartfelt desire to see the poem as an extension of the suffering (or joy or diffidence or . . .) of the composer.

The relation of poem to autobiography is metonymic rather than representational; it is *indexical* not *iconic*, to use Charles Sanders Peirce's terms.

We can never historicize or contextualize too much if we acknowledge that we historicize and contextualize not the composer but the composed. The singer becomes the song, but it's the singing that allows this metamorphosis.

Tragedy can provoke anger or grief and every shade in between (and outside). But it doesn't make a poem. Poetry emerges from difficult life *in spite of* as much as *a result of*.

So much depends upon spite.

The promise of a poem, the kind of poetry I want, is that it refuses reality, even if nothing can succeed at that.

Americans appear to be more interested in accounts of personal experience than in the aesthetics of a poem: Ted Talks and "real-life stories." I accept that those preferences have more weight than mine. But my obsessions are not entirely without merit, just different—and here's the sharp kick in the kishkes—unpopular and unfashionable. Poetry, the kind I want, the kind I am, shows up at the ball with mismatched socks, a stain on the tie, and thinking it's a rally.

Poems can be read as imaginary and symbolic—rhetorical—constructions that we read *against* everyday life, in a dialectical manner—rather than as representations of everyday life. So that the ancient enmity that Bei Dao, echoing Rilke, evokes is also the promise of art's freedom.

The promise is made by Osip Mandelstam in 1937, the year before his death on the cusp of the extermination of the European Jews:

If they dare to keep me like an animal
And fling my food on the floor—
I won't fall silent or deaden the agony,
But will write what I am free to write,
And yoking ten oxen to my voice
Will move my hand in the darkness like a plough
And fall with the full heaviness of the harvest[1]

In his essay, Bei Dao evokes, in order to complicate, the apparent impossibilities of a happy life and the creation of a masterpiece, though we might well see Lucretius's Epicureanism as a counterweight to this view and his masterpiece, *De Rerum Natura* (Of Thing's Nature) as the proof. Perhaps my perverse view here is the revenge, or privilege, of someone who has lived, if not necessarily a happy life, then one with greater personal and economic security than most.

Great poetry abhors a safe space. In evoking the "ancient enmity" between poetry and security, Bei Dao points to dissent and internal conflict along with economic, social, and political oppression. I share his focus on resistance, the misfit between poetry and the wor(l)d that can mean all manner of not getting along: the ancient enmity between the artist and family, society, God. The kind of poetry I want is as averse to expression of solidarity and community as it is to univocal self-identity.

Most American poets and poetry officials would take these phantasmagoric aversions as akin to career suicide. They mock and jeer those who follow such crooked courses. And they would be right to note that there are more great poems that affirm nation or religion or group than those that do not.

Any political sentiment, left, right, center, or anti-, can fall prey to conformity. Conformity is the aim of most poets, poetry teachers, and arbiters. Aesthetic justice remains associated with the degenerate or decadent and is contested with ever new and improved normalizations, which colonize

1. Translation by James Green in *Poems for the Millennium: Volume One,* ed. Jerome Rothenberg and Pierre Joris (Berkeley: University of California Press, 1995), p. 396.

previous areas of dissent or stigma under the umbrella of affirmation, community, and rectitude.

If we value not the poem but the iconized life experience of the poet, we discount the poet's work, adding insult to injury. Pity (or its rich cousin empathy) replaces awe; piety trumps fancy.

The moral approach to art is not just a matter of outmoded or conservative or reactionary values; morality may also underpin appeals for racial, gender, social, economic, and environmental justice. Aesthetic justice is not so much an outlaw as antinomian, beside the law, as the poem puts me beside myself, rips my soul into rippling patterns. Aesthetic justice is fundamental to those other forms of justice, but it is not in their service. Its field of action is symbolic, necessarily at odds with everyday life.

Maybe I have lived a happy life, as best I could, which means with my share of unhappiness (real and imagined). Do I seem grumpy? Is being a curmudgeon the essence of poetry?

Why not just get along?
I prefer not to.
Because I can.

[2017: first presented November 23 at "Ancient Enmity," International Poetry Nights in Hong Kong. The essay responds to Bei Dao's "Ancient Enmity," tr. Fiona Sze-Lorrain, *Mānoa* 24 (Summer 2012): pp. 1–5. *Critical Inquiry* 44 (2018).]

95 Theses

"95 Theses" commemorates both "Frame Lock," a talk I presented at the 1992 MLA Annual Convention, and which was collected in My Way: Speeches and Poems *and "The Practice of Poetics" written a decade ago for* Introduction to Scholarship in Modern Languages and Literature *(David Nicholls, editor; MLA, 2007), collected in* Attack of the Difficult Poems.

In "Frame Lock," using terms adapted from Erving Goffman's Frame Analysis, *I made the case for shifts in mood and style in scholarly writing; not only made the case, I performed it. Contrary to what some members feel, I have always found the MLA convention, with its knowledgeable and often enthusiastic listeners, an ideal place to present my work. In 1990, I got my first full-time academic job at SUNY Buffalo. It was astounding to start at Buffalo, having had virtually no prior academic affiliation since I had graduated college two decades earlier. I am sure that unusual experience gives me an odd perspective. In 1992, I had just cofounded the Poetics Program at Buffalo with Susan Howe, Raymond Federman, Robert Creeley, and Dennis Tedlock. The program was a model for literary artists teaching in PhD programs—not creative writing but literary history and poetics. Over the years, my briefs for the essay as art have shifted to keep up with the changing environment and also because I don't like to repeat myself, even though I am sure I do.*

I retired a few years after writing this, so take it as something of a swan song, or, anyway, duck soup. I leave the remainder of the theses to be filled in by you.

1. Professionalism is a means not an end. Less is more. Professors are better off when they professionalize less and risk extinction when professionalization is primary.

2. Professionalized scholarly writing often seems to play off a list of master-theorists who must be cited, even if the subject is overcoming mastery. A modest proposal: In your next essays and books don't make any reference to the ten most cited authors in your field. Apply the death of the author to the ones that authorize that idea.

3.   Don't cite authors, become an author. Then undo your own authority.

4.   If you write, you are a writer. It is as simple as that and no amount of research, findings, conclusions, proposals, projects, and laboratories will change it a whit.

5.   Writing is a laboratory for the mind, its experiments are in syntax as much as analysis, arrangement as much as argument.

6.   Frame Lock was not built in a day.
Tone jam is not a marmalade.

7.   Contradiction is closer to truth than consistency, so don't consistently emphasize contradiction.

8.   The truth is not the end of the essay but its point of departure.

9.   The fragment is more important for criticism today than for poetry.

10.   Not fragments: constellations.

11.   Positivism is as rhetorical as negativism.

12.   Reason abhors a rationalist.

13.   Which does not mean anything goes: anything is possible but only a very few things get through that eye of a needle that separates charm from harm. And often what appears as harm has got the charm.

14.   We're better with alternatives to STEM
Than when we go on imitating them.

15.   A recent Digital Humanities lecture presented both a fount and a font of information about a poem's unusual digital typeface but not a word about the font's meaning or ideology or how the visual display affected the interpretation of the poem. This was New Criticism with close reading not of the words of a text but the technology for generating its letters.

16.   Distant reading without reading is not reading. Close reading without toggling frames is myopia.

17.   Information everywhere but not a drop to think.

18.   The question for macro and distant sociological approaches in the humanities, digital or otherwise, is not just *what happens* but also *so what?* and *what for?*

19.   "The fact you tell is of no value, but only the impression."—Emerson on Thoreau (1862)

20.   Criticism, scholarship, and poetry are all fonts of rhetoric. The aversion of rhetoric is an unkind kind of rhetoric.

21.   There is no formula for avoiding formulas.

22.   Sometimes what appears as unformulated is just new jeans with fashionable rips.

23. Not that there is anything wrong with that.

24. One size doesn't fit all. (*Each to his own goo, be true.*)

25. Not interdisciplinarity: non-disciplinarity. (Call it pragmatism.)

26. If we want to emulate the natural sciences let us do so by stressing speculation and collaboration (through multiple author essays).

27. Expository writing needs to be balanced by nonexpository writing.

28. I don't want trans-national studies I want non-national studies. Non-national studies would look at language-speaking groups and conversations among languages and across languages not based only on nation-states but also affinities, immigration, refugees, the displaced and diasporic, the nomadic, the national-non-conforming. Examples would be born-digital arts, poets writing in English irrespective of their national or first language, Yiddish, or to give a more historical example, the medieval and European cultures approach of David Wallace here at Penn that looks not at discrete national literatures but rather "sequences of interconnected places."

29. Nothing suits us like our union suits, as the old ILGWU (International Ladies Garment Workers Union) ad put it.

30. Don't mourn: unionize.

31. There are no themes, histories, ideologies, ideas, terms, or categories uninflected (uninfected) by the often fractal, fractured, and fraught signifying practices that make them so. Ideas bleed re(a)d blood; the imaginary weeps wet tears. The real is no less so minding the body than embodying mind.

32. Language is never more than an extension of reality.

33. Form and style are not ornamental to meaning.

34. No flapjacks without eggs.

35. Impersonality is the hobgoblin of frightened prose.

36. Autobiography and personal narrative are not a prophylactic against formulaic expression of received ideas.

37. Contentious rhetoric opens dialog more than professionalized prose. But contentiousness as a mode of dominance is tyranny. Denunciation and defamation, even in the name of a good cause, destroys dialog.

38. All professional rhetoric is pre-professional.

39. The real cannot disappear. Even the appearance of disappearance is real.

40. The absence of expressed identity is a form of identity.

41. The expression of identity is, also, a mask.

42. The poetry and poetics I read and write are not a product of the world financial system but of the world semantic system.

43. Whenever you walk on a new road, you can be sure no one has spoilt it yet.—Menachem Mendel (Kotsker Rebbe)

44. Whenever you think you have walked down a new road, you can be sure others have been there first. Try to find and acknowledge them.

45. Feeling superior to the self-righteous makes you that.

46. Taking pleasure in piety is piteous.

47. The good longs for us but we are unworthy.

48. Recently, a dean at my college declined to allow a class for a "diversity" requirement even though the syllabus included poetry in a dozen languages from the Americas, Asia, Europe, Africa. The dean said *diversity* needed to focus on only one group, one language. *Diversity without uniformity is poetry and don't count.*

49. For the colonial mind, decolonization is a new frontier to settle.

50. It never hurts to add a joke.

51. You know the one: three Jews four opinions? What you don't hear is that two of them, the schmucks, have the same opinion, while the third . . .

52. To write prose after Auschwitz is barbaric.

53. "Away then with all those prophets who say to the community of Christ, 'Peace, peace,' and there is no peace."

54. My concern is more *What is false?* than *What is truth?*

55. "This is our task: to imagine no whole from all that has been smashed."

56. A bird at heel is better than a heel with a bird.

57. Redefine English in "English department" as the host language not the disciplinary boundary, where English is understood neither as origin nor destination.

58. The aversion of disciplinarity requires discipline.

59. The arts, including the literary arts, are as foundational for literary studies as criticism. Literary studies without aesthetics is like science without nature.

60. There are nowadays many professors of culture but few originators, since origination has been mostly assigned to the realm of fantasy, of unicorns and fairies. "The success of great scholars and thinkers is commonly a courtier-like success," Thoreau writes in *Walden.* "They make shift to live merely by conformity, practically as their fathers did, and are in no sense the progenitors of a noble race of men." Nor is Thoreau ironic when he insists, "Yet it is admirable to profess because it was once admirable to live."

61. Lyric Theory: The spouting of a whale is freer than the lyric of most poets.

62.   Coming before any public in this month requires a loud denuncia-
      tion of Donald Trump, who poses a grave danger to this republic, a
      requirement made all the more urgent when so many young people,
      perhaps even some here at the University of Pennsylvania, seem
      reluctant to support Hillary Clinton. *I'm with her.*

63.   Pataquerics cannot be schooled. It cannot be, which is to say rest as,
      itself. Pataquerics questions its own questioning.

64.   The rest of these 95 theses intentionally left blank.

[2016: *Profession*. Written for "Aversive Prose," a panel convened by Eric Keenaghan and Josephine
Park at Kelly Writers House, University of Pennsylvania, September 16. The panel title comes from a
graduate seminar I led in 2015, which presented an abbreviated history of exceptional and aversive
approaches to essays and discursive prose (upper-limit poetry / lower-limit manifestos) <writing.upenn
.edu/bernstein/syllabi/prose.html>].

The Unreliable Lyric

If story's other is narrative, what is lyric's other? *Lyric* is so generic that it's difficult to find a term to contrast with it, unless one moves to another genre, typically *epic*. Even so, the hegemony of a single-voice, "scenic" lyric, the Vampiric heart of Romantic Ideology, has been contested since Blake, Byron, Swinburne, Poe, Dickinson, and the slave songs, in the nineteenth century, and Stein, Loy, Williams, Pound, Eliot, Tolson, and Riding in the early twentieth. The conventional lyric's American other in the 1930s was the "objectivist" poem, in the 1950s "Projective Verse" and the "serial poem." In the 1960s, Antin and Jerome Rothenberg suggested "deep image" and Amiri Baraka and company, "Black Arts." There was a time in the early 1980s that poets advocated against the scenic lyric with terms such as "analytic lyric" or "transcendental lyric." Ron Silliman's "new sentence" and David Antin's "talk poems," as with "language-centered," specifically presented themselves against the vanilla lyric.

Not voice, voices; not craft, process; not absorption, artifice; not virtue, irreverence; not figuration, abstraction; not the standard, dialect; not regional, cosmopolitan; not normal, the strange; not emotion, sensation; not expressive, conceptual; not story, narrative; not idealism, materialism.

For binary oppositions to intensify their aesthetic engagement, and not become self-parody, it helps if they fall apart, so that you question the difference, confuse one with the other, or understand the distinctions as situational, as six is up from five but down from infinity, diction so low its high, solipsism so radical it dissolves into pure realism.

Narrative and story are made of the same cloth, share a genre, might, paradoxically, be the same, the way a broke clock is right twice a day but always impecunious, but on a lonely night in Georgia the clock's not right any time, because the morning refuses to come. For the longest time I thought *signified* was a crypt term for *signifier*, but then I learned to tango to the music of the Pragmatics in the House of Lost Spades.

Or such is the confession of a high functioning fyslecic {dyslecic} {dusleci} [dyslexic]. There is no left or right just degrees of left and right in relation to other points in space. [*Hey! Who are you calling a point in space!*]

To be against binary oppositions is what it's against. *Dedualize*, yes, in the sense of *always dialecticize* and *historicize*. Which is to say, don't neutralize conflicts in pursuit of reconciliation: the rhetorical heightening of conflict is the sine qua non of an activist poetics. It's de rigueur for those poetry practices formally known as the avant-garde (PPFKAAG [Brit. /ˈpʌfkɔːɡ/, U.S. /ˈpəfˌkɔɡ/]) to be shamed for a lack of lyricism, emotion, humanity, even if those poetry practices reject the whole God-damn avant-garde schtick (as I done done).

Even those in the PPFKAAG hate it and there is nothing they hate more than other sectors of PPFKAAG or those whose work they most envy in their own sector.[1]

A tried and false path to transient official verse culture acceptance (TOVCA) is to attack the avant-garde for its lack of virtue (LoV) and total affect failure (TAF). *Transient* because it is unable to form a stable relationship.

Hatred of the avant-garde / opens doors / that slam / behind you.

But what do I know? I am just an unreliable lyric poet peddling tales, singing the same song all the day long.

And into the night.

[2017: The motif of story versus narrative is extended in "UP against Storytelling, for David Antin" in Act Three of this collection.]

---

1. See my study *Avant-Garde Self-Hatred* (Brooklyn Free State: Hungadunga, Hungadunga, Hungadunga, and McCormack, 2018).

A Fabric of Expectation

VICKI HUDSPITH: *What are you working on right now?*

I've been interested in how various kinds of phrases and phraseologies tend to shape the ways in which the world gets seen, so that in writing I almost feel I'm exploring the way in which—the material with which—social reality gets created. It's as if by looking at these phrases and their combinations like they were in themselves coercive or controlling you could get out from under their compelling force. But it's not this idea about control that I'm working on, it's the material of the phrases and their combinations, seeing how the most common kinds of phrases put together create a fabric of expectation one to the next that links them together. And what I really want to do is to create this fabric, or, another way of saying it, to make a kind of music. Not music in the sense of using rhythmic or structural patterns based on musical composition, but rather, to use a phrase of Don Byrd's, a "music of content," of different kinds of meaning configurations. By moving from one element to another and seeing the different kinds of balances and harmonies that are created, the world sort of comes into an attunement, and that begins to be the poem. Certainly, this is also true just of the sounds of words when attention is paid to each vowel and consonant and syllable. I'm interested in what might be called fragmentation, although I don't see it as that. For instance the kind of expectation that develops when you cut a phrase off supposedly in the middle, which is simply using a kind of rhythm, using the expectations and projections—the momentum—that any given phrase has, so that if you stop something at any given point in the normal syntactical pattern or even in a more imagined pattern, you have almost a shadow which continues along or underneath, when you move on into the next series of words. That desire for certain sound resolutions creates the music.

Do you work from the content first or from a formal problem you want to solve?

I don't have any idea before I start to write what I'm going to write. I work from the inside out. When I'm in the middle of something certain formal things are on my mind. After I'm a few pages into it, I begin to become conscious of an overall shape the work is taking. It is important to me not to continually rely on the same ways of making phrases and making them go together. In one poem I'll accentuate certain structures and in another they'll be very submerged. The genesis of the next poem is something I'm always concerned with: how it's going to be different, have I said everything I have to say?

How does nonreferential language fit into what you've been describing?

Reference is a very central element to what reading is. You really can't strip yourself of the associative qualities that words have. It's interesting and inevitable to deal with the vectors of reference, but I think only a limited amount can be done with trying to totally block reference off.

In terms of the magazine L=A=N=G=U=A=G=E *of which you're an editor, I think a number of people would say that you were trying to fetishize a certain kind of style of writing . . .*

The magazine has actually been involved in exploring how writing doesn't have to operate primarily out of fixed styles. I always saw *L=A=N=G=U=A=G=E* as a method of exploring broader issues of poetry in relation to social consciousness.

Even though I recognize a number of different formal styles in your work, the personal or referential element is always present.

Having some kind of *concern* palpably present that centers the poem—is something I'm very interested in. Not starting out with a given preexisting conception of the style or genre, the vocabulary or the rhythmic patterns—but that all these things are the material with which the poem is made. What centers the concern has most to do with the process of composition and the power any word added to another word has over you, enough to bring a world into being.

[1980: *Poetry Project Newsletter* 75, June/July]

Offbeat

1. Leap for Li Zhimin

Poetry is more than meets the eye. It's more than meets the ear too. It's total mind expansion through verbal, vocal, and visual extravagances. Poetry is not just an expansion of the mind, but of perception and heart. But it can't be understood by trying to figure it out. You need to take a leap of faith into the poem, jump into it as if you were jumping into a hole in a frozen lake, fearing perhaps that you will drown or freeze. But once in the water, it's as warm as a hot spring, and even if you can't swim, all of a sudden, you'll be floating on the poem's surface, then plunging deep. It just takes a leap of poetic faith.

2. Poetry Month Will Come a Little Late This Year

Poetry's freedom, which to say poetry's essential contribution to American culture, is grounded in its aversion of conformity and in its resistance to the restrictions of market-driven popularity. Indeed, contemporary American poetry thrives through its small scale and radical differences of form. There is no one sort of American poetry and certainly no right sort—this is what makes aesthetic invention so necessary.

Free verse is not a type of nonmetrical poetry but an imperative to liberate verse from the constraints of obligatory convention and regulation. In that sense, free verse is an aspiration, and its stuttering breathlessness is a mark of its impossibility.

I want not just a politics of identity but an aesthetics of identity.

While some may choose the straight path of self-righteousness, do not give up hope that they will return to the crooked roads that have no certainties.

The goal is to find wilderness in bewilderment. Or is that the process?

I am the shell of the person I once was. The shell of the shell. But then the person I once was is a shell of the person I now am.

"The more realistic a poet is, the more distant from reality." (Sutzkever)[1]

I cannot make it decohere.

The world doesn't make sense; we do. (Sense is of the word and in the world. The nonhuman is also beyond the human.)

Assisted living. As opposed to what?

Poetry is reacquired taste. (after David Bergman)

Nearly touching are the ethical realm of our obligation to others and the aesthetic world of our freedom from such obligations. (for Rachel Levitsky)

"The loss of a public is in fact the artist's withdrawal from his public, as a consequence of his faithfulness to his art. The public is lost to art because they are readying themselves for war, for life by the gun. They are also lost because of art, because art maintains itself against their assaults, and because, almost against its will, it unsettles the illusions by means of which civilized people conduct themselves." (Cavell)[2]

Those ardent in their beliefs and certain of God's will are the faithless ones.

The thing is: life *is* a one-way street.

Gods need us more than we need them because without us they would not exist but without them we do.

---

1. Avrom [Abraham] Sutzkever, "My Life and My Poetry," in *Still My Word Sings: Poems*, ed. and tr. Heather Valencia (Dusseldorf: Dusseldorf University Press, 2011), p. 33

2. Stanley Cavell, "More of *The World Viewed*," in *The World Viewed: Reflections on the Ontology of Film—Enlarged Edition* (Cambridge, MA: Harvard University Press, 1979), p. 290

I am for a single prayer initiative: God loves those who think for themself.

Physical distance / social intimacy: a kind of poetry.

How the music learned to write.

The poem that is true for all people and all times is a true for no one and no time.

I never met a person who cried "fire" when confronted by a snowball. But there are many today who cry "freedom" when confronted with tyranny. My aggrievement may be absolute to me, but that does not make it greater than yours. My freedom is only that to the extent it guarantees yours. Anything different, to the extent of the difference, is not liberty; it is oppression.

Like a memorial except we're all alive. Or we imagine we're alive even though we died weeks ago.

The fight for truthfulness is a fight against the claim of a single truth. At best, science and poetry both move toward truth through an insistence on truthfulness; religion and politics, sometimes; demagoguery, never.

The temporary loss of our physical commons is devastating. But the commons needed now is imaginary not territorial.

Those who know God's truth won't say; those who say don't know. (after Abraham Sutzkever)

Injury to the imaginary is trauma.

The imaginary commons is art.

[2020: University of Chicago Press blog.]

3. Eventuality

One of my worst habits of mind is to assume that a work of poetry deemed "notable" by the leading cultural organs must not be any good. After all, just being singled out for praise by one of these publications or prizes doesn't guarantee humdrummery; mistakes can be made. Sometimes I've been one.

But it's fair to say that very few of the poets I most care about have been deemed "notable" outside the inner sanctum of dedicated readers focused on pataquerical poetry.

I won't provide a year-end roundup of this year's most notable poetry-related books, but just say there were plenty and they were plenty ignored. But notability does not make an event. Events in poetry are more likely to ripple underwater than be a splash, though I aspire to both.

Event is one of those words long mangled in the threshing machines of philosophical analysis. You know: the only true event is a non-event. Or you don't know what an event is until you see it and when you do you are likely to repress it (or it will repress you).

Or, as we used to say, *It's not an event, man, it's a happening, I mean it's happening man, can you dig?—Don't bring me down with all this event claptrap.*

Then there are the religious connotations. But like the schnorrer says— messiahs keep coming and going but waiting's not going anywhere.

Or am I confusing *event* with *advent*?

I guess if I really wanted to be theological, I'd say my concern is not the *event* but the *eventual.* That sounds good, but God knows what it means. Or maybe Emerson might—only a moving toward, never a grand finale. To Tagore's marvelous paradox that "inconsistency" is both the greatest vice and virtue, I'd add *inconstancy.* I just mean that sometimes in the spluttering of rethinking and reconsidering and recalculating, there is the possibility of an ingenuity necessary for both the event and the eventual.

I seem to be saying that for something to be an event it can't be named and, especially can't be named *notable.* But that can't be right. I'm no gnostic. I acknowledge and celebrate the poets I admire, as I do Paul Celan, whose one-hundredth birthday is upon us. If any poet's work is an eventuality rather than event, it's Celan.

Acknowledgment and celebration allow eventualities to become events (and the other way around). Right now it starts here, in conversation, at *Literary Activism.*

[2020: In response to Amit Chaudhuri's forum question for *Literary Activism*—"What do you think of as a notable cultural event from recent times?"]

4. Paraenigma (Paradigma)

Reading is a plural event.

I've specialized in creating books that contain works, poems, and essays, that cannot be read in one way. They defy not only a unified theory but also, sometimes, even the semblance of plain sense (and at other times offer the palpable semblance of sense, unmoored from rational explanation). I like to think the relation of one work to the next in one of my books is comparable to the twisting, inside-out movement of a Möbius strip. Reframing is the reader's response, at least if the reader wants to take the ride offered for the sheer hell of it, which turns out to be for the sheer heaven of it too.

Most critical theories operate on the replacement model, mandating an ever-revisionist framing of the critical paradigm for reading, with a built-in obsolescence of five to ten years: close, distant, symptomatic, surface, deep, affective, impersonal, political, psychoanalytic, linguistic, sociological, na-tionalist, transnational, pessimistic, optimistic, projective, historical, for-mal, and so on. All those frames of reading come into play in reading one of the Henry James passages that Marjorie Perloff mentions in her essay "Microreading/Microwriting."[3] And, indeed, Perloff is exemplary in her advocacy of a mobile, pragmatic rather than axiomatic, approach to frames. In this respect I think also of Jerome McGann, Johanna Drucker, Leslie Scalapino, Susan Stewart, Tracie Morris, and Thomas McEvilley. All these follow on work as discrepant as Michel Foucault, Roland Barthes, Thelo-nious Monk, Deleuze/Guattari, Mel Brooks, Erving Goffman, Arakawa/ Gins, George Lakoff, Shulamith Firestone, John Berger—which in turn follow the Lucretian lead of Dickinson, Stein, Wittgenstein, and Benja-min. Or such have been the models I have written about.

L=A=N=G=U=A=G=E was an invitation to read with and through a *multripillocation* of frames, "InOutside" in Kyoo Lee's sense.[4] It's that multiplicity that makes the work still largely repugnant to official verse culture, no matter the exceptional (and welcome) exceptions. Poems, the kind of poetry I want, use reframing as a process. They allow readers (Lee's "U") to shift frames "InOutside" without settling onto an individual one. Jackson Mac Low called this "reader-centered writing" because it puts the reader, not the poem, in the driver's seat. This doesn't mean the poem isn't a well-wrought submersible. But in this kind of poem, readers navigate through the textual waters, actively not passively: they earn their reading. Or indeed, as Perloff and Lee remind us, *listening*, since the audiotext of a work presents a whole new set of frames, which is to say possibilities, for the reader/listener.

In 2019, I had a poem accepted by the *Paris Review*. I was glad for that,

---

3. Marjorie Perloff, "Microreading/Microwriting," *PN Review* 249, 46:1 (2019) and *Theoretical Studies in Literature and Art* 39:3 (2019)

4. Kyoo Lee in "A Close-up: On U, the Reader InOutside," *Theoretical Studies in Literature and Art* 39:3 (2019). My essay is a response, in part, to Lee's and Perloff's.

as my work is often unwelcome at such places. A few weeks later a young assistant editor sent me a proof with dozens of changes. I would have been less disappointed if the magazine had queried before making the changes. I had to backtrack through the poem and hand correct each of the unauthorized alterations. House Style at this place trumps author's choices, and I must have been the rare author to object. My *101* became *one-hundred-one* (I wanted the numeration to seem wonkish). In other cases, the editor changed my wording from sharp and particular to bland. "Sudden move" became "sudden moves"; a man appearing with a *sudden gift* was changed to sudden *gifts*. "Orient Eastward" lost its caps, losing the sense of Orient and East both. I stetted most of the changes. Even so, on the third round, the earnest assistant editor told me that the chief editor had asked that I please be consistent in how I capitalize "dark matter," as I had it both capped and lowercase. They were concerned readers would think the editors had made a mistake. Their professional competence would be questioned. I just couldn't write another email saying I intend my Inconsistencies, that they are the heart of my Dark Matter. I didn't want to put them in harm's way.

And indeed, this short response to Lee and Perloff (and a much longer one that put this essay in the context of my earlier essays) was rejected, after being solicited, by *Theoretical Studies in Literature and Art*, because it did not follow their idea of professional decorum. Just my point about the sort of clueless, frame-locked editorial practices that are as theoretically misinformed as they are aversive to both art and literature.

I remember in Marjorie Perloff's first review of my work, a crucial introduction to L=A=N=G=U=A=G=E poetry in 1984:

> Charles Bernstein takes this sort of word play a step further, almost to the point of unintelligibility. In "The Sheds of Our Webs," neologisms abound: "a lacrity," "sumpter" ("marshy" or "low-lying" on the model of "sump"?), "plentitude." More important; grammatical position is frequently ambiguous: is "sheds" a noun or gerund ("sheddings")? "Abandon skirts" a verb followed by its direct object or a subject—verb clause? "Tender" a verb or adjective or noun? There is no way to be sure, especially since many of the words in ambiguous syntactic position are homonyms.[5]

That's "microreading/microwriting" in action. Thirty-five years later, and after a lifetime of being known, if not notorious, for my ideosyncratic [*sic*] approach to style, I can still get a bright young editor's puzzled response. If

---

5. Marjorie Perloff, "The Word as Such: L=A=N=G=U=A=G=E Poetry in the Eighties," in *The Dance of the Intellect: Studies in the Poetry of the Pound Tradition* (Cambridge: Cambridge University Press, 1985), p. 216. Originally published in *American Poetry Review* (May–June 1984), 13(3).

such smart folks don't know how to read poetry and see THOU SHALT
NOT at any slight wandering from convention, then there is no hope.

And that is why, and how, reading matters.

[2020: *Foreign Language and Literature Research* (Wuhan, China)]

5. Offbeat

if you say I'm offbeat, my dear
you know it hurts me, ain't that clear?
only the privileged
have ears like yours
all I got's what's given by my dear Lord

if you insist my behavior is unsuitable
classifying my compositions unmusical
my argument, maybe untenable
is that it's Bossa nova
that is the most natural

what you don't know
what you refuse to sense
is my off beats come straight from the heart
I photographed you with my Rolleiflex
what I see is that you don't love my art

don't talk about my love
it's far more than you are capable of
you and your music forget the key—
the sounds inside me beat offkey
deep and quietly
inside of me
the beat's offkey
to hit the heart, but you don't see

inspired by the lyrics of "Desafinado" (1958)
by Antonio Carlos Jobim and Newton Mendonça

[There are over 350 recordings of this song, in Portuguese and using the adaptions by Gene Lees ("Off Key") and Jon Hendricks and Jessie Cavanaugh, a.k.a. Howie Richmond ("Slightly Out of Tune"). Most notable performances: João Gilberto, Jobim, and Caetano Veloso. Augusto de Campos championed the song in *Balanço da Bossa e Outras Bossas* (1974). Published here with thanks to, and the permission of, the Estate of Newton Mendonça.]

6. From a Letter to Jerome Rothenberg: On Wilderness & Language

Wilderness for me means diving back into the language, the density and unchartable courses that sweep us in there, in that, about as wild as you can get. But anyway this is more about the social world, the attempt to build that "wilderness" *back in*: so a certain kind of skid and you don't know where you are, can begin to get bearings for the first time. Just the items piling up, the numerousness of them, the sorting them out. Every thing, every item, image, fact is a wilderness—that would be, though, to reduce that concept to a status quo, not the ideology of it, but the sheer fact, experience, at every moment. If "space" has been a central fact to "American" literature [Olson], the fact of being able to move into parts unknown—an ever-expanding frontier to the wilds & all that, well now that's got to go into, onto, itself—the next available space is as much a vertical movement as a horizontal one. Anyway, the thing is: "All spots are taken but we will let you have the next available place." Displacement. Next to us. Our own despair, the de-construction of the social world, the labyrinthine irritation, wavy sensation—bands of intensity—that place us up against, to face——. And the gravity that pulls us back, "centers" to the Imperial center as much as "self's center" whatever that might be.

[*New Wilderness Letter* 7 (1979)]

7. The Tugboat and the Quail

Sound precedes form.

Neeli Cherkovski

Zoom is where poetry goes to die. Or where we, dying, go for poetry. Or is it the best available platform for poetry in the age of covidity?

Zoom may also be where teaching goes to die. But it doesn't have to be that way if interaction and discussion is favored over lecture and recitation:

dialogue over the monologue. *Poetry should be at least as interesting as television.* Which means, for one thing, not making sitting in front of a laptop the default posture. For poetry to be art it needs to stand . . . and stand back. It needs to dance.

Zoom's "live" streaming hiccups may be its prime aesthetic given, if only we could dwell in those gaps. (Whose got the Bufferin?) *I don't want to watch myself watching or watch you watching.* In which case, it's a society of spectacle all over again, with facial icons muted to simulate presence in an overwhelming experience of absence—the body of the poem anesthetized.

Poetry's medium is sound and rhythm, bodily gesture (signed and performance poetry), visual inscription (poetry plastique). Digital resources for poetry have been fundamental for poetry for twenty-five years. The Poetics List, PennSound, EPC, Eclipse, Ubuweb, ModPo are just a few noncorporate possibilities. The audio of a reading can be sublime in a way a video of the same reading often isn't (but could be).

I want poems that are ecstatic in the sense that they exceed moral and political discourse. Poems as sensation, as performance, as aesthetic, *doing* rather than *stating*. Difficult poems that put readers in the middle of difficult circumstance and that cannot be resolved through conventional position-taking. More than exaggeration, extravagance—an insistence that the rhetorical subsumes the expressive. [for Amiri Baraka]

Containing poetry, or anyway its unruly aesthetic dimension, will always be more convincing than radicalizing poetry. Especially if the taming is pitched as care or cure.

As Perry Bathos says, If young poets want conventional success, they need to aim for a reassuring balance between mediocrity and profundity. Anything else will ruin a promising career.

My poems are ruined more than ruins. They are curiosities.

"Is it elegiac, is it satiric?" Jerome McGann asks of Byron's *Don Juan*, citing this passage—

Between two worlds life hovers like a star,
　'Twixt night and morn, upon the horizon's verge.
How little do we know that which we are!
　How less what we may be!

The oscillation between pathos and comedy consumes and ignites me. I run amuck of moral seriousness, which is as far from serious as "firmament to fin," as McGann puts it.

Like as to as and like to like
the seeming holds out promise
false, breaking on double-edged
shores of *might*: power, worry.

Runa Bandyopadhyay asks me what I meant by including the Graeae in the list of dramatis personae that I added as a decorative flourish after finishing "The Pataquerical Imagination," in *Pitch of Poetry*, what she calls my "melody for the malady." Perhaps the presence of the Graeae suggests that rather than sharing one eye, every eye should have three within it. That's a good working definition of pataquerical.

Love me for who I am not what I am.

But who am I, outside of what I am?

—A straw in the wind, a cry in the wilderness, a wave on the sea, a moment in time.

We may *all be in this together*, depending on what *this* means. Whatever the common menace, the outcomes will never be the same. Deep below our difference is not "interconnection" but *incommensurability*. Humanness is not so much shared as contested. Empathy and solidarity are crucial local investments. But acknowledging our uncommonness alongside our commonness grounds struggles to resist the hegemony of the universal.

My poems are not an expression of my identity but of my relationship to identity. Their value is as much for what they refuse as what they embrace.

Not poem nor revolution erases the irreparable.

In their aesthetic and moral unsettling, poems are provisional sanctuaries of freedom, unstable sites of imaginative reflection that can inform, but not enact, political transformation. Poets, and other artists, are (or could be) fantasists of unacknowledged worlds. But they also are canaries in the mines of the acknowledged world, carrying its viruses, tripped by its traps, crying wolf long after the fox has slaughtered the hens, and all the while pleading for credit.

The need now is not (just) for the underrepresented but (also) for the unrepresentable.

I cannot accord sympathy to those who do not recognize the human comedy.

[2020: *Literary Activism*]

8. The Untimely

If a poem fails in a forest because no one hears it, is it still a poem? If a poem denies time, is it any less timely? Might we speak of a timely poem but also an untimely one? The more a poem is *in time* the more it becomes part of the folds and veils of *deep time*. In other words, a poem is always in now time, with one foot in before, one foot in after, and another in neither.

Time is a daydream to which we escape. Meaning meanders in the meantime, meaning by means of means at hand. If most people have no time for art, I want a poetry that inhabits that no time.

Most days I am happy if a poem can make it through the night.

9. Race and Poetry

Dear Claudia,

I take RACE to be the central fact for those born in the Americas. I spell it large because it comes large here. Large and without mercy.[6]

We are all of us from somewhere else: some came running, some came screaming, some were moved from where they were at home to reservations and plantations that were, at times, akin to killing fields. Most of us just found ourselves here, with a history we never asked for, understood, or can ever fully right.

And there are all the languages: the ones lost in the prairie and on the high plains, wiped out systemically as if they were smallpox; the ones given up to start anew and the ones forbidden at pain of social or economic failure. And the ones retained, the resistant strains that bubble up through our speech like sparks of light; the voices, accents, pitches, tones, vocabulary, dialects, and ideolects that are as ineradicable as the will for freedom or the need for poetry (that is: precarious).

Language is poetry's business, so it is with these resistant strains that I have been most concerned: the way that poetry resists, transforms, and remakes the standard.

---

6. Adapted from the opening of Charles Olson's *Call Me Ishmael*.

Questions of race are never just about narrative or images or
stereotypes, they pervade our grammars, our styles, our forms,
and above all our unstated system of preferences, of aesthetic
value. You say well-wrought urn, I say stunningly tedious; you
say stuttering with incompetence, I say that is a new music
for our age.

You ask for "a discussion pertinent to the more important
issue of the creative imagination and race" and I agree with
your insistence that this is necessary. Poetry can't be left
to its own devices. We need the conversation, commentary,
contention. Sometimes it hurts and sometimes it hurts too much
and sometimes it's illuminating and sometimes stupefying and
sometimes just silly or uninformed.

I am interested in how our projections as readers, or as
citizens, taint the images we encounter. I don't think you
can ever transcend that tainting, but I think it's possible to
acknowledge it, or at least come to speaking terms with it.
"In Particular" (in *Girly Man*) constituted itself as a Möbius
strip of imaginary identity formations and actions, beginning
and ending in black and white. What I wanted to create was a
counter-bachelor-machine, bachelor machine being Duchamp's
term for self-enclosing, non-procreative processes. Along
with this poem, two of my essays provide the most detailed
response, which I am capable of, to the racial mountain
in American poetry: "Poetics of the Americas" from *My Way:
Speeches and Poems* and "Objectivist Blues: Scoring Speech in
Second-Wave Modernist Poetry and Lyrics" from *Attack of the
Difficult Poems: Essays and Inventions*.

                    Truly, yours
                    Charles

[2013: *The Racial Imaginary: Writers on Race in the Life of the Mind*, ed. Claudia Rankine, Beth Lof-
freda, Cap Max King (Hudson, NY: Fence Books)]

10. No Hiding Place

I thought language poetry was against emotion in the name of sensation
I thought language poetry was against theory in favor of praxis
I thought language poetry was lots of words making the most of meaning
I thought language poetry was the diehard foe of the massed mediocracy
I thought language poetry was a big tent without roof or floor
I thought language poetry was sympathy without tea

I thought language poetry was ambient sound in serial locomotion
I thought language poetry has branches in Paris, New York, Toronto, and
Palm Springs
I thought language poetry was Marxist
I thought language poetry was anarchist
I thought language poetry was the antichrist
I thought language poetry was bourgeois aestheticism
I thought language poetry hated the voice
I thought language poetry was all voicing and never content
I thought language poetry was against realism
I thought language poetry was a new form of realism
I thought language poetry was against dogma
I thought language poetry refused its commissars
I thought language poetry was against closed groups
I thought language poetry was all thought in pursuit of potential action
I thought language poetry was Gertrude Stein all over again
I thought language poetry was trying to make the reader feel smart
I thought language poetry was wary of proclamations of sincere expression
I thought language poetry was a lot of nonsense packaged to look important
I thought language poetry was the possibility for freedom
I thought language poetry was the major precursor to word-salad email spam
I thought language poetry was short for L=A=N=G=U=A=G=E poetry
I thought language poetry favored style over manner
I thought language poetry was too intellectual
I thought language poetry was too difficult to ignore
I thought language poetry was the cat's scratch
I thought language poetry was neither a school nor a movement but a
transient moment
I thought language poetry was a chimerical constellation
I thought language poetry was tendencies and investments not rules or
orders
I thought language poetry was minor literature with a vengeance
I thought language poetry was a collective figment of a collective imagination
I thought language poetry was an illusion
I thought language poetry was over
I thought language poetry resists the authority of language poetry

[2007: *Work*]

11. Firewood/Foreword

Give me a place to sit and I can *mysthink* the world.

That is to say, every attempt to instrumentalize poetry diminishes its power. In other words, two steps behind, three steps over.

Or to translate: depth is just another kind of surface and surface is either the stutter of inconsequence or a concretization of the sublime.

Let's put it this way: don't mind the store, mine words.

Or then again—if you bought it, you have to live with it, and life ain't worth the paper it's printed on if you lose heart.

A reign of dullness is not the fate of poetry but a bad weather condition.

Wind alert: Efforts to avert the conventional are met with every possible defamation and denunciation.

Ice storm: Poetry of ethical, aesthetic, and social challenge is dismissed as morally deranged, aesthetically inadequate, and politically wrongheaded.

The history of poetry is pockmarked by innovation and invention, by the struggle for the new *not as novelty but as necessity*. And this aesthetic struggle has often, though not always, been led by those previously denied a place in literary history. Over the past two centuries, this *pataquerical* imperative has become Western poetry's activist center. The macadamized verse of conventional poetry (MVCP) proliferates like lawn ornaments in a museum of suburban life. In such works, coherence and expression metamorphose into a Coke and Pepsi mélange, concocted for sipping on a smoky, hot day. MVCP abhors aesthetic pleasure and semantic license, supposing it can save meaning by suffocating it.

Williams Carlos Williams, *Paterson*:

Without invention nothing is well spaced,
unless the mind change, unless
the stars are new measured, according
to their relative positions, the
line will not change, the necessity
will not matriculate: unless there is
a new mind there cannot be a new
line, the old will go on
repeating itself with recurring
deadliness: without invention
nothing lies under the witch-hazel
bush, the alder does not grow from among

the hummocks margining the all
but spent channel of the old swale,
the small foot-prints
of the mice under the overhanging
tufts of the bunch-grass will not
appear: without invention the line
will never again take on its ancient
divisions when the word, a supple word,
lived in it, crumbled now to chalk.[7]

"unless there is / a new mind there cannot be a new / line" is the motto of an Emersonian poetics, echoing a Romanticism that resists lyric containment, even if it elides the material and social barriers to such transformation. Even so, this remains a motto for a poetics of democratic social space, whether we call it avant-garde, experimental, exploratory, innovative—or, and here's the rub, *rootless cosmopolitism*.

Ezra Pound's attack on Jews as rootless cosmopolitans echoes in today's culture debates. The ahistorical/revanchist quest for a deep or authentic identity as the sole property of a single group, which has fueled the rise of the global right, is toxic for the kind of poetry I want.

In contrast, identity remains a volatile issue for the poetics of invention: the identity of the poet as well as the poem, the identity of language as well as the social world, the identity of politics as well as emotion. The kind of poetry I want reveals in every line that meaning is as plural as human consciousness. In this light, avant-garde aggrievement is the malaise of a poetry that is under siege from those who reject its calling as epistemological inquiry, as secular, as resisting closure, as anti-authoritarian. Aggrievement negates the sublimity of the formalist imaginary, turning what can be an exhilarating agonism into self-destructive resentment.

In large measure, the poetry canon is a history of heterodoxy. That is why it's worth noting that the 2018, sixth edition of the *Norton Anthology of English Poetry*, has turned against the values of the tradition it proposes to profess. While this always problematic flagship anthology includes a fair number of the poets who comprise a radical tradition of invention in English language poetry over hundreds of years, among the several dozen living poets, there is a total shut-out of US and UK poets recognized as, or

7. William Carlos Williams, *Paterson: Revised Edition*, ed. Christopher MacGowan (New York: New Directions, 1992), p. 50. Thanks to Richard Cureton for citing this passage.

championing, the necessity of aesthetic invention in poetry (as reflected by inclusions in the major British, US, International, African American, Asian American, and women's anthologies and annuals recognizing such work, not to mention the poets discussed in this collection). People talk about the crisis of the humanities: this is no small part of it. The publisher and editors necrotize their own authority by turning away from poetry as a living art. To exclude mavericks and pioneers also trivializes the work of many worthy poets who are included and deserve to have more robust company.

The lesson is not new: official verse culture is pernicious not so much for formally radical poetries, which have developed alternate means of production and reproduction, but for the history of poetry and the centrality of poetry within contemporary culture. The Norton peddles its wares as a valuable introduction while proclaiming poetry's death.

But *it's alive!* This collection continues the necessary work of both celebration and reflection on poetry as a living art.

[2018: Foreword to *Reading Experimental Writing*, ed. Georgina Colby (Edinburgh: Edinburgh University Press, 2019)]

Groucho and Me

ROBERT WOOD: *In* Pitch of Poetry, *one gets a sense of your role in a critical community. This commitment to the forms and perspectives of others has been there for a long time, not only in* L=A=N=G=U=A=G=E, *but also in the Electronic Poetry Center and at PennSound.*[1] *You have spoken about these in relation to editing, technology, and other poets. But one other place where you see the collective in this new release is in the interviews in the section "Echopoetics." Why does 'the interview' matter in* Pitch of Poetry?

I only know what I think when I am in conversation. Conversation's an art: my thinking comes alive in dialog. I don't have doctrines or positions, I have modes of engagement, situational rejoinders, reaction deformations. It takes two to tangle, three to rumble, four to do the Brooklyn trot. I want my writing to dance to the changing beats of the house band. Dialog's the center of what I do: my collaborations with coeditors, composers, artists, and other poets; my work as host of the *LINEbreak* and *Close Listening* radio shows; my teaching. Beyond that I want poems that avert the single lyric voice expressing itself to the reader in favor of poems that deploy multiple voices and discourses calling out for response, poetry that comes alive when readers or listeners project their own psyches onto them, poems that find ways to be in conversation—*interenact*—with readers/listeners. "Echopoetics" locates writing as a form of listening, with reverb as rhythm's ungainly gait.—I am less interested in answering a question than bouncing off it, finding out where it takes me.

A sense of the collective also comes through in how you resist a hegemonic poetics that would dissolve aesthetic difference and often depoliticizes verse or even resurrect troubling aspects of Heidegger. You and I have spoken privately about

---

1. PennSound is at <writing.upenn.edu/pennsound>; subsequent references listed as "PennSound."

antisemitism in places as far away as Australian poetry. And there is a height-
ened concern about the limits of free speech. What do you make of all this?

I'm listening . . . because my first responses often strike me as tone deaf.
I come into both my political and aesthetic consciousness in, around &
about 1968. I recognize that some of my 60s/70s shibboleths fail in the
face of persistent economic and social inequality. But the problem with
neo-illiberalism and lyric atavism is that they quickly get absorbed by the
right. As Heidegger might have recognized, an acute sense of "aggrieve-
ment" often fuels right-wing attacks on those, like Jews, who are desig-
nated as foreigners and who are stigmatized as cultural/national invaders
and appropriators. A nightmare is haunting America and Europe; it's
slogan could be: "I am aggrieved by your aggrievement." The danger is
depoliticization in a reversion to instinctual loyalties. Aggrievement is
not the end of politics but its beginning. And yet, it's true that freedom
of speech (including tolerating pernicious ideas, though hopefully not
with silence but with vocal dissent) benefits those with power more than
those without it, which is a given in a perjurocracy (my neologism for rule
by those who violate the public trust, which echoes Pound's neologism,
pejorocracy, rule by the worst).

I find it useful to focus on the parts of Heidegger's late poetics that are
most compelling—not to spin that off from his illiberalism nor to taint
it as a siren song. Rather, it's a reminder that some of the most liberating
thinking about poetry is at the same time a poison: the cure that is a curse
(which means it is possible to mistake one for the other).

Curing might be good for meat but perhaps not thought, lest salami
turn to baloney.

I want a poetics that gets by without cures and where the curses curtsy
in time to unheard maladies.

—I am most Jewish in my aversion of *halakha*. My homeland is
diasporic.

You champion a polyvalent formalism and a progressive materialism. With
all that in mind, I was interested to see that you work at defining terms in
"Pataquericals & Poetics" in Pitch of Poetry. *It is a list of keywords that helps*
us with the primary work of sharing language with each other. How does defi-
nition matter as the first step in creating a community?

Over the past forty years, I've made up lots of terms as a way of resisting
linguistic reification—that is relying on a limited number of SuperNouns
as shorthand for entangled semantic complexes (ESCs). If you are making

a stump speech in a political campaign, the buzzwords may be necessary. But when they are used to police thought, under the sign of legibility, resistance is called for. I am erratic in the use of my own coinages and formulation, often restricting them to a single essay. I am not trying to introduce a new set of terms for general use and, indeed, many of my terms are sufficiently ludicrous to prevent general use.

In 1968, many of us objected to the reductive language of the old Left and the way it described the ills of the world with ten Super Nouns. Every one of those nouns were both revelatory and reductive. Like many, I was looking for nonbinary alternatives. One term I made up in the '70s is ready for a revival, *com(op)posing*: Writing resistance to established norms, including received ideas of how the world is represented. This is also why I often find myself persona non grata. That's been my perverse joy all along: to create resistance to assimilation in order to provoke thought and pleasure.

Com(op)posing: Poesis as a pose, a come-on that flaunts itself as such, *opposing* oscillating with *composing*.

Building on from that, there are implications for thinking about poetry and poetics when it comes to revisioning one's own historicization. We see this in "The Pataquerical Imagination," which features the words of others woven together to manifest a future for "Bent Studies." Talk to us about your historical materialism and explain what "Bent Studies" might become.

"Bent Studies" and "pataqueroid," from *Pitch of Poetry*, are among my most recent coinages, which link, in the final essay, to "midrashic antinomianism." Antinomianism is the refusal to be governed by moral (or religious) law. This is disobedience not lawlessness (as, paradigmatically, in the teaching of St. Paul). Antinomianism is an active aesthetic that rejects morality decreed by authority in favor of an ethics that is founded in social praxis. Obedience by our own lights, not searchlights from on-high. Susan Howe reads Dickinson as an antinomian, working in the wake of Anne Hutchinson. But there is also a Jewish antinomianism—an aversion of *halakha* (in particular ritual law). The antinomian frees midrash (commentary, interpretation) from proscribed meaning, allowing for allegorical and associative readings (and for poetry that does not have an intended moral message).

Poetry, the kind of poetry I want, is not the unmediated expression of truth or virtue but the bent refractions, echoes, that express the material and historical particulars of lived experience. My poems don't instruct, nor do they signal my virtue; they don't translate into easily assimilable anecdotes and messages. Rather, the poems provide a thinking/feeling/ perceptual field that readers enter at their own (imaginary) peril. They provide a place for *interenacting*.

I think all these aspects also matter to Near/Miss. *Other critics have noted its disruptive openness and how you break the heart of cliché. Yours is not an authentic voice expressing its inner self in language that is easily accepted and readily acceptable. What is it pitched towards and for whom?*

Pitched toward the moon. And just for you.

   Pitch is defined in the preface to *Pitch of Poetry* as frequency of a voice (highness or lowness), sales rhetoric, black gummy matter from wood tar or turpentine, inclination (as on a boat), degree of intensity, and the throw of a baseball. But I want to add, in respect to *Near/Miss*: the place you choose to station yourself, as when you pitch a tent.

One of the qualities I noticed in the book is the enmeshment of language with technology. It does help me think about Near/Miss *as part of your longer interests from the Xerox machine to your blog. I was wondering if you could unpack the social relations of this in light of the multinational digital corporation.*

The slash in the title of *Near/Miss* is, possibly, the mark of mediation. Verbal language is one kind of mediation, writing is another, the recorded voice yet another. *Near/Miss* was issued in cloth and paper as well as a digital and an audiobook. Susan Bee's cover image is based on a still from Robert Bresson's *Pickpocket*. It represents the lover's visit to the prison, where she is separated from her beloved by bars or a grate, something that also brings to mind the grate of a confessional. The painting offers itself as an allegory of mediation, of language: that a grate separates us from that which we are closest. The grate is a gate.

Daniel Benjamin in Chicago Weekly *asked you about being a "trickster and a charmer" but I prefer to think of you as a Groucho Marxist. I always appreciated that you had a childhood with vaudeville, Lenny Bruce, and gallows humor. In this collection, you use the pun, the dad joke, and irony to great effect. Your humor never sits still but it always plays around. What makes poetry fun?*

There is a direct connection with what I do and the work of Groucho Marx. His comedy is grounded in puns, on tripping on the material conditions of words, and on context switching. The jokes are embodied, situational, and antic. They reflect the shrewd intelligence of the second-

language speaker: the making of the diasporic, the condition of immigra-
tion, a home ground filled with delight. Bringing to mind another great
Jewish entertainer, Harry Houdini, Groucho Marx's jokes are allegories of
escape, and especially escape from being defined. The Jewish comic, like
the Jewish poet, dodges, deflects, evades, ducks.

Why a duck? Because someone may be throwing a punch.

"Certainly there be that delight in giddiness, and count it a bondage
to fix a belief; affecting free-will in thinking, as well as in acting," Francis
Bacon writes in "Of Truth."[2] I don't want to run from this warning so
much as up the ante. I use something Bacon writes a few sentences later
as an epigraph to "Professing Poetics" in *Attack of the Difficult Poems*: "But
it is not the lie that passeth through the mind, but the lie that sinketh in,
and settleth in it, that doth the hurt, such as we spake of before." That's
perjurocracy.

The illicitness of the comic, like the radical impersonality of the
scientific method, has the potential of unsettling truth, of setting it free.
Where freedom is not an end but precariously transitory. The comic as a
method of aesthetic intensification is best when its giddiness is measured
by its ability to resist redemption.

In Near/Miss *you use a lot of repetition, from list poems to rehashed slant
phrases to other passages that recur. What draws you to repetition and what do
you think it negates?*

The poems with reiterating structures, for example with every line repeat-
ing the same word or phrase, fall under my rubric *radical legibility.* Several
poems of this kind appeared in *Girly Man*, though my first use of radical
legibility goes back to one of my earliest works, from 1974, "My/My/
My."[3] Since the lines of these poems tend to be short, each one is riveting
and it's impossible to get lost. Even if you miss a line, when your mind
drifts, the poem stays in the groove. The structure marshals attention in
a way that borders on coercive. At the same time, the poems don't have a
conventional anecdotal or scenic coherence; the array of lines is concep-
tually divergent. So the form allows for simultaneous discontinuity and
continuity at a high level. In some ways, radical legibility has a similarity
to the overlapping repetitions in the music of Steve Reich but with the
glaring difference that the line-for-line shifts are semantically disruptive

2. <en.wikisource.org/wiki/Bacon%27s_Essays/Of_Truth>

3. *Asylums* (New York: Asylum's Press, 1975)

rather than modulating. The coerciveness is countered by the porousness of the array, so the works approach what Tan Lin discusses as "ambient." Moreover, each of these poems is a patacosmology, that is, each generates *a* world but not *the* world.

You also attend to the rhythm, musicality, and aural qualities in these latest poems; ear work and close listening have been well noted by other critics and interviewers. But tell us about the other senses in Near/Miss; *or, its corporeal imaginary?*

The sense of unknowing, not being able to put your finger on it. That so-called sixth sense of the intuitive. Going by ear rather than by eye or idea.

Near/Miss *could also be read as a fulcrum. After this, will there be a confessional turn to liberal lyric that is palatable to the burghers of official verse culture? I want to know your pitch for tomorrow in our poetry and poetics.*

Tastes morph and sheer persistence—persistence of resistance—has its power. When I got the Bollingen Prize for American Poetry last month I was stunned and happy. I take it that the prize was partly for my sticking with my poetics by not staying the same, for opening myself and my work to changing forms, but also for acknowledging continuity (and warping) in the shifts. The more I change the more I encounter myself. "My/My/My" was already listing all the things that I could call mine as both incommensurable and a barrier. When the Bollingen was announced, I got a flood of letters and congratulations. I'm grateful for each one. "You deserve it," many wrote; I was heartened. But I know "you deserve it" is also what one says to someone who is made to walk the plank. The jury is always out on poetry: each reader delivers the verdict for a poem every time they read it. And in that lies poetry's freedom.

[2019: *Los Angeles Review of Books Blog*]

Shadows

Duncan, Pritchard, Gins & Arakawa,
Blaser, Ott, Creeley, Bromige, Federman,
Zukofsky, Cavell, Schwerner

ἐγὼ δέ τοι ἐγγυαλίξω . . .
ἦ μάλα τοῦτο ἔπος θυμαλγὲς ἔειπες
(In my care?
Words that grieve)

Odyssey, 16:69–70

1. Two Minutes for Robert Duncan [1919–1988]

It's funny to have to be brief about Robert Duncan, since there is nothing brief about his work or my responses to it.

There seems no limit to the breadth and scope Duncan envisioned as a poet's project. Because his endeavor so overwhelms any of the traditional ways we have of defining poetic work—as, say, lyric poems or critical essays—he continually provoked a reexamination of the smallness of scale that characterizes the conception of poetry of many of his more mainstream contemporaries. His research and scholarly preoccupations, his insistence that linguistics and the Dark, Saussure and gnosticism, are sources of the poetic remain an important alternative to residual anti-intellectualism and emotion-fetishizing of much contemporary verse. The fact that Duncan's poetry remained controversial because it was thought to be too intellectual or not plain-spoken enough has given encouragement to at least two subsequent generations of poets, who have taken off on his "permissions" while interpreting them in wildly different ways.

For me, the heterodox range of Duncan's sources has had impact even beyond any of his specific enthusiasms. Anyone who visited his house could attest to the sheer exuberant fantasy and marvelous humor of Duncan and Jess's transformations of these "sources" into a home as rich with whimsy as accumulated knowledge. Duncan inspires one not to accept the given narrative of cultural history but to look to a multiplicity of hidden and suppressed and vilified sources for myth-shattering revelations about the past and present. This insistence that poetic material is to be found not only, or even primarily, in the hallowed texts of Literature but also in those sources that are without authority is a foundation of his consistently anti-authoritarian, liberatory politics and poetics. It would be ironic if his own explorations and wanderings are sanctified into a new curriculum of required study.

The first time I met Robert Duncan, after a performance I did in San Francisco in the mid-70s, he handed me a poem he had written while I was reading and in response to my work. I've often thought about the generosity of the gesture of entrusting me with his only copy of this poem, which went so much beyond any friendly words he might have said at the time.

Here is something of what he wrote in the poem:

She appeared in a shift
waiting for shifters. From one sentence to the other
a world is declared necessary. Time
has to count to be counted. In phrases.
In phase. In consequences. In place.
In this place I is an event without a hat.
I meanwhile mean my own hat.
What I does is natural
in a sentence referring to me me occurs.

Duncan's last book, *In the Dark*, will always be associated for many of us with the news of his death. Thinking about that marvelously evocative title—suggesting both the terrors of unknown and the grace of fallibility—I kept hearing Lil Green (born, like Duncan, in 1919) singing her bluesy "Romance in the Dark," a sound transported from almost fifty years ago, that seemed to meet this occasion with full force.

In the dark, it's just you and I
Not a sound, there's not one sigh
Just the beat of my poor heart in the dark.
In the dark, in the dark, I get such a thrill
When he presses his fingertips upon my lips
And he begs me to please keep still in the dark.
But soon, this dance will be endin'
And you're gonna be missed . . .

Just let them dance, we're gonna find romance
In the dark, in the dark

[1988: Presented at a memorial tribute to Robert Duncan on October 9, at the Poetry Project, St. Mark's.]

2. N. H. Pritchard [1939–1996]

I found N. H. (Norman) Pritchard's *The Matrix: Poems 1960–1970* just a few years ago—perhaps 2002—at the Ark, a used bookstore on the Upper West Side of Manhattan. It is an elegant clothbound book with a large photo of Pritchard, featuring his stylish handlebar moustache—he looks a bit like a soulful Salvador Dali—staring, eerily, from the front cover (or is it from the great beyond?). The book was published by Doubleday in 1970 but the only sustained references I know to Pritchard's work are A. L. Nielsen's immensely useful discussion in his 1997 *Black Chant: Languages of African-American Postmodernism* and a much earlier essay by Lorenzo Thomas, "The Shadow World: New York's Umbra Workshop & Origins of the Black Arts Movement," published in *Callaloo* in 1978. (Nielsen mentions a 1992 essay by Kevin Young, "Signs of Repression: N. H. Pritchard's *The Matrix*.")

Pritchard is a gloriously iconoclastic poet, who combines syntactic wildness, visual daring, and conceptual scatting. *The Matrix* is a strikingly designed volume, composed of seventy-one poems in three parts, mostly visual or "concrete" poems, which are at the same time "sound" poems. It is one of the most interesting works of its kind from this period of American poetry. Nielsen mentions the connection to scat, a jazz vocalist's style of intoning "vocables" (vocal sounds not immediately processed as words), while Thomas notes the connection with the "vocal styles and tones" of African languages. Pritchard hops, skips, and jumps with his syncopated words, creating spaces inside words in a way that makes one word many. It's a rhythmic concatenation that relies on multiplicity and ambiguity. When I first read these poems, I realized Pritchard was a perfect example of the "ideolectical," about which I write in "The Poetics of the Americas" in *My Way: Speeches and Poems*. The ideolectical is meant to suggest a synthesis of dialect and idiolect, centering on the use of nonstandard words and syntax—whether invented or based on the vernacular.

The opening page of *The Matrix* gives virtually all the information I know about Pritchard: Born in New York City in 1939, graduated from NYU, published in *Umbra* (a crucial magazine of the Black Arts movement), *The New Black Poetry*, as well as *The East Village Other*. He also performs his poetry on the 1967 Broadside album, compiled by Walter Lowenfels, *New Jazz Poets*. The bio ends with a notice that he teaches a workshop at the New School and is poet-in-residence at Friends Seminary.

Subsequently, I found a copy of his second book, *Eecchhooeess*, published by New York University Press in 1971. The book continues the complex, often letter-for-letter linguistic, visual, and sound play of *The Matrix*. Taken together, Pritchard's two books anticipate several of the formally inventive techniques that would gain greater circulation in the United States later in the 1970s, though his work is almost never referenced in these contexts because, within a few years of these two books, the work seemed to disappear from the poetry horizon. (I recognize the circular reasoning here: lack of reference erases, the erased are not well enough known to reference; after all, the work was out there to find.)

Other traces of Pritchard: a magnificent, very short piece on a 1999 album by Bill Dixon, playing with Tony Oxley, entitled "Quadro Di N.H. Pritchard"; I am listening to it now—and the majestic space between each note seems to open up a universe inside the one we so often think we are living in. The album is called *Papyrus* and it reminds me about what is not yet lost in our vast trove of paper and digital archives: if only we know where to look or how to read what we find.

Over time, in which we are all lost, some words, or almost words, jolt us, jam us, join us, as this from *EECCHHOOEESS*:

junt

mool oio clash brodge

cense anis oio

mek me isto plawe

[2004: *Dark Horses: Poets on Lost Poems,* ed. Joy Katz and Kevin Prufer (Champaign: University of Illinois Press). For the collection of poems, I selected "Epilogue" from *The Matrix*.]

* * *

P.S.: In an interview in the March 2023 issue of the *Brooklyn Rail*, N. H. Pritchard's friend Ishmael Reed, referring to him, says: "Charles Bernstein appropriates him as a Language poet, but you know, his basis, his stuff was Black, his rhythms were Black. And he was doing hip-hop before it was popular—well, we all were." David Grundy cites two letters from Pritchard to Reed (June 2, 1970, and August 23, 1971), in which he writes of a planned anthology, *Origins: A Contribution to the Monophysiticy of Form*, later named *Origins: An Anthology of Transreal Writing*. "Further, undated notes for the Transreal Anthology," Grundy writes, "list potential participants ranging from Bruce Andrews and Clark Coolidge through to Amiri Baraka, Ginsberg, and Richard Brautigan."[1] When I wrote this essay two decades ago, I was able to find out very little of Pritchard. But in the last few years, there has been an upsurge of interest in his work. In 2021, both of his books were reprinted by Primary Information/Ugly Duckling Presse and DABA (the imprint of artist Adam Pendleton). Also in 2021, I located an autobiographical interview Pritchard did with Judd Tully for the CETA Artists Project in 1978. We were able to make that available at *Jacket2*/PennSound.[2] This recording gives the best account of Pritchard's story and greatly expands knowledge of his work. By a strange poetic logic, in 1978 I was working as the associate director of the CETA Artists Project, and just beginning to coedit *L=A=N=G=U=A=G=E*, but I knew nothing about Pritchard. In 1980, we also appeared together at the 12th Annual International Sound Poetry Festival in New York, but I missed his performance. I remain stunned, and disappointed, that I didn't know about him while he was alive. But it's poetic justice that his work, and its many contexts, are now being rediscovered.

3. A +/- G

Shusaku Arakawa (1936–2010)
Madeline Gins (1941–2014)

Beauty is momentary in the mind—
The fitful tracing of a portal;
But in the flesh it is immortal.

The body dies; the body's beauty lives.
So evenings die, in their green going,

1. David Grundy, "'mistish liftings': N. H. Pritchard manuscript notes" (2021) at <jacket2.org /commentary/grundy-pritchard>

2. <jacket2.org/commentary/pritchard-1978>. The recording was found by Molly Garfinkel of City Lore as part of archival work on the CETA Artists Project. In this *Jacket2* post, I include references to recent scholarship on Pritchard as well as a summary of the interview and photographs. See Pritchard's PennSound page for all available recordings.

A wave, interminably flowing.
So gardens die, their meek breath scenting
The cowl of Winter, done repenting.

—Wallace Stevens[3]

I found a deep connection with the early paintings of Arakawa and with Arakawa and Madeline Gins's paradigmatic *The Mechanism of Meaning* (1971), as well as various early writings by Gins, particularly her essay on multidimensional architecture, which I published in *boundary 2*, thirty years ago (this work that anticipates much of Gins and Arakawa's later work in what they called "procedural architecture").[4] Gins is the author of two literary masterpieces, *The Mechanism of Meaning* and *Helen Keller or Arakawa* (1994). These works, as well as Arakawa and Gins's later works, share a space with many of the poets and artists with whom I have been most engaged.

Susan Bee and I met Arakawa and Gins through Hannah Weiner in the late 1970s. Indeed, Susan and I wrote one of our few collaborative essays, in 1981, "Meaning the Meaning: Arakawa's Critique of Space," in which we looked at Arakawa's early painting and *The Mechanism of Meaning* in terms of a critique of Euclidean and Cartesian conception of space-time, what Robin Blaser, thinking of Olson and Whitehead, called the Western Box, but which also relates to Donald Ault's work on Blake, *Visionary Physics*.[5]

In my poetics, an artwork takes on its greatest significance when seen in the context of works by other contemporary artists as well as in terms of the social and historical, and indeed biographic, contexts in which it emerges. For this reason, and going against the grain of Arakawa and Gins's own troubling self-projections as working beyond comparison, I want to be explicit in refusing to isolate the collaborative work of these two artists via a Romantic exceptionalism or philosophical idealism both of which risk subliming the material grounding, generic specificity, and social force of the art work, which is fundamentally embedded in its time and is always and primarily part of a collective project. For this reason, I would want to emphasize the value of placing work of Arakawa and Gins among their contemporaries in poetry and the visual arts (painting, site-specific and

3. "Peter Quince at the Clavier," in *Collected Poetry and Prose,* ed. Frank Kermode and Joan Richardson (New York: Library of America, 2008), p. 72

4. Madeline Gins, "From an Essay on Multidimensional Architecture," in *43 Poets* (1984), ed. Charles Bernstein, *boundary 2* 14: 1–2 (1985–1986)

5. Collected in *Content's Dream: 1975–1984*. I also discuss Arakawa and Gins in "Every Which Way but Loose," in *Attack of the Difficult Poems: Essay and Inventions* and in the preface to *With Strings*.

installation work, conceptual art) rather than considering their work as disembodied ideas relating primarily to speculative philosophy. While I appreciate the references to Deleuze or to Nietzsche, or indeed Blake in my account in "Every Which Way but Loose," I find it more telling to think of Gins in the context of Hannah Weiner, Richard Foreman, Ron Silliman, Leslie Scalapino, Robert Grenier, Joseph Kosuth, and Eva Hesse; and, specifically in the visual arts, let me use the shorthand "Poetry Plastique," the show I co-curated with Jay Sanders in 2001, which focused on work with words that moved off the page. We were happy to have Gins and Arakawa as part of that show, where they found a solid grounding, along with—and I mention these names advisedly—Jackson Mac Low, Robert Smithson, Philip Guston, and Wallace Berman.

In 2002, Hank Lazer and I published Arakawa and Gins's *Architectural Body* in our modern and contemporary poetics series. Like the essay on multidimensional architecture, I consider this and related work not to be theory, philosophy, or science, but rather to be a conceptual poem or more precisely pata-conceptual, for I see Alfred Jarry, as much as Duchamp, as the presiding angel of these works. If we read Arakawa and Gins as philosophy, then they will seem like so many Sancho Panzas, and come out short. But as pataphysics, Arakawa/Gins enter into a still active set of swerving quests.

Arakawa and Gins's swerve to architecture and the folly of their assertion of efficacy (of reversing mortality) was not only a turn from poetry and art but also from pataphysics. Yet it is the refusal of that turn, returning their procedural architecture to the realm of imaginary solutions, which reclaims their most significant work for poetry and art.

One further telegraphic point: No full account of Arakawa's work—from the productive—but now often overlooked—engagement with blank and painting as "thinking fields" to the more recent work on what he and Gins call "reversible destiny" should fail to note that Arakawa is the same half-generation as the group of poets I discuss in a late '80s essay of mine called "The Second War and Postmodern Memory" (in *A Poetics*)—all born during, like Gins, or in the first years of, the Second World War; and in Arakawa's case—more specifically and distinctly from anyone else I have mentioned, growing up in Japan and being around eight years old at the time of the bombing of Hiroshima and Nagasaki, which is made explicit in his early "coffins," made while still living in Japan.

They say, "We may have decided not to die," but I say, we will anyway, each of us, often painfully for those in whose care we have lived. The task of art is as much to mourn the dead as it is to listen to their voices as we move into an ever-flickering present. Immortality only works as a metaphor if it reminds us of its opposite: our fragility in the world. This is known / deep in the bones / of those born in an apocalypse.

The body dies; the body's beauty lives.

War is so real we can't even imagine it, so real we can't do anything else but imagine it over and over again. Let's just say these works—theirs and ours—become crystalline structures of loss: imagined/fabricated dystopias, closed or trapped worlds. Or what I lately keep calling (thinking of works of my own), bachelor machines after Duchamp and Kafka's *Penal Colony*: nonprocreative, self-collapsing systems—or let me already rename what I have just named: these are para- or anti- or indeed pata-bachelor machines. Their uselessness is their greatest claim to our engagement.

[2009: The core of this essay was written before Arakawa and Madeline Gins died. I wrote it for a conference on their work at Barnard College, Gins's alma mater, organized by Serge Gavronsky. While Arakawa was too sick to attend (he died of ALS soon after), Gins was present, and we continued to discuss these issues over the next few years.]

4. Blaser's Fire [1925–2009]

The Fire: Collected Essays of Robin Blaser, ed. Miriam Nichols (Berkeley: University of California Press, 2006)

Robin Blaser's best known essay is "The Practice of Outside," his extended introduction to the poetry of Jack Spicer that appeared in *The Collected Books* (1975). This is one of the key works of poetics to emerge from the New American Poetry, comparable, in its own way, to "Projective Verse" by Charles Olson, Jack Spicer's Vancouver lectures, and Robert Creeley's *A Quick Graph*. Unlike Olson or Creeley, though, Blaser published his first essay only in 1967, after he turned forty and after he had established himself as a poet. Indeed, the bulk of the collected essays are from after 1980; the signal exceptions being "The Fire" (1967), "Particles" (1969), and "The Stadium of the Mirror" (1974). His poetics has the advantage of its belatedness, but its belatedness is also exemplary of an aversion to the programmatic and his commitment to a space of in-between that refuses the abstract binary logic of contradiction in favor of a generative "polar logic" of nonidentity and disjunction. This could be described as the ethical basis of Blaser's aesthetics.

There are internal reasons, aesthetic reasons, for Blaser's aversion of canonical publication. This is the first collection of his essays, and it is being published simultaneously with an expanded American edition of his collected poems, *The Holy Forest*, also from the University of California Press. For one thing, his work insists on elusiveness as a social investment not just as a literary trope. It questions a semiotic economy of accumulation (intersecting with both Baudrillard's and Bataille's interest in a "general economy").

Miriam Nichols has done a meticulous job as editor for both the poems and essays. She has provided a set of notes that are both useful and comprehensive: uncredited citations are documented; allusive references are made concrete. Nichols's insistence on providing these paratexts make this edition definitive. Her introduction details the main contributions of these essays and their historical significance. Indeed, she has turned what could have been a valuable essay collection into a superb scholarly edition.

Compared to the essays by his immediate contemporaries, Blaser's are, by design, philosophically more sophisticated. While Blaser wears his polymathy lightly—often in the form of allusive citation—he is deeply informed by, but by no means entirely in synch with, many of the poststructuralist thinkers of the 1970s and 1980s, and also with the key currents in European philosophy from phenomenology to existentialism to the Frankfurt school. At the same time, his poetics is best understood as a deepening and a socializing/historicizing of the poetics of the New American Poetry. There are certainly many productive differences—and productive continuities—between his work and the philosophers with whom he affiliates himself. Blaser's essays also make more apparent the affinities with, and the differences between, the New American Poetics and the poetics of the next generation.

Blaser's essays do not lend themselves to quotation since they come to life not so much in any given sentence or gloss but rather in a process of thinking that moves from one citation to another. He cultivated insubstantiality and evanescence in a genre better known for hyperbole, imperviousness, and arrogance. Blaser comes as close as anyone to having created a poetics that manifests itself as a tissue of citation rather than substantive exposition or proposition (and he surely has in mind Walter Benjamin's idea of a text composed entirely of quotations). The result is that he practices what he preaches: his "self" is subsumed by his "great companions" and by the language through which he encounters them. His submerged voice (let's just say, *voicelessness*) is exemplary in the classical sense. Blaser's is a poetics of deep listening, introjective rather than projective.

If "The Practice of Outside" remains the defining essay on Spicer, "The Violets: Charles Olson and Alfred North Whitehead" is a crucial essay on

Olson's poetics. Using Whitehead as the avatar of a poetics of process (in a way that also calls to mind Dewey, Peirce, and Wittgenstein, but most of all Mallarmé and Blake), Blaser makes a powerful case for the limits of technorationality (what could also be called logocentrism) in the "Western box" (Olson's term). Among the fundamental issues of poetics that Blaser addresses here and elsewhere is the need to think through analogy and resemblance—to think serially, in opposition to the radical epistemological limits of positivism (a recurring pole of critique throughout). Nichols usefully refers to Blaser's "affective rendering of reflexivity." Blaser questions the stable lyric expressive "I" without ever abandoning the possibility of poetic agency, through an inspired understanding of the relation of language itself, as the social, as "outside."

[2006]

5. Gil's Shadow: Gil Ott [1950–2004]

We remembered Gil Ott last night at the Chax Press reading in Chelsea, a few months after his death. Gil cast a big, dark, deep shadow over the event. At times like this I am reminded that shadows are the foundation of imagination.

Charles Alexander, Chax's editor and publisher, came to New York to celebrate the twentieth anniversary of his press but also his new collection, *near or random acts*, which is, as it happens, Gil's last Singing Horse Press release and, at the same time, the first book in the new life of the press, under the very capable hands of Paul Naylor.

I am glad I got to see Gil last week at the University of Pennsylvania hospital intensive care unit. Bob Perelman and I went on Tuesday afternoon. Gil was miraculously self-possessed, engaged with the conversation, ironic, barbed. If my eyes had been closed, I imagine I could have been across the street, chatting in my office; there was little in his voice that reflected the grim intensity of the surroundings or his physical circumstances. Gil spoke of his forthcoming book, *The Amputated Toe*, from Kyle Schlesinger's Cuneiform Press, as his "last" book and wondered if Kyle knew it was his last. Bob and I offered an alternative meaning to last: "you mean your most recent book." Then Gil told us the story of how anxious Franco Beltrametti had been for Gil to bring out his Singing Horse book, though Beltrametti never explained to Gil that he was dying, that this was to be his last book (which, indeed, he did see before he died). Then Gil said, "Let's talk about something else."

Gil spoke of how extraordinary his prolonged life had been, the gift of living without his own kidneys for a quarter of a century. He said he was one of the longest surviving members of that class of early kidney transplant patients and almost all we know of Gil and his work as a poet, editor, organizer, has been in the period of grace provided by his renal subversions.

My first memory of Gil is walking down Spring Street in the late 1970s, going east from the Ear Inn, in the year or so after an unsuccessful transplant. I remember how slow he walked, how cumbersome and heavy his body seemed. And how, just a year later, he came into a new life and new sense of physical and cultural possibility, after his first successful transplant.

I remember *Paper Air*, Gil's magazine, especially the Mac Low and Taggart issues. And I remember *Artifice of Absorption*, my essay-in-verse, which was first published as an issue of *Paper Air* in 1987 and which may have been part of Gil's turn from magazine to book publishing. This was Gil's and my first experiment with producing a book directly from a computer file. There were so many errors that crept in, that the process seemed to be insisting on a level of textual impermeability well beyond the desires of author and publisher.

But no number of anecdotes will bring Gil back from the dead: Gil, father of a daughter just the age of my son—eleven—, life companion to Julia Blumenreich, friend to so many of us.

Dead poets have one trick left: they live in our ears, in our minds, in our personal hereafter.

[2004]

6. Creeley's Eye and the Fiction of Self [1926–2005]

Robert Creeley's work, poems and prose alike, is preoccupied by self-reflection. His work is not so much an expression of an already defined 'I' but an exploration, or perhaps better to say, excavation of self: an extrapolation (estimation of unknown facts from a limited range of the known) of self: the "self" forming and reforming, through a serial process of poesis.

In one sense, the *I* in Creeley's work plays the role of a third-person character submerged in the tidal pulls of the experiential (most famously noted by his revisionist cogito, "As soon as / I speak I / speaks"—"The Pattern" in *Words*). In another sense, the *I* is always in the process of un-covering/re-covering itself, is always adjacent, hence never fully occupied or possessed, except perhaps at birth or death. (The self in Creeley is a virtual reality: it resides in the past or future but is a contemporary fiction.)

A key poem of this preoccupation, also from *Words*, is entitled "I." The poem begins by quoting from a local newspaper account that identifies the author by means of his patrilineal relations and their properties; that is, circumstances doubly adjacent ("adjoined," "extended") to whomever "I," the "present" Creeley of the poem, turns out to be:

I

"is the grandson
of Thomas L. Creeley, who acquired
eight acres of Belmont land around 1880 and

continued

"His house was numbered 375
Common st.
and his farm lands,
through the heart of which the present Creeley
rd. runs, adjoined

the Chenery holdings and extended
toward Waverly from the upper
Common St.
        The author's father, the late
Dr. Oscar Creeley,
was a prominent Watertown physician
for many years
        and headed
the staff of Symmes Hospital in Arlington."

I's—Robert's—belatedness to this scene is made explicit in the next lines, where we learn of the death of the grandfather's, T. L.'s, two sons, but most particularly the death of I's—the present author's—father:

I, is late

But I saw a picture of him once, T.L.
in a chair in Belmont, or it was his invalid

and patient wife they told me sat there, he
was standing, long and steady faced,
a burden to him she was, and the son. The
other child had died

They waited, so my father
who also died when I is four gave all
to something like
the word "adjoined," "extended"
so I feels
I sees the time as long and wavering
grass in all about the lot in all that
cemetery again the old man owned a part of
so they couldn't dig him up.[6]

Discussing this poem with Creeley in a graduate seminar in poetics at
the University at Buffalo, a student well-versed in poststructuralism was
excited that Creeley had come early to ideas about the dispersed, or belated,
subject. Nonetheless, alluding to the poem's grounding in an anecdote
rather than a philosophical proposition, the student ended by saying, "I was
disappointed." Without losing a beat, Creeley replied "I was disappointed
too," referring to the circumstances related in the poem, e.g., I would have
liked to have been that "I," able to occupy that space, but it was not pos-
sible. For Creeley, lack of self-possession is not a theory but a given—the
"common" circumstance, the "haunts and habits" of the places one's life
adjoins and extends, a "lot" in which "I" waits.

The autobiographical scene of "I" is much extended in *Autobiography*,
which is exemplary of Creeley's approach to the narrative demands of
prose fiction, particularly since the genre of autobiography typifies Cree-
ley's genre interests in his other fictional works. But more pertinent to my
preoccupation here, *Autobiography* offers an uncanny perspective on the
construction of the self if one exchanges, as I propose to do, an *eye* for an *I*.
In other words, what does it mean to lose an eye, or an *I*? Or lose an eye at
two and a father two years later? What *I* survives such lateness?

In the second paragraph of *Autobiography* the ontological scene is set:
Amid the onslaught of events, the self provides only an *apparent* centering
or agency, always subject to readjustments and recentering: "The great flood

6. Robert Creeley, *The Collected Poems* (Berkeley: University of California Press, 1982), pp. 279–80

of seeming chaos had only apparent agency for its signifying order, and that was oneself. . . . 'Mine eyes have seen the glory.'"[7] Mine I's indeed! Contingency intrudes early, in the form of a shower of broken glass, bringing with it the end of transparency, figuratively and literally: When two years old, Creeley's eye is "damaged" when he is "showered with broken glass full in the face when a stray lump of coal shattered the side window" of the car in which he is riding, sitting beside his father (pp. 19–20).

The damaged I: In Lacan's "stadium of the mirror," the child, looking into a mirror, claims herself for the first time as an integral physical entity separate from the external environment. In Creeley's "shower of broken glass," the child finds the external world impinging on his fragmenting body. Looking into the shattered glass, the child realizes, Ah ha! I am not whole, my self and sight are precarious, on the brink. Nor can the loss of the eye/I be mourned, for the tiny New England subject is warned that crying will only cause "further damage." Creeley continues: "For some time, then, the damaged eye was kept in place although it seems to have had little function" (20). So poetic function in this account is an act of reclamation, not, Romantically, of the self as an autonomous agent, but as a site of a series of encounters with a *forming real*.

"When I was five, just a year after my father's death, the eye was taken out." One day, waking from anesthesia, the subject "came to with a great bandage covering my head and the eye gone"—his mother had not warned him, as she had not explained what had happened to the father who the previous year had been "taken away" in an ambulance, gone forever (pp. 20–21). Again, this is not a psychoanalytic theory—the father and the eye/I taken out at the onset of the age of reason—but excruciatingly painful, acutely particular, events visited on the person, the body. To speak of the uncanny is to note these piercing homologies, that the (proprioceptive) history of the poet's body becomes itself an exemplary tale.

Creeley, in conversation, related that as a child he would take his glass eye out and put it next to his bedside; it had no necessity and he abandoned it as one might a prop: "Each evening one would take out the eye and put it in boric acid. You couldn't wear the eye continually. I wore that eye from five to eighteen—all of my adolescence, all of my formative years."—The *I* is not something you can assume, prefabricated, but must find a way to do without—"more a fact of places . . . than of changing progression," as Creeley says of his childhood in *Autobiography* (p. 28). (The glass "I" is an

---

7. Robert Creeley, *Autobiography* (Madras: Hanuman, 1990), p. 9. All subsequent page references are to this text.

eerie image of the sort of neat-persona verse and fiction of which Creeley's work is so much the antithesis.)

In *Autobiography*, as elsewhere in his work, Creeley says he lacked a "sense of what constitutes manhood," relating this particularly to his father's death when he was four (p. 43). Creeley doesn't celebrate this fact, as the student seemed to want him to celebrate the decentered self, because it is not for him a virtue. Nor does he gleefully wish to undo Whitman's self-celebration. Negative capability is not a bugle call. His "sudden losses" (p. 28) are a disappointment, for *this* subject expected to occupy, less self-consciously, the position of a self, and a man to boot. It didn't work out that way. ". . . the world has hardly been a nice place to live in" (p. 83). But from these star-crossed circumstances, a fictive poetry and a poetic fiction with ferocious commitment to the particular over and against the generalized was born.

[1995: *Review of Contemporary Fiction* XV:3]

7. The Difference Is Scale [David Bromige (1933–2009)]

"Cognition requires exaggeration," writes David Bromige in "Indictable Sobourners"—and the converse would apply equally to explain his method: *exaggeration requires cognition.* In extremus luminatus ludicrus.

However, it is an ungracious task, as the oxymoron says, to try to explain a joke. You get it or better yet (a) it gets you (b) you don't get it. That is, in these works it's not "subject matter" (shopworn hangnail) but form (allopathic progenitor) that's made intrinsically funny. "It is easier to see through my little tales than it is to see through the pernicious society we are trapped within. But the difference is merely scale." And this may begin to account for why each poem is approached (and so apprehended) in a determinately different way. "When you start to doubt your own skepticism, look out!" Bromige has never "fixed" on any one style or mode (there are characteristic reverberations of course) but tackles (targets) new turf (segmentation sections) with each tussle (six of one, couple of half-dozen of other). "It was very dark inside the fish." "This is among the most poignant: thoughts I know." This is a good deal different and more humanly refreshing—in the sense that a breath is more refreshing than a cough—than the idea of form as *plastique.* For Bromige, the question becomes what color plastic and why not rubber.

As to subject (subsequent) matters, Bromige makes mincemeat of the fashions of the "contemporary" "mind" ("The era had a milky density, tepid and torpid, mildly disgusting like a one-acre homesite; this disgust had spoken of the rebuttal to its final vestige of candid spontaneity, except that the toothache of the times looped a, scarf over everybody's ears,") and builds from there. An Englishman who came to the U.S. of A. by way of British Columbia (a.k.a. Canada's grey sunbelt) he has made cultural distance into a prosodic measure that leans on device without being devisive. "There is an intense pleasure of experience in the juxtaposing of the two polysyllabic words with the staccato monosyllables—*greift* and *Spuk* particularly spook me." [In this passage from *Threads* Bromige is referring to a quote from Heidegger; for the present context, *hot tub / retotalization* would do as well, as in there'll be a hot tub at the totalization tonight (requiring a further introjection into our unconscious episiotomies).]

"Doesn't all innovation in knowing happen much as a pun: the thread of likeness enables one to articulate what is in one sense the utterly dissimilar, since new. Or what had been forgotten." Eternity and paternity become avenues of access; the reader is left to draw the moral after Bromige has provided the tone and tonic.

"And still we hold there are times when we can bear witness to the present condition of absolute things."

"For language can take us there—wherever it is."

[1987: *The Difficulties*: David Bromige issue (1990). All quotes from Bromige: *The Uneven Steps of Hang Chow* (Berkeley: Little Dinosaur Press, 1982), p. 28; *Tight Corners and What's Around Them* (Los Angeles: Black Sparrow Press, 1974), p. 37; *Threads* (Black Sparrow Press, 1971), pp. 48 and 66; and *My Poetry* (Berkeley: The Figures Press, 1980), pp. 83 and 84. In 1988, Bromige's *Selected Poems, 1963–1987*, was published by Black Sparrow. I provided this endorsement: "David Bromige's *Desire* is a guide for the lovelorn and love-drenched, a devilish excursion into a psychorealism for which laughter is the exact analogue to human breath and paranoia an antidote (anecdote) for keeping your mind in view. In *Desire*, the bottom of everyday life drops through, as land mines are triggered by the reader's darting glances. *Desire* is a "blow struck for meaning"—&, boy, do these poems *blow*. David Bromige's hour has come—and it begins here."]

8. Raymond Federman: Double Portrait [1928–2009]

QUESTIONS

Raymond, what is the use of fiction? What is the use of stories? And what is the use of telling them, the same ones or different ones, over and again?

How about historical memory? Collective memory? Does fiction serve to spark or to spank memory? To make sure people don't forget or to be sure they remember the right things, and also remember the right things about the right things? You are a survivor of the Holocaust; your family was killed during the systematic extermination of the European Jews during World War II. We have many memorials of this systematic extermination. What do you think that such memorials should represent? Your work, which I would say is one of the most significant of the memorials to the systematic extermination process, in many ways veers into abstraction and digression—it refuses to represent those events. Why do you evade history? Is it that facts, or not any facts but those facts, refuse representation? But then do they refuse memory too? In any case, you make light of facts rooted (or is it rotting?) in that dark history. But whose history? Your history? Our history? You refuse to be solemn in the face of those horrendous events that have, in all actuality, in living color and dead black and white, occurred historically, but also hysterically. What gives you the right—moreover, what gives you the nerve—to be funny about this? Why aren't you, not only a real survivor, but also a famous one, terribly solemn and profoundly serious, like the memorials that we have all grown accustomed to, that make us weep and in our weeping comfort us? Your work seems to mock not only the possibility of accurate representation, but also the idea that mourning should be dignified. Do you think mourning is a joke? Why do you make readers so uncomfortable with your laughter, your self-consciousness? Why do you still kick up a fuss instead of writing with poignant, eloquent, tearful resignation?

What is 'The Voice in the Closet'? Whose voice? What is the voice saying?

When you speak of *Federman*, is that you? If so, why do you refer to yourself in the third person? Or are you not you to yourself? Did you lose that you in the closet? Or later? Who or what are you calling attention to when you name yourself, as you do so often, so insistently? Why do you call so much attention to this anxious act of self-naming? Is it because the name names an absence? Or is because in the absence of this naming you cease to exist to yourself, for yourself? Or for "us"?

Do you think your work is better understood in Germany or in Europe than it is in the United States? In Germany, do you represent a response to a German catastrophe and is that why you take a place of honor as a witness of, and commentator on, that catastrophe? In the U.S., are you seen as just another unintelligible experimental novelist refusing to give the dignity of sense to the catastrophes of your lifetime? Is your work *American* in its refusal to represent, in its insistence that response and representation are mutually exclusive? Were your works made possible because they are grounded in a cultural space that is non-European or anyway (for you) post-European? In what ways would you say your works portray a coming of age in America that is also the coming of age of America?

Ray, are you a poet or are you a fiction writer, and does it make any difference?

Your work is often immersed in some of the seamier sides of male culture, and it has sometimes been read as sexist. Yet, why is there is so little reference to the outdoors, to men doing virile things in open spaces? Why is there so little male bonding? And what about the sexual desperation of the men in your books? How do you imagine male sexuality?

Who is this guy who drops down by parachute into an Army barracks in the South in the 1950s? Why tell your story from the point of view of the man who fell to earth, or let's say to America? Why do you blur memoir with fiction? Why don't you take out the rough edges of that first encounter with America? Why does what is most 'experimental' about your books— the typography, the digressions, the multiple point of view, the insistent intrusion of aesthetics and philosophy—seem at first playful and then deadly, uncannily serious?

How about improvisation, Raymond? Your work plays a lot with a feeling of spontaneity, of just going on, with the pleasure of telling the story as it is happening. But if that's true, why does your work seem so composed that it decomposes in its own afterburn?

ANSWERS

For Raymond Federman fiction is useless.

Fiction is a delusion we use to screen ourselves from reality and reality is largely, though not entirely, delusional. This is why Federman is a storyteller and not a novelist. And assuredly not a writer of fiction.

And if he tells the same stories over and again it is because the story is never the same in any telling because, if it were, *that* would be fiction. And Federman writes nonfiction. Historical nonfiction.

Or else what he writes is a bed of lies. (A hole inside a gap.)

And anyway it is never the same story and Federman tells it over and again because what he has to tell, like history, cannot be told once and for all.

Like the same dream you keep having only it's not the same and this time you can't wake up.

Federman wakes us up.

Federman is a spelunker of either historical memory or collective forgetting, depending on the reader. He is not interested in the well-lit paths through the cave nor even the once-marked off-roads. What's a cave to him or he to a cave that we should weep so? Memory has become a way of forgetting, the recovered forgetting of the professional memoirist. Federman prefers the musings of Stan and Oliver, or Vladimir and Estragon. He speaks of his life like a defrocked poet at a coroner's inquest.

O, inconstant heart!

Digression is as much a foil as progression. Federman's digressions are as direct as "an arrow from the Almighty's bow." They pierce but don't wound. The wound is the condition, the voice in the closet that comes out, like Tinker Bell, only if you say you believe it. And you believe it only at your peril. (Pauline will fend for herself.)

The elementary error of the literature of self-help and affirmation, the preferred fiction of the mediocracy, is that trauma is overcome, that you get better, that there is healing. That there can be understanding. Federman neither dwells on the abyss, nor theatricalizes it, nor explains it, nor looks away.

The Dark is the ground of his being and his becoming.

Go nameless so that the name you are called by becomes you.

Federman is an improper noun full of signs and stories signifying (precisely) nothing. *Federman* names that which is *(k)not here.*

He is our American Jabès, only the rabbis have been subsumed into the bouillabaisse and the ladder loaned to the roofer.

And from that roof we shout to the crowd assembling below: Break it up! Go back to where you came from, if you can find it! *There is nothing to see here.*

The truth you seek is not on this earth nor in Heaven either.

Then Federman begins again.

One more time.

The words, at least the words, are indelible, even if we are not.

Or so the story goes. . . .

[Questions, 1995: *The Laugh That Laughs at the Laugh: Writing from and about the Pen Man, Raymond Federman*, ed. Eckhard Gerdes (based on our *LINEbreak* interview) and *Journal of Experimental Fiction*, 2002. Answers, 2007: Preface, *Federman's Fictions: Innovation, Theory, and the Holocaust*, ed. Jeffrey R. Di Leo, State University of New York Press, 2010.]

9. Zukofsky's Prepositions [1904–1978]

American poetics of the late twentieth century is saturated with the terms and techniques developed in *Prepositions*, Louis Zukofsky's only collection of literary essays. As the title of this book suggests, these articles are both prefatory and relational, providing an active thinking field in which the propositions of any particular poem may interact.

The essays collected in *Prepositions* span from 1924 to 1971. The collection begins with three essays that define Zukofsky's poetics of "sincerity" and "objectification" and continues with tributes to William Carlos Williams, Wallace Stevens, and Ezra Pound, poets from the generation preceding Zukofsky's who were of utmost importance for him. In addition, the collection includes short notes on some of Zukofsky's own works as well as reflections on Marianne Moore, Hart Crane, William Blake, George Santayana, Spinoza, Charlie Chaplin, Lewis Carroll, Henry Adams, and "outsider" painter Dometer Guczul. The book ends with Zukofsky's own list of key words, an "Index to Definitions" that composes its own poem of motifs, as, for example, in the thirteen words that begin with *m*: mass, meaning, measure, melody, memories, metaphor, mind, modern, montage, morality, motion, mysticism, myth.

One of the most influential essays in *Prepositions*, "An Objective," is based on three essays that Zukofsky wrote in 1930 and 1931, when he was in his late 20s, two of which were published in the breakthrough "Objectivists" issue of *Poetry* (1931), which Zukofsky edited. As a supplement to this edition of *Prepositions*, Mark Scroggins has assembled the original, far longer, versions of these essays, along with the most substantive interview with the poet, originally published in *Contemporary Literature* in 1968. Together with *Bottom: On Shakespeare* (1963), and *A Test of Poetry* (1948), this expanded edition of *Prepositions* provides the essential record of Zukofsky's published critical writings.

Zukofsky was born on January 23, 1904, in New York City, just a year after his mother had emigrated from what was then Russia and is now Lithuania (his father had come ahead a few years earlier). His first major publication was "Poem Beginning 'The'" in 1926, a trenchant response to Eliot's *The Waste Land* and a foundational poem for Jewish American modernism. His 24-movement long poem, *"A,"* written over the course of his entire writing life, was published in its first complete edition in 1978, the year of the poet's death. His *Complete Shorter Poems*, an extension of the succinctly titled *All*, was published in 1991.

Prepositions was constructed as a distillation or abstraction of Zukofsky's poetic thinking. Since complex structure and elision were Zukofsky's tools of the trade, it is not surprising that these essays reflect the result of a historical process of "getting it down to the bare bones," as he tells L. S. Dembo in the 1968 interview included here. The objective of these elisions is to keep the essays open to active thinking, to enable them to move into new historical and social and poetic contexts, all the while constantly transforming themselves. The context-specific buttresses of earlier versions of the essays weigh the pieces down into literary history; here the aspiration is for the words to stand on their own. Precisely because of the fundamental ambiguity of many of Zukofsky's terms, his essays, in their final form, remain available to reinterpretation and therefore reintegration into contemporary poetic thought and practice. This achievement is both prescient and exemplary.

For all the technical and quasi-logical qualities of the first set of essays in *Prepositions*, this is a work not of philosophy or aesthetics but of poetics. These are compositions not explanations, where the sincerity (care for the details) and objectification (structural solidity) of the writing take precedence over any putative argument. The image of an objective lens, which Zukofsky uses in "An Objective," is illustrative of the technique. The lens focuses the rays coming from an object, making the image ready for projection or microscopic examination. The image in the lens remains virtual or immanent, available for use. Zukofsky's poetics, like his poems, invite the reader's projection or introjection, to fill in the blanks.

Zukofsky was wary of philosophical abstractions and generalizations and his irritation with metaphysical poeticizing is evident throughout this volume: he thought such theorizing a lot of "gas" (p. 169). For Zukofsky, concepts such as *reality* or *knowledge* are disembodied and inert. Knowing, he insisted, takes place in particular acts of perception: "No thought exists / Completely abstracted from action" ("*A*"-8). Moreover, Zukofsky rejected that much-cherished humanist idea of poetry as a source of a generalized human truth: "*Impossible* to communicate anything but particulars— historical and contemporary—things," as he puts it in "An Objective" (p. 16). Specificity, detail, the concrete—these are, for him, the solid-state components of any poetics. And indeed, Zukofsky's poetics of the particular were significant not only for his closest contemporaries—Charles Reznikoff, George Oppen, Basil Bunting, and Lorine Niedecker—but also were formative for the poetics of Robert Creeley, especially as articulated in *A Quick Graph* (1970).

Certainly, Zukofsky does call for a poetry that "can speak to all" (p. 8), a formulation that is hardly particularistic; but the way to this objective is not through mythopoetic or thematic universalizing, nor through developing a theory of knowledge, but through the most concrete verbal attention humanly possible. When Zukofsky writes that "a case can be made out for the poet giving some of his life to the use of the words *the* and *a*" (p. 10), he is being deliciously provocative. He is also defining the shape of his own body of work, from "Poem Beginning 'The'" to "*A*" (eleven of whose sections begin with the letters *an*). The movement suggested here from the definite to the indefinite article is as telling as anything else in this poet's work.

In "An Objective," Zukofsky writes of a "Desire for what is objectively perfect" (p. 12). Poetry is not the realization of such a utopia but, in contrast, what is *aimed at*: an aspiration grounded in the historical practice of the art of configuring words. These essays are neither theories nor theorems but "steps" in a process sounded as "stops" on an organ: recursive, recombinant, resourceful, even restless. "Rested totality" (p. 13) is not the final stage at the top of the stairs but the *process* cast as "thing."

Several times in *Prepositions* Zukofsky notes that poetry approaches (or has as its "upper limit," as he puts it in *"A"*-12) the "wordless art of music" (p. 18). The recourse to music emphasizes the thingness of poetry (its object status), the sound value of poetry (its song), as well as poetry's durational space (its temporality). Unlike music, however, poetry's sound is verbal. For Zukofsky sound, pitch, rhythm, and tone do not accompany meaning, neither are they arbitrary nor conventionally associated with meaning: they *make* meaning (pp. 17, 19). When words are heard as sound, the poetic mode of perception has taken hold. The result is not free verse but an acoustically charged poetry whose patterns are not derived from manuals but newly invented. "Technique" is stressed but as a matter of innovation not of finesse: the "immediacy" (p. 78) of "invented technique" (p. 72) is valued over the imposition of received form (p. 23).

For Zukofsky, "objectification" marks an insistence on "the detail, not mirage, of seeing" (p. 12); the desire is to represent not the appearance of nature but its conditions—autonomy, completeness, self-sufficiency, particularity. Never words over world but words as world. In Zukofsky's poetics, "sincerity" is not an affect but the truth in the materials: "thinking with things as they exist" (p. 12), where things are not only objects but also persons. To adapt the familiar Kantian phrase, neither sincerity nor objectification pertains to *the thing itself*; rather, they are means of grappling with the structures and conditions through which things come into perception and by means of which we come into contact with them and live alongside them.

Zukofsky's poetics intricately elaborate on a key tenet of William Carlos Williams's, quoted in "A Statement for Poetry": "A poem is a small (or large) machine made of words" (p. 19). Zukofsky defines a modernist practice in which the poem is not an extension or expression of the self but an entity in itself, "another created thing" (p. 20). The value of a poem—*conviction* is Zukofsky's word—is not measured in terms of the work's "attitudes and beliefs" (p. 20) but by means of its style and technique. What matters is not the person standing behind the poem but the poem standing on its own prosodic feet, a construction set apart from the person who made it. The poem, that is, presents not the poet him or herself "but that order that of itself can speak" (p. 8). In Zukofsky's lucid analysis in "Poetry: *For My Son When He Can Read*," modernist composition is a constructivist practice involving the serial ordering of syllables, words, phrases, and lines, in which the articulation of a particular ordering defines the aesthetic of the poem ("the awareness of order," as Zukofsky puts it [p. 8]).

In a constructivist poetics, the politics of a poem are exhibited as much by its composition as by its statement. For Zukofsky, belaboring the poet's piety or compassion compromises the sincerity of the poem's enactments—a view that put Zukofsky at odds, during the 1930s, with such journals as *The New Masses*, with whom he shared a left political perspective. Zukofsky's poetics challenged the socialist realism of his time, just as it challenges the multicultural populism of the present—not because of their socialism or multiculturalism but because of possible insufficiencies in this regard.

The longest—and earliest—essay in *Prepositions* is a montage of luminous passages taken from the writings of Henry Adams. The technique appears to anticipate Zukofsky's later, and far more intricate, use of quotations in both *"A"* and *Bottom: On Shakespeare*, and brings to mind the fact that Zukofsky, as much as Walter Benjamin, could envision a literary work composed solely of citations. In any case, Zukofsky's elected affinity with Adams, in which he casts Adams as poet in the cloak of historian, sets the stage for his use of Adams in *"A"*-8, where it might be said that he casts himself as historian in the cloak of poet. Zukofsky's imaginative identification with Henry Adams has affinities with several other poet's extensively citational studies in American affinity, such as Susan Howe's C. S. Peirce (*Pierce-Arrow*, 1999) and Paul Metcalf's Herman Melville (*Genoa*, 1965).

Like the theory of knowledge, the philosophy of history was a major preoccupation of the poet, and his writing weaves together public and private history, autobiography and politics, in a manner that addresses the interdependence of seeming contraries. Zukofsky touches on this in a statement he made for the publication of *All*: "In a sense *All* is an autobiography: the words are my life. . . . The poet's form is never an imposition of history, but the desirability of making order out of history as it is felt and conceived." One might conjugate this, with a Wittgensteinian twist, to say: The facts compose a life as they do a history. The poet's form is never an imposition of facts, or autobiography, but the desirability of making order out of facts, and life, as they are felt and conceived. While Henry Adams's philosophy of history was an important influence on Zukofsky, as was Karl Marx's, it is Benjamin's "Messianic moment" that comes to mind when considering Zukofsky's aspiration, in his first statement of poetics, written six years after the Adams essay, for "rested totality" and "what is objectively perfect," suggesting as it does a desire for something beyond history's transitory instability and its inevitably partial (not to say *mis-*) representation. (Ron Silliman first suggested the connection between Benjamin and Zukofsky in *L=A=N=G=U=A=G=E* #4 [1978]).

An intriguing, but little discussed, essay in *Prepositions* concerns "BASIC" English, that curious 1920s and 1930s experiment of C. K. Ogden and I. A. Richards to create a simplified noun-centered English as a universal second language. Zukofsky clearly had an attraction for making English more concrete and this essay suggests a relation between this experiment and his own insistence on making every word count and on resisting verbal ornamentation. Indeed, his own radically reductivist impulses played out in his poetic practice of condensation and elision. Zukofsky's interest in BASIC elucidates the fact that while his poems may appear rhetorical, verbally acrobatic, and suffused with intellect, he was aiming for an embodied language free of vague or ungrounded thought (even to the point of undervaluing the contingent imperfections that compose the everyday). Yet Zukofsky's at times hilarious send-up of BASIC shows how his commitment to complexity and specificity put him at odds with lexical essentialism and linguistic positivism, where the cure is worse than the disease. In *"A"*-8, he diagnoses the problem this way: "The simple will be discovered beneath the complex / Then the complex under the simple / Then again the simple under the complex." (For another perspective on the implications of BASIC, by one of Zukofsky's most immediate poet-contemporaries, see Laura [Riding] Jackson and Schuyler Jackson's *Rational Meaning: A New Foundation for the Definition of Words*.)

While the references to translation are brief in *Prepositions*, the topic is important in the light of Zukofsky's pervasive use of inventive translation in *"A"* and Celia and Louis Zukofsky's paradigmatic homophonic translation of Catullus. Zukofsky saw translation as a way of achieving objectification: translating oneself into a poem/object or personae, as he says in his essay on Pound (p. 71). At the same time, he saw translation not as a means of assimilating a foreign poem into a fluent English but rather as a means to bring into English "unexplored poetic forms" (p. 71).

These essays do not provide a skeleton key to Zukofsky's poems but, like the rest of this poet's work, are often complex and refractory. The idea that there is an underlying meaning to the poems, hidden from view but available by scholarly excavation, is rejected: "just read the words," Zukofsky advises (p. 24). He shows that complexity and multiplicity of meaning are part of the experience of the work, not a veil to be lifted away. The structures and elisions of Zukofsky's poems often are made almost indiscernible, creating the particularly exquisite experiential richness in the perceptible unfathomability. While Zukofsky's work opens itself to, indeed inspires, elucidation through the use of source material, through the consideration of historical and social contexts, and through detailed structural and prosodic analysis, the objective of such critical interpretation is to be subsumed within the poem's affective elusiveness. Deciphering the codes may supplement the experience but it cannot explain it. Explanation is beside the point, beside the poem. Zukofsky's poems play to the ear; the truth of the work is in the music, not the underlying webs that produce it. As the poet says, talking about an ambiguous gesture by Charlie Chaplin that ends *Modern Times*: "what can the action of the shot mean but what it *does*—it *performs*" (p. 64). And this is Zukofsky's point about his own poetry as well, it means by doing, it performs.

In his lifetime, Zukofsky's readers were small in number. He provided few hooks for the casual reader and chose to work in accordance with his own exacting standards rather than to assimilate his work to contemporary literary or market considerations. The result is a work remarkably durable, to use a word that Zukofsky applies, with admiration, to Wallace Stevens. This durability is currently resulting in a steady and accumulating interest in Zukofsky's work in the English-speaking world as well as in Europe. In France, his poetry is greatly revered by such poets as Claude Royet-Journoud, Emmanuel Hocquard, and Anne-Marie Albiach.

In the Dembo interview, Zukofsky quotes a line from Elizabethan poet George Chapman, "the unspeakable good liquor there," adding, "Obviously, the man who wrote that knew what it was to gargle something down his throat." The person who wrote this book knew what it was to write poetry *in*—and to write poetry *for*—the twentieth century.

"Poetry never exaggerates or destroys the things it is" (p. 10), says Zukofsky, who tests this principle in every passage he writes. *Prepositions* is the work of a poet who created poetry not of attitude nor ideas nor moral views nor lifestyle but as a bearing in and toward language, in and as language. In *Prepositions* he does not tell about poetry, he shows it. For "how else can the poet speak . . . but as a poet" (p. 11).

[2000: Foreword to *Prepositions +: The Collected Critical Essays*, ed. Mark Scroggins (Middletown: CT: Wesleyan University Press). Parenthetical page references refer to this edition.]

10. Finding Cavell [1926–2018]

I met Stanley Cavell fifty years ago. I was eighteen, a freshman at a college I found infuriatingly opaque and dominated by a markedly gentile, prep school consciousness. I was furiously engaged with the antiwar movement in the spring of 1969, but also groping to find my way in, about, and around cultural and political history—and also trying to find the present of both. Twice a week Cavell talked about nineteenth- and twentieth-century philosophers in the ground floor lecture hall at Emerson Hall. It was a large class, a few hundred, and I don't recall he ever took questions, but he answered every single one of mine. I felt an immediacy and intimacy. It was my dream of what college could be. And, somehow, I got to know him, maybe because I would hang out with him after the class. From conversations in his office I then went to visit him, and Cathleen, at their house in Brookline—memorable trips to me because I didn't leave the campus much and otherwise never went to anyone's house, since the only people I knew in the area were my fellow students.

In that first year at college, I had no way to evaluate what was going on or why I was having such a hard time. I didn't even know there was a category for first generation to attend college (because my parents, children of immigrants, only focused on my being that first generation and had no idea what it would be like to be at a college like the one I ended up at). And, since I had never experienced snobbism, combined with antisemitism, before, I didn't fully recognize it.

I was completely enthralled by reading, writing, and talking—and Cavell not only recognized that, but also acknowledged it, in ways both explicit and inexplicit. He was a lifeline.

Must We Mean What We Say? was published in 1969 and I was completely absorbed by it. Cavell's philosophic approach to literary works and aesthetics seemed more compelling than anything being done in literary criticism (at least the little I knew about it at the time) and set the foundation for my essays.

I participated in three other courses with Cavell. One was a set of improvisations on *Walden*, which set the stage for *Senses of Walden*, published in 1972. At each session, Cavell would do improvisations, variations, and midrashic commentaries on a passage of the book. His only text was Thoreau's, all the rest was pure fantasy and invention. Cavell's performances were the closest thing a talker could do to echo the style of solo saxophone improvisation. He turned phrases of Thoreau's around the way Miles Davis turned a musical phrase of Irving Berlin's "How Deep Is the Ocean" or Thelonius Monk (a favorite of his) lifted and reworked the chord changes of "Blue Skies." *In Walked Stanley.* That is to say, Cavell was not restricted to *Walden* but used it as a trampoline, to bounce himself, bounce ourselves, to parts unknown. I don't mean to say he didn't adhere to the text but that he understood the text to have resonance. By sounding the sentences of *Walden*, Cavell was able to sound the limits and possibilities of his thought, as Thoreau had sounded the depth of Walden Pond.

I think jazz improvisation is the best way to describe Cavell's talks. He would start with a leading phrase, test out every intonation, circle back around to its converses and blanks, go for minor dissonances, then come round to the major chords. These were not lectures or monologues, they were unscripted performances. Perhaps not exactly "talk poems" in David Antin's sense, but there is a strong family resemblance. Perhaps more talking philosophy, the talking cure for the virus of analytic philosophy infecting Emerson Hall at the time, no doubt marked by Wittgenstein's paradigmatic talks in Cambridge and the tradition of Socratic dialog championed by Cavell's great colleague Rogers Albritton. Contra Albritton, Cavell perfected a form of writing that embodies his dialogic talk performances, but the performances were in no way secondary to his writing. Performance is the foundation of his writing.

Harvard's philosophy department at the time I was there was spiked with remarkable people, Cavell and Albritton standing out from the rest. Van Quine was a brilliant and witty author, but in the undergraduate classroom (symbolic logic) he showed an extreme disregard for teaching or any serious engagement with the ideas in his book as something that might be discussed rather than learned by rote. To those of us demonstrating against US war crimes in Vietnam, he made his position clear: we should be locked up like the juntas did in South America. At the other end of the spectrum (or was it?), Hilary Putnam was an avid Maoist. I have heard that he moved on, but I haven't, since that perspective was so destructive of the Left at the time, far more so than Quine, whose politics were, for many of us, an object of ridicule. Robert Nozick was only a decade older than me, but it felt like a century. I remember he once asked me why I didn't brush my hair down (I wish I still had enough hair for a Jewfro); but then you wonder about his pompadour. He provided my first close encounter with a neo-con; how apt that his work could become the butt of a joke on *The Sopranos*. Of course, John Rawls was and is a hero, but so dull. And Norman Goodman, perhaps the closest to my own aesthetic idealism, in my more wigged-out moments anyway, seemed to my youthfully idealistic gaze more to be about playing sophisticated games than having an engagement with art. I probably got that wrong (and much else). I wonder what the significance was of this concentration of Jewish intellectuals in the department—Cavell (Goldstein), Putnam, Goodman, Nozick (Cohen), Morton White (Weisberger)—something about which I was not conscious at the time.

In this and any context, Stanley Cavell stood out as a voice of reason. *The Claim of Reason* (1979) was based on his dissertation, *The Claim to Rationality: Knowledge and the Basis of Morality* (1961). I remember reading the dissertation—a copy was on deposit at Widener Library—and coming upon a penciled comment in the margin pointing to an open parenthesis and saying there was no close. But Cavell was no Charles Olson (who used unclosed parenthesis in his work)—someone else had marked, on the next page—*here it is*. I love the compound complexity of Cavell's sentences, and how a paragraph would not just say but think, where thinking is a process not a result of a deduction. This is the difference between the rationality of Quine and the reason of Cavell. Cavell's work is a series of long parentheticals, extenuations, revisions, recognitions, second and third thoughts.

The third class I took with Cavell was on the later philosophy of Wittgenstein. This one was in small classroom on the second floor of Emerson Hall, where Cavell talked from the stage about passages in *Philosophical Investigations*, weaving his way through the book as a flaneur might have weaved a way through the Paris arcades, as evoked by Walter Benjamin, whose writing style has a strong kinship with Cavell's. I remember talking to Cavell before one of these performances and he said he felt jittery—he had the nervous energy of a performer taking a risk. In his lectures, Cavell talked not at you but *with you* (and with Wittgenstein too).

One summer after my sophomore year, Susan Bee and I had rented an apartment on Dana Street with Steve Holt, Don Goldberg, and Ned Stucky-French. A classmate of ours, a brilliant thinker, came over very agitated, spooked by voices and hallucinations. I had no idea what to do and my immediate thought was to call Stanley and Cathy, since Stanley knew this young man. After that, we found the best way to help him, though I never saw my young friend again. I mention this because it gives a sense of how intimately connected I felt to Cavell at this point in my life, that I knew he and Cathy would be able to respond to this young man's suffering. There was no one else I thought to turn to.

The last class I took with Cavell was a small seminar on Rousseau's *Emile*, a foundational work on modern education. I remember a long discussion on the passage in which Rousseau warns against swaddling Emile too tightly, lest the restrictions on his free bodily movement be internalized. Cavell refused to internalize the swaddling of symbolic logic, of systematizing moral thought, of traditional teaching, of formal student/teacher relationship, of the subject-verb-object sentence, of the rationalized lesson-plan lecture.

I didn't enter a classroom for almost two decades after taking these classes with Cavell and I am teaching my final classes, after thirty years, this Fall. In all my teaching, Cavell has been a model. I was lucky to find him in 1968. Luckier still, he found me.

[2018: *ASAP Journal*]

11. Missing Tablet

for Armand Schwerner (1927–1999)

The last time I saw MISSING SEGMENT Armand Schwerner INDE-CIPHERABLE PART best time. UNTRANSLATABLE WORDS had come to Buffalo to appear as part of a mini-translation ELIDED that Dennis Tedlock and I had organized, and he read and gave a talk. The other speaker was INDECIPHERABLE Felstiner, author ELIDED *Celan: Poet Survivor* UNDECIDABLE WORD POSSIBLY FOREIGNER POS-SIBLY ALIEN POSSIBLY JEW. In talking about translation and in the multiple POSSIBLY FRAGRANCES AROMAS I was reminded of the significance of the fact that Armand, like so many MISSING INTER-PRETATION American POSSIBLY WRITERS POSSIBLY SING-ERS POSSIBLY MAKERS before him, was a second language speaker of UNTRANSLATABLE PART a condition of secondness about INDE-CIPHERABLE WORD that I have long associated with a greater MISS-ING SEGMENT of the UNTRANSLATABLE and materiality, call it the plasticity of the new POSSIBLY EARTH POSSIBLY HISTORY POSSIBLY BECOMING-WORLD. That quality of secondness and ma-teriality pervades Schwerner's INDECIPHERABLE and it is worthwhile, with a renewed UNDECIDABLE SEGMENT in textual material and the materiality of textuality to acknowledge the significance of POSSI-BLY SONG POSSIBLY ARCHITECTURE for certainly in *The Tablets* the fact of ellipsis, disjunction, indeterminacy, indecipherability, referential distortion MISSING SECTION

Armand once told me, in the early POSSIBLY LONG TIME INTO THE LIFE POSSIBLY NOT TOO LONG AGO that he felt that now, as an elder, there was an INDECIPHERABLE of discipleship for him or toward him among the poets POSSIBLY AFTER OR IN THE PATH OF APPARENTLY SELF-REFLECTIVE SO POSSIBLY IN THE PATH OF OR AFTER HIMSELF with whom he had a sense of UNTRANSLATABLE RELATED TO CONTINUITY OR KIN-SHIP. I knew that one way or another he was talking of ELIDED but not MISSING SEGMENT and a sense that perhaps his own work had been ELIDED the poets with whom he may have associated MISSING SEGMENT he surely knew me the best among such, and had, throughout all, some sense of connection, some sense of relation, even some sense of UNTRANSLATABLE POSSIBLY FAMILY TIE POSSIBLY AFFILIATION POSSIBLY INTERCONNECTEDNESS POSSIBLY COMMUNITY POSSIBLY TRADITION so that it reminded me of something of SECTION EXCISED Armand had accepted an idea of mastery and discipleship that seemed to me, and no doubt to many of my ELIDED not really viable, and maybe that's because poetry is such a youth-driven phenomenon, so it seems as if it works from the bottom up and not the other way around or maybe like most poets Armand simply felt INDECIPHERABLE INTERPRETATION acknowledged.

The first time I heard Armand Schwerner was the best time. I had just gotten my first issue of *Alcheringa* and the thing I did was to put an UNTRANSLATABLE WORD POSSIBLY NYLON POSSIBLY MICA POSSIBLY CARBON SHEET POSSIBLY COMPRESSED MEMORY DISK inserted into the magazine on the LITERALLY TABLE THAT TURNS. It was Armand reading from the INDECIPHERABLE. I played it to everyone who came over to my UNDECIDABLE SEGMENT in the next weeks: it was the closest thing to Lenny Bruce I had ever heard in poetry: cut-up, in all the senses, hysterical, a send-up and yet also none of UNTRANSLATABLE. I continued to admire the comic if not to say satiric aspects of MISSING PART, but when I first met Armand I was surprised to see that much of the surface giddiness I had expected wasn't UNINTERPRETABLE PORTION Armand had a seriousness and a sense of discipline that was at odds with ELIDED. Maybe Armand had moved on to hone into the archaic or even epic qualities of MISSING PART maybe it was only increasing identification with Buddhist practice, or simply a change in his ELIDED or maybe I simply misunderstood the work, though I have to say I don't really think MISSING SECTION

I didn't know Armand nearly as well as ELIDED, but I was in touch with him on and off for about 20 UNTRANSLATABLE PORTION think I ever recall him sounding so happy as he did when he called me from a train somewhere I think in MISSING WORD Island he was with the troupe that had just performed his libretto for INDECIPHERABLE at the Japan MISSING WORD. Susan and Felix and I had gone to this great cross-cultural ELIDED great in part because of the POSSIBLY VIRTUOSITY POSSIBLY EXCELLENCE POSSIBLY VIRTUE of the performances but also for the quite amazing LITERALLY CROSS SECTION OF DIFFERENCE and dance of juxtaposition within and between: very much an extension of his aesthetic. Felix was MISSING WORDS by the performance and we all sat in the UNTRANSLATABLE PART action. I don't quite know why Armand called me that day—he was on his cell phone and I remember being somewhat surprised he had a cell phone—but I MISSING PART he felt we had made a kind of POSSI- BLY CONNECTION POSSIBLY TOUCHING POSSIBLY INTER- SECTION through this work that perhaps sometimes MISSING PART. I got the sense he was calling all his friends MISSING PART

UNTRANSLATABLE PART
INDECIPHERABLE PART
MISSING PART
MISSING PART
MISSING PART
MISSING PART
MISSING PART
MISSING PART
MISSING PART
MISSING PART
MISSING PART
MISSING PART
MISSING PART

[1999]

Pesapalabra
Interview

BRAULIO PAZ: *So why poetry? We're in the middle of a pandemic, even before that the political landscape globally seemed to steer everything to the right of the spectrum. There's climate crisis, economic crisis, political crisis, spiritual crisis, personal crisis, etc. Why write, why read, why give a damn and why not just suffocate in our own nihilism?*

I don't make art for a "reason," but against the reasons you pile on. Or maybe I take those reasons as the warp and weft of my multi-ply, pleated, pleading work. I came into a world in crisis, and I expect the world I leave will also be in crisis. So the question is: what to make of the time we are here, which is to say *make with*, abiding time. A former student, who is a literary center director, just posted on social media—"Surprised to find myself repeatedly saying, 'This is not a time for fiction, this is not a time for poetry. This is a time to face the truth.'" She then posted the New York *Times*'s nonfiction best sellers.

Poetry is (or can be) *facing* the truth. To turn away from that at this time is to turn away from the possibility of transformation.

The pandemic we are in the middle of is not just racism or capitalism or climate change. It is the human crisis.

JUAN IGNACIO CHAVEZ: *Your poetry faces the truth by making normality less normal, or finding the uncanny within ordinariness, in a similar fashion to objectivist poets, such as Louis Zukofsky. Is poetry here to wake up people? How uncanny is uncanny in uncanny times?*

It's a cliché of our present moment to say it's surreal. *Surreal* was dubbed the 2016 "word of the year" by Merriam-Webster, the dictionary maker. A certain level of dystopian reality can begin to seem normal: police violence, digital surveillance, constant stream of disinformation from the government, disinformation that denounces disinformation.

What's a poet to do?

The normal has never been normal.

My concern is with the imposition of the frame of normal on the everyday, something that is constantly reinforced within official verse culture, where withdrawal from normalization is viewed as unintelligible, elitist, or a crime against universal human sentiment. My work, despite its sometimes wide distribution, is usually unpublishable within the strongholds of the liberal mainstream because it doesn't operate through mandated normalizations of empathy, legibility, and shame. Just as political activism means going out on the streets and organizing opposition, poetic activism means challenging the prevailing "order" of representation and regurgitation.

Near/Miss, my most recent collection, received overwhelming acknowledgment. At the same time, the central oppositional political poem in the collection, "Our United Fates," was rejected by the official culture organ that commissioned it. National Public Radio's *This American Life* asked me to write a poem to air on the day of the Lyin' Don's inauguration. Had I written a poem about my "feelings" or filled the poem with nostalgic anecdotes of my struggles with antisemitism seen through the eyes of my brave parents, my disappointments tempered by my optimism, a bittersweet sense of injustice, or perhaps poems made of anodyne comments on the difficulty of achieving the America dream, no doubt it would have been broadcast to NPR's millions of listeners. Instead, I wrote a poem that confronted America's racism and genocide without personalizing it and without nostalgia—and NPR would not accept that. Or maybe just to say: my rhetoric was too challenging. But I am also tempted to say that the form of the poem might be too difficult for NPR—the poem's refusal to talk down to the listener/reader. So it's the politics or the form. The principle that governs the massed media presentation of poetry is *banality über alles*. The mediocracy loves to talk about the death of poetry when the real story is their attempts to kill it. And I did get a kill fee.

Ben Lerner's book about the *hatred* of poetry has received accolades from US mainstream publications that would not give the time of day to the love of poetry. What is hated about poetry is its difficult truths, its refusal to assimilate or standardize, its resistance to equating a love of poetry with love poems, its epistemic intransigence. There are plenty of poets lining up to write poems for people who hate poetry, not because they hate poetry but because they are willing to use it to score points.

My poetic process is always contrary and counterintuitive: I want to make the uncanny seem canny and verse vice-a. But I get them confused.

Maybe it's my dyslexia/dyspraxia but more likely my dyspepsia. I love "making strange," "alienation effect," "foreground the device," "*detour-nement*," "derangement of the senses." But it's rhythmic oscillation among perspectives that is my obsession: here / not here / where / there / what / when / O! / oh / wow / when / %&^*#^$ [sorry, delete that, it's the password to my bank account], ooh-la-la, come dance with.

The only poem that isn't strange is a blank page.

And a blank page's no poem at all.

JUAN: *Though at a certain point you stated later that performance [as opposed to writing] has . . . the advantage of letting the listener get lost. In the last months, however, where poetry has been shared more and more in short videos we get the chance to [constantly rewind], as if we could plunge into the tone and rhythm of the performance and yet avoid losing its "content" in the lapse of time, a suspiciously optimal transaction. How do you feel about this? What awaits poetry performance and its "consumption"? Are we heading towards a world of singles?*

I like social media as much as the next guy. But you are pointing to a limitation of this medium. I can make a thirty-second poetry video and I know it will get more response, more quick hits, than if I posted a far denser essay on which I worked for months but which would take hours to read (and moreover would require moving to another site). I have plenty of work that is perfect for Instagram. At the same time, that essay has the potential to sink in deeper and perhaps stick around longer. Then again, social media posts can serve as "loss leader" (announcements, links) enticing readers onward or outward, to the unknown or untried, maybe even outside the gilded ghetto of English.

In my business, we get readers one at a time, so if you get one to connect, it's worth the transient traffic.

—I understand that attention spans are frazzled but I remain committed to long-form poems and poetry collections and difficult, historically and conceptually complex, critical thinking. Otherwise, we pledge allegiance to freedom with our "clicks" while locking ourselves into what Blake called our "mind forg'd" manacles of consumer passivity—starved by a "chartered" diet of information that may convey some new facts yet fails to inform just because it refuses to challenge form, refuses, that is, the aesthetic. It's a Faustian bargain: to think you can convey information with what Audre Lorde famously called "the master's tools." That isn't to say that a short lyric poem can't be as powerful as a long poem, or a performance as mind-altering as a book. Blake's "London," is, after all, something like a short lyric. But it is not a single "song" of Experience but part of a book of "songs." And it cannot just be heard, or sung, but must be seen.

And that makes all the difference.

In other words: I want to rewind all of language, the whole shebang, not just a clip.

BRAULIO . . . *Let's say there's literature and there's writing. I don't mean a distinction between the critical and creative aspects of writing, since I believe that creation is an exercise of criticism, but a distinction between that which is created and the institutions that process it. That which chews, standardizes and sometimes even nullifies the creation. Let's say, academia, for example, the old institutions that were created and function surrounding an idea of writing (which we traditionally call literature) and the forms of creation that exist to-day (which are a far cry from what we used to call literature) are in dissonance. Do they need to be reconciled? Should we attempt a new set of institutions to process these new forms of creation? Is there something to reconcile or perhaps it is better to let them each sing their own song?*

Reconciliation is a dream that serves no one, not the "tradition" or the new. Conflict is welcome most where it is valued least. Every conversation, collective action, magazine, small press, web site, book, is a newly forming institution. I don't just resist existing intuitions but endeavor to make new ones that work for new times. Endeavor, that is, to make institutions not that become popular but that do the necessary work that you and your comrades, if comrades you have, or, if not, your imaginary comrades, deem necessary; which is to say, what is otherwise not being done. The idea that you can resist institutionalization is just as troubling, as you need to em-brace existing institutions (or institutional operating systems) in order to succeed. *We* both are (are born into) and become institutions. So I say—*occupy institutions*: resist them, take responsibility for them, *invent* them, mean them, be conscious of what and how they work, actively reshape them. *Be them better.* Counterhegemonic resistance is necessary to achieve hegemony, not as an end in itself, which romanticizes opposition or the bohemian. Not that we ever get there; the road is long, and success comes in fits and starts. Besides, there is no *there* to get to.

—Oh sure, opposition is cool. But being cool is part of the problem.

JUAN: *Larry Tesler, who died a couple of months ago, invented the copy-and-paste computer function in 1974. In 1975 you cut-up—though using a typewriter—Goffman's* Asylums *for your first book*: Asylum. *Would estab-*

lishing a connection imply getting into conspiracy theory? If yes, what was the
process of taking that decision at the beginning of your poetic production?

I didn't get a computer till the mid-1980s. The immediate precedent for
cut-ups would have been Jackson Mac Low's great work, starting in the
1950s and also William Burroughs and Brion Gysin's cut-ups. These prec-
edents used chance-derived procedures to select and organize the texts. In
"Asylum," I selected the parts of Goffman's work I used. Robin Seguy has
mapped out the process in this digital edition, along with Craig Dwor-
kin's Eclipse scans of the pages of the original book, which was xeroxed
and side-stapled from pages made with a manual typewriter.[1] I allude to
Goffman above, when I say we are always inside institutions, that even a
conversation is an institution. "Asylum" explores that reality, with lan-
guage echoing the state of being trapped inside walls, visible and invisible.
    Seguy's edition relies on digital technology to give a textual X-ray
of the poem and source. Eclipse, like the Electronic Poetry Center and
PennSound, uses digital technology to make available, free, noncommer-
cial poetry resources. I think the web has allowed for a greater access to,
and appreciation of, the material and visual aspects of poetry, by giving
far greater circulation to materials that had limited first runs. Collage and
juxtaposition (parataxis), including cut-ups, may now seem more "natural"
just because the artificial world of the web and digital composition make
them more ubiquitous. The kind of associative trail of clicking on links,
of drift from site to site, bring to mind a set of poetic hypertexts avant la
lettre, works that suggest a digital hyperspace but were done well before
the advent of digital technology. Then again, the early premonitions of
a new digital textuality have been mostly reined in by social media and
commercial web design. The *Electronic Book Review* just relaunched a 1997
hypertext essay of mine, "An Mosaic for Convergence."[2] At the time, it
may have suggested a future direction, but now it seems as anachronistic
as a 1928 Buck Rogers comic strip.
    So I'd call it synchronicity more than conspiracy. Tesla's and related
innovations certainly made more legible otherwise aspects of poetic
composition.

JUAN: *You have stated that you understand books in an architectural way: a*
book as something that is built, a grammatical space with relative clarity or

1. <writing.upenn.edu/epc/authors/bernstein/books/Asylums.html>

2. <electronicbookreview.com/essay/an-mosaic-for-convergence>

opaqueness. What do you think will be the next techne that best metaphorizes the way we understand books? Programming? Sampling? Composting? Something else?

Books and print formats are paradigmatic as are live poetry performances. Those remain my primary mediums. Digital periodicals, newspapers, and books remain in many ways tied to book format, just as poetry audio and video is often an extension of a live performance. Among the biggest difference, since the advent of the web, is the availability of color reproduction as well as video and sound files, not only distribution but also making videos and audios as technically easy and inexpensive as writing. I find the immediacy of email, combined with the availability of machine translations, immensely appealing, especially in terms of exchanges outside one's immediate neighborhood. The ability to exchange books by email, with no postage cost, is a lifesaver for poetry, which relies on keeping overhead (operating expenses) to the minimum. These may not be the glitziest features of the digital revolution, but they are probably the most significant.

Because so much of my energy has gone into PennSound, I think a lot about audio files and the way they have radically transformed the archive of poetry. It's been less than two decades since you could become as familiar with a poet's readings as their books. For a long time, I have imagined using that archive of poetry recordings for the kind of sampling and collage I did in "Asylum." And indeed I have pursued making audio works and have recently been making short videos, in the absence of being able to do live readings.[3] But an advantage of being old is that I am thinking backward more than forward, or anyway hovering in the present and trying to make the most of that.

BRAULIO: *Lou Reed or Leonard Cohen?*

I was just seventeen, you know what I mean, when Leonard Cohen's first LP came out; the same year I went to see Ravi Shankar play at Lincoln Center. I listened to *Songs of Leonard Cohen* incessantly and many of my friends shared that enthusiasm. I am sure I had all the songs on that record memorized: I could sing most of them to you now (and maybe just as off-key as Cohen). (So a good thing there is no audio file for this conversation.) At the time, I was also listening to lots of "folk and jazz": Phil Ochs, Richie Havens, Buffy St. Marie, Peter Seeger, Paul Robeson, Pearls Before Swine, Bob Dylan, Bessie Smith, The Incredible String

3. Collected at the "audio" and "video" sections of my PennSound page.

Band, John Coltrane, Joan Baez, Miles Davis, Leadbelly, Judy Collins, Laura Nyro, B. B. King, Thelonious Monk, Lightnin' Hopkins, Arlo Guthrie, Billie Holiday. But also taking in the world of Western classical music—Gregorian Chants, John Dowland, Debussy & Satie, John Cage & Alban Berg.

The first time I connected to Lou Reed was *Transformer* in 1972, just after I graduated from college. I liked it quite a lot; still do. Lou Reed was so hip and cool.

But as I say, I have a preference for the uncool.

BRAULIO: *You've always defended self-publishing. . . . Down here almost everybody self-publishes but at the same time it is somewhat frowned upon. It would also be interesting to know what projects did you look up in regard to self-publishing in your youth, before* L=A=N=G=U=A=G=E?

It's imperative to publish collectively, one's own work (poetry and poetics) and the work one values. Small press / independent magazines, presses, and websites are necessary to give a place to counternarratives, or perhaps better to say, ever newly forming aesthetic and literary constellations and frames. Not just nice or well-meaning poems but poems that *matter*; and not just individual poems, but constellations of poems that articulate aesthetic possibility.

I don't see an alternative.

Much of what I most value in poetry is "frowned upon," at least some of the time or by some people. This doesn't make it good or bad; it's a given, if not for poetry, at least for the life in poetry I've lived. Most poets, even the most successful ones, rely primarily on small and independent presses and—let's face it—cultural prestige in poetry lies more often with the off-sites than the on-sites, with the "frowned upon" more than the "smiled upon." When "Our United Fates" got axed by NPR, it got picked up by Hortense Spiller's great new independent web magazine, *The A-Line*, which was the right place for it all along. As much as anyone, I like to be published by nationally circulated magazines or newspapers. Moreover, I think the struggle to change mainstream culture is crucial and I celebrate those occasions when poets I care about are recognized in the widest possible contexts. I just wish it happened more and earlier.

I am not waiting for that.

—Do your own thing or it won't get done at all.

I suppose the stigma you talk about is especially associated with publishing books of your own poetry through your own press, which some would call "vanity" publishing. That's a bit different than what we did with *L=A=N=G=U=A=G=E*, though through *L=A=N=G=U=A=G=E*, we did publish a long collaborative poem, *Legend*, by the two editors and three of our friends, which has just now been republished in a beautiful edition from the University of New Mexico Press. Like my first two books, which I published myself, there was simply no other way to get this work out.

While there are many examples, I think of Charles Reznikoff, publishing many of his own poetry books on a press in his basement. I'm not sure they've gotten their due even to this day. But maybe more to the point are the self-published collaborations between Russian Futurist artists and poets. In their immediacy, in their wildness, in their utopian imagination of a Russian Revolution that never arrived, their work remains a model of the thrilling precariousness of unsanctioned possibility.

[2020: *Pesapalabra* 6 (Peru) in Spanish translation. I subsequently did a video conversation with Chavez and Paz, archived at my PennSound page.]

The Brink of Continuity

John Ashbery [1927–2017]

1.

On September 5, 2017, a few days after John Ashbery died, *Le Monde* published an obituary for him by Olivier Brossard: "Pour le poète américain, l'écriture était ouverture, fuite ou fugue, le refus d'une identité ou d'un poème qui soient clos ou définis à jamais": For this American poet, writing was an opening, flight or fugue, the refusal of an identity for a poem that is closed or defined forever.[1]

I appreciate that Brossard addresses the identity of the *poem* in this opening paragraph, something sometimes lost in America, where there is so much attention given to the identity of the poet that the identity of the poem is eclipsed.

Not that a poem can ever be separated from the person who wrote it.

It's just that with a poem you start with the *flight and fugue* of the words, not with what the poem represents.

The day Ashbery died the New York *Times* posted an obituary by its official obituary writer, the talented Dinitia Smith (with "Maggie Astor and David Orr contributed reporting" appended at the end).[2] The oddest thing about Smith's obit (O-1) was a paragraph on Ashbery's relation to his parents:

> When I was about 3 or 4 years old, [my father] said to me one day, 'Who do you love more, me or your mother?' and I said, 'My mother.'"

1. Olivier Brossard, "Mort de John Ashbery, poète américain," *Le Monde*, September 5, 2017

2. O-1: <web.archive.org/web/20170903231633/https://www.nytimes.com/2017/09/03/arts/john-ashbery-dead-prize-winning-poet.html>: Dinitia Smith, "John Ashbery, Prize-Winning Poet, Is Dead at 90," New York *Times*, September 3, 2017

No doubt the bored masses of *Times* readers could find *at least this* something they could relate to. I might have said the same to my father when I was three, but I hope it doesn't land in any obituaries.

Smith had the historical sense to mention Barbara Guest as one of the company of poets most closely associated with Ashbery, even if she called "Frank O'Hara," *John*, which I am sure Ashbery and O'Hara would have found amusing:

> Mr. Ashbery was originally associated with the New York school of poetry of the 1950s and '60s, joining Kenneth Koch, Barbara Guest, John O'Hara and others as they swam in the currents of modernism, surrealism and Abstract Expressionism then coursing through the city, drawing from and befriending artists like Jackson Pollock, Willem de Kooning and Jane Freilicher.

When David Orr's byline was added to Smith's the next morning (O-2), "Frank" was back and the poets were no longer *swimming* in the "currents of modernism" but, less aptly, *reveling*.[3] But, alas! Guest was out, and the New York School was just guys:

> Mr. Ashbery was originally associated with the New York school of poetry of the 1950s and '60s, joining Kenneth Koch, James Schuyler, Frank O'Hara and others as they reveled in the currents of modernism.

The anecdote about the poet's mother was also excised, making way for a bit more ideological clean-up.

David Orr is most notable for his April 2, 2006, front-page *Times Book Review* rave for a favorite of Ashbery's, Elizabeth Bishop. The piece begins:

> You are living in a world created by Elizabeth Bishop. Granted, our culture owes its shape to plenty of other forces—Hollywood, Microsoft, Rachael Ray—but nothing matches the impact of a great artist, and in the second half of the 20th century, no American artist in any medium was greater than Bishop.[4]

This claim is so wacky that it can only be understood as a fetish for Bishop and her patron Robert Lowell, two of the central ideological icons of Cold

---

3. O-2 <nytimes.com/2017/09/03/arts/john-ashbery-dead-prize-winning-poet.html>, and McGrath on Lowell <nytimes.com/2003/06/15/magazine/the-vicissitudes-of-literary-reputation.html>: Dinitia Smith and David Orr, "John Ashbery Is Dead at 90; a Poetic Voice Often Echoed, Never Matched," in the New York *Times*, September 3, 2017

4. David Orr, "Rough Gems: 'Edgar Allan Poe & The Juke-Box,' by Elizabeth Bishop," in the New York *Times* Sunday *Book Review*, April 2, 2006

War Official Verse Culture. And like all such fetishes, it reduces the poetry to propaganda.

Ashbery and his New American Poetry comrades were the proponents of an alternative to the "cooked" (a.k.a. half-baked) poetry of Official Verse Culture—sometimes called "raw," meaning grounded in process. (Lowell makes the deceptive distinction between open-form "raw" poems and closed-form "cooked" poems in his 1960 National Book Award acceptance speech.) So Brossard's elegant, Ashberian phrase, "clos ou définis à jamais," is quite specific and delightfully so.

O-1 mentions a key issue of Cold War aesthetic ideology:

> But [Ashbery's] most significant artistic relationships were with other poets, including James Schuyler, who were rebelling against the formalism of Allen Tate and Robert Lowell.

O-2 deletes this statement and with that any sense that this poet, now beloved of all, was "rebelling" against anything. In the Orr-revised version, Ashbery's "Self-Portrait in a Convex Mirror"—long can(n)on fodder for those conservative critics who dismissed much of Ashbery's earlier work along with that of his more radical contemporaries—is juxtaposed with Harold Bloom's triumphalist claims for Ashbery. Yet also cut from O-2 is this tender morsel about "Self-Portrait," which found its way into Smith's first version:

> Though it became the signature piece in the collection that won Mr. Ashbery the Pulitzer and other prizes, Mr. Ashbery had reservations about the poem. "It's not one of my favorite poems, despite all the attention," he said. "I was always very unsure of the quality."

Ashbery's comment is a marvel of wit and self-consciousness. Ashbery also distanced himself from the book many of us on the L=A=N=G=U=A=G=E side of the street especially liked, *The Tennis Court Oath*. At one point, Ashbery said it was the *only* poem of his we liked, which certainly wasn't true for me, but this, again, was Ashbery's way of deconstructing (*there I've said it*) false boundaries. He said somewhere he didn't want his work to become a political football. There was no American poet more adept at eliding polemic and refusing mantles.

Ashbery resisted becoming a polarizing figure because of the exquisite demands of his aesthetic. His greatness is connected to his poetics of aversion, deftness, deflection, humor, and, above all, privacy. For Ashbery pri-

vacy is a kind of politics, as is not wanting to be pinned down. This is one
of many qualities in his work that is fundamental for me.

Both versions of the *Times* obit included a British authority's put
down of Ashbery as "boring." Both have a quote from a *Times* review
that calls Ashbery "incomprehensible," but in a possibly OK way; still,
an offhand slap at poetic difficulty that traffics in anti-intellectuality and
anti-aestheticism. O-2 both resists the aesthetic and claims its mantel. The
shibboleth of "human experience" is meant to anoint with a humanist piety
that is explicitly anti-political and non-denominational:

> But if his poetry is rarely argumentative or polemical, this does not mean it
> avoids the more difficult areas of human experience.

O-2's revisions gut the *polemical* force of Ashbery's argument for poetic
freedom, drift, and the imagination uncontrolled by the forces of rational-
ization and accessibility:

> But while other eminent poets of his generation became widely known for
> social activism (Adrienne Rich and Gary Snyder, for example) or forays into
> fiction (James Dickey) or the details of their own harrowing lives (Sylvia
> Plath), Mr. Ashbery was known primarily for one thing: writing poetry.

Orr and collaborators erase the key New American Poets of Ashbery's
generation outside the New York School—Amiri Baraka, Robert Creeley,
Jackson Mac Low, Allen Ginsberg, Jack Spicer, Hannah Weiner—the list
could go on—in favor of apparently more mainstream poets, only to make
the claim that they are less significant as artists than as icons, something
each of these poets worked fiercely *against*. Ashbery no more resists becom-
ing iconic than any of these poets, he is just iconic in his own way.

Here is Orr & Co.'s coup de grâce (a passage not in O-1):

> Charles McGrath, the editor of *The New York Times Book Review* from 1995 to
> 2004, recalled that a large portion of new poetry titles during his tenure could
> be (and often were) tossed into a pile labeled "Ashbery impersonations." And
> Mr. Ashbery remains far and away the most imitated American poet.

The authority of McGrath and Orr is based on their mutual pledges of
allegiance to Lowell and Bishop—not as poets, though, but as Cold War
icons, forged in McGrath's case by his long apprenticeship to *New Yorker*
editor William Shawn. McGrath, in a June 15, 2003, piece in the *Times*

Book Review, is worshipful of Lowell while condescending to Ginsberg as a "self-caricature" and dismissing contemporary poets as never able to be as serious as his "master."

> Unlike so many contemporary poets, Lowell never wrote poetry about poetry, or worried about the insufficiency of words to stand for what they signify. Lowell may have belonged to the last generation to believe seriously in the poetic vocation.[5]

I suppose the swipe here about poets who write about poetry is a reference to Ashbery; if not, it might as well have been. But McGrath's remark about the "insufficiency of words to stand for what they signify" is the giveaway, for what Ashbery shows, as Olivier Brossard notes, is the sufficiency of words to say more than "what they signify." To say otherwise is not just to dismiss Ashbery, or the rest of us, but to dismiss the possibility of poetry and, indeed, of language.

It is to consign us to the tawdry world of poets as icons.

While there are many imitators of Ashbery, though no more than imitators of other poets, what the McGrath quote in O-2 suggests is that those who depart from the straight and narrow of convention, who follow Ashbery's example of freedom, will be put in the discard pile. The burden of this obituary is to make Ashbery the exception, not the rule. It buries Ashbery in its praising of him.

But we know from Ashbery, hero of the pataquerical: once discarded, twice derided, thrice's the trick:

> So many of these things have been discarded, and they now tower on the brink of the continuity, hemming it in like dark crags above a valley stream.[6]

2.

One of PennSound's most extensive author pages is for John Ashbery. The page includes dozens of audio and video recordings of Ashbery readings, starting with a 1951 Poets Theater performance of "Everyman." We have

---

5. Charles McGrath, "The Vicissitudes of Literary Reputation," in the New York *Times Magazine*, June 15, 2003

6. "The System," from *Three Poems* in *Collected Poems: 1956–1987*, ed. Mark Ford (New York: Library of America), p. 316

about a hundred Ashbery recordings on PennSound, including a *Close Listening* radio conversation I did with John on March 18, 2016. To record the show, my son Felix and I went to see John at his Chelsea apartment. It was the last time I saw him.

John and David Kermani were deeply committed to PennSound—the largest archive of poetry recordings on the web. All PennSound recordings are available free for streaming or downloading (and we have no advertising). David insisted that any place making a recording of John's work, or digitizing an older reading, give a copy to PennSound. As a result, anyone with an internet connection can hear a comprehensive collection of Ashbery readings.

John's death is a terrible blow, just as his life was a marvelous whoosh! And his voice lives on: hypnotic, radiant, and sublime.

Once David and I started to work on the Ashbery PennSound page, I would meet David at the Moonstruck Diner, near their apartment. After lunch, he would hand me shopping bags full of cassette tapes, videos, and CDs. Over time PennSound sorted it all out, carefully documenting each event.

A few years later, David proposed that I work with John and him on a big manuscript-focused digital project. They were intrigued by the new digital version of *The Waste Land* that had just come out, but also unhappy with pirated digital editions of John's work that, in addition to being unauthorized, were chock full of errors. I said I'd love to do something with "The Skaters." David laughed. "I knew you would say that—and you are the only one that would ask for that poem first."

Some weeks later, David handed me two gigantic white binders that included two hand-corrected typescripts for the "The Skaters" (with many canceled lines) and a raft of poems written at the same time but never published. I was ecstatic. I suggested to Robin Seguy, then a graduate student at the University of Pennsylvania, that he take on the project. Robin scanned and transcribed everything in the notebook, creating code that provides novel ways of reading through and searching the poems, including quantitative data about the poem; a set of evocative grouping of textual features of the works, such as place names, personal names, pronouns, foreign words, seasons, references to color, light, and weather; plus a hypertext index to every word in "The Skaters." There is also a text-voice version aligned of Ashbery reading the poem and to the source text he used in writing it.

There is nothing that gives a more thrilling sense of Ashbery at work. Many of the rejected lines are as good as the ones included—and the unpublished poems are endlessly appealing.

3.

In 1991, John, David Kermani, and I were waiting to get on a flight to Milan for a poetry festival there. John and David were in a convivial mood and the subject turned to John Shoptaw, who a few years later published a study of Ashbery called *On the Outside Looking Out*. Shoptaw's book was one of the first studies of Ashbery's work that included references to his being gay, which Shoptaw read in terms of what he calls "homotextuality." Before the early 1990s, Ashbery's homosexuality was not commonly addressed in print. As far as I know, this is how Ashbery wanted it.

The introduction to Shoptaw's book is called "Misrepresentive Poetry." This title speaks of both being out of a closet and elusive.

At the airport, John and I were drinking, though all I remember is that John was. He said he was uncomfortable with Shoptaw writing about him as a gay poet, that he was concerned that this might be a reductive way to see his work, especially if it became a primary frame. I said the obvious, knowing that John knew it better than me—that his being identified as gay was welcome, indeed liberatory, and, in the case of Shoptaw's work, elucidating.

As we three New Yorkers waited for the plane that would take us to Europe, I thought of John's coming of age in the 1940s and '50s. Ashbery's poetic response to the Second European War, the defining event of his youth, is remarkable for its obliqueness, indirection, aversion—for its intimate rather than grand scale, its particularities of registration rather than largeness of statement. Ashbery's reaction to fascism (and to the Cold War) was not proclamations and denunciations but deflationary rhetoric, *profoundly superficial*, as an oxymoron might say.

Poetry is best that governs least. That's my motto for Ashbery's work—this great project of Unrepresentative Verse, a search for an alternative to reductive forms of representation, whether it be representation of a person, a place, a group, a nation, a species, or simply of an object. Unrepresentative Verse entails an abiding skepticism toward the authoritative voice of both public and market discourse in a society that moved from the centrist conformism of the '50s to the more complex varieties of boutique or pluralist conformisms of the present, where the values that reign are moral, market, and atavistic.

Of all the many "difficult" American poets of the twentieth century, none was so admired and beloved as Ashbery. He was essential for those of us who searched for formal extravagance and technical wildness in poetry, while he was charming enough to the poetry scolds to win not only awards and prizes, but also, sometimes begrudgingly, consent.

Ashbery was the least polarizing of polarizing radical poets. He joins a small group of twentieth-century American poets highly esteemed by the conventionals and inventors alike, up there with William Carlos Williams, Wallace Stevens, Gwendolyn Brooks, and T. S. Eliot; poets whose work is seen in very different ways depending on from which side of the aesthetic line you are looking.

In the mid-1960s, and especially in "The Skaters," Ashbery introduced into American poetry a nonlinear associative logic that averts both exposition and disjunction. As I wrote in *Pitch of Poetry*, Ashbery's aversion (after *The Tennis Court Oath*) to abrupt disjunction gives his collage-like work the feeling of continuously flowing voices, even though few of the features of traditional voice-centered lyrics are present in his work. The connection between any two lines or sentences in an Ashbery poem has a contingent consecutiveness that registers transition but not discontinuity. However, the lack of logical or contingent connections between one line and the next opens the work to fractal patterning. To create a "third way" between the hypotaxis of conventional lyric and the parataxis of Ezra Pound and Charles Olson, Ashbery places temporal conjunctions ("meanwhile," "at the same time") between discrepant collage elements, giving the spatial sensation of overlay and the temporal sensation of meandering thought.

"The Skaters," published in *Rivers and Mountains* in 1966, realizes this contingent connection between lines as "vanishing points."

The lines that draw nearer together are said to "vanish."
The point where they meet is their vanishing point. //
Spaces, as they recede, become smaller.

As we were getting onto the plane for Milan, John was so wobbly that David and I had to hold him as we walked the gangway. In "As One Put Drunk into the Packet-Boat" (1975), he writes:

A look of glass stops you
And you walk on shaken: was I the perceived?
Did they notice me, this time, as I am,
Or is it postponed again?

Halfway down the plank John turned to me and said, "Well, I guess I am a role model."

The summer demands and takes away too much,
But night, the reserved, the reticent, gives more than it takes.

4. 87 Words for John Ashbery at 88

curvilinear	surround
bequeathed	slope
propaedeutic	loping
emblazoned	procrastination
blazer	prognostication
bemoan	prostate
befuddle	peripheralize
boomerang	puckish
procrustean	nasturtium
pediment	foment
Piedmont	slide
Yangtze	immobilization
elastic	surety
arboreal	sensation
aerial	fancy
miscellaneous	farmed
moribund	locomotion
feckless	mystic
freakish	mosaic
free-floating	mazurka
arrested	marbles
interruption	momentary
hypobolic	mesh
cryptography	Mercurial
cello	temporarilyness
churn	tumble
salience	thimbled
succulence	thud
sherbet	encrustate
billowing	gong
swank	fluting
swallow	floridly
swell	flatten
swarm	foregone
swoop	inconclusion
sweep	gust
weep	crust
worrisome	intubation
weary	burble
waver	curdle

flavor	opalescent
float	sentient
buoyancy	prescience
girlancy	. . . ¶§®§´´¢´∞¢∑ɛ!!

[2017: (1) *Postmodern Culture* 27: 2 (2) *Bomb* (September 8), (3) excerpts in *Reader's Almanac* blog of the Library of America (September 7), and (4) 2015: tribute assembled by Adam Fitzgerald and subsequently published by John Tranter in *Cordite*. The Ashbery poems cited can be found in *John Ashbery: Collected Poems 1956–1987*, ed. Mark Ford (New York: Library of America, 2008). The digital edition of "The Skaters" is linked at the bottom of Ashbery's PennSound page and at the EPC Digital Library, quotations from this edition.]

The Poetics List

1. Preface to *Poetics@*

Above the world-weary horizons
New obstacles for exchange arise
Or unfold, O ye postmasters!

The Poetics List was founded in late 1993 with this epigraph serving as its first message. I had been on email for only about a year at that time, but from the first was fascinated by the possibilities for group exchange made available by the listserv format. I remember endless conversations with friends explaining the mechanism: you send out one message to the list address and everyone subscribed gets the message almost instantaneously. And to reply, you simply hit "R" on the keypad and write your new message. My friends listened in something as close to astonishment as poets doing hard time ever can. It was as if I were explaining the marvels of xerography to letterpress printers.

In 1993, most of the poets I knew who had email had those accounts provided by universities and the history of the Poetics List is marked by the change, within a few years, from the dominance of ".edu" (university) email addresses to ".com" (commercial) addresses. At that time, writing email was far more cumbersome than it is today. For the first several years of the Poetics List, most of the messages were written online using early versions of Pine or more primitive mail programs, with very limited editing tools available. Typing could be slow, and the possibility of revision was limited—especially for those who chose to engage in the spirit of improvised list exchange by spontaneously typing their messages and immediately sending them out. Indeed, it is worth noting that a number of people on the list, working with email systems that had no text buffers, could not retype the lines prior to the one they were typing—making a post to Poetics more like a telegram than a letter. And indeed it was the telegraphic immediacy of this new writing genre that was so electrifying. Group exchange of texts had never been faster or easier.

Initially, I was amazed at how close the Poetics List mimed "live" exchanges in bars, cafés, readings, and apartments that so characterize the social environment of poetry. It was all here: the quick dismissals and the brilliant précis, the idle chat and the meticulous scholarship, the silly and the self-important, the smug arrogance and startling generosity, the noise and music. I never imagined that there could be a textual equivalent of the temporary and "in the air" exchange among poets that literally surrounds, and provides crucial contexts for, individual poems. Thanks to the internet, the intensities of day-to-day poetry conversation, previously restricted to a few urban centers, were now available to a far more geographically diffuse group; indeed, poets living in those urban centers have been the least likely to participate in the Poetics List, possibly because of the many "live" alternatives available to them.

The Poetics List is not, of course, just a US or North American phenomenon, but it should be acknowledged that, in terms of content and participation, the Poetics List is US-centered. Nonetheless, the international access to the list is one of its fundamental dynamics and it offers something uniquely useful to those living particularly far from its geographic center, since for such participants, the information and discussion that the list provides would be virtually impossible to find elsewhere. At the same time, the list has allowed a greater amount of exchange among English-writing poets in the United Kingdom, Australia, Canada, Ireland, and the United States than previously had been common.

One of the central features of the Poetics List is the exchange of small and independent press information as well as announcements of poetry readings. Distribution remains one of the most difficult aspects of poetry book and magazine publishing; the list has provided an ideal site for publicizing, selling, and indeed giving away such publications. Over time, as more and more poetry emerged on the web, the list also became a prime site for announcements about web publications. Although such announcements are not included in this collection, the fact that the discussions presented here were accompanied by such information is a crucial frame.

LISTSERVs like Poetics have inaugurated a new genre of writing that is a cross between letters and essays. Most of the pieces of this book were quickly typed prose improvisations that should not be mistaken for carefully revised articles. The unedited quality of the originals has been retained for this collection: enjoy the writing for what it is, keeping in mind the informal setting of the list environment.

The Poetics List, while committed to openness, has always been a private list with an articulated editorial focus and a restricted format. Initially, the Poetics List had about 150 subscribers and it has continued to grow to its present level of 750 subscribers. Because of the vastness of the internet, I tried to make the list available primarily to those for whom it would be of greatest interest, realizing that the broader and more diffuse its participants, and the more voluminous its posts, the less valuable it would be to a core group of poets and critics and readers who might be reluctant to stick with highly generalized or elementary discussion—whether on how to write poems or how to get published. The trick is to keep those who have been around the block one time too many while entertaining the urgent concerns of those who just found out the block exists, perhaps because it's not on the standard-issue maps.

During the first five years of the list, individual posts of participants were sent directly to all subscribers and no one approved any specific post. Nonetheless, the editorial function of the list was promoted, or perhaps better to say cajoled, in other ways, including our editorial statement sent to all new subscribers and posted each month on the list. As I put it in the welcome message: "The definition of this editorial project, while provisional, and while open to continual redefinition by list participants, is nonetheless aversive to a generalized discussion of poetry. Rather, the aim is to support, inform, and extend those directions in poetry that are committed to innovations, renovations, and investigations of form and/or/as content, to the questioning of received forms and styles, and to the creation of the otherwise unimagined, untried, unexpected, improbable, and impossible."

Starting in the beginning of 1999, Christopher Alexander became the list moderator and editor; under a new format, subscribers were no longer able to post messages directly to the list. Unfortunately, as the list became bigger and more prominent, it became impossible to continue with unrestricted posting. Simply put, we were too easily open to abuse of the list by those unwilling to work within our stated editorial guidelines. I had made the mistake of holding onto the unrestricted format longer than it was manageable, at the cost of putting in jeopardy what the list, at its best, could achieve. The issue is significant in terms of the internet as a whole, where endless chatter often produces little in the way of political or aesthetic exchange but, on the contrary, can be understood as a way of defusing or swamping any such possibility. The Poetics List has tried to find a way to enable greater participation in the discussion of the range of poetics to which it is committed. And indeed, since we initiated the moderated format, the size of the list has grown and participation among its subscribers has been more balanced. In one sense, it is not as open as a newsgroup or a chat list because some constraints are put in place. Without these constraints, however, I believe that the range and depth of contributions would be diminished. In the age of the internet, more editing, not less, is required.

The Poetics List is one part of a much larger internet project-for-poetry, the Electronic Poetry Center, founded and directed by Loss Pequeño Glazier. Full archives of the list, plus of course much more, are available at the EPC. From 1997 to 1998, Joel Kuszai managed the list's day-to-day operations, while at the same time working on this selection. Anyone who knows the list from its daily manifestations will have a shock reading the substantial and sustained collection of poetics Kuszai has culled from the far more chaotic "list itself." At this point in time, experiences with lists are common enough not to require a print equivalent of list dynamics; in any case, no print version could adequately reproduce the look and feel of the Poetics list or other longtime active lists. Instead, Kuszai has picked a set of works important not just for where they were said but for what they are saying. And, tellingly, he has picked a set of texts that are useful to him as a practicing poet and scholar: this is not the "best of" the Poetics List but something even more interesting, a reading of the Poetics List. Other readers would no doubt have followed quite different paths through the wealth of material available. In shaping this selection, from the early years of the list, Kuszai provides a window onto an ongoing, highly articulate, intensely percolating poetics-in-the-making that is a fundamental feature of the most engaging and active poetry of our time. If anyone wonders what today's poets are thinking, what they are concerned about, what they value, this is a good place to start finding out.

[1993. *Poetics* @ ed. Joel Kuszai (New York: Roof Books, 1999) is available at the EPC along with the full poetics list archive <writing.upenn.edu/epc/poetics>. Subsequent references to this site are given as "EPC."]

2. Hermit Crabs Don't Cry

On one of my frequent trips to the Folded Place
inside the Ethernet's Thirteenth Passage,
with the new translation into Idiophone
of Moses Maimonides's Guide for the Perplexed
in my left hand, I had occasion to jot
down some rules of conduct (not so much

community standards as uncommunity striations)
into my Blake's Newton Feelpad (TM pending)
(a pad is after all a kind of home,
or used to be). The Feelpad, as many
of you will know (and I use the word "you"
carelessly), is able to convert inner feeling
processes into linguistic signs. The
protocols of the Blake's Newton Feelpad
do not allow me to review the file before
downloading directly onto your screens
(and I also use the word "your" carelessly):

All of these proposed Listserve Rules
will be enforced through a fully automated
new version of the Youngman Listserve Program
(Henny 33.95). As I am sure you will agree
(and I use "you" loosely), Total Automation
of rule enforcement is the only way to ensure
fair and impartial Rule Maintenance:

1. Postings on Poetics@UBVM shall be
neither in prose nor verse. Rather,
all postings shall conform to shifting
character/line formats, announced
periodically on the list. Initially,
lines shall have at least 43 and no more
than 51 characters; hyphenation is
discouraged.

2. No messages shall be posted between
:43 and :52 minutes after the hour.

3. All postings shall be made from
"Dos"-type platforms; Apple users
may post from "IBM"-type computers
but the graphic orientation of

Macs make these environments
inappropriate for Poetics postings.

4. You have to sound 30 or show ID.

5. On the third Friday of every month, only short
"chat" messages to friends on the list may be posted.
For those without, or who no longer have, friends
on the list, a message service will be available
to provide names of friends as well as appropriate
messages.

6. The Listowner will provide a name
purging service to permit anonymous
postings. Purged names will remain
strictly confidential, although, at
the Listowner's discretion, they may be
sold, on condition of continued
confidentiality, to benefit the outreach
services at Poetics@UBVM provided
by Whitewater Development Company.

7. Subscribers to Poetics@UBVM agree to
end all "back channel" communication. All
communication among subscribers shall be
sent to the list as a whole: no individual
e-mails, or conventional mail may be
exchanged, no face-to-face verbal
communications will be permitted
(nonverbal communication is in no
way restricted by this rule).
At first, this may be difficult
for those who live in the same area.
But, over time, the enormous advantages
to community-building will become
apparent.

8. In order to cut down on those repulsive
smile icons that are used on Other Lists
to indicate humorous intent (as we used
to say in Method Acting class—DON'T
INDICATE) [Remember the one about the actor, who
asked the director what his motivation was to
walk across the set and light a cigarette, to
which the director replied, "your motivation is,
that if you don't, you'll be fired"?]—
where was I? even when I write I lose track
of where I am—oh yeah,
in order to cut down on those smile icons,
and for other reasons that should be
obvious to all of you (I use the word
"you" inadvisedly), all irony
(including sarcasm, schtick,
mocking, jokes, and comic innuendo)
will be prohibited from the list.
This is a particularly difficult rule
to enforce automatically, but recent,
unpublishable research, indicates
that there may be genetic markers of
sarcasm and our team of crack(ed?) computer
experts are working around the clock
to find programs to detect this "irony
gene" in linguistic expression.

>FINALLY<
For those who have asked that this
listspace move toward *reality* rather than
float in talky virtuality, the following rule
implementation procedure will be adopted:

If there is significant sentiment on the
list in favor of these rules, they will
not be adopted; if, in contrast, there

is strong opposition to these rules,
they will become effective immediately.

In addition, to bring even more reality
into the system, between three and five
Listserve Rules will remain concealed
from all subscribers AND about one percent
of all messages will be randomly deleted
before they are delivered.

PS
Our public relations team at Hungadunga,
Hungadunga, and McCormack is currently considering
two campaigns. They will be making their
decision in the next few weeks:

POETICS@UBVM—we're taking the unity
out of community! Unsubscribe today!

Or

Not getting enough community at home?
Subscribe to POETICS@UBVM.

Yours in virtuality,
    C * h * a * r * l * e * s
B * e * r * n * s * t * e * i * n
(rest area)

[1994: Posted to the Buffalo Poetics List March 5, three months after I founded it.]

3. Community and the Individual Talent

[One of the first, and most sustained, discussions on the Poetics List was on the subject of poetry communities, particularly in the context of other discussions on the internet of the "virtual" communities possible in "cyberspace." I was slow to

join the conversation, so my post on the subject also served as a reply to several specific comments made earlier.]

I had a number of thoughts, over these past weeks of posts, about community, but I've misplaced them.

Every time I hear the words *literary community* I reach for my bivalent AutoCAD simulation card emulator.

Poetry is (or can be) an aversion of community in pursuit of new constellations of relationship.

In other words, community is as much about what I am trying to get away from—reform—as form.

So there is a spectrum of communities, from the closed community modeled on the family, to communities fixed by location (what might otherwise be called, for example, neighborhoods) or civic identification (the community bounding a literal and figurative commons or commonplace) or political ideology, to utopian communities that have either sought to form a new place or to remain open by refusing to be grounded by a place.

Literary communities have often been understood in terms of place—the "local"—as Michael Davidson writes about the emergence of a literary community on the West Coast in his book on the SF Renaissance, or in terms of scene (a local hub within a place) or group. Black Mountain remains crucial because it forged an arts community from writers and artists from many places. The connections of writers within ethnic, gender, or racial groups have been designated as communities. Schools or movements have not usually been called communities, although Ron Silliman, among others, has wanted to insist that a shared aesthetic project among writers in different locations can best be understood on this model of community. It's possible to speak of the "poetry community" in the sense of "the poetry world" (in the sense of "the art world")—but such a formulation immediately suggests that arts-funding agencies are nearby (more commonly, one speaks of the "small press community"). I would say "poetry communities," but this begs the questions even as it suggests relief. Many poets that I know experience poetry communities, say scenes, as places of their initial exclusion from publication, readings, recognition. Being inside, a part of, is often far less striking than being left out, apart.

Communities, defined by what they have in common—a place, an ideal, a practice, a heritage, a tradition—cannot immunize themselves against what they do not find common. To have a community is to make an imaginary inscription against what is outside the community. & outside is where some poetry will want to be. That is, some poetry will want to work against received ideas of place, group, ethnicity, gender, sexuality, person, member, individuality, tradition, aesthetic tendency: either not using collective nouns or at least not without skepticism (if not anxiety).

Robert von Hallberg, in *Culture and Value*, argues for a poetry that reflects community values; this is what he calls a poetry of accommodation and also, for the United States in the 1970s and '80s, a suburban poetry.

I suppose it has something to do with how comfortable you feel about the confines of family or nation (fine or confining). As the critic asked the poet who had slipped on the ice and was lying in the middle of the road— "Are you comfortable?"—"I make a good living."

(I take it Steve Evans's comment in his introduction to the "Technique" volume in *o.blek / Writing from the New Coast* about his generational "hatred of identity" could also apply to a hatred of community, and perhaps that is implicit in his recent discussion of "hating society properly" and also "hating" tradition. Would this include a hatred of virtual, or for that matter unavowable, communities? Echoing W. C. Fields's famous riposte to being corrected about his insistence that Jews were running the Studio— Catholics, worst kind of Jews—might we say: Virtual communities, worst kind of communities!?)

Any discussion of community would do well to start with the idea of institution rather than association. For the rules of our associations, one on one or one with many, is fundamentally an institutional matter (in the sense that Erving Goffman details in his many works). So that I would say the first fact about the "community" made possible through modems hooked up to mainframes that are teleconnected is that the access and protocols of this community are predetermined by the institutions that give us entry into them; for most of us on this particular list "membership" in the university "community"—(and for the few on commercial services bearing the insignia of ".com" at the end of their email addresses, they have simply paid to have access to this already formed nexus).

This is changing but that only makes more crucial the need to acknowledge the overlay of different institutional interests that mediate our interactions in these spaces. We don't shed old institutional habits as we inhabit new institutional spaces so much as project our old ways onto the new spaces. A great deal of sociological analysis is sure to follow us here. But it is interesting to consider, what patters [patterns] of "who speaks?" in "live" group settings—meetings, seminars—are also present in listserv situations, which may at first appear to be free of the need to interrupt or speak up or find a temporary opening in the discussion.

For example, I will soon begin monitoring how long each of you spends online with Poetics@UBVM or whether and what you download. The potential for monitoring such transactions, as well as doing various forms of statistical analysis of posts and activity, is part of the medium of our communing here. Several subscribers have noted that one of us has chosen to conceal his identity from the publicly available list of subscribers; am I right to "out" Chris Funkhauser of our SUNY-Albany node?

I have set up this listserv so that anyone can subscribe and I am automatically notified, but also so that the list itself is not listed in any directories of listservs. At some point, to keep the list at a scale small enough, or "common" enough, to work, will it be worth considering eliminating open subscriptions?

The idea of possibly hidden listeners is something a listserv invokes insofar as the communication is considered interpersonal, private in the way a letter is, or even a seminar or meeting; although we accept that we never know who buys our books (or checks them out from the library). But perhaps the situation here is more like a performance, where we make our récits individually to an audience that is able to see one another, even if, when on stage, our view of the audience may be blocked by the klieg lights.

That, anyway, would bring to mind Jean-Jacques Rousseau's preference for public meetings over and against public spectacles (theater): the public convenes to consider its circumstance, its common needs.

What is public space and why does there seem so little of it, as if the public had become a commodity no longer in much demand, but still available for import at high prices, free trade notwithstanding? (We import it from ourselves, and the tariffs are high.) So little public space, that is, so much public spectacle.

This suggests the civic values of spaces like these: not reinforcing existing communities but taking up the constitution of social space.

If I resist the idea of a literary community, while working to support the "actually existing" communities of poets among which I find myself, it is because I want to imagine reading and writing, performing and listening, as sites of conversation as much as collectivity. I want to imagine a constellation of readers who write, to and for one another, with the links always open at the end, spiraling outward—centrifugally—not closing in.

At one point in these parts—posts—a message identified as from Lolpoet (Loss Pequeño Glazier), echoed G. E. Moore's shaking of fists at the skeptics ("at least I know two things that are real!"): "We are physical beings, not virtual ones." My heart sank, for it is our virtuality that allows for hope. V139HLA3 (at Buffalo it is an institutional privilege to have your name be used as part of your user ID), a.k.a. Martin Spinelli, wanting to put off the idea that this space of exchange is unreal, insisted, "We are *really* here with our *real* eyes at *real* monitors" (but unfortunately no real italics): yet my real eyes do me no good if I aspire to something else than what I see, and what I want to monitor is neither real nor unreal.

So my hope for electronic communication is not that it engenders virtual communities, but rather virtual uncommunities.

[February 20, 1994: *Witz* (1994) and *Diacritics* 26:3–4 (1996). Unedited (no italic, "email"). The comment about monitoring time on the site and downloads would have been recognized as a joke in 1994.]

The Swerve of Verse

Lucretius's *Of Things' Nature* and the Necessity of Poetic Form

The de-versification of Lucretius—treating it as prose—is an unintended theme of the most famous contemporary account of *Of Things' Nature*, Stephen Greenblatt's *The Swerve: How the World Became Modern* (2011). Greenblatt begins *The Swerve* with an account of his youthful discovery of Lucretius through Martin Ferguson Smith's excellent prose translation. Greenblatt pretty much sticks to citing this prose version throughout his book, despite his nod to Dryden as the best for conveying Lucretius's "ardor" and noting that he consulted all the translations.

Greenblatt provides several pages of lucid, useful, and judicious summary of Lucretius's doctrines in *Of Things' Nature* (Smith's edition also provides a helpful and detailed outline of each book of the poem). Of course, I swerve from Greenblatt's basic orientation in his book. *The Swerve* is principally an engrossing yarn about the discovery of the manuscript of Lucretius's poem by Poggio Bracciolini in the fifteenth century. Greenblatt's précis is a text-book case of the heresy of paraphrase—a heresy, if that is what it is, that pervades the book and its appreciation of Lucretius for his "dangerous" ideas, ideas that appeal to Greenblatt as much as they do to me for their apparently proto-secular humanism (or proto-materialism).

(I first got hooked on Lucretius in 1971 with The Doors' song, "Atoms in the Void": "Into this world we're thrown / Like a dog without a bone.")

Apart from Greenblatt's swooning appreciation of the beauty of the poem, he does not address why it's a poem or the uses Lucretius makes of poetic form.

In a review of the superb Ronald Melville translation of Lucretius's *De Rerum Natura* (I offer here a new translation of the title: *Of Things' Nature*), Richard Jenkyns gives an explanation of why this work was written in verse. (He repeats this explanation in his introduction to Alicia Stalling's 2007 translation.)

> In the Rome of the first century BC serious philosophy in verse, if not quite
> as bizarre as it would be now, was none the less markedly eccentric . . . to
> many of his contemporaries, Epicureanism must have given the impression
> of [being] peculiarly unpoetic. . . . The doctrine is materialist, but Lucretius'
> colouring is religious. . . . You cannot command someone into a feeling. . . .
> Instead, [you] must coax and seduce. His purpose is to recast Epicureanism
> to show that it can be apprehended religiously and poetically. . . . The medium
> really is the message.[1]

Of Things' Nature was written in the first century BCE, at the time of Ci-
cero, the greatest advocate (and teacher) of oratorical/rhetorical discourse.
If the point was to "coax and seduce" readers to accept the truth of Epi-
curus's and Demosthenes's views, then why not follow Cicero's approach
to eloquence and persuasion? For Jenkyns, the reason is that Lucretius's
doctrine requires something like religious conversion rather than persua-
sion by argument. You might persuade someone that a political leader is
corrupt but to "coax and seduce" a reader to accept a new (and aversive)
cosmology requires nothing short of poetry. But the problem with this
account of the necessity for verse in *Of Things' Nature* is that Lucretius
advocated a turning away from religious superstition and seduction and
toward reason.

   Lucretius's own explanation for choosing verse is that it is the spoonful
of sugar that makes the truth of the real go down:

For as with children, when the doctors try
To give them loathsome wormwood, first they smear
Sweet yellow honey on the goblet's rim,
That childhood all unheeding may be deceived
At the lip's edge, and so drink up the juice
Of bitter medicine, tricked but not betrayed,
And by such means gain health and strength again,
So now do I: for oft my doctrine seems
Distasteful to those that have not sampled it
And most shrink back from it. My purpose is
With the sweet voices of Pierian song
To expound my doctrine, and as it were to touch it
With the delicious honey of the Muses;
So in this way perchance my poetry

---

1. Richard Jenkyns, "Coaxing and Seducing," London *Review of Books*, 20:17 (1998)

Can hold your mind, while you attempt to grasp
The great design and pattern of its making.[2]

Does this mean that reason is less palatable than superstition? For the modern "humanist" sensibility, prose is more palatable than poetry. Greenblatt, wanting to persuade and cajole us about the importance of Lucretius, necessarily writes his account in prose. A contemporary verse work with Lucretius's purpose and scope would be rejected in today's poetry climate, which prizes poems of personal experience above all else, just as it would be rejected in today's scientific climate, which insists on its own version of empirical prose explanation. Indeed, one of the sentimental appeals of poetry in our time is that it is free of science (and knowledge not earned by personal experience), just the sentimental appeal of science is that is free both of bias and of the jargon of sweetening. Does Lucretius offer a bait and switch: my songs can be as sweet as your myths—but no bull? Can truth ever be beautiful as superstition? Does truth need to put on luring makeup just to get noticed at the party? Does reason rim us with perverse pleasure? Or is Lucretius just tipping us off to how it works?

I propose a radical swerve from Greenblatt's and Jenkyns's view. The verse in *Of Things' Nature* is there to ensnare, to pull readers into an aesthetic/conceptual experience that cannot be put into prose. It goes beyond the resources of prose in making palpable its (initially) counterintuitive philosophy, which contests the naturalizing assumptions of superstition and religion. The appeal of the Latin poets in first century BCE—Lucretius, Virgil, Catullus—is their powerful, uncanny frankness, an appeal that remains fresh. For Epicureans, religion is the poison cup rimmed with honey that dispels fear of death at the cost of the appreciation of life as it is. *Of Things' Nature* dispels not fear but unnecessary fears, and that is a bitter pill to swallow. The virtue of its verse is that it embodies reason, directing, in rime, your eyes and ears to thing's nature.

So my questions are—what is it about the poem that is changed by its form?—or is the form just cosmetic?—a spoonful of poetry makes the medicine go down. Is the medicine (the doctrine) affected by the verse or just a neutral candy-coating?

Reason without poetry is like the body without a soul. Verse is the
    clinamen in action.
Round, angular, soft, brittle, dry, cold, warm,

2. Tr. Ronald Melville (Oxford: Oxford University Press, 1998), 1:935–40 and 2:11–15

Things are their qualities: things are their form
And these in combination, even as bees,
Not singly but combined, make up the swarm[3]

Prose suggests unambiguous
doctrine or
description. Verse
allows for an
order
of in-
determinacy. Verse
is swerve.
Verse echoes
Lucretius's cosmology.
Prose's faster.

Jane McIntosh Snyder's *Puns and Poetry in Lucretius's De Rerum Natura*
(1980) offers concrete example of how this works. Lucretius's incessant
punning (paronomasia) and *figura etymologica* (words in a passage that
share the same etymology but have different meanings) make sensuous
the conceptually challenging view of world making in *Of Things' Nature*.
The word play is metonymic of Lucretius's cosmology, fomenting constant
etymological and linguistic collisions that engender new meanings.

   Think of translations of Lucretius as offering a set of commentaries on
his poem. A couple of lines in Book V (lines 735 and 736, below) help to
make that point. These lines are difficult to translate for a reason that goes
to the heart of what the poem is doing (swerving not saying). The subject of
the passage from Book V can be read as the problem of translating a non-
sensuous view of reality into words. A central problem for Lucretius was
how to articulate a view of the world that is aversive to (that swerves from)
what is visible, that seems to push against what intuitively seems to be the
case. This is the Lucretian imperative.

   Lucretius confronts a problem that scientists and mathematicians have
faced from well before his time to the present: that their findings seem
implausible or counterintuitive. The world feels flat, waves and particles
are irreconcilable, atoms colliding in space could not produce the world
as we know it. Let's put it this way: You can't put into believable descrip-

---

3. *Lucretius on Life and Death: In the Metre of Omar Khayyam*, tr. W. H. Mallock (New York: John Lane
[the Bodley Head], 1900), III:viii, p. 17

tive prose E=MC², much less algebra or calculus or, well, non-Euclidean geometry or, as here's the rub, evolution, Mr. Darwin's dangerous theory (or for that matter Mr. Marx's or Mr. Spinoza's). Once you go beyond the visible reality of "ratio"—as Blake so powerfully notes in his visionary physics (to use Donald Ault's phrase), all prose bets are off. The alternative to "ratio" and to the direct evidence of the senses is not irrationalism or religion or superstition—but reason. And reason is neither visible nor consistent.

Of the translations: I prefer Smith's prose to Alicia Stallings's verse, which is too cute and cloying; but I also love the Mallock adaption, which creates a kind of self-help or wisdom verse modeled on Fitzgerald's *Rubaiyat*. I like Melville best.

I include here two new translations by Richard Tuttle. In 2014, Tuttle and I collaborated on "Echologs," after the poetry match in Virgil's *Eclogues*, III (collected in *Topsy-Turvy*). Tuttle's gleanings are possible because *Of Things' Nature* is poetry not doctrine. His versions locate precisely Lucretius's poetics.

Book V: 735–736

difficilest ratione docere et   vincere verbis,
difficult rational teach and conquer words
ordine cum videas tam certo   multa creari.
order with see   so   certain much created
→?
difficult to teach rationally and subdue words
seeing so certain an order in so much created

Literal / Tim Chandler (2015)

It is difficult to teach with reason and prevail with words
when you see many things to be created with so certain an order

Richard Tuttle (2015)

It is difficult to accept words can
describe what can repeat itself
but cannot describe what cannot

John Selby Watson (1851)

Further, when you see so many things produced in a certain order, it
   is difficult to demonstrate by reason, and to evince by argument,
   why a new moon may not be generated every day . . .

John Mason Good (1851)

Both words and reasoning arduous find alike,
Since things throughout in order flow precise.

H.A.J. Munro (1866/1891)

It is not easy to teach by reasoning or prove by words, since so many
   things can be born in such a regular succession.

William Ellery Leonard (1916) (reversed line order)

Can be create with fixed successions:
To prove absurd—since, lo, so many things'
Tis hard to show by reason, or by words

W.D. Ross (1924)

. . . it is difficult to explain by reasoning and to prove in words,
   seeing that one sees many things produced in so fixed an order.

Martin Ferguson Smith (1969)

Lastly, it is difficult to give any convincing reason why a new moon
   should not be created every day, with a fixed succession of phases
   and forms, each new-created moon being extinguished each day
   and replaced by another: one sees many things created in so fixed
   an order.

Ronald Melville (1997)

That is difficult to explain by reasoning
And prove by words, seeing that many things
Are created in so fixed and sure an order.

Alicia Stallings (2007)

You'd have your work cut out for you to prove it can't be so,
When so many other things arise in order, as you know

Book V: 747–750

quo minus est mirum se certo tempore luna
gignitur et certo deletur tempore rursus,
cum fieri possint tam certo tempore multa

Smith (1969)

Seeing that many things can occur at so fixed a time, it is not
surprising if the moon is created at a fixed time and again at a
fixed time is destroyed.

Melville (1997)

No marvel then, if at fixed times the moon
Is born and at fixed times again destroyed,
Seeing that in this world so many things
Come into being at so fixed a time

Tuttle (2015)

How great to see uncertainty
when everything else is fixed!

"Too Philosophical for a Poet"

A Conversation with Andrew David King

ταῦτ' ἄρ' ἀοιδὸς ἄειδε περικλυτός
(this the noted minstrel sang)

Odyssey 8:521

ANDREW DAVID KING: *I wanted to start by asking about the phenomenon of the book—as object and as commodity. In 2010, you spoke with Thom Donovan about the process and rationale behind putting together your selected poems,* All the Whiskey in Heaven.[1] *Certain types of work (non-poems; this is, of course, a tricky distinction) were excluded: the essays and libretti, for instance, whose presentations alongside poems in* My Way *unsettle more mainstream, big-publishing-house attitudes toward the compilation of written work. You said that the final product "has a very strong connection from beginning to end," but that "it's not in the way that the poems look, or the tone, or the style": a connection, instead, in the "potentiating recombinations among parts," which, at the same time, were linearly fused via your decision to exclude book titles from the text proper (making "a kind of text opera"–and there's your libretto!) from the chronological selections, or, as the case may be, excerpts. You recently released* Recalculating, *your first full-length volume of new poems in seven years, and so I wanted to know if there was anything significantly different for you about the act of putting a collection together now, after curating* All the Whiskey in Heaven—*or, alternatively, if there's anything significantly different about the project of assembling a "new" collection versus a selected poems. As Donovan pointed out in the interview, the concept of the "selected poems" is "obviously a genre at this particular cultural moment"—but so is the notion of the "new collection" as such. How do you confront, think about, and move through (or across, or over, or beneath) the presuppositions of these categories, which are so often market-driven and which I imagine exert many pressures—conscious and unconscious—on you as you work toward the completion of a particular project? What was it like to face these forces in the arena of another author's*

1. *Harriet*, Poetry Foundation blog, 2010

*work, such as Zukofsky's, when you edited his selected poems for the Library of
America?"*

My original manuscript for *All the Whiskey in Heaven* had about one-third
more poetry than the published book. While the longer version is closer
to my sense of the range of what I do, I thought the publisher, Jonathan
Galassi, was right to keep this book to just over three hundred pages,
forcing me to sculpt—from a large mass of writing—a new work that
has its own logic (if you can call it that), one I found as I whittled away.
The truth is in the materials, like they say, or the lie; it is much the same
to me. I would enjoy doing another selected with entirely different works,
including essays and libretti, though I don't see that in the cards.

My other experience with selecteds was with translation: over the last
years, I have been working with a number of poet/translators who have
edited, for the most part, either collections of poems or essays. For all my
translated books I have asked the translators to make their own selections
and I don't kibbitz, well not too much, since what these poets want to
translate seems to me the best possible choice, far better than any sense
I might have of representativeness. Same thing for the translations: the
main focus has gotta be on how the new poems being created work on
their own terms, fidelity be damned. Anyway, fidelity to what? The words,
the concept, the structure, the form, the style, or the exchange?

My most amazing experience of translation was when James Byrne
handed me a copy of a selection of essays and interviews translated into
Burmese by Zeyer Lynn, published a few years earlier. I loved the fact
that I knew nothing of this book, loved the fact that the translated work
spoke to a world I knew not at all. But, as the world turns, Zeyer Lynn is
coming to New York next month. I am eager to meet him.[2]

In a funny way, I wanted *All the Whiskey in Heaven* to be as close to
a generic poetry collection as possible; I didn't even come close. Let's
just say it's a generic poetry collection in drag. And while I do think
it's a good introduction to my work, that is because, if anything, it is
misrepresentative.

But I can't say that I had market considerations in mind for that book
any more than for any of my others. I started with a long and intractable
poem, "Asylum," which I think makes sense in terms of the inner logic
of the book but not in terms of any easy idea of a market or an easy way
to enter the book. But then I figure that is what the people who come to

2. Go to PennSound's Burma page for a recording of our first meeting.

the book will want, or what I want for them. To put it crassly, capitalism is not necessarily about providing a familiar cultural product but also about market differentiation. But every difference does not make a difference. Every thorn does not have a rose.

I am just so obsessed with creating the work, with composing the book in a way that works for me, which means, to some degree, that pushes to the limits of what I can make sense of.

You are probably right to think of the Zukofsky selected as a model for me, though that book was so extremely short. Still, I wanted to make it a sampler, which meant excerpting and also leaving out a couple of the best-known works in favor of the constellation.

I have been making books for almost forty years. During most of that time, I thought of the book as my basic unit of composition, though now, perhaps as a result of *All the Whiskey in Heaven* and the translations, I see my books as provisional exhibitions: other constellations are implicit, but implicit because of, and in terms of, the specific makeup of each book. There was a longer gap between *Recalculating* and *Girly Man* than between any of my other full-length collections, and some works in the book go back well before *Girly Man*, so that made for new possibilities in terms of the scale and the way the narrative of the book unfolds and refolds and finally disappears.

On the topic of publications, of publishing, let's talk about L=A=N=G=U=A=G=E and its role in both populating, shaping, and record- ing the community of poets working in avant-garde modes in the last forty years or so to today.

In a 1997 essay printed in Steve Evans and Jennifer Moxley's The Im- percipient Lecture Series, *Kate Lilley quotes Bob Perelman's point in* The Marginalization of Poetry: Language Writing and Literary History *that though "language writing" had become a recognizable buzzword by the mid-nineties, "there was never any self-consciously organized group known as the language writers or poets—not even a fixed name."*[3] *Lilly appeals to Perelman's idea of an "ad hoc" beginning of the movement, a group of individ- uals unified instead by "opposition to the prevailing institutions of American Poetry," not all that dissimilar from Steve Benson's description in* In the American Tree *of a group of writers who "markedly propose conscious value*

3. Kate Lilley, "This L=A=N=G=U=A=G=E," Impercipient Lecture Series, ed. Steve Evans and Jennifer Moxley (I: 4, 1997), reprinted in *Jacket* </jacketmagazine.com/02/lilley02.html>. Perelman is quoted from *The Marginalization of Poetry* (Princeton, NJ: Princeton University Press, 1996), pp. 11–12.

to what could otherwise be taken as impingements in a literature of autono-
mous display."[4] *Keeping a Barthesian trepidation about naming and titling*
in mind—one that seems closely related to the concerns of many of the writers
in L=A=N=G=U=A=G=E—*do you find these post hoc, historical character-*
izations accurate? What happens when a gathering of writers simultaneously
working through the same concepts and questions begins to enter into a name,
begins to gather under a banner? To what extent did L=A=N=G=U=A=G=E
document a preexisting community as opposed to acting as an agent of its crea-
tion?

Last August [2012] you posted to Jacket2 *a list of alternative titles for*
L=A=N=G=U=A=G=E *that you and Bruce Andrews had come up with.*
They range from the fittingly esoteric and material ("S/s," "T. C. W.," "'An'")
to the comic ("Rasta," "Scum O' the Earth," "Just Another Poetry Magazine,"
"Ron Silliman's Interview*") to the dryly droll ("Wordness," "Present Tense,"*
"Language Bound").[5] *This, to me, evidences both anxiety and humor at the*
task of naming: why L=A=N=G=U=A=G=E, *that moniker which, so to*
speak, stuck? Lyn Hejinian, commenting on her essay "If Written Is Writing"
in The Language of Inquiry, *says that you and Andrews, via the publication,*
"proposed that the theory need not be extrinsic to the poetry," and therefore
the fetter of a "normalized, expository style" could be discarded.[6] *Fittingly, the*
first issue in February 1978 begins with a piece by Larry Eigner, written in
a Stein-esque prose, asking questions about language's role and materiality;
there are echoes of the same concerns that emerged in This *in 1971—cf. Clark*
Coolidge's poem from the inaugural issue, "MADE THOUGHT," the first
line of which reads "made thought which of it."[7] *Was there something mimetic*
about L=A=N=G=U=A=G=E *that pushed you and Andrews to it as a title,*
and later—intentionally or not—as the calling card of your poetic commu-
nity? And can I ask, facetiously, why it's not =L=A=N=G=U=A=G=E=—
beginning and ending with equals signs, inviting conjunctions—as a professor
here at Berkeley (Geoffrey G. O'Brien, speaking on Stein as a forerunner of the
movement in his American Poetry class) rhetorically asked?

L=A=N=G=U=A=G=E pulled together different strands: it was a constel-
lation created by an editorial vision (that is to say, decision), things Bruce

4. Steve Benson, *In the American Tree*, ed. Ron Silliman (Orono, ME: National Poetry Foundation, 1986), p. 487

5. <jacket2.org/commentary/you-know-it-dont-come-easy-alternate-titles-language-1977>

6. Lyn Hejinian, *The Language of Inquiry* (Berkeley: University of California Press, 2000), p. 25

7. *L=A=N=G=U=A=G=E: The Complete Facsimile Edition*, ed. Matt Hofer and Michael Golston (Albuquerque: University of New Mexico Press, 2020). Scans of all issues at Eclipse.org.

and I felt needed to be connected, but were otherwise not or not explicitly. Our choices were speculative and conceptual: not based on (or only on) an already existing template or community but one suggested by our virtual mappings of the field. We were adamant in not wanting the locus of our map to be people in one city or people we personally knew or even people who necessarily felt connected to one another. We saw connections and wanted to make them explicit. No doubt the fact that we were in New York, where there were few poets interested in our approach and even fewer outside poetry aware of what we were doing, made a virtue out of a necessity. We were not old friends (though some of us have surely become that), college classmates, or even a tight social circle—we were working in an environment where our approach was both novel and greeted with a fair amount of disinterest if not scorn, which is why what held us together was more an aversion to a set of commonly accepted poetic ploys than a set of stylistic dictates of our own. But I'd argue that aversion is defining in poetics and does carry with it a set of preferences and procedures, including a preference for heterogeneous forms and for the sort of apoetics I am articulating here.

A number of poets were doing work we felt related—there was a marvelous collective sprit that, happily, pulled in many directions. There was the historical part: insisting on a set of precedents in American and European poetry. But I think more important, and often harder to see: we wanted to find poetry contexts for the philosophical, political, and aesthetic thinking that engaged us. This is quite the opposite of applying theoretical principles to poetic practice. Bruce and I were very conscious of giving a skeleton to the magazine in the form of our featured poets. And the lists of magazines and books, with addressees and prices, were a crucial feature in trying to establish lines of discussion. But this was a conversation, not a school; a movement not a doctrine. We were mostly focused on enlisting people and those interested in being part of the conversation we pretty much welcomed; we rejected almost nothing that was sent to us for the magazine, because the people who did send us things were self-selected and small in number.

Bruce and I are consummate collagists, and the issues are highly orchestrated. We would go to crazy lengths to excerpt things. I remember Eric Mottram telling me he was shocked to see his 150-page book on concrete poetry cut to five hundred words—sampling the whole book by selecting discrete sentences. We did something similar with Richard Foreman—well maybe it wasn't excerpted as radically as Mottram, but we picked some paragraphs of his from a theater program that we found relevant. Richard found the magazine in a bookstore and wrote us a note:

he was delighted. We've been friends since. There was no preexisting connection between Foreman and what we were doing as poets: it just seemed to us fundamental and once we put it in the magazine, well, then there was a connection.

We insisted on short pieces, no more than five hundred words. This was a way to involve more people and also to cut to the chase. Most of what needed to be said could be said at that length, so we thought—I was and remain wary of the padding that goes in typical expository prose and indeed I have gone on at great length (!) about that. The short pieces also allowed for greater participation for those who were poetics-shy, since writing poetics was not common (or was resisted) for many of the poets we wanted to contribute.

Ours was a "hard" editorial collaboration. Bruce and I had to both agree on anything we included in the magazine, any piece we solicited, any poet we featured, right down to every magazine or book listing or excerpt. This meant we had to justify to one another our choices and their relevance to our editorial approach. Our conception of what counted was not that it conformed to some theory; I have always been against theory in this sense. But the work we included needed to contribute to the conversation we were organizing: our choices were self-consciously partial and focused, which means there were aesthetically convincing poems outside our frame. But equally important, we turned a cold shoulder to a range of "experimental" poetry that might have seemed relevant but that we did not like; we were averse to the narcotic of, on the one hand, inclusivity of all experimental or avant-garde work, and, on the other hand, of the preeminence of prior friendships or sceney clubbiness, both of which debunk aesthetic choice (as uncool, judgmental, bourgeois, exclusionary, controlling). The intense fallout from our approach is still visible, though there is often a conflation, by those unsympathetic, of theory-driven schoolishness and aesthetic judgment. Our selections were based primarily on our aesthetic preferences within the frame we created, which we then did our best to provide an account of, both to each other and in our poetics. Poems or poetics that might seem to belong to L=A=N=G=U=A=G=E "in theory" might well fall short on aesthetic criteria, which remained primary, not just for us, but for the editors of magazines and presses such as *Roof*, *Hills*, *This*, *Là Bas*, Tuumba, and *Tottel's*. Which is not to say that I don't see errors in judgment, looking back; and indeed judgments complicated by friendship and alliances. Judgments are always interested, both invested and investments. I have some lines in "Foreign Body Sensation" on this—

Judge
less you not
be judged
& the world slip
by unknown
you to it
it to you.[8]

Lyn is quite right to emphasize that we wanted the poetics to be just as formally engaged in its writing as the poetry we wrote. There is nothing more fundamental about the magazine than that and also nothing rarer in the other magazines of the time or after.

Why say something in prose when you can say it as easily in poetry (in poetics)?

On the equal signs: once we decided to use the name "language," we came up against the fact that this was the title of the journal of the Linguistics Society of America, as made famous for us all by Jack Spicer's *Language*. So we faced the practical problem of differentiating. The idea was to find a graphical difference and Bruce and I decided on the equal signs, though I can't say why. It looked good. We asked Susan Bee to make a logo. The actual logo that appears atop the first issue was made by Susan in conjunction with her father Sigmund Laufer, who was a graphic designer and also had the Compugraphic machine to generate the type. But he had to physically paste the letters and equal signs in because the machine couldn't get them close enough together.

Last fall here at Berkeley the English Department hosted a colloquium entitled Boundless Poetics, *which brought together a parade of critics, poets, professors, critic-poet-professors, to discuss, descriptively and prescriptively, the enterprise of poetics. . . . Your discussion of poetics in terms of, as you say, wanting such (a) poetics to be "just as formally engaged in its writing as the poetry we wrote" brings to mind something a mentor of mine, Prof. Eric Falci, mentioned in a statement he prepared for that colloquium. To paraphrase and, doubtlessly, to oversimplify him . . . just what is poetics? If it is "boundless," so to speak (and this isn't, of course, an unquestionable tenet), can it be anything? And if it's not anything—if it's not a definite, determinate object we can direct our inten-*

---

8. *The Sophist* (Los Angeles: Sun & Moon Press, 1987; rpt., Cambridge, UK: Salt Publishing, 2004), p. 103

tionality at, not something "out there" in the world—is it, can it be, a sort of Heraclitan flux, a movement, some sort of activity? Its presence, and its importance, is palpable, but when pressed to give an account of just what it is, I come up blank. The question of poetics is one you've taken up throughout your career; I see it also in "Writing and Method" from Content's Dream, *where one might take your account of the traditional distinctions between philosophy and poetry as a corollary for an account of the distinctions between poetics and scholarship.*

Setting aside the status of poetics and pedagogy in the university more generally . . . I wanted to ask about your essay, "The Practice of Poetics," which appears in David Nicholls's Introduction to Scholarship in Modern Languages and Literature *(published by the Modern Language Association in 2007). The form of this essay is especially curious to me when considered in relation to the propositions that populate it; it has the patina, the poise, of traditional philosophical discourse, but it also, somehow, enacts just the sort of paratactic thinking it exonerates: "Paratactic writing, thinking by association, is no less cogent or persuasive than hypotactic exposition, with its demands that one thought be subordinated to the next."[9] The essay is "divided" (a loaded word in this context, to be sure) into eleven parts, each possessing its own distinctiveness but also possessed by the demands of the whole and its numbered progression. One remarkable thing about it is how it manages to tease out an overall liminality from what looks, at first, like the brickwork of traditional syllogistic argumentation—a quiet but comic way of commenting even further on hypotactic exposition's status as a preferred discourse. I can't get away with failing to note the volleys of aphoristic assertion. The last of these intrigues me most, and calls to mind another writer's speculation (pp. 75, 77, 78): "Scholarship requires poetics." "Read globally, write locally." "Poetics is a prerequisite for literary study." "Poetry is a name we use to discount what we fear to acknowledge." The last of these intrigues me most, and calls to mind another writer's speculation (it's buried in my unconscious—maybe it was you?) about Plato's banishment of the poets from his ideal city: that any rejection of poetry on the grounds of its supposed lack of utility and even danger can't help but, by this very refusal, designate poetry as a discourse in possession of some sort of autonomous power— something, in other words, formidable enough to ban; something, or as you said, to be feared.*

Beginning a project like "The Practice of Poetics," how do you manage what I imagine must be the various formal impetuses to write in expositional as well as poetic modes? I suppose what I want to ask here is how the very questions you raise in such essays turn back on themselves, if they do, to influence or even

---

9. "The Practice of Poetics," collected in *Attack of the Difficult Poems: Essays and Inventions* (Chicago: University of Chicago Press, 2011), p. 75

obliterate a given instance of their formulation. I tried to get at what I thought to be a leading formal tension—that between parataxis and hypotaxis—in the essay, but realize that other forces may have inclined you to write it how you did. Can we ever "get outside of form" enough to comment on it from the privileged position of some metadiscourse, or are we to be content (no pun!) with an understanding of form as inexorably present, or perhaps dialectically persistent, as I tried to outline above? To press this a bit, one might ask whether or not arguing that "Clarity in writing is a rhetorical effect, not a natural fact" frames itself, or must frame itself, in turn as another rhetorical effect (p. 75). And given some sort of positive answer to the last question, one could go on to ask whether or not this reflexive self-framing—the implications of criticisms of normative discourse for those criticisms themselves, especially when they're so often structured in terms of that normative discourse—is actually problematic or not.

Poetics is always bound (and bounded) and what I am arguing for, in the MLA essay, is that poetics—the kind of poetics I want—distinguishes itself from other forms of philosophical and critical writing in its acknowledgment of its situatedness and its dress. This comes up elsewhere in *Attack of the Difficult Poems*, so that the essay reads quite differently in the context of that book than in the MLA volume. Specifically, citing a remark of Stanley Cavell, I contrast writing philosophy in a gorilla suit versus a business suit, so then I am proposing that guerrilla poetry be done in a gorilla suit. (I think by association, so it's hard for me to avoid that pun but also not to think of the ILGWU [International Ladies Garment Workers Union] slogan: "Nothing suits us like our union suits," with the four senses of suits: fits, uniform, garment, and legal.) You could say that this desire to mark, or call into play, the boundaries of the discourse in which I am operating (often without a license, which is to say *with license*) is also a mark of my poetry. If I insist that my poems, as much as poetics, are rhetorical, it's not that I don't think other poetics or poems are. And by rhetorical I also have in mind more than to persuade. Charley Altieri and I had a sustained discussion of our differences on this in an email exchange in 2012, because I felt his sense of rhetoric was insufficient in a way that fatally undermined the position he was taking. Rhetoric to me is always imbued with sophistry, but a sophistry that lays bare its good faith. I think of Jerome McGann's formulation, "truth in the body of falsehood."[10] For someone so apparently critical of lucid expository writing,

---

10. "Truth in the Body of Falsehood" [Clark Coolidge's Poetry], in *The Point Is to Change It* (Tuscaloosa: University of Alabama Press, 2007)

my essays might seem an odd lot of lucidity and flights of fancy; but the truth is I am not averse to lucidity any more than to obscurity; neither is a sine qua non, if you'll pardon my Latin. In $L=A=N=G=U=A=G=E$ days, I found the lack of reflection on critical terms and aesthetic values in poetry reviews demoralizing, but this lack of reflection was a mark not of expository clarity but of aestheticonormativity.

In a recent commentary on a short poem, "Why I Am Not a Buddhist," I wrote, "My concern is more *What is false?* than *What is truth?* All true poetry comes from deep fear, immobility, timidity."[11] So here I go again: using the "all true poetry is" right after undermining any such claims. It's not that I contradict myself or even that I want to have it both ways, though both of those are surely true, but that I want to create a space where the enthusiasm of the latter claim is framed by prior acknowledgment (the way a prior arrest compromises your claim to innocence.)

I am guilty but I didn't do it.

Could you tell me more about the differences between you and Altieri when it comes to your respective accounts of rhetoric?

I'm trying to comb through what I can remember of the many references to rhetoric in what works of his I've read. In The Particulars of Rapture: An Aesthetics of the Affects, *he discusses what he sees as the attempt by modernist poets to pit what he describes as "the feelings" against "the emotions," given that any project to idealize the latter was arrested due to the emotions' long-term contamination by "centuries of rhetoric" and the socially imposed associations of classed behaviors and privileges with particular emotions.[12] And in* Enlarging the Temple, *to pull another example, he characterizes New Criticism as reconciling, via the promotion of irony, a cleavage in the prevailing Romantic attitude toward poetry and poetics between an understanding of the poem "as a rhetorical artifact" and the poem "as somehow containing experience within itself," where maybe what's meant in the latter case is that the poem's linguistic structure serves as a proxy referent for something more properly understood as existing independently of it.[13] Your inversion of Wordsworth in* My Way—*your claim that poetry is "tranquility recollected in emotion," a return to a conception of poetry that respects its instigations of chaos as well as*

11. See <jacket2.org/commentary/why-i-am-not-a-buddhist>.

12. Charles Altieri, *The Particulars of Rapture: An Aesthetics of the Affects* (Ithaca, NY: Cornell University Press, 2003), p. 50

13. Charles Altieri, *Enlarging the Temple* (Lewisburg, PA: Bucknell University Press, 1979), p. 23

its productions of order—surfaces here, also.[14] *Keeping rhetoric in mind, how do you confront this fluctuation between the idea of the poem-as-referent-to-external/empirical-experience and the poem-as-independent-rhetorical-object? Is this schism (supposing we can hold onto it for a second) relevant at all to poetic praxis, or in need of refinement or abandonment; does irony sufficiently fuse these two positions? Altieri goes on to say in* Enlarging the Temple *that the critic's task "is to recognize the falseness of the opposition between artifact and experience in terms more philosophically defensible than those proposed by the founders of New Criticism" (p. 23). My guess would be that you'd agree with this, at the very least on the assertion of the opposition's falseness. But I was wondering if you think there might be a case to be made that rhetoric, seen here as a close cousin of poetry, fabricates a very particular type of experience, one both ontologically and phenomenologically different from the experiences about which poems that purport to describe things that happen "out in the world," as Altieri says (p. 23).*

For those under the sway of Romantic ideology (to use Jerome McGann's formulation), sincerity and rhetoric are at odds. (Romantic ideology elides the rhetoric of Romantic poetry.) What this often means is that the rhetoric of sincerity and authenticity in contemporary poetry is naturalized and lays exclusive claim to the true expression of emotion. As a result, those most phobic to rhetoric become slaves to it. Like authenticity, emotion is a social and textual dynamic in a poem. That's why the "ideal" has an agonistic relation to rhetoric, going back to Heraclitus v. Plato. I remain on the side of the Angel Sophists. I lay claim to the fake expression of emotion, or anyway the messy or deformed or difficult to categorize or ambivalent. Perhaps better words would be *affect* or *feelings* or *sensation*. Resistance to the reification of emotion comes off to some emotionally dead readers as the absence of emotion. Emotional deadness is also emotion. The absence of emotion is the emotion of absence.

Anyway, such is the view from the formative years of *L=A=N=G=U=A=G=E* and *Content's Dream*, to which I think Charlie Altieri is largely sympathetic. I would characterize that moment in the 1970s as a turn away from proscribed (scenic) forms of expression of emotion to more polysemic and polymorphous realizations, no more powerfully achieved than in the work of Leslie Scalapino.

14. "Revenge of the Poet-Critic," in *My Way: Speeches and Poems* (Chicago: University of Chicago Press, 1999), p. 11

Coming of age in the 1960s, I learned so much about the gender of emotions through reading Shulamith Firestone's *Dialectics of Sex* and related works. I came to see that so much sanctified emotional expression was part of a system of regulation that appeared to be hard-wired into the language but was not. The poetry and poetics, my social, or constructivist, formalism, followed. As Peter Middleton reminds me in an email, this approach connects to Altieri's description, in *Painterly Abstraction in Modernist American Poetry*, of "the deliberate foregrounding of the syntactic activity of a work of art (either noniconically or in conjunction with representational content)," so that "the formal properties take on extraformal content."[15]

The essay Charlie and I were recently discussing is "What Theory Can Learn from New Directions in Contemporary American Poetry,"[16] which is a very generous response to my work but also raises some major problems that are worth addressing:

> Bernstein can do a brilliant job of getting his audience to hear rhetorical gestures and to indicate the fault lines where these gestures are likely to come apart. What he cannot do consistently within his poetics, although he often succeeds in his recent practice, is transpose the satirical deconstruction of rhetoric into a register that can take seriously not only the ideas in the rhetorical processes but the idea of what is at stake in the processes themselves. I will argue that only an explicit sense of purposive activity can fully engage the world in a way that addresses the density of our sense of the event-making poetic powers that have an impact on history, albeit usually local versions of history. We need an understanding of rhetoric that sponsors the poetic, without being absorbed into what remains, in Bernstein, the dominant logic of the aesthetic. (Altieri, 71)

The problem is that Charlie's call for "recovering and transforming ideals of rhetoric" (70) undermines the full aesthetic and philosophical force of rhetoric unbound to such ideals, as I wrote to him in my initial email:[17]

> There is a kind of historical amnesia at work if you want to claim a return to rhetoric in the face of my, anyway, hectoring insistence of poetry as rhetoric for as long as we have been in conversation. I'd have said, overall, that your own critical position had an insufficiently robust view of rhetoric; I'd say that especially now when you cry rhetoric but mean a kind of cancelation of rhet-

15. Charles Altieri, *Painterly Abstraction in Modernist American Poetry* (New York: Cambridge University Press, 1999), pp. 56–57

16. *New Literary History* 43:1 (2012)

17. My email to Altieri, May 25, 2012; in the email I excerpted his essay and responded below.

oric . . . but I don't have the need to deny that your view is also a version of rhetoric. . . . And that's the rub, because I see your championing of the poets you like, I'd say that suit your taste, actually undervalues their work, at least in the case of [Juliana] Spahr and [Lisa] Robertson. . . .

> And the poet is not Wordsworth's man speaking to other men, but the lonely exile from public language trying to redeem aspects of experience for the solitary reader by rendering a sense of the world in the form of an objective structure. (Altieri, p. 69)

. . . let's just say, I don't feel alienated from public language nor think of the reader as solitary nor imagine poems as objective structures.

> As Bernstein puts it, quoting Niklas Luhmann, poetry forms "a perceptual system distinct from a social system," just as visual art does—this from the poet who has gone furthest amongst his contemporaries in developing Wordsworth's ideal of a poet speaking to other people in a common language. (Altieri, p. 69)

The quote is from Jed Rasula's piece in [Craig] Dworkin's anthology [*The Consequence of Innovation: 21st Century Poetics*], not mine! I don't know Luhmann and don't agree with the statement: I can't imagine making perception distinct from the social, which I think is part of where we disagree. Also, not sure if in your view here I am closest to, or furthest from, Wordsworth's ideal.

> But the more poetry becomes an internal system, the more difficult it becomes to specify how it might affect life beyond the poem, even though it seems to have more resources than sharpened attention to the material properties of words and images. . . . Because poets cannot trust discursive understanding and because the poem is primarily an object that establishes a play of imaginative energies, the primary modality of reception for the audience is not one of understanding an object held in common as a structure of meanings, but rather experiencing subjective intensities sparked by the object. . . . But I am bothered by the way such formulations subordinate the poet to the poem, meaning to experience, and the domain of historical being to sheer ontology or to states of immediate presentation that ignore the terms of interpersonal social and psychological relations. (Altieri, pp. 69–70)

Why not be as bothered, in your formulation, with the subordination of the poems to the poet [or experience to idealized meaning, ontology to the idea of history]? To me this is just dualism, at best, or sentimental humanism at worst. The relation in all such binaries is dialectical. You wish to have the poet dominate but usually when the rhetoric of the poet dominating is in play, it's a matter of ideology not persons, of fiat not fact. So I read this comment as a ceding of any real struggle for subjectivity or individual articulation.

Poetry is born "sheer" but everywhere in frames. "The formal properties take on extraformal content." Because of its unacknowledged absorption of Romantic ideology, the idealization of one frame, that of "an object held in common as a structure of meanings," negates the deregulating power of rhetoric in poetry, which is, indeed, not "sheer" but a historical probe. The trump card of a "domain of historical being," as applied to the fundamentally imaginative and symbolic spaces of poems, is historicism without a historical method. The rhetoric of cuing "historical being" in a poem has itself to be historicized; it is never sheer historical being. Indeed, the structure of meaning for one is a regulation of emotion for another. The commons is a site of incommensurability that calls for dialogue.

I ended my email with a parodic reversal, substituting Charlie's name for mine in the passage of the essay that I quote at the beginning of this response, also reversing his key terms. I turned his words inside out not to articulate my view of his argument, but rather to show how I hear that argument as circular, much in the way he hears mine:

> What Altieri cannot do consistently within his critical thought is transpose the reification of rhetorical processes as an ultimate arbitrating value of what is held in common between poet and reader into a register that can move beyond his thematized self-seriousness as a form of aesthetic prophylaxis. The result is a failure to grapple with processes that underlie rhetoric, meaning, and expressivity, that is, what is not ideally, but in fact, held common. I will argue that only an explicit sense of the purposelessness of poetic activity can fully engage the social in a way that addresses the multiplicity of our senses of the world, so that poetry's impact on history is not entirely subsumed within representations of it. We need an understanding of the aesthetic that sponsors rhetoric, without being absorbed into what remains, for Altieri, the dominant logic of idealization under the guise of imputed authorial activity.[18]

Charlie and I went on to have a rare and valuable exchange, opening onto common ground and deeper engagement with the issues at hand. This is what I said to him:

> We share the sense that "rhetoric" as a term of art needs to be decoupled from *persuasion*. On poet/poem: I don't see that the presentation of "self" in

18. My email to Altieri, May 25, 2012. Contrast with Altieri's original: "What he cannot do consistently within his poetics, although he often succeeds in his recent practice, is transpose the satirical deconstruction of rhetoric into a register that can take seriously not only the ideas in the rhetorical processes but the idea of what is at stake in the processes themselves. I will argue that only an explicit sense of purposive activity can fully engage the world in a way that addresses the density of our sense of the event-making poetic powers that have an impact on history, albeit usually local versions of history. We need an understanding of rhetoric that sponsors the poetic, without being absorbed into what remains, in Bernstein, the dominant logic of the aesthetic." (p. 71)

a poem does that much to actually put the reader in contact with a historical author: whatever the textual or stylistic features of a work, a historical method would need to read the work against the grain and in terms of its time, place, and through a grappling with the particulars of the author (e.g., context). I don't think attending to the poem ever need divert us from attending to the poet; that is what makes poems powerful. However poems that wear their self-representations on their sleeves are often the most resistant to a robust—let me use that word again—reading of/for/through the author. So this is where I find your argument "circular" (to turn your criticism of me around). The author function can be read equally in Robert Hass and Bruce Andrews; the fact that Hass writes about himself does not aid in this reading but often hides it. Yes, it creates a representation of the author in a virtually scenic way, but that is hardly really coming to terms with how selves are articulated in poems. It's a conceit, man speaking to man; I use it myself, many the time. There is no escape from such conceits (rhetorics) but hiding the author in the guise of the self may often pay too high a price in relegating the author function (the actual person) to ideology. Maybe that's the crux of our difference: I don't see the kind of self-representations you seem to be advancing as in any way eliding ideology; it is an ideology that masks its ideological character.

What I think is more important here is what we may hold in common on these issues. The social also always poses "possible agreements"—I have no problem there. I also have no problem with your formulation, "how poems establish intelligence in their dealing with the world and with the history of dealing with the aspects of the world relevant to the poem." Though again I'd say Andrews is more revealing on this score than Hass. I'd only add, reflexively perhaps, that structure is always in a dialectical relation to other extra-structural factors, and vice versa. Content is never more than an extension of structure, and the reverse. But then while I say *reverse*, there are often incommensurabilities among levels (so I take the "abilities" in that word to heart). That gets interesting. The move away from close reading often got drowned in the bathwater, even if we could never find the baby. So, to use my word of the week again, we need a robust close reading . . . an inherently multilevel process (forms not form). I also like this because it suggests a criterion for aesthetic judgment, an ability to value one work over another. A historical method would insist on reading structure in context. The work may cast light on the socio-bio-historical contexts, but those contexts do not determine the work. The writer's decisions are not limited to any particular style or mode of self-representation (or self-cancellation), though the decisions are articulated through choices over just such issues. The writer's decisions, that is, are necessarily multilevel, and individual works will cue a reader to the primacy of different frames (to use Erving Goffman lingo). One of the intelligences in a body of poetry is that it is able to reframe where the decision-making is occurring. This way a—ohmygod!—robust sense of intentionality is needed (while we are often subjected to an abandonment of intentionality). The "purposelessness" of an artwork is meant to potentate the ability to read intentionality not in utilitarian terms but in aesthetic ones: a willing suspension of the utilitarian in pursuit of the aesthetic.[19]

Because I'm interested in the relationship between aesthetics and history (and the aesthetics of history, the history of aesthetics, and other inversions), your claim that "only an explicit sense of the purposelessness of poetic activity"— even if made in an illustrative attempt to bring out the circularity you find in Altieri's argument—"can fully engage the social in a way that addresses the multiplicity of our senses of the world, so that poetry's impact on history is not entirely subsumed within representations of it" strikes me. It seems a likely candidate for success as a theoretical alternative to what Altieri proposes. A related concern of mine came up a little earlier when I asked you whether it might be possible to "get outside" form, or ideology, and comment on it—to get some degree of distance that provides, at the same time, the necessary proximity. Your comments on this point, as well the insights volleyed between you and Altieri, are well-taken when they rest on a set of (as you say) dialectical relationships such as those between the poet and the poem, experience and meaning, ontology and history; in this sense, it's tough to see how a return to an idealized version of poetic rhetoric promises anything but a temporary suppression of these inextricable, alternating binaries for the sake of something like authorial assuredness. I wonder, though, what you might say to the charge that because even the privileging of these dialectic relationships is itself a form of rhetoric that it's no less exempt from ideology in the end—and that it, as well as neoliberalism and the modes of self-representation you take Altieri to be advancing, must inevitably cede its claim to any particular transparency on questions of rhetoric and its relation to controversial ideologies. An even more skeptical critique might ask whether it's not the ideological indebtedness of any particular species of linguistic expression (in an atomic sense: corpuses, poems, works, words, symbols of any sort, anything that hazards or pretends an almost irreducible coherence) that we ought to be concerned with, but the medium—the genera, so to speak— from which these particulars descend: something larger, say, a given language, idiom, or soundscape. Even if this critique might be difficult to play out because of inevitable problems with classification . . . , I don't want to give up on what it's getting at. This is an insidious skepticism, even cynicism, I'm toying with. And perhaps it becomes the sort of self-defeating relativism nobody wants. But I'd be interested in hearing whether you think it has anything to do with your reaction to Altieri. I recognize the possibility, of course, that an agreement with the criticism I've put forth here may nonetheless not alter the urgency or efficacy of attempts to debunk this renewed emphasis on "idealized meaning."

19. My email to Altieri, May 27, 2012

There's also the question of how these interpretational binaries play out not just in the space of the poem but in time, i.e., through the rise and fall of various critical apparatuses, ideological inclinations, political beliefs, institutional changes, and so on. Maybe the best we can hope for is a return to Altieri's notion of "recovering and transforming ideals of rhetoric," but a return that falters as soon as it steadies—a constant giving and taking of ground. I can see how this might be politically or pragmatically unacceptable though.

My life is replete with inversions. I have something like (mild) dyslexia, where I go left when I ought to go right (well, that's a virtue, but not on the road) or call Joan Jane and Jane Jan.[20] It's not a happy condition, but I can't imagine any other way to negotiate the world. It's hard for me to hear any expression without hearing the reverse, a variation, or pun. Substitution is not a literary device that I try out, it's integral to my perception: a verso occurs to me, unprompted, almost at the moment I recognize a recto. Into every life a little pain must fall, say; the minute I think of one I think of the other. (Zukofsky's "See sun, and think shadow"[21] [or is it the other way around?].) You know the way the brain flips the images we see upright? Mine flips everything around one more time or maybe one and a half. When I make an argument, I see the hole in the other side before I finish my first thought. My experience is *second thought, first thought*. I call what I do an echopoetics of translation, transformation, variance, hyperbole, parody, satire, and reversal. That would be the rhetoric of the purposivelessness, the sieve of purpose, that you say you like; just about Kantian, after all is said and undone. Why can't we all just . . . refract reflection. But no, I hate *mise en abymes* as much as the next bloke, and I wouldn't want to be stuck with one on a long train ride. Someone recently referred to me as polemical, but I'd say raucous is more like it. And while such excess has its lineage, from Blake and Poe to Tzara to Richard Foreman, John Zorn, Steve McCaffery, Tan Lin, Will Alexander, Maggie O'Sullivan, Susan Howe, Arkadii Dragomoshchenko, Henry Hills, Tom Raworth, Gil Scott-Heron, George Kuchar, Caroline Bergvall, Will Alexander, Bruce Andrews, Amy Sillman, Christian Bök, Harryette Mullen, Nick Cave (the artist), Robert Grenier, Ken Jacobs, Tracie Morris, Mei-mei Berssenbrugge (perhaps we could call this a branch of neobaroque?)—I see it so vividly in the work of Felix and Emma Bernstein and Susan Bee—I also realize what a distance it puts me from the

20. It's a cognitive dyspraxia: directional, letter, and word reversal.

21. *Louis Zukofsky: Selected Poems*, ed. Charles Bernstein (New York: Library of America, 2006); *Anew* 21

button-down decorum that masquerades as serious poetry. I suppose this is very different than the aspiration to get outside anything (or get to a core)—form or history or ideology. I do respect the need we have, citizens!, to get next to our interest values and consider the good of the polis (not the police); but, unlike John Rawls or Richard Rorty, I think there's as much chance of that as for a rich man to get through the eye of a needle on a camel ride to Hades. In other words (it's always that): it's the best chance we got and I'm putting all my chips on it. As an artist, it's not my responsibility to be responsible but to foment response, to toque the showboat here and there, thither and yon, fort and da, so we can have the mental space to breathe, in the in between. Fred Wah takes over that Johnny Mercer song, "Ac-Cen-Tchu-Ate the Positive" ("Don't mess with Mister In-Between"): but let's just say accentuate the accent.[22] Bob Dylan has a remark in his February 1966 *Playboy* interview, "As far as I'm concerned, I don't consider myself outside of anything. I just consider myself *not around*";[23] I loved that for its immediate social sense of turning the tables on insiders, but looking at it literally it's always the issue that can't be overcome. Everybody's gotta be somewhere. . . . It's just that too often people confuse being somewhere with being everywhere; even God can't pull that off. I'm no relativist, but I am sick at heart. Let me see if I can find a way to tell you one more time.

    . . .

Ron Silliman . . . observed in his 1988 essay "Poetry and the Politics of the Subject" that the purveyors of so-called "marginal" literatures tend to emphasize the reliability of some first-person position or voice (this is what, at least, I take it he means by "conventional"); the passage is worth quoting at length:

> *Progressive poets who identify as members of groups that have been the subject of history—many white male heterosexuals, for example—are apt to challenge all that is supposedly "natural" about the formation of their own subjectivity. That their writing today is apt to call into question, if not actually explode, such conventions as narrative, persona and even reference can hardly be surprising. At the other end of the spectrum are poets who do not identify as members of groups that have been the subject of history, for they instead have been its objects. The narrative of history has led not to their self-actualization, but to their exclusion and domination. These writers and readers—women, people of color, sexual minorities, the*

22. Fred Wah, "Mr. In-Between," in *Is a Door* (Vancouver, BC: Talonbooks, 2009)

23. <www.interferenza.com/bcs/interw/66-jan.htm>

entire spectrum of the "marginal"—have a manifest political need to have their stories told. That their writing should often appear much more conventional, with the notable difference as to who is the subject of these conventions, illuminates the relationship between form and audience.[24]

Silliman qualifies this in other contexts. Harryette Mullen, in The Cracks Between What We Are and What We Are Supposed to Be, *brings up his argument that many readers and critical institutions tend to suppose a dichotomy between poetry that stands in for the "codes of oppressed peoples" as opposed to "purely aesthetic" undertakings, by which, he argues, the writings of unprivileged or underprivileged groups is automatically pegged as falling into the former category, a classification that produces just another restriction of agency for a group that, by that very classification, was supposed to have gained a space for agency.*[25] *One idea here seems to be that critical institutions inadvertently reiterate the inequalities inherent in the distribution of privilege by attempting to make privileges visible.*

This passage bears some resemblance to Rae Armantrout's response roughly ten years earlier to your question about a perceived lack of women in "language-oriented writing," an absence she explained by saying that women need "to describe the conditions of their lives," that this "entails representation," that they feel "too much anger" to participate in modernism's "analytical tendencies."[26] *What interests me in these approaches—besides, in Armantrout's case, the contention that anger can act as a significant force in the determination, or self-determination, of voice—is the assumption or claim that there's something "basic" about the voice-position which many of these groups have perceived themselves to be deprived of, and have been deprived of. And it's the same position which, in the hands of a more privileged and materially enabled population, becomes, on this view, a breeding ground for illusions about its supposed transparency, though it remains hardly much more than a dominant racial, sexual, social, political, etc., ideology in sheep's clothing. I think back, here, to your essay "Stray Straws and Straw Men" from a 1977* Open Letter *symposium, where you write about "the natural look," a constructed and structurally consistent aesthetic intent on masking the agency behind its construction so as to claim special access to an objective reality—another strategy familiar to Barthes, who dedicates a good portion of the work that would become* Mythologies

24. Ron Silliman, "Poetry and the Politics of the Subject," *Socialist Review* 88/3 (1988), pp. 61–68

25. Harryette Mullen, *The Cracks between What We Are and What We Are Supposed to Be: Essays and Interviews* (Tuscaloosa: University of Alabama Press, 2012), p. 12

26. Rae Armantrout, "Why Don't Women Do Language-Oriented Writing?," *L=A=N=G=U=A=G=E* 1 (1978)

deriding similar pretensions of naturalness. There you assert, plausibly I think, that despite a multiplicity of naturally occurring aesthetic "modes," there is no master "natural mode."[27]

Is it fair of me to ask what your position offers these parties? Or, as an alternative, what it might say to Silliman's attempt at a sociological explanation of why we see a preference for a "voice," however much a rhetorical artifact, in certain groups, if we do? And about the pragmatic consequences of the approach you advocate: I'd suspect you have some confidence that it effectively undermines or elides, to use your words, the (or a) dominant ideology, but I'd be interested in hearing, in good faith, how you think this will work, and if there is ever a point where maybe we can return to some workable concept of self-representation that weds the democratic facets of your approach with an acknowledgment—if one is merited—of the utility of 'voice' in certain social contexts, or of the author function that Altieri emphasizes.

Will there be a time when all this flux of voicing disappears in favor of the "utility" of a "workably" solid, intelligible voice which we can rely on? I'm a pragmatist who relies on such provisional assurances. (After all, much of this discussion utilizes just such a voice.) But I also rely on a space for overturning such assurances. That is the (or anyway *a*) space of art. In my aesthetics, art is not a utility. If we close off that nonutilitarian realm, we create a fantasy of the end of history, but without actually ending history. So that's a problem.

"Let's just say that the aim is not to win but not to lose too bad."[28]

Forming in the wake of the civil rights movement, feminism, and the anti-Vietnam-war movement, $L=A=N=G=U=A=G=E$, and my subsequent editorial work, endeavored to bring to the forefront a set of poets who had been, mostly anyway, excluded from the canon. Fundamental to these acts of reclamation was also to insist on the relevance of social, historical, and biographical contexts in reading form (not just subject matter), that is, the politics (and social identities) of poetic form.[29] This emphasis on social politics has been a red flag—antagonizing the powers that be / of the poetry blandoisie. The classical example would be Gertrude Stein: was she excluded from the High Modernist canon because she was a woman, a lesbian, a Jew, or because of her radical formal invention—or was the combination toxic for the blandoisie (one or two of those things would

27. "Stray Straws and Straw Men," in *Content's Dream: 1975–1984* (Los Angeles: Sun & Moon Press, 1985)

28. "Let's Just Say" in *Girly Man* (Chicago: University of Chicago Press, 2006), p. 11

29. See *The Politics of Poetic Form: Poetry and Public Policy* (1990), which I edited.

be acceptable but not all of them)? I've wanted to address these issues variously through consideration of, for example, Emily Dickinson, Paul Laurence Dunbar, Mina Loy, Sterling Brown, Louis Zukofsky, Claude McKay, Lorine Neidecker, Melvin Tolson, Hannah Weiner, and Larry Eigner.[30]

My question to Rae Armantrout in 1978 was ironic, meant to dispel an illusion. (It didn't.) As to Ron Silliman's essay, Leslie Scalapino provided an immediate and persuasive rejoinder:

> My response, briefly stated, was that people's conditions of suffering, an el-
> ement of which is continual re-definition by a ruling group, people pressed
> even to the point of revolution, do not necessarily respond by creating con-
> ventional narratives as such definitions of reality that arise from within the
> ruling group's perspective and dictation. It is like saying the Russian Revo-
> lution was accomplished solely by aristocratic men because they had leisure
> time. One may respond to constraint of oppression by creating a language
> whose syntax/structure is (as such, does) its conception—thereby altering
> the ruling language.[31]

Echoing Leslie, I don't accept the premise that adopting normalizing rhetoric gives voice to the otherwise voiceless; you could just as well say the opposite, that such normalization abrogates or ventriloquizes, which is to say silences, such voices by proving a prefabricated template for what counts as intelligible and legitimate. Audre Lorde, famously, put it this way: "For the master's tools will never dismantle the master's house. They may allow us temporarily to beat him at his own game, but they will never enable us to bring about genuine change."[32] Many writers who come "late" into official literary history do, indeed, challenge that template, but they are often *initially* marginalized in favor of writers who work in more conventionally legible forms. That, for me, is the lesson of radical politi-cal thinkers from Mary Wollstonecraft to W. E. B Du Bois, from Amiri Baraka to Shulamith Firestone. Who gets counted as "avant-garde" is subject to sanitization by both proponents and detractors. But the most

---

30. See, especially, "Poetics of the Americas" in *My Way: Speeches and Poems* and "Objectivist Blues: Scoring Speech in Second-Wave Modernist Poetry and Lyrics" in *Attack of the Difficult Poems: Essays and Inventions.*

31. "Disbelief," in *How Phenomenon Appear to Unfold* (Brooklyn: Litmus Press, 2011, pp. 220–21). Scalapino's stinging original response to Silliman was called "What Person?" (1999) and is collected in *A Guide to Poetics Journal: Writing in the Expanded Field, 1982–1998* (Middletown, CT, Wesleyan University Press, 2013).

32. "The Master's Tools Will Never Dismantle the Master's House," in *Sister Outsider: Essays and Speeches* (Berkeley, CA: Crossing Press, 1984), p. 111

radical transformations of American poetry are unthinkable without putting those previously unrecorded at the center.[33]

Blacks, Jews, queers, women, immigrants, the dispossessed (by circumstance or election), speakers of broken or brokered English, outsiders and sick-at-heart insiders, the mad (as hell or just plain), apostate WASPS & language bootleggers, workers and those out of work, irregulars & incorrigibles, the disagreeable & divisive, unfit & uncomfortable, betrayers & betrayed, misfit & marginal—the whole pataquerical crew—are the shock troupes of the avant-garde, an elite force specializing in unconventional operations.[34] When it comes to the symbolic space of American poetry, projected identifications are as important as origins: *you can't judge a book by its biography*. Art is judged by outcomes not inputs, and that is intrinsically unfair because privilege is real and art can't change—by fiat or desire—the debilitating effect of inequalities (including access to the historical record). Mean people can create *mean* (in the sense of edgy) poetry, and a victim can write in the voice of the victimizer (sometimes better than the victimizer can). Woe be it, but the value of a poem is not commensurate with the social value of the person who created it.

Even so, those who have had a long run as the "subjects of history," that is, the ones who have *subjected the rest of us to their history*, are both likely to cling to the truth of their rhetoric and unlikely to see their normalcy as perversity. And that is a big aesthetic disadvantage for them.

In other words, you can't use the minister's bible to dismantle the minister's religion. In other words, use the minister's bible to dismantle the minister's religion. In other words, there is more than one way to cook kale. In other words, voice is kind of ministry, mimicry, melody, memory. . . . In other words, the broad masses ain't no woman.

I've written till, well, I was blue in the face (I think I must be purple by now) about the social history and aesthetic force of nonstandard approaches to voice, voicing, dialect, and accent and how they are, in American poetry, specifically linked to a counterhegemonic resistance to

33. A. L. Nielson emphasizes this point in *Reading Race: White American Poets and the Racial Discourse in the Twentieth Century* (1990) and *Black Chant: Languages of African-American Postmodernism* (1997). See also the discussion of Kamau Brathwaite, Claudia Rankine, Harryette Mullen, M. NourbeSe Philip, Nathaniel Mackey, and N. H. Pritchard in Anthony Reed, *Freedom Time: The Poetics of Black Experimental Writing* (Baltimore: John Hopkins University Press, 2014).

34. This riff is extended in "The Pataquerical Imagination: Midrashic Antinominanism and the Promise of Bent Studies" in *Pitch of Poetry*. See also the fifth volume of Jerome Rothenberg's Poems for the Millennium series, *Barbaric Vast & Wide: A Gathering of Outside and Subterranean Poetry from Origins to Present*, coedited by John Bloomberg-Rissman (2015).

assimilation.[35] It's often the *outs* who change the *ins* rather than the other way around. But that point is rhetorical because we are each in and out in so many different ways that you *can't never* give a full accounting; and there is plenty of room for invention, refinement, conformity, and iconoclasm coming from all sorts of people, often in unpredictable and unexpected ways. In this respect, anomaly *is* poetic destiny.

I came at this again in a recent piece on Gertrude Stein, discussing her suffragette opera, *The Mother of Us All*:

> The problem Stein keeps coming back to in her last work is that, if the structures of power are not changed, then bringing women into power, getting the vote, doesn't change a thing. "You have only got the name, you have not got the game," says Jo the Loiterer, who cannot vote, even after women's suffrage, because he, like a nomadic play by Gertrude Stein, has no fixed address.[36]

The attraction to dominant (or standard) forms of discourse (including voice) is like the attraction to money: it seems to buy you a lot, seems to have the most rhetorical punch for the dollar. The problem is you may end up punching the wrong thing. And, then again, what's defined as innovation is so often a betrayal of the poetics of invention. If you focus on stylistic change, you can get hung up on intention, as opposed to what Kenneth Burke calls motivation. Fresh eyes (voices fresh and being fresh to history) are needed. If that freshness poses limitations, so does jadedness. The base limits (the given of our social and biological identities, the author function, as you call it) that each of us brings to the conversation are not chosen. We choose what to do about, or with, or without, them. They don't disappear. Look at it this way: those who never got a slice of the pie want it, while those who've had their fill think they own it. Still, some of the haves and some of the have nots may say, *hey, the pie's not so good*, and maybe someone will make a better pie or maybe show us how we can dine on air—or on poetry or on virtue (to echo Baudelaire).

Such points require reiteration because one way "dominant discourse" stays dominant is by undermining all challenges to its exclusive authority.[37]

35. I discuss "mastering form" versus "deforming mastery" in "Poetics of the Americas" and the continuation on mashugana miscegenation in "Objectivist Blues." Assimilation is necessarily a context-depended figure. For some, writing in a style deemed European or white is a kind of selling out of your identity, de-ethnicizing, passing. For others, standardized writing practices amount to the same. But neither mainstreaming nor innovating is tied to any one American identity, and both can be gloriously inauthentic or deliriously real.

36. *Pitch of Poetry* (Chicago: University of Chicago Press, 2016), p. 99

37. Forgive the personification: think of it as a cartoon image.

Attacks on the "avant-garde" as racist or sexist—a charge that rightly could be made about all cultural sectors in the United States—imply either that aesthetically radical work should be held to a higher moral standard or that such work is morally worse than the mainstream, or both. The "avant-garde" *is* worse because it makes a hash of such standards.

Radical modernist and contemporary art is tainted by the cultural values of its times, and its dystopian geniuses are notorious for being as vile as, if not viler than, the times in which they lived. Radical art and poetry are not necessarily "nice" or "supportive" or models of ideal communities. Still, much depends upon who gets to determine the borders of the "avant-garde" (itself a detestable designation that I would never use in a strictly positive sense). At its most radical, poetry challenges and reforms those borders. Poets who are deeply committed to assimilation and intelligibility, often for the loftiest of reasons, may want to be "avant-garde" but they want it "clean"—they want to be part of it without being pulled into the mud by it. Because to get your wish and be "avant-garde" is to become the problem, not the solution; it is to become the accused and not the accuser.

In "Disfiguring Abstraction" (in *Pitch of Poetry*), I recount my experience at two advisory meetings for the Museum of Modern Art's "invention" of abstraction show. The canon put forward by the curator stripped modernist abstraction from its connection to decorative work (often by women) and to the art of Africa and other non-Western cultures. This beached and bleached view of abstraction was neither a reflection of the radical aesthetic practice a century ago nor of the inchoate views of the great artists that were presented in the show. The problem was the way MoMA claimed and framed this work. At one point, Hal Foster, who was vociferously defending the status quo, turned on me, saying he was tired of my attack on art history. For Foster, the history had already been written and the task of the museum was to retell that story. But the art tells another story—and that one's still unfolding. To rethink and resituate works of art is not to attack art history; it is to refuse the authority of those who would claim sovereignty over it.

McGann's claim about rhetoric and sincerity being at odds reminds me of something another Jerome—Rothenberg—said in an interview with William Spanos in Dialectical Anthropology *in 1986. Spanos asked about his interest in oral traditions, and Rothenberg responded by emphasizing the depth of many communities' investments in what he called the "subterranean culture" of the "tribal-&-oral," and by arguing that an oral tradition is itself created in the pursuit in pursuit of "recovering" "the idea . . . 'per se' of the oral tradition . . ."—something more foundational than any localized, empirical oral phenomenon in particular.*[38] *And this in turn brings to mind a related, but somewhat narrower, comment William Corbett made about Rothenberg in* Erato *in 1987: "He is concerned to write a public poetry that will stand for more than just his experiences. What he has made is a poetry that relies upon the rhetorical power of the chant, the Whitmanic list, testimony, and American colloquial speech."*[39] *In both comments, something like a universal language—or if not language, then sentiment—is referenced; and I wonder if you see such an idea as at all enticing or perhaps even dangerous.*

You described a little while back the undertaking of "writing poetics" as uncommon even in the days of L=A=N=G=U=A=G=E's *advent; that observation of uncommonality seems just as relevant today. Should the practice of poetics, the adoption of poetics as a modus operandi for anything like criticism, analysis, and engagement with poetry, be seen as the proper (and not only de facto) purview of poets? Something like this seems to be, from my pinhole view, how things stand today with English departments. A fairly apparent division is set up between what is seen as poetics and, on the other hand, scholarship.*

But in your keynote address to the Northeast Modern Language Association's Buffalo meeting in 1992, you suggested that literature classes, in response to a certain type of institutionalization of literature, could be "transformed from a knowledge-acquisition approach to creative reading workshops, replacing tests with poetic response in the form of free-form journals, poems, and literary imitations."[40] *And of course you suggest as much in several other essays. Is there something to be said, maybe, for preserving the party-line division? Is it only in the case of literary study—rather than other disciplines also—that engagement in poetics, or something analogous to it, can be fruitful? In one sense, it seems to me that a position such as yours could go hand in hand with commitment to the view that there's some ur-language to be sought out, something to unify the traditional and nontraditional fields of study, but I'm not at all sure you see it that way.*

In my poetics of pitched tents and collapsible space modules, sincerity is a form of rhetoric and rhetoric is sincere, if acknowledged. I know I've got

---

38. Jerome Rothenberg and William Spanos, "Comment," *Dialectical Anthropology* 11:2 (1986), pp. 211–12

39. William Corbett, review of *New Selected Poems* by Jerome Rothenberg, *Erato* 4 (1987), p. 8

40. "What's Art Got to Do with It? The Status of the Subject of the Humanities in an Age of Cultural Studies," in *My Way: Speeches and Poems*, p. 50

it backwards. Recovering, uncovering, and covering are part of an imper-
fect (more perfect) dialectical process. Tradition, as Rothenberg uses the
term in your citation, is what is buried alive. The culture we recover (are
recovering from) is one we are bound to, but out of touch with. To get
back in touch we have to—Oy!—make it newer. Or better: *Make it now.*
(Even though that sounds so yesterday.) Nower. (*More now.*) Contra the
Whit-manic: there's a need for a poetry that is *less* than my experience,
because, in my experience, experience can be the problem. Let's just say,
experience is an albatross (a sign of loss). Force of conviction's not the
same as universalist doxa: I hear plenty of particularity and resistance in
Rothenberg's songs.

I find it helpful to remind myself that there are worlds outside my
worlds. Call them universes, if you like; but I am less interested in the
"uni" than the verses.

Everybody talks about poetics, but nobody does anything about it.

Poetics is the last resort of poetry, but, then, poetry is an art of last
resorts. The either/or you present (citing Hass) leaves poetics stranded
between the Hardy of grandiosity and the Laurel of triviality. But I
keep saying poetics differs from more rationalized forms of philoso-
phy or criticism by being embedded in the situational. Contra Thomas
Nagel, it's a *view from somewhere* because it is implicated in making
specific art works (not coining universal values à la Nagel's "view from
nowhere").

The aim of poetry is to show the fly it's in a bottle.

If literary criticism veers toward scientific/rationalized "rigor" rather
than more associative forms of research and investigation, that's not
poetry versus scholarship, it's a pinched, overly professionalized view of
scholarship. Deprofessionalization is stigmatized as *poetic* because it chal-
lenges positivism (while also challenging the idea that any method reveals
an ur-language: in my view, all methods are veils). But that was the prob-
lem we faced in starting the Poetics Program at Buffalo twenty-five years
ago. I've never thought there should be one approach to literary studies
but rather have made a case for not standardizing methods of scholar-
ship or core bibliographies. My paranoia is that the literary academy has
turned its back on aesthetics in pursuit of didactic historical and socio-
logical studies, where art is not a value or exemplary of ways of perceiving
but, rather, a crime against moral codes. But I get it: everybody's weary of
questions so seek the sensation of answers.

I'm for the plenty of nothing, to twist Ira Gershwin's lyric to an inch of
truth.

You talked about translation a little earlier. I was looking over Modernist
Archaist: Selected Poems by Osip Mandelstam[41] *and noticed that you had
done a few translations with Kevin M. F. Platt. Platt's introduction begins
with a quote that leads into something else I want to ask, something from an
essay titled "The Word and Culture" (translated by Platt):*

> *Poetry is a plough, turning over time so that its deep layers, its fertile black soil, ends
> up on the surface. There are periods when mankind, not satisfied with the present
> day, yearning like a ploughman, craves the virgin soil of time. Revolution in the
> arts inevitably leads to classicism. (p. 7)*

*Besides the reference to the boustrophedon—that type of bi-directional text
seen in ancient manuscripts whose etymology in Greek means something like
"as an ox turns in plowing"—another kind of recurrence caught my attention
here: that of cycles of taste and purpose, aesthetics and ethics, in the history of the
practice of poetry. There are other references to this "primality," too, in the poetry
itself; the speaker in "Notre Dame"—which you translated—talks of the "pre-
ternatural ribs" of the basilica at Notre Dame and how "from crude weight /
Someday I too will fashion the beautiful" (p. 35).*

*At any rate, I wanted to contextualize the recycling that Mandelstam
posits here with reference to the Language school's interest in Russian artists,
theorists, and critics, particularly the Formalists. Who or what, besides exper-
imental poets working in Russia with whom you sustained dialogues (Dra-
gomoshchenko, etc.), sparked this attraction to the aesthetic wealth of Russian
modernisms and avant-gardes, stretching from Pasternak, Akhmatova, and
Ivanov to Velimir Khlebnikov, Mayakovsky, the poets of Berdyaev's Silver Age,
even Jakobson as he began his career—across Symbolism, Futurism, Formalism,
and hybrids of these? The aesthetic variety is diverse; Platt, for one, describes
Mandelstam as "a committed Modernist," but I've also come across a video of
your reading, with Ian Probstein, of Khlebnikov's "Incantation by Laughter,"
which seems decidedly postmodern.[42]*

*What was it about these Russian movements and authors that drew you and
others to them? In reverence (or correspondence) is there any acknowledgment,
implicit or not, of Mandelstam's dictum about the cyclicality of revolution and
classicism (and classism)? I suppose I'm asking, in part, about how you see the
structure of the various relationships of modernisms and postmodernisms to
their predecessors, however recent or ancient. And, in addition to this, whether*

41. *Modernist Archaist,* ed. Kevin Platt (Miami: Whale and Star Press, 2008)

42. At PennSound's Khlebnikov page

or not the global political situation in which such modernisms take place has
changed more than its window dressing. Mandelstam's quoted as saying—
though I couldn't find a definitive source for this—"Only in Russia is poetry
respected—it gets people killed. Is there anywhere else where poetry is so com-
mon a motive for murder?"[43] *Mandelstam himself died in a transit camp near*
Vladivostok in 1938. But maybe you have an answer to his question, too.

In *Recalculating*, I included two of the Mandelstam translations I did
with Kevin Platt. "I've been given a body. What should I do with it?"
is from *Stone*, Mandelstam's first book from 1909; you might say it's an
ur-modernist poem of the preconditions of authorial voice. The other
Mandelstam I included is the first half of his last poem from 1937, whose
first line answers the question of that early poem: "To empty earth falling
unwilled." But what transfixed me in the last poem are the two lines "She
is propelled by the stifled freedom / Of inspiring deficiency."[44] *Inspiring*
deficiency comes as close to my poetics as I can imagine.

   These are part of a set of translations in *Recalculating* that makes
possible other voices for myself or, perhaps better to say, other selves for
my voices. The translations bring into the American something precisely
related to the original poems: I try to channel the poems into my present-
in-language. I am a medium. Sure, that's a working fiction: any translator
has a way with words that's her or his own. Being a medium is not the
same as being faithful: it's a form of listening. If you can hear what is
being transmitted, then you have all the liberty in the world. Still, these
translations are not stylistically rewritten to be like my poems: I am sick
of my own style and thought patterns and turns of phrase and quirks. I
am seeking something that is not mine (though becomes me). If you want
to have formal heterogeneity in a book of poems, then translations are
essential. And yet (one more turn): the translations in *Recalculating* are
leitmotifs in the opera that is *Recalculating*. I use them, and they are an
integral part of the work, serving my purpose as they adhere to their own.
So that connects, albeit tenuously, to Mandelstam's sense of digging up
the past and plowing it back under.
   I have remained deeply engaged with the Russian futurists from when
I first began to read their work in the mid-1970s, starting with *Snake*
Train, Gary Kern's 1976 selection of Khlebnikov; dear and much-missed

---

43. John High and Matvei Yankelevich quote this at the beginning of their note accompanying their
translation of Mandelstam's "Yet to die. Unalone still." in *Poetry* 194:1 (2009), p. 42.

44. From ["To empty earth falling unwilled"] in *Recalculating* (Chicago: University of Chicago Press,
2013), p. 100

Paul Schmidt did several volumes of translation of Khlebnikov that were of immense value to me in *Artifice of Absorption*. So it was with Khlebnikov that I began, but I quickly found Kruchenykh, Shklovsky, Mayakovsky, Bakhtin, Volosinov, and Jakobson. The 1980 Stephanie Barron exhibition of Russian futurism at the Los Angeles County Museum of Art was the first time many of us got a chance to see the full sweep of Russian Futurist art beyond—already so important to me—the related work of Kandinsky and Malevich: Popova above all (who is a character in "Entitlement," a short play collected in *The Sophist*), but also Goncharova, Tatlin, Rodchenko, and Stepanova. I loved the collective action of the Russian futurists, outside official art institutions, and also the book collaborations between painters and poets. As we were working on *L=A=N=G=U=A=G=E*, this was a great inspiration.

More recently I have been very taken with Daniil Kharms and Alexander Vvedensky. I became aware of OBERIU (second-wave radical modernists) only in the past decade through the translations of Matvei Yankelevitch and Eugene Ostashevsky, with whom I have been lucky to be able to talk about Russian modernist and contemporary poetry. I have a connection to a few contemporary Russian poets of my generation: Arkadii Dragomoshchenko, Dmitri Prigov, Lev Rubinstein, and Alexei Parshchikov. Parshchikov and friends translated *Artifice of Absorption*. And over the past few years, I have entered into an intense dialog with Ian Probstein, who lives in New York, has been translating and publishing scores of my poems and plans to collect them in a book.[45]

Arkadii's recent death haunts me, as do the deaths of Prigov and Parshchikov.[46] I felt uncannily close to Arkadii. It's an affinity I'd call non-national rather than cross-national—not that my communication with him was more than sporadic over the twenty-five years I knew him. I first met Arkadii, via Lyn Hejinian, when Arkadii came to New York in the late 1980s. I set up a reading for him at James Sherry's loft. We

---

45. Probstein's translation, *Sign Under Test: Selected Poems and Essays*, was published by Russian Gulliver (Moscow) in 2020; an English translation of Probstein's introduction was included in *Charles Bernstein: The Poetry of Idiomatic Insistences*, ed. Paul Bové, *boundary 2* 48:4 (2021). Probstein subsequently published a collection of Mandelstam translations. See also his *The River of Time: Time-Space, History, and Language in Avant-Garde, Modernist, and Contemporary Russian and Anglo-American Poetry* (New York: Academic Studies Press, 2017). In 2023, Probstein's translation, *Zeno's Way: Selected Poems*, was published by Tiptop Street (New York). See also my interview with Natalia Fedorova in *The Poetry of Idiomatic Insistences*.

46. As I was reviewing the copyediting of this book, word came of Rubinstein's death. In an obituary in the New York *Times* (January 20, 2024), his work was compared to Charles Bukowski: perhaps a kind of unintended Russian joke. Both this obituary and one in the *New Yorker* (January 19, 2024), focusing on Rubinstein's anti-Putin activism, suppressed any reference to his American-published translations.

invited him, and his wife Zena, to come to the Poetics Program in Buffalo for a semester in the early 1990s. Susan, Felix, and I went to see Arkadii and Zena in St. Petersburg in the summer of 2001. Most recently Arkadii came to Penn in the Fall of 2010, two years before he died. Dragomoshchenko transformed Russian poetics by exploring a meditative and introspective approach to both rhythm and content. The constantly metamorphosing detail is his constant companion through the often harsh times of the Cold War and what came after.

Anyway, to backtrack: there was something about the way Mandelstam was put forward in Cold War ideology that made him hard to hear: the Cold Warriors had turned him from poet to symbol, at least for me. So my translations were part of a reframing I needed to do. I began to think of Mandelstam as related to Zukofsky, both negotiating their Jewish particularism with a yearning, to use Mandelstam's phrase that you quote, for "the virgin soil of time," or what Zukofsky called "rested totality" and "objectively perfect"[47]—something beyond the trap of the utility of voice given to you (what Stein called human identity in contrast to human nature). In "Notre Dame," from 1912, that *annus mirabilis*, Mandelstam addresses his quest to be part of something beyond himself, something that both dwarfs him and exhilarates him (as Platt and I translate it):

But, citadel of Notre Dame, the closer
I studied your preternatural ribs,
The more I thought: from crude weight
Someday I too will fashion the beautiful.

In such moments, Mandelstam writes, "the cocky vault's battering ram is still." But I am not sure we can count on that!

The emphasis on retaining the same formal considerations in poetics/expository writing (I hinge those categories together with some hesitation, of course) as with poetry seems like it can, and maybe should, extend itself, somehow, to a consideration of the book-object, and not only because we live in a time when the very materials that convey knowledge and facilitate knowledge acquisition are uncertainly changing. Is there—or should there be, maybe—a desire to get out of the "form" of the book and into a freer field of hypertext, for instance, or

47. Zukofsky, "Sincerity and Objectification," in *Prepositions+: The Collected Critical Essays* (Middletown, CT: Wesleyan University Press, 2001), pp. 193–202; and "A"-6 in *Selected Poems*

is this form somehow integral to, somehow inseparable from, literary texts as they've for so long been conceived? Could L=A=N=G=U=A=G=E *happen again, digitally? Do certain media have intrinsic values and capacities as such?*

I like your phrase "uncertainly changing." I am infatuated by the difference between *sure* and *certain*, as in, *there are a lot of things I am sure about, but few I am certain of.*

A couple of days ago I came upon a few letters my father wrote me after I left for college. He was critical of my sureness, which he found arrogant and unmerited. He mentioned "the generation gap" since it was the 1960s and my strident anti-Vietnam War views bothered him.

When I was young, I denounced my father as racist and sexist, but now I see it was not because he was, but because I was, and, no doubt still am, since that is not a malady you can ever rid yourself of. And I hated that about myself.

But now I am old and have put aside adolescent rages.

I appreciate your trepidation about speaking of the "same" formal devices for poems and essays because it's, well, the same only different. The same device would mean the converse (not the sneaker) in the different genres. That's what it means to read identity as a form and not (just) a content.

L=A=N=G=U=A=G=E used the technology at hand: the self-correcting Selectric typewriter and cheap offset printing and photocopying. In some ways, our articles anticipated blog posts. So, yes, for sure, specific media do have inner lives, and it's a pleasure when the medium is the masseur.

The book remains for me a central organizing structure for my work. It may be anachronistic but that's a blessing.

If you are locked in a cage, it's shrewd to be cagey. Trapped in time, just give me one more chance at bat.

I wanted to round out this interview—which has, perhaps appropriately, given its concern for form, taken place over a sizable stretch of space and time—with a few last questions. The first has to do with how you see the relationship between poetry and philosophy. So put, that question might seem opaque, or such as to give rise to a hopelessly trivial answer. But your work, both your poetry and your critical writing (not to mention plenty you've said in this interview), make it evident that the question of their relationship is one that you've thought about for quite some time. To cite some of the more obvious pieces of evidence, one of your books is titled The Sophist—*and you studied philosophy as an undergraduate at Harvard, even writing a thesis on Stein's*

The Making of Americans *and Wittgenstein's* Philosophical Investiga-
tions.[48] *I was struck by your comments in the thesis on the affinities shared by
the poet and the philosopher. You said that they both "dramatize the breakdown
of a one-to-one correspondence between word and object," and that you felt
Stein was invested in something like the problem of other minds. (Connected to
this, you also mention Cavell's writings on skepticism; did you ever work with
him?) At one point in the thesis you write: "I felt, still do, that this philosoph-
ical conundrum [the problem of giving a theory of reference] directly bears on
the meaning and reference of not just words or phrases in poems but of poems
themselves, which certainly mean, designate, and express, but do not necessarily
refer to 'things,' if things are assumed to be already existing and named objects."
So, I have several more and less specific questions. The more specific are these,
some of which relate to our discussion of Altieri. What are your thoughts, now,
on a theory of reference for poems-as-wholes? What might be at stake in such
a theory? And should we expect the answer to this question to depart radically,
or at all, from the answer we give to the question of how individual words
refer? The less specific are these: How do you, now, understand the relationship
of philosophy to poetry, and vice versa? Does—or should—one learn more from
the other? I'm not necessarily asking about the division between philosophy as
practiced in (analytic) philosophy departments and literary studies and poetics
as practiced in English departments, unless that's where this leads you.*

I studied with Stanley Cavell when I was in college and have been a close
reader of his work, and we've remained friends, since.[49] *Pitch of Poetry*
takes its title from Cavell's *The Pitch of Philosophy* and so takes up the
difference in the pitches of poetry and philosophy. I was at the top of my
philosophical form with my essay on Stein and Wittgenstein because in
college I was so immersed in philosophy, both analytic and continental,
as the split was then characterized (before so-called continental philos-
ophy morphed into literary theory). The analogy would be precarious (but
better a precarious analogy than an impecunious simile), but I can't help
associating the more formally traditional "product"-oriented poets with
the analytics and the more formally radical "process"-oriented poets with
the continentals. That's because I associate the postwar peri-antimodernists
with a commitment to rationalism and naturalized conceptions of rep-
resentation and reference while I think of the continentals as insisting
on skepticism and frames for reference (epistemological conditions). It's

48. *Three Compositions on Philosophy and Literature* (1972, Asylum's Press Digital Edition, 2012), pdf:
<writing.upenn.edu/epc/3-Steins.php>

49. Cavell's PennSound page has my 2012 *Close Listening* conversation with him.

the difference, in poetry, between seeing metaphors as descriptive of a preexisting state (analytical studies of a state of mind or place or historical event to which the poem refers) and the "turn toward language" in which metaphors are, to quote George Lakoff's title, what we live by because they condition not only the way we see but what we perceive. Conditions handsome and unhandsome, as Cavell has it in one of his titles.

These two diverging roads are so engrained by now that even the one less traveled by is a superhighway.

I see the difference between philosophy and poetry in terms of genre and rhetoric, the claims to reason or knowledge or truth or impartiality (or claims to falsity, skepticism, uncertainty, affect).[50] In other words, I don't see the distinction between truth claims, on the side of philosophy, and affective expressions, on the side of poetry; perversely, I am interested in affective expressions in philosophy and truth claims in poetry, and I distrust the rationalistic basis of much poetry (its so-called "empiricism"). Maybe the better one-on-one comparison is poetics and philosophy.[51] Is one regulating and the other irregular? So much depends on what you're hauling in the wheelbarrow or whether the point is the haul, or hailing the wheelbarrow as "read," or whether you just want to forget about all this thinking and go home but can't find it.

Can philosophy be written as a kind of poetry? Wittgenstein's *Tractatus* might be read as a poem, and a great poem at that, but still, it's not a poem. There is a compelling sense of the genre of philosophy—that it be written as prose. Anything else would put the attention on the language and not the argument, though that might be the point. Can poetry be written as a kind of philosophy? Is that the same question? Isn't poetry a kind of outer limit for philosophy? When philosophy traffics in poetry, doesn't it cease to be philosophy? Yet we wouldn't say philosophy is an outer limit for poetry: poetry has little risk (or a fat chance) of becoming philosophy.

Poetry and philosophy used to share the foundational work of world making or cosmology. But that seems to have gone out of style with Lucretius, or maybe Leibniz's *Monadology* or Descartes's *Meditations*, or Spinoza's *Ethics*, at least for philosophy, since poets never stopped being cosmologists (often for their own fantasy worlds, but that's another story). To the baked goods of epic cosmologies, add the open-pit barbeque of anti-cosmologies, from Heraclitus to Dickinson ("This world is not con-

50. "Writing and Method," in *Content's Dream*, provides a more thorough consideration of the relation of poetry to philosophy.

51. See "The Practice of Poetics" in *Attack of the Difficult Poems: Essays and Inventions*.

clusion"[52]) to Celan. Or consider that Nietzsche and Kierkegaard wrote works that appear to be anti-cosmological prose poems. I seem to be creating an Ouroboros (the figurative snake with its head eating its tale):

I used to be a philosopher, but now I am philosophized.
Used to be a poet but now am the words.
Used to be critical but now take the local.
I used to be emotional, but now I've got affect.
Used to be empirical, but now I am in the dark.
Used to believe in process but now can't get it to stop.
I used to be cosmological, but now I am pataposterous.
I used to make arguments but now am argumentative.
Used to be historical but now can't work up the energy even for that.
Used to dream of answers but no longer remember the questions.
I used to love knowledge but now know language.
Used to go to school but now vagabond.
Used to be, but now am.

Poets like to quote philosophers because they got a theory that explains or a morality that proclaims. As so and so says, every time you hit a brick wall it's because some bugger put it there to keep you in your place. But it's not really a brick wall; it's a glass ceiling. And even glass ceilings have legs. Then again, philosophers like to quote poetry because it adds a superficial layer of depth to the proceedings, which generally end in poetry being found guilty of a crime it only wishes it could have committed.

People say Cavell is too literary for a philosopher. I aspire to be too philosophical for a poet.

The problem of reference is like finding the pea under the shell in a street corner scam. There is a pea all right, but it's the system, baby, always the system.

It's a mug's game.

My last question is about the last poem in Recalculating. *"Before You Go" seems to be in conversation with a quotation from your daughter, Emma, that appears at the beginning of the book, in which she speaks imperatively: "The*

---

52. *The Poems of Emily Dickinson*, ed. T. H. Johnson (Cambridge: The Belknap Press of Harvard University Press, 1955), p. 501

road tells you what to do. . . . Retrace your route in reflection, but look only as far / as the blur of passing yellow lines to see the present. Race your future to the finish line" (p. xi). It's eerie and wonderful to hear echoes of your voices in each other's: a playfulness bolstered by directness, clever uses of common phrases, an overall confidence. I was moved by "Before You Go"; it's a poem as formally smart as any other of yours, but one primitively informed by grief, and the conclusion in particular—when the line-ending refrain "before you go," effaced by parts, is finally gone, replaced by the satori of "Two lane blacktop, undulating light" (p. 185)—is unqualified arresting, even gutting. It produced a physical reaction in me, which is not something I can say about too many poems.

What was the significance of putting this poem at the end of the book, especially given that its ending involves the destruction of the titular phrase? It almost seems the sort of "understanding by subtraction" that poetry, in virtue of being composition, is not—and yet, insofar as it involves excision, at the same time is. I'm reminded of Beckett's claim that artwork is a "desecration of silence"; this might be understood as a claim about the costs of art, or about the impermissibility of art, or both or more.[53] (Relatedly, I think Warhol said—sincerely, I take it—that he preferred blank space to space with an artwork in it.[54]) "Before You Go" also stands in a curious relation to "Chimera," the penultimate poem in Recalculating, *the speaker of which concludes "Resigned that tunes will never bind / Shimmering shadows tossed in time" (p. 185). That poem gives off a jadedness or exhaustion with poetry, but the book, in spite of this, goes on to issue this final piece, which—to add to the stakes—is an instance of that most 'serious' of poetic genres, the elegy. I suppose what I'm trying to suggest is that there seems to be this theme of the ineffectiveness or superfluousness of poetry toward the end of the collection—one expressed, almost necessarily, in verse, and with a seriousness that seems pronounced for a collection otherwise sprinkled with overt comedy. I was wondering if you saw the collection ending in this way, too; and, if so, if there was any purposeful connection between that theme and this final poem, which seemed to speak to your daughter, or perhaps to your family more generally—you seem close to them not just in the common sense but artistically, too.*

---

53. The exact history of this phrase is unclear. Jean-Michel Rabaté provides a story of its origins: "In January 1968, Beckett and Adorno met more cordially, for a last time, in Paris where Adorno had come to give a lecture at the Collège de France. He talked for two hours with Beckett. During that conversation, Beckett stated (in English) that his work amounted to a "desecration of silence," a phrase which found its way into the pages of *Aesthetic Theory*." See "Philosophizing with Beckett: Adorno and Badiou," in *A Companion to Samuel Beckett*, ed. S. E. Gontarski (Hoboken, NJ: John Wiley & Sons, 2010), pp. 97–117.

54. See, for instance, Andy Warhol, *The Philosophy of Andy Warhol: From A to B and Back Again* (Orlando, FL: Harcourt, 1975), p. 143.

Latently, I'm interested in how what seems to be a popular folk criticism of language poetry, namely that it's too "impersonal" or "inhuman" (or, put negatively, insufficiently "personal" and "human"), appears refuted, or at least nullified, by the poem—which for me contains so much unfiltered, irreconcilable energy, but an energy that's nonetheless conditioned by the formal constraints you've imposed on it, and it you.

I'm not interested in emotion tranquilized into legible form. My register goes from rapture to rupture, often in the same breath; from despair to hysteria to preternatural calm, from anxiety to dissociation, from agitation to evanescence. In my book, dyslexia is emotional and fragmentation a kind of aesthetic melodrama approaching tragedy. Interruption and inscrutability enthrall me. I desire impersonality, but every time I get close, it shakes me off.

Being human is a condition (animalady), not a positive value. Being human is not something poems I like or don't like are more or less invested in. Though being "insufficiently" human sounds like a good direction for poetry, even if I have not been able to go there, keep getting pulled back into the muck.

Emma's death was an amputation. As with a chimeric (phantom) limb, I feel it. Recovery (covering over) is not an option. Recalculating is a different measure.

When the child dies, the father dies. It's a mortal wound. What disappears in death grows wild in imagination.

[2012–2015: questions abridged: uncut version in *boundary 2* 44:3 (2017)]

ACT TWO
Kinds
(*andante*)

A poetry the quality of which
Is a stand made against intellectual apathy,
Its material founded, like Gray's, on difficult knowledge . . .
But, more than that, its words coming from a mind
Which has experienced the sifted layers on layers
Of human lives—aware of the innumerable dead
And the innumerable to-be-born . . .
—Rich in its discoveries of new problems,
Important questions so far unsuspected,
For which field research does not yet supply
The data necessary to answer them. . . .
A poetry that is—to use the terms of red dog—
High, low, jack, and the goddamn game.

Hugh MacDiarmid, "The Kind of Poetry I Want" (1965)

Free Thinking

Spring and All versus *The Waste Land* at 100

Two roads diverged . . .

Robert Frost, "The Road Not Taken" (1916)

Oh life, bizarre fowl, what color are your wings? Green, blue, red, yellow, purple, white, brown, orange, black, grey? In the imagination, flying above the wreck of ten thousand million souls . . . Your great wings flap as you disappear in the distance over the pre-Columbian acres of floating weed.

William Carlos Williams, *Spring and All* (1924)

Therefore, the best among the young, the most intelligent, the most interested, like only works which have a high moral and sociological, even religious, bearing. (Ainsi la meilleure partie de la jeunesse, la plus intelligente, la plus intéressée, n'aimait-elle plus que les oeuvres ayant une haute portée morale et sociologique, même religieuse.)

Marcel Proust, *Time Refound* (1927)

What I mean by tradition involves all those habitual actions, habits and customs . . . which represent the blood kinship of 'the same people living in the same place.'. . . I think that the chances for the re-establishment of a native culture are perhaps better here [in Virginia] than in New England. You are farther away from New York; you have been less industrialised, less invaded by foreign races. . . . Reasons of race and religion combine to make any large number of free-thinking Jews undesirable.

T. S. Eliot, *After Strange Gods: A Primer of Modern Heresy* (1933)

I come to you today at the 138th Annual Convention of the Modern Language Association in San Francisco, California, on land in which Ohlone was once the dominant language, on the fortieth anniversary of my speech, "The Academy in Peril: William Carlos Williams Meets the MLA" and on the centenary of both Williams's *Spring and All* (1923) and T. S. Eliot's *The Waste Land* (1922): the one an anthem of free thinking and the other an enactment of it.

Free thinking is akin to free jazz and free (in the sense of liberated) verse. I come here to talk about a way American poetry can wrest itself from the chaos of such free thinking. I come here today to tell you about the possibility of redemption.

I myself have been redeemed through my turbulent induction into Offi-

cial Verse Culture, in a secret ceremony this past Halloween. My new status
has entailed changing course. I am still finding my sea legs, so expect some
backsliding; OVC programmers are at work to fix the glitches. Those of us
accepted into OVC need to have the good manners to stop calling it out,
lest we be tarred with beating an old horse and feathered with "look whose
talkin'." The only thing worse than an old avant-gardist railing, as if noth-
ing has changed, against a mainstream that has embraced him, is a young
avant-gardist railing against a mainstream that has not. To age with dignity,
and avoid appearing bitter, best accept the status quo or at least keep your
grumblings to yourself (and close family members).

I am here today to show how poetry can turn from the waste land of
miscegenation and the strange gods of free thinking by anchoring itself
in lyric self-expression (LSE) and compulsory confessionalism. The model
for LSE is the white, male, heterosexual Christian confessionalism of
Robert Lowell, which gives us a paradigm for our current age of post-
confessionalism. Only when a poem can be read as confessional—that is,
as expressing the personal and historical experience of the poet—does it
have the potential for redemption from aestheticism and artifice. The more
a poem requires an allegorical reading, the more it is able to redeem itself
from the heresy of free thinking. Allegory, as Paul Bové shows in *Love's
Shadow*, allows a poem to be read as something other than itself—a story,
a lesson, a moral, message, a representation of a period or a group. Unless
a poem comes to readers in this package it "won't translate to our pages,"
as an OVC editor explained to me: the role of such editors is to protect
readers from untranslated aesthetic experience.

Don't get me wrong: I am not advocating identity-centered poetry but
rather a self-centered poetry grounded by biographicalismo that rejects not
only poetry-centeredness but also indulgent binges of unsanctioned subjec-
tivity. All poetry reflects the time, place, and personal history of its author.
Identity is much too complicated and messy to make for successful post-
confessional poems (PCPs). Identity poetics is best left to free thinkers.
PCPs have only a tenuous relationship to identity, even when identity is
its putative subject. *Putative* not *punitive*: I have too often confused those
words. By the way, no association is intended between the acronym PCP
and the dangerous drug; if anything, I'd associate free-thinking poetry with
the kind of malignant mental warp produced by PCP.

The Library of Congress proclaims that the poet laureate should be "the
nation's official lightning rod for the poetic impulse of Americans." This is
what PCP offers: poems that deflect lightening to avoid aesthetic damage.

Here is the bottom line: Never trust a poet who hasn't written a memoir
or, if not a memoir, at least a novel, and whose life story, summarized in less

than fifty words, can't be the defining frame for reading their work. To be sure, I am not talking about free thinkers and free feelers who use the genre of memoir or novel to warp and distort reality.

Great lyric poetry (GLP) is a genuine expression (GE) of the poet's feelings (PF): GLP = GE/PF. GE is our most important product as GLP crafters. Shame on those heretics who have turned against GLP. I know that some in this audience will decry the anonymous social media attacks, several years ago, against poetry free-thinking (not to be confused with free-basing, despite the resemblance). However, race-baiting (plausibly deniable), antisemitism (an artform itself), and unfounded personal and political attacks were justified to purge degenerate elements from the margins of poetry and to keep poetry a safe space. The anonymity was necessary because if the real class and ethnic identity of the authors were revealed, their message might have been undermined. Moreover, the postings have a marvelously buoyant literary style and show that the pseudo-cultural-left (PCL) can be just as inventive as the hard right.

Here's my take-away: Only anti-elitist poetry should win elite prizes.

Let me make this plain: the hatred of avant-garde poetry is prerequisite for entry into any official verse culture worth its smelling salts. The avant-garde is a good target because it is, indeed, populated by fascists, miscreants, and malcontents, along with communists and saints, hopeless Romantics, and middle-class idlers. But how much more exhilarating, and what an effective distraction, to attack the avant-garde for sins found equally in the mainstream. And how convenient to redeem non-white poets from such censure, albeit with a wink: those often-overlooked poets who blazed a path for radical aesthetics and miscegenated free thinking in American poetry, without whom avant-garde American poetry, whatever that could possibly be, could not exist.

We are all sinners in the clutches of a dyspeptic God. But there is a Blesséd Election that allows for redemption of some poets *for whom they are* (Eliot's "blood kinship"), irrespective of the conduct or misconduct of their works; just as—ever again—some are excommunicated regardless of their works. While Election ensures redemption, fear wrath still: such exemption does not license free thinking or free feeling in the poem. To be saved, even an Elect's poem needs a biographicalist hook or some other value that lies outside it, a value that can be extracted, such as the poet's suffering, identification with suffering, or, if nothing else, moral sentiment. Poetry, like pornography, requires redeeming social value. But mark my words: not all suffering, backstories, or moralities, just as not all poets, are Elect in any one epoch. In the cold war, it was Great Men's struggle against Godless Communism and WASP angst. Progress occurs with the acknowledgment of some of those overlooked in the past; aesthetic value is then determined by a zero-sum calculus: if one group is promoted, another group must be demoted. In contrast, free-thinking poetry wallows in wanton irredemption and an aversion of biographicalism, along with a refusal of the zero-sum. Such poetry claims to be free of pre-text, but isn't its aestheticism, its siren shrieks of art of art's sake, a pretext?

Spring & All: "The only realism in art is of the imagination. It is only thus that the work escapes plagiarism after nature and becomes a creation. // Invention of new forms to embody this reality of art, the one thing which art is, must occupy all serious minds concerned."

Forty years ago, here at the MLA, and in L=A=N=G=U=A=G=E more generally, I missed the boat for the trees by including "white" poets as among those neglected in American poetry history, along with non-white poets, falsely imagining that the work is intertwined. But let me zero in on the problem with this troubling reclamation of free-thinking and free-feeling white poets. Are they really white, in the sense of Christian? Are they even men? It has gone almost unremarked that *L=A=N=G=U=A=G=E* encompassed, through its contributors but also its sources and references, the greatest convergence of free-thinking Jews in any non-Jewish-focused poetry publication in American history; it was a place where Jewishness was just one, unmarked, part of an inclusive and troubling comradery. It's time to call out this hidden danger. Surely, American Jews born after the Systematic Extermination of the European Jews have had a better time in American poetry than earlier generations; it's a struggle to keep Jewish clannishness at bay, but we can do it we are not afraid to call it out when we see it, and, preemptively, even when we don't. At the same time, we need to resist the push to gain recognition for earlier generations of free-thinking Jews who, like other non-Elects, were struggling for inclusion in American literary life and who cannot be sublated into Christian whiteness. As far as first- and second-wave modernist American poetry, white revisionism, which necessarily includes any number of free-thinking Jews, needs to be stigmatized lest the historical white, male Protestant canon be breached.

Let me be clear—even worse than free-thinking Jews are free-thinking Protestants, immigrants, second language speakers . . . like William Carlos Williams, as I am sure T. S. would agree. Let there be no mistake: Eliot is the Greatest Poet of All Time (GPOT), though certainly Sappho is a contender for that title as is *The Song of Solomon*, but who is the poet there—we only have a first name, and I suspect the author may have been a free-thinking Jew but without a last name we can't be sure. At the same time, I would be less than candid if I didn't note that Eliot's work is antipathetic to PCP—he is far too abstract, elusive, and impersonal, too in love with poetic artifice, to be a model for PCP. Indeed, in "Prufrock" and *The Waste Land*, he falls prey to the free thinking he later so bravely decries. However, by 1933, with works like *After Strange Gods*, Eliot's cultural acumen becomes clear: *none dare call it heresy.*

As we turn to the present, I often see the attempt to redeem for PCP some "language poets," as if they were just fellow travelers. But there is no such thing as a little-bit-language poet. There is no redemption possible for free thinking. The era of ambiguity is over. This is a particular problem for teachers. Students should not be subjected to poems whose interpretation cannot be controlled and used as an example of something worthwhile, either historically or as a personal story. Otherwise, a trigger warning is mandatory: *Watch out. Your imagination may be activated. You may be asked to think. You may be subjected to a way of looking at the world which you will find morally repugnant.*

But now, I want to turn to redemption through statistics. For the humanities to succeed we must emulate the sciences, using empirical studies, graphs, and acronyms (ESGA). It's less important that this work say anything than that it looks scientific. Above all, the literary academy needs to stop focusing on the aesthetic dimensions of literary works.

I have developed a highly unreliable tally for the combined mentions of a poet by the *New Yorker* and New York *Review of Books* (search by "first and last name" and including, letters, poems, and listings). Mentions don't distinguish between positive and negative citations, so free-thinking Jew Gertrude Stein gets a high rating based on lots of convincing, albeit unscrupulous, attacks. One conclusion: those concerned about the detrimental effects of acknowledging neglected "white" poets can rest easy. The status of the great poets remains firmly in place according to the *New Yorker / NYRB* ratings (NYR), and otherwise undesirable free thinkers, Jewish and non-Jewish, Black and white, have not violated this hallowed ground.

Among the modernists, Eliot (956) and Frost (343) are the tops; Williams rates well, coming in with a NYR one-third Eliot's (but note: *The Waste Land* 334 vs. *Spring and All* 6). Happily, we can report that efforts to acknowledge the poetry of free-thinking, or really any thinking, modernist Jews have failed, apart from Stein. Only Laura (Riding) Jackson (24) rates statistical significance (>20), coming in at .1589404 of her old friend Alan Tate (that 404 is quite intriguing and possibly a hidden message). The other modernist L=A=N=G=U=A=G=E Jews, such as the Objectivists and Mina Loy, come in too low to attain statistical significance, just as is free-thinking non-Jewish fellow traveler Lorine Niedecker's NYR at 3: rest assured, those three mentions are unsubstantial: undesirable woman stay undesirable. Strange gods stay strange. As for comparable Black poetic innovators—Hughes scores best, close to Williams. But Melvin Tolson (the syncretic Eliot) and Sterling Brown are as invisible as their counterparts in what I once called the "Objectivist blues."

The unassailable criticism of the avant-garde's "whiteness" serves as an effective check against cosmopolitan rootlessness. Intersectionality is too difficult for the general poetry audience being sold on PCV and is best left to free thinkers. Class, gender, sexual orientation, disability, and ethnic background—as with the epithet "Christian"—only muddy the waters, and I am not talking about Muddy Waters, the blues singer. The generality of the critique avoids the awkward fact that the Christian whiteness of Eliot is not the same as the Jewish whiteness of Louis Zukofsky (who had the impudence to call out the bias of *The Waste Land* in 1927), any more than the white avant-garde of John Wheelwright is the same as that of Samuel Greenberg. The important thing is to keep Wheelwright and Greenberg off the charts, since their work represents unprecedented disruptive free-thinking as well as a social, ethnic, and class challenge.

If we turn to the "New American Poetry," we can take comfort that the cooked is, mostly, stiffing the raw, at least as far as Official Verse Culture is concerned. Robert Lowell (480) is tops and even bests Frost, as does W. H. Auden (467). Even so, free-thinking Jew Allen Ginsberg (380), a celebrity like Stein, fares well in the chart. John Ashbery bests Ginsberg, but only by a little. Charles Olson, Robert Duncan, and Robert Creeley show, but their combined score is less than half of Lowell's alone. Not so the Jews of this generation that were part of the L=A=N=G=U=A=G=E conversations, who fail to come up to statistical significance—Jerome Rothenberg, David Antin, Jackson Mac Low, but that's also true of Jack Spicer. Hannah Weiner and Larry Eigner both come up a perfect zero.

NYR shows a principled rejection of liberal two-sidism: these publications know what counts and they make sure readers are protected against alternate views. Despite being a free-thinking Jew himself, Harold Bloom was right, and NYRs show it, when he proclaimed the near impossibility of a major American poet to be Jewish. Bloom's argument has a kinship with Eliot's conception that poetry must be read within a defined tradition, in this case Protestant. Keep in mind: Nobody likes free-thinking Jews, especially other free-thinking Jews. Don't get me started.

Coda: Doing the Police in Voices

There are developments on the international front that might give us pause. Consider a comment by Luigi Ballerini a few months ago at "The Re-

Appearing Pheasant" conference, talking about editing an anthology of Italian poetry in English translation. We are "ecumenical but biased," he said: "We include all those who work for poetry, who understand that poetry is made of language. And we exclude those who understand lyricism as confessionalism. If your pain and strong emotions don't bend the language, you're not in the anthology."

Perhaps this remark, coming from outside American poetics, suggests a different possibility for PCP, something that is really *after* the familiar god of confessional poetry and that opens up to the mongrel wilderness of a poetry that turns decisively away from being held together by the "blood kinship of the same people living in the same place," as in Eliot's conception, in *After Strange Gods*, of a culturally homogeneous Virginia venerated for having "no difference of language or race," that is, a place wholly white and Christian.

In a free-thinking and free-feeling poetry, the god of strangers is no longer estranged and the foreign and heterogeneous is home ground.

We are all strangers in the wilderness of language. *Spring and All* imagines that. And it's not the "spring" but the "all."

In the kinds of poetry I want, we come together not despite, but because of, our differences.

And do it for Elsie.

The Elsies in us.

Eliot and Williams are both—the tops, both poets of supernal achievement. But they are the tops of different mountains.

Only in free thinking and free feeling poetry can we—Black and white, Jew and gentile, immigrant and native, possessed and dispossessed, queer and not, *against all odds*—read and reread *The Waste Land* and *Spring and All*, and celebrate, prompted by Williams, Eliot's wild aesthetics liberated from supremacism. For even Eliot needs reinvention (not redemption), despite himself and against the grain of his canonical status.

"I will make a truce with you" Tom Eliot. "We have one sap and one root— / Let there be commerce between us."

And then, you and I, "when the evening is spread out against the sky," will find someone to drive the car.

Even if we don't know where.

It will be a joy ride.

[2022: Presented at the MLA Annual Convention on January 7, in San Francisco, at "*Spring and All at One Hundred Meets 'The Academy in Peril' at Forty*," sponsored by the William Carlos Williams Society and convened by Elin Käck. "The Academy in Peril: William Carlos Williams Meets the MLA" was presented at "Poets' Centennial Tribute to William Carlos Williams" at the MLA convention in New York on December 29, 1983; it was first published in *Sulfur* 10 (1984) and collected in *Contents Dream:*

Essays 1975–1984. Sources and background for this essay can be found at <writing.upenn.edu/epc /authors/bernstein/essays/OVC.html>. Echoes in the final lines from Ezra Pound, "A Pact," Eliot, "The Love Song of J. Alfred Prufrock," and XVII (for Elsie) in *Spring and All*. The Library of Congress quote is from Librarian of Congress James Billington in 2015 <blogs.loc.gov/loc/2015/04/national-poets>. Thanks to Peter Middleton.]

#CageFreePoetry

Now, who shall arbitrate?
Ten men love what I hate,
Shun what I follow, slight what I receive;
Ten, who in ears and eyes
Match me: we all surmise,
They, this thing, and I, that: whom shall my soul believe?

Robert Browning, "Rabbi Ben Ezra" (1864)[1]

There is no perfect in poetry, but there can be more perfection. Every success has a countermeasure of failure: the better you do one thing, the more you fail to do something else. That is why monotheism in poetry is a crime against aesthetics. Which does not mean anything goes: anything is possible but only a very few things get through that eye of a needle that separates charm from harm. And often what appears as harm has got the charm.

Harder for a rich man to write a good poem than to buy a good painting. The hardest part: *why bother*?

When you are on the losing side of literary judgment as long as I have been, you count your losses as gains, in the poetry economy. For every poem I love, a baker's dozen hate it, and sometimes I feel (delusions of agency) my endorsement of a poem is sufficient cause for others to shun it. Those ten, or ten times ten, will say *Robert Lowell* to my *Larry Eigner*. Who do I think I am, Sancho Panza? Am I just a voice crying in the wilderness, or am I a just voice pleading aggrievement? Indeed, my gang's outlier taste is often viewed as canonical by those who feel their mainstream taste is slighted by a cognoscenti that shuns them. Is anyone in poetry free of aggrievement? The ones who get the prizes say, "Why has no one heard of me?" The ones that don't sing in unison, *the system is rigged*, as if they are at a Bernie Sanders rally (or maybe shills for Donald Trump). I have composed many arrangements for this chorus. Being Jewish helps with the cacophonies. There hasn't been a *real* Jewish poet since Solomon and his *Songs*, but at least we can agree that he was pretty God-damn good.

My soul believes only its own ears, Ibn Ezra. I can't be wrong about that.

---

1. *Poems of Robert Browning*, ed. Charlotte Porter and Helen A. Clarke (New York: Thomas Y. Crowell & Company, 1896), pp. 207–12. Browning based "Rabbi Ben Ezra" on poet and philosopher Abraham Ibn Ezra (c. 1089–1167). "Ibn" is the Arabic form for *ben* (son of).

If I love a poem, can I love it tastelessly? Or is it that I love its tastelessness? Reb Bint Eliza would say that the discussion of taste is more important than the preference for one taste over another.[2] "I don't want to know what you prefer but rather what's your criteria?" the rebbe would always say.

Once two poets came to King Solomon each insisting that the poet they most revered was the greater poet. Solomon said that each of them should burn the books of the poets and read only the Torah. *What a jerk!* (Don't confuse the author of *The Song of Songs* with the earlier king; King S. would surely resent that he is best known for poetry he couldn't and wouldn't have written.)

Even so maybe King Solomon would have echoed his poet avatar and said that it is not the poem but its kiss that matters: let the poem kiss you with the kisses of its mouth, for love is better than wine. There are many poets who say the kiss of a lover is far greater than any poem.—But kisses grow cold and hard while a poem will never betray you.

"Rebbe, are you arguing that the Bible says that sex is better than art?"

"No. The kiss in *The Song of Songs* symbolizes aesthetic experience, which is akin to *shekinah*, the presence of God. And while each of us might say our lover is the best of all lovers, we accept the plurality of loves as it would be monstrous to think there are only a few great loves and the rest are minor. Love is plentiful and always next to us. The difficulty is in acknowledging its presence rather than shunning it."

I am in mortal danger, but not from an erotic
Lovesickness of a desperate suitor;
My desire is to be with the mighty Monarch who has
No weakness; He is the fountain of my craving;
My anguish is hidden in the recess
Of my heart; my face does not show it,
 Lest they say of me: "His base passion killed him
 Why does he put on airs?" (Ibn Ezra)[3]

In 1974, I was doing a drug-education talk for teenagers at Camarillo State Mental Hospital near Los Angeles. The place Charlie Parker made famous with "Relaxin' at Camarillo." At the time, I was the health edu-

2. Rabbi Eliza first appears in "Sign Under Test," a poem of mine collected in *Girly Man*. Bint is the Arabic form for *bat* (daughter of).

3. *Twilight of a Golden Age: Selected Poems of Abraham Ibn Ezra*, ed. and tr. Leon J. Weinberger (Tuscaloosa: University of Alabama Press, 1997), p. 31

cator at Freedom Community Clinic in Santa Barbara. My friend Stu Ru-
binstein and I were talking about LSD and marijuana when one of the
teenagers mentioned sniffing glue. I must have blanched because the kid
came back hard: "I get just as high on my glue as you do on your LSD." I
interpreted this as his saying, "You contemptible bourgeois snobs, you think
your Courvoisier is so much better than my Thunderbird, but isn't what
you want same as me?" Democratic vistas; but after all, glue causes brain
damage, so whatever its potency, it's a "bad" way to get high. But then, lots
of popular entertainment also causes brain damage, even if we call it mind
damage. Is potency the issue or is it the kind of potency or is it the pedigree
of the potency? You could certainly make a case that "low-grade" poetry is
less intense than what you get from "high" art.—and if you can't make that
case then I will. *I'll take my Creeley over your Bukowski any day of the week,
buddy.* For the lover of Bukowski, Creeley will seem too elusive, while for
the lover of Creeley, Bukowski will seem not elusive enough.

So is what's most significant the poem itself or the experience a reader
gets from the poem? I could write a Creeley-like poem that might have
the same power for someone who never read him. Sometimes imitations
will have more impact because they cut to the chase quicker. "Candy / Is
dandy / But liquor / Is quicker." Who said that? Was it Dorothy Parker,
Tim Leary, or Ogden Nash?[4] We aesthetes will always insist that when
you go back to the original, you'll see the difference. The copy is a gateway
drug for the power of the real thing. But it could as easily be said that the
great poem initiates the reader into taking aesthetic pleasures beyond the
poem: listening with a livelier consciousness and seeing with a crocked eye.

The poem is not the end of aesthetic experience but its beginning.

Feeling superior to the self-righteous makes you that. If I say my taste
is better than yours, I have just proven my tastelessness. My taste is better
than no one, but it is mine. Even so, I don't own it, it owns me.

Nowadays the professors of culture speak more of "distinction" than
"value" since distinction can be quantified in a way value can't. Western
poetry from the Romantic period on has accorded the greatest value to
poets who had, in their own lifetime, the least distinction. It is a measure
of distinction to have a poem in the *New Yorker*, but I have never heard
anyone argue for the aesthetic merit of the poems in the *New Yorker*.[5] The
magazine sets the bar so low for poetry that when it does on occasion pub-
lish a poem that breaks the mold, it generates attention that overshadows

4. Ogden Nash, "Reflection on Ice-Breaking," in *Hard Lines* (New York: Simon and Schuster, 1931), p. 83

5. See my related commentary in "The Pataquerical Imagination: Midrashic Antinomianism and the Promise of Bent Studies," section CII, in *Pitch of Poetry*.

its more typical commitment to the mundane. The distinction of having a poem in the *New Yorker* is similar to the prestige of a prize: everyone wants it, but few get it. But there can also be another level of distinction involved: showing you can write an aesthetically good poem in such a way that it can "pass" muster, like having your cake and eating it too, or being a cool nerd. The ultimate prestige is for the great poet who manages, against all odds, to get recognized as great. The great but obscure poet is still a loser. Even if the system is rigged, the point is to beat the odds. That's far more prestigious than writing a poem could ever be.

If one of your criteria for the value of poems is that they unsettle, it doesn't mean that every poem that aims to unsettle is equally good or that a poem that is deeply conservative might not be better than one that is all about undermining received opinions. But still I'd prefer to read poems that are at least trying to unsettle than ones that treat poetry as a dead art.

Taste is a matter of experience. You can educate your taste as you can open your experiences to new vistas. Knowledge and awareness are not opposed to judgment; they are its foundation. As a poem is an opening to experience, so taste is not the end of aesthetics but the onset, as of a fever. Judgment is never final; it is a place to begin a journey in art, a point of departure on a trip without a fixed destination.

Taste is rooted in perceived preference. To deny or invalidate your preferences is not modesty but travesty. Tastes are *essentially* provisional even if you remain locked in the prison house of your predilections.

Aesthetic judgment is more precisely articulated by comparison with poems that are alike than by comparing poems of wildly different forms or periods.

Taste is not a matter of wrong or right. Moral principles of wrong and right impede the grasp of taste: that is the still-scandalous principle of aestheticism.

For many readers of poetry, identification with the poet, solidarity with the moral or political sentiment of the poem, or prior knowledge of the prestige of the poet is more important than the formal, stylistic, or aesthetic qualities of a poem. Psychologists will talk about branding or affectional projection and sociologists about predetermined ideological dispositions. How can taste be any more than an extension of tribalism, class, or commodification? Capitalists may celebrate the triumph of the market while anti-capitalists will stress the importance of counterhegemonic alternatives. The idea that taste could ever be more than a puppet of economic and ideological forces seems as precarious as a piece of china in *The Spoils of Poynton*.

Changes of taste require changes of consciousness: the aesthetic clash between refinement and coarseness is a symptom of discordant senses of the world. I prefer Larry Eigner to Robert Lowell and find Eigner the more refined, but it's a different kind of refinement from the patrician Lowell, as different as Cambridge from Swampscott or gentile to Jew. To prefer Eigner requires a readjustment of aesthetic criteria. It is not a matter of what Eigner stands for but what he does ("thro' acts uncouth, / Toward making," as Browning puts it in "Rabbi Ben Ezra").

The proof of Eigner's poems is in the experience they allow. Depending on where you are coming from, Eigner may well be an acquired taste. But for the kind of aestheticism I want, all tastes are acquired. You feel it on the tongue before you prize it in the mind. It stings before it stuns. And yes, there is something of a conversion narrative here, a transvaluation that can only come after habitual or received judgments are called into question, suspended for a moment in an imaginary place of possibility. The dialectical process of aversive judgment, pushing against the given of authority or moral law toward the possible, is grounded in taste just as experience is the ground of ethical judgment.

It is a shibboleth (שִׁבֹּלֶת) for those who turned against the New Criticism that the meaning of a poem is essentially bound to its historical context and the identity of the author (except we would avoid the word *essentially*). Much ink has been spent on redressing how this doctrine has turned critics and professors from close reading to distant learning. Here's my three and three-quarters sense: it is the dialectical relationship of the form of the poem to its social context that makes aesthetic meaning possible. A failure to address the ethnic and local particulars of Robert Frost fails to grapple with his poems even if that is the basis of his hegemony. Similarly, reading the work of a "minority" writer only in terms of her or his subaltern experience robs the poem of its aesthetic particularity. The history of racist exclusion of black poets from the canon is most powerfully addressed by a discussion of the forms and styles of specific poems and their contribution to the art of poetry. Valuing poems thematically, exclusively as expressions of the subaltern, risks reinscribing racist ideas of authenticity. The answer to the problem of the color line in American poetry is not primitivist paternalism but a prolonged and detailed consideration of the history of poetry, language, and song by African Americans, with special attention to the formal inventions that have been an unacknowledged foundation of radical North American poetry.

Reception of poems is dogged by asymmetrical patterns of evaluation. The "same" poem by a male or female (white or black) poet will be evaluated differently—both by the proponents of an identity-free canon and those whose priority is the inclusion of underrepresented voices in the canon. Eccentricity by a male poet might be valued as formally innovative while formal innovation by a woman poet is written off as eccentric or affective.

I am under no illusion: my prioritizing of the aesthetic and formal aspect of a poem is fundamentally out of step with the preference of many readers for personal stories and moving anecdotes. My criteria for what make a poem good are irreconcilable with those who favor narrative continuity and emotional expression achieved through the overcoming of language play and ambiguity.

Evaluation is always interested. The construction of disinterestedness is itself a form of interest. If, as the cliché has it, Western "high" culture favors those perceived as white Christian heterosexual men, this form of identity preference does not favor all white people or all men or all heterosexuals but rather those whose work is marked by, and conforms to, an idealized identity.

Is Elsa von Freytag-Loringhoven a better poet than Frost? It depends on the criteria.[6] Surely she is the better Dada poet.

"No Images," from 1926, is the only poem I know by Waring Cuney (1906–1976). Its value is not diminished for me by its being singular, even if that means that this often-anthologized poem is both obscure and famous.

She does not know
her beauty,
she thinks her brown body
has no glory.

If she could dance
naked
under palm trees
and see her image in the river,
she would know.

But there are no palm trees
on the street,

---

6. I read the Baroness's "Teke Heart" at the Museum of Modern Art for a Dada show: <jacket2.org /commentary/teke-baroness-elsa>.

and dish water gives back
no images.[7]

Each stanza is a broken sentence with the middle stanza's five lines being one line longer than the first and third stanza. The "echo" theme of seeing one's reflection in the water takes a startling turn in "No Images," connecting it to the radical modernist aesthetic of resisting mimesis. "No Images" transforms the modernist aversion of representation into a dialectical engagement with racialized images. The second stanza projects an unalienated site that evokes Africa but avoids the primitivist romanticizing of the "jungle," common at the time. The stanza's opening word *if* insists on the role of the imaginary not as a prior reality but as a counterpoint within the present. The elegant syncopation of the Williams-like lines of this stanza is free of any trace of traditional poetic diction. "Naked" stands alone on its own line, unbaring the image, bringing us up not only against the *naked* word, but also against the "brown body" that is at the center of both the poem's gaze and aversion of gaze. This nakedness is contrasted with the inability to "know," echoed from the first line of the poem. In "No Images," this inability is self-knowledge and recognition of value ("glory"). It is only in the penultimate line of the poem that the site of alienation is located: dirty (and so opaque) "dish water." The dish water could be the subject's own, but there is the suggestion that she works as a domestic worker, where her life is taken away from her rather than being "given back." Through Cuney's negative dialectics, the loss of image literally *reflects* the loss of the beauty of her body.

Compare this poem to "Man and Wife" by Robert Lowell. What would happen if I gave the kind of flatfooted, clueless, exoticizing reading of this canonical poem that so many champions of Lowell give to poems that are not to their taste:

Written in the New England section of the U.S. and first published three decades after "No Images" in 1958. Robert Lowell's poem begins—

7. (William) Waring Cuney, *Storefront Church* (20 pp.), Heritage Series 23 (London: Paul Breman, 1973) p. 7; digital edition at <jacket2.org/commentary/cuney>. Cuney's only other poetry collection is *Puzzles*, ed. Bremen (Utrecht: DeRoos, 1960); 76 pp, illustrated, limited to 175 numbered copies. Cuney wrote "No Images" when he was eighteen; it won the 1926 *Opportunity* literary contest. Lorenzo Thomas calls Cuney "a minor poet who produced a major poem." Thomas discusses several of Cuney's poems as well as the blues lyrics he wrote with Josh White. See Thomas's "Whose Images: Waring Cuney and the Harlem Renaissance Idea of the Poet's Work," in *The Heritage Series of Black Poetry: 1962–1975*, ed. Lauri Ramey in consultation with Breman. I first heard "No Images" sung, a cappella, by Nina Simone.

Tamed by *Miltown*, we lie on Mother's bed;
the rising sun in war paint dyes us red;[8]

In contrast to "No Images," the diction is stiff and suggests that the poem is possibly written by a second-language speaker (as suggested by the missing personal pronoun before "Mother" and the overpunctuation). The poem is strikingly anachronistic—almost sixty years after *Un coup de dés*, it fails to reflect the poetic revolution of Stein, Pound, Eliot, or Hughes: consider the naive rhyme of "bed" and "red" and the primitivist idea associating a red sun with war. But this first impression can be overcome if we take into consideration the cultural background of the author and read the poem from an ethnographic point of view. The cultural limitations of the poem—it's "uptightness" and recognition of the difficulty of sustaining heterosexual relationships ("Now twelve years later, you turn your back")—become its strength. "Man and Wife" seems to be bruising up against a "high" education and breeding that hamper a freer emotional life ("too boiled and shy / and poker-faced to make a pass") and acceptance of more open form ("tamed," "you / hold your pillow to your hollows like a child"). That is, once we see that the poet comes out of a repressed, alcoholism-prone ("boiled," as in aesthetically cooked[9]) Anglo-Protestant-American background, once we take in its class origins ("all air and nerve"), we can see its immediate appeal to other Anglo-Protestant-Americans, who may suffer from the same problems, such as emotional and intellectual sedation, drug addiction, or overdosing (*Miltown* is not a reference to a factory town but to a prescription sedative, a popular form of legal doping in the late 1950s). Yet while "Man and Wife" would be primarily of interest to heterosexual Anglo-Protestant-Americans of the upper crust, the poem gives other readers insight into this unique form of life.

　　—But enough of such costume foolery! Both poems are great, in their fashion, and both turn their forms on themselves. Lowell's poem is less interesting for what it "confesses" than how its candor works like acid on the form.

　　I prefer art that opens up possibilities rather than art that perfects a possibility. That may mean liking "lesser" poems to "greater" ones. Of course, nowadays, *minor* is *major* and the concept of "minor literature" is the new critic's siren song. The signal work on this distinction, for the thirtieth consecutive year, is *Kafka: Toward a Minor Literature* by Gilles Deleuze and

8. <poets.org/poetsorg/poem/man-and-wife>

9. Lowell makes the deceptive distinction between open-form "raw" poems and closed-form "cooked" poems in his 1960 National Book Award acceptance speech <www.nationalbook.org /nbaacceptspeech_rlowell.html>.

Félix Guattari, though if Kafka is minor, what does that make all the other twentieth-century fiction writers far more minor than he is? Oh but: they mean minor as a modality not as a marker of diminished achievement. It is a commonplace that "outsiders" later become insiders. The most conventional poets are dying to be called "avant-garde" even though they detest actual avant-garde practices, in the process trashing their weirder fellow-poets for taking up the oxygen that God designated for the conforming. It all gets so confusing. I want to make a case for genuinely "minor" figures—poets who didn't write as much, have the impact, or achieve the level of innovation as their "major" counterparts. At the same time, I want to sing the praises of reading a range of innovative and iconoclastic modernist and contemporary poets, not just the "best"—not so we can rescue a neglected poet for the canon (though I am all for that), but because poetry is best read through multiplicity rather than singularity. I do not, however, extend this same capacious interest to the ensemble of conforming poets. In that case, I do prefer only the best! But that is because my interest lies in nonconforming poetry from the past century and more.

A Bach fugue is a closed experience, even if infinite in its variations and transcendental in its feel. Familiarity allows even the startling changes of tempo in Glenn Gould's Bach performances to feel fresh while confirming a received idea of perfection. The experience of Brian Ferneyhough's music is different: it remains provisional and unexpectable, averting a listener's ability to fully come to terms with it. Ferneyhough's music is open in the sense that its value is undetermined (is it great?), but also undeterminable (it averts perfection).

Canonical art does not offer a challenge to the arts of invention but rather to the arts of convention, to artwork that offers a pale imitation of values no longer fully obtainable.

Francis Janosco, a high school teacher in Darien, Connecticut, recently asked me and a few others to nominate poems written since 2000 so that his senior class could exercise their judgments by picking what they perceived to be the best.[10] I was thinking of Robert Duncan's remark in 1963 ("Pages from a Notebook"): "I make poetry as other men make war or make love or make states or revolutions: to exercise my faculties at large." I asked the teacher to tell his students that I don't believe in "best" in the abstract since what I may most value in a poem is likely to be despised by other readers. Poetry is more like politics in that sense, but the stakes are aesthetic. In making this list, I assumed the students were relatively new to poetry and I selected works that are very different in approach, so their

10. Links for the poems are at <writing.upenn.edu/bernstein/syllabi/Janosco-best-poems.html>.

preferences would reflect as much the kind of poem they are interested in as the "best." I picked the following poems to raise issues that I hoped would spark discussion.

Lyn Hejinian, *The Unfollowing*, Hejinian's new book, where each line is supposed to be a non sequitur. The poems are each fourteen lines, but she says they are not sonnets. Would other combinations of the lines make for equally good poems? Why do non sequiturs put into this form become connected to one another? Could this be a structural allegory for human organization in families, groups, cities, nations?

David Antin, "Hiccups"—Antin gives improvised "talk poems" and then transcribes the talks. You can read the written version and also listen to the audio on which Antin based the text. What's the difference in experiencing the recording versus reading the poem? Is it one poem or two? Why call this a poem?

Maggie O'Sullivan, *All Origins Are Lonely*. O'Sullivan is the only poet here from Great Britain. She sometimes publishes her work with her own collages.

Tracie Morris, From "Slave Sho to Video aka Black but Beautiful" (audio file). There is no "text" version of this poem, only the recording of the performance.

Felix Bernstein, "If Loving You Is Wrong." This one is by my son. How does nepotism affect the selection of the "best"? The poem lists the number of Google search hits for each of the dozens of contemporary poets listed. Is this a legitimate form for a poem? Do "hits" represent popularity, distinction, or value? The poem ends with a reference to David Antin's quip, "if robert lowell is a poet i dont want to be a poet   if robert frost was a poet i dont want to be a poet   if socrates was a poet i'll consider it."[11]

Ron Silliman, "from Caledonia." Silliman has been publishing since 1970. This is his most recent online magazine appearance.

Tonya Foster, "In/Somniloquies" in *A Swarm of Bees in High Court* along with a commentary I wrote on the work. Do you read the poem differently after reading the commentary?

Robert Grenier, two "scrawl" (hand-drawn, visual) poems with rough translations. Many people would not consider these drawn works poems at all. How does handwriting affect the meaning?

Christian Bök, *Eunoia* ("o"). Each chapter is composed with just one vowel (lipogram).

11. David Antin, *Radical Coherency: Selected Essays on Art and Literature, 1966 to 2005* (Chicago: University of Chicago Press, 2011), p. 273

Elizabeth Willis, "The Witch." Are you one?

Charles Bernstein, "War Stories." This is not my best poem, but a good one for discussion. Does that make it a better candidate for this classroom use?

Ibn Ezra as channeled by Browning:

Rather I prize the doubt
Low kinds exist without,
Finished and finite clods, untroubled by a spark.

In a recent letter to our mutual friend Li Zhimin, Susan Stewart wrote, "I expect art to create new knowledge and new feelings."[12] No doubt she was echoing Wallace Stevens's "new knowledge of reality."[13]

A *here* we've never been. Where we've always been. Where we are now.

Feng Yi, a visiting scholar at Penn this year, puts it this way: "This is the moment for me to test whether I can be an immigrant to the uncertain, the unknown and the foreign, whether I am acceptable and open enough, whether I can adapt to the new or not."[14]

Once Reb Bint Eliza was asked, "What poems will abet making the next world?"—"None," she answered. After a few minutes three people walked by, talking wildly and bursting into uncontrollable laughter.—"What those people are exchanging is making the world to come."

I can't get no perfection. But I can get new possibilities, new directions, new horizons.

Then, welcome each rebuff
That turns earth's smoothness rough,
Each sting that bids nor sit nor stand but go!
Be our joys three-parts pain!
Learn, nor account the pang; dare, never grudge the throe!
        ("Rabbi Ben Ezra")

[2016: *Evaluations: U.S. Poetry Since 1950: Volume One*, ed. Robert Faggen and Robert von Hallberg (Albuquerque: University of New Mexico Press, 2021)]

12. E-mail, August 1, 2016. See Stewart's *The Poet's Freedom* (2011).

13. "Not Ideas About the Thing But the Thing Itself," in *Collected Poetry and Prose* (New York: Library of America, 1997), p. 451

14. E-mail, April 26, 2016

Forewords & Backwords

Waldrop, Armantrout, Drucker, Foster,
López Cuenca, Joris, Pearson, Clark, Sheppard,
Serbian Poetry, Morris, Royet-Journoud,
Perloff, Lin, Hejinian

1. 80 Words for Rosmarie Waldrop at 80

sojourner

intuit

investivagation

florescence

flip

bodilihood

engesture

rereproduction

clamp

insoupiance

cluster

bookish

trans(n)actional

alien

counteralienation

mmirrorr

traffic

transmogrification

crystalime

tongued

hanky

sobriquet

bordering

boding

brooding

bents

bristle

languagish

scoot

dililquessence

drape

drip

drop

druidical

détournement

distantiationism

o

oh

ah

ach

ache

it

itch

its

sort

sore

sure

insolvenerable

so

olé

hole

wool

would

workings

silhouette

duets

thinkamajig

thung

scrum	improviden
fliction	provisolo
beauty	precariosity
arrowtics	thimble
perspicuously	tumble
twinnings	tremble
rhymings	asynchronicitylessness
trimmings	singe
fillllings	hinge
disrequited	fringe
dehiscence	flotilla

[2015: *For Rosmarie on Her Eightieth* (Brooklyn: Ugly Duckling Presse); *Plume*, 2016.]

2. Rhythms of Dislocation and Relocation [Rae Armantrout]

I. SUNY Buffalo Poetics Program, February 15, 1995

Rae Armantrout's poem "Extremities" ends with the line "the charmed verges of presence"; and, indeed, her poems are charms, virtual presents.[1] Armantrout's poetry is notable for its precision and elegance, its preternatural ability to chart the slightest shifts of social register on the city streets, in the suburban malls, and in the university corridors. In an early poem she writes "the smallest / distance / inexhaustible"[2]—a poetic credo of commitment to the specific scale of an unadorning everyday life, words lived in their pajamas as much as their toupee. "the smallest / distance / inexhaustible"—providing a reservoir of wry, wacky, wicked, torqued and torquing observations, skewering any bloated sense of proportion, skewing lines of logic to make poems of sentient, radiant sense: returning us to the pleasures of reflection and to consoling, indomitable wit.

II. The 92nd St. Y, March 12, 2009

I first met Rae Armantrout in 1977 in San Francisco, or maybe 1975, or maybe it was San Diego or New York. It must have been somewhere. I

1. *Extremities* (Berkeley: The Figures, 1978), p. 7; Armantrout's first book, available at <eclipsearchive.org>.

2. "Processional," in *Extremities*, p. 34

really can't be sure. I know I know her and met her. But my recollection is no match for my desire to extemporize and I've learned not to trust anyone who does that.

Well, I do remember that in 1977, Bruce Andrews and I wanted to have an essay on gender issues in the first issue of the magazine we were planning. Thinking of Rae as a primary practitioner of the work that was our magazine's subject, I asked her, I thought ironically, "Why Don't Women Do Language-Centered Writing?," which became the title of her influential essay. Thirty years later I think it would have been better to ask the less ironic question, "Why Don't Men Do Language-Centered Writing?" This has been one of the main issues I have tried to tackle in my work and is central to the collection of essays I am working on now, to be called *The Attack of the Difficult Poems*.

Which reminds me . . . As we speak now, the audience for Richard Foreman's *Astronome* at the Ontological Hysteric Theater at St. Mark's Church is being given ear plugs in case John Zorn's music is too loud. I want to suggest to you at the outset that for those who find severe dislocation disturbing, please put on your blindfolds immediately following this introduction. For those comfortable with the dissonance of contemporary poetry, the blindfolds won't be necessary. But if you are unsure, I suggest you use the blindfolds as a prophylactic.

Well perhaps I have jumped too fast to Armantrout's work. I first want to say something about Rae herself.

Rae is frank, straightforward, even blunt in her honesty and directness. She always gives you a straight answer. Yet her work is wry, sly, and spry; indirect; slant, in an Emily Dickinson kind of way. You read a poem and you sort of get it, but then realize you didn't, then reread and are sure you didn't. That's when you got it, or it got you.

Armantrout's work is not surrealism, not realism, but para- or peri-realism: it is constructed of precisely articulated observations that seem to logically follow one another but that, like everyday life, don't or better to say, *don't quite.* Her rhythms are of dislocation and relocation. Armantrout's signature is serial displacement: incommensurability torques from one iteration to another, like Marcel Marceau miming a mime miming. Such an approach can be used for many ends. Armantrout's engagement is often social and cultural dysfunction, giving her work its dark undertones and muted overtones. In this way, she depicts the sociocultural logic of late Capitalism; dark matter, indeed. So yeah, sure, please be sure to note: her work enacts, through its multifoliate insights, an ideological critique, as when you lose your balance but don't fall; you realize something must be wrong but don't know what. Preston Sturges said it best: *if you can't sleep at night, it's not the coffee it's the bunk.*

So, yes, Armantrout is one of the grand masters of our beloved radical disjunction of the 1970s and '80s. If one were to chart the vectors of each of her lines, you would get a field of skewed angles. Her motto might be: *One perception must lead tangentially to the next.* But tangential is not arbitrary or disconnected. Tangential is the mark of contingency but also motivated relation. To follow associative and peripheral connections— non-rationalizable, nonexpository, non-narrative—offers a constantly reiterated possibility of new perceptions.

Next to us is not the world we know so well, which we use to do our bidding, but the world that could be, the world we might make. I jump the line because I am so tired of waiting in it. I am not me if my little pigeon ignores me. And in not being me I become I, the maker of my perceptions, as the morning follows the night only once in a while, and even that is imaginary.

A couple of years ago death came calling for Rae. She wouldn't listen and just went about her business. That business is what we call poetry, and you are about to see her do her business tonight. The state of the art is in for a thorough interrogation. Who's minding the store? Where are the stairs? If I say it, do I have to buy it? Are those words she is reading or are you just the kind of people that admire her sensibility?

Join me in welcoming Rae Armantrout to the stage of this old house, this old city, this old art . . .

3. *Figuring the Word* [Johanna Drucker]

During the 1960s and 1970s, the New York Public Library acquired an admirable collection of contemporary small press magazines, including many of the xerox, mimeo, and side-stapled publications featured in the 1998 show, *A Secret Location on the Lower East Side: Adventures in Writing 1960–1980*. This was the heyday of a writing storage medium called microfiche, which the librarians embraced as a space-age space saver: no sooner had they committed these publications to fiche than they disposed of the cumbersome objects, as one would discard the husks around an ear of corn. However, it wasn't too long before the library found itself recollecting, and prominently displaying, the material artifacts that they had earlier so abruptly deaccessioned.

What difference does it make? What's the fuss about these material imprintings of language—isn't it the content that matters? Does the method of storage really make a difference?

The work of Johanna Drucker reflects a radical change in understanding the semantic contribution of the visual representation of language—not just for visual poetry or artists' books, not just for poetry, but for all forms of written language. To be sure, Drucker has focused her attention on language works in which visual materiality is foregrounded. But the lessons she has to teach—historical, philosophical, and aesthetic—apply to all the technologies human beings have invented to store and explore language. *All language is visual when read.* In her work, Drucker reverses a common assumption even among writers, typographers, and visual poets that the visual dimension of writing is ornamental, decorative, extrasemantic—a matter of design, not signs that matter. "The single, conservative constant in my work," she says, "is that I always intend for the language to have meaning. My interest is in extending the communicative potential of writing, not in eliminating or negating it."

In these pages, Drucker presents herself as a visual artist, a literary writer, a scholar/historian, and an aesthetician. In each of these areas, Drucker has made substantial contributions. But it is her synthesis of these fields that is her most extraordinary achievement and that links her late twentieth-century work in the United States to the work of two towering British scholar-book artists of the previous fin-de-siècles: William Blake of the late eighteenth century and William Morris of the late nineteenth. Like these men of letters, this modern-day person of books bends and stretches the nature of art practice well beyond its conventional generic constraints. She questions and transforms the gender codings of the intellectual, the polymath, the scholar, the printer, and the artist. Indeed, Drucker is more a satirist than a visionary or utopian, reveling in, rather more than reviling, the "carnival of grotesque human folly." For all its extraordinary detail and formidable erudition, Drucker's work is rigorously anti-systematic, emblematically anti-authoritarian, and often giddily eccentric.

Figuring the Word is a work of poetics rather than criticism or theory in that these essays are the products of doing as much as thinking, of printing as much as writing, of designing as much as researching, of typography as much as composition, of autobiography as much as theory. The mark of the practitioner-critic is everywhere present in these pieces: it is as notable in Drucker's insistence on discussing her process of making things as it is when she reveals her process of hiding things. Moreover, even as she has learned the history of her medium, she remains insistent that current practice, not precedent, is her guiding impulse: "The idea that there were precedents for such activity seemed a lot less important than that there was a future in it."

Figuring the Word is a wide-ranging collection of Drucker's essays from the early 1980s to the present. Written in a variety of styles and presented in a variety of formats, the book reflects many divergent aspects of her work and thinking, while at the same time demonstrating how cohesive her project has been. Drucker begins with a wonderfully digressive discussion of her work as a book artist in which she gives an account of what led her not only to her book art, but also to her related scholarly investigations. She then provides a series of close readings of the work of several contemporary language artists, providing in other essays overviews of the historical precedents for this work. The book includes not only a perceptive essay about the use of language in the landscape, but also a prescient essay about the use of language in the new electronic frontier of cyberspace. In several sections, Drucker narrates her personal history as a way to explore the affinity with the genre fiction and tabloid prose that underlies much of her writing. And throughout the collection, she interrogates the role and significance of gender, not only for her own work, but for the genres within which she works. Drucker insists that "the place for women is not *as the Other* but as the one who shows that *that Other has always been present*," a position that is, to a remarkable degree, analogous to her view about the material features of language.

Susan Bee and I first met Johanna Drucker in 1977 in a large tent in Bryant Park, on the grounds of the New York Public Library, during a Small Press Book Fair. Drucker was exhibiting her first few letterpress books, which immediately caught my attention as just the kind of work that I wanted to focus on in a new journal Bruce Andrews and I were just starting, *L=A=N=G=U=A=G=E*. Indeed, I reviewed Drucker's *From A to Z* in the first issue of *L=A=N=G=U=A=G=E*, commenting on its uncanny fusing of constructivist constraints (she had set every piece of type from a set of forty-five type drawers she had acquired), sumptuous physical detail (a vision of textual excess and density), and wry metanarrative commentary.

Drucker's works, including her unlikely and necessary creation of a supernal body of scholarship exploring the history of alphabets and the theory of the visual representation of language, have remained central to my own sense of writing in the years since. In a wider context, her work has become ever more relevant with the introduction of new writing reproduction and distribution technologies.

When we met, Drucker already knew what the folks in the library would celebrate two decades later: What matters in language is not just the edifices that we make to rise towards the heavens or bore deep below ground. The mud on the floor at Bryant Park that day may have dirtied our shoes, but it also kept us in mind of the material ground of our writing practices—of the significance of making by marking.

[1998: Introduction to *Figuring the Word* (New York: Granary Books)]

4. Tonya's Place [Tonya Foster]

In Harlem, one can
never get a room dark enough
to lose sight of things.

In Harlem, one can
or can seem to make peace with
a tour bus of eyes.

I first heard Tonya Foster read at St. Mark's of the Vieux Carré church in New Orleans on December 29, 2001. It was one of our annual "off-site" readings during the Modern Language Association convention, this one sponsored by Lit City and coordinated by Camille Martin. About fifteen poets read, and Foster was the only one entirely new to me. When she read the place lit up, and I lit up with it; the echoing cadences of her voice filled the church space. Her poetry was rooted in New Orleans, where she grew up, but it wasn't a New Orleans legible from the outside. As she's shown over the years since, to be a poet of New Orleans is not only to be a poet of an actual place, but also of a place of the imagination. Her work is site-specific but also re-citing, re-splicing, and re-sounding.

> *The disaster has no single origin, no single moment of birth. Like the wave bruising the shore, it is an unapologetic accretion of uninterrupted motion.*

Foster revisits New Orleans post-Katrina in a long mixed-genre work called "A Mathematics of Chaos: Pay Attention to Where You At/From," which, when she presented it at a 2008 reading (you can hear the audio on PennSound), was accompanied by photographs and a short video. The work comes off as part elegy and part reconnaissance. Reconnaissance turns out to be crucial for Foster: second site, knowing again, diving into a wreck that is not only all-too-real but all-too-imaginary.

Waterlikelanguagelikewaterlikelanguagelikewaterlikelanguage
likeotterslikelanguagelikedaughterslikeotterslikelickinglikelapping
   languagewagonwaters

Foster's engagement with repetition and lists is a mark of her continual
return not to the same but to the *site as reciting*. She is a poet of a place that
is displaced: the place of her place is its displacement, her emplacement and
replacement of it, as she returns and turns away, as she turns. Here / *not here*,
the fundamental rhythm presence and absence, take center stage in Foster's
emerging poetics of emplacement.

> *My sisters and I could drive each other crazy by mimicking each other, repeating*
> *every word and gesture again and again. We took pleasure in making language we*
> *all knew strange, pleasure in accentuating the strangeness of words and in holding*
> *up that strangeness.*

This is a series devoted to emerging poets and I don't want simply to
be coy in locating Foster's poetics as *emerging*; but I take that as a tenet
of her approach, as we used to talk about process. There are a number of
ways that Foster's work can be located within a contemporary moment of
site-specific poetry, which often focuses on the environmental context of a
work, how it situates in terms of its surround. Indeed, Foster's work is at the
intersection of site-specific writing, ecopoetics (poetics read or written as
an ecological system), and the poetics of identity. But what distinguishes it
from these approaches is its insistence of emergence, which means that site
and identity have not yet been actualized and the system not yet realized.
Emergence here is a sign of crisis, of emergency, in which the provisional
is valued for its register of immediacy. Repetition and lists in Fos-
ter's work is not a legacy of modernist composition so much as a mapping
device.

Blackity-black girl
sitting in a dark lit by
t.v and streetlight.

Blackity-black girl,
at play on the court of your skin—
imminent domain.

The work often leads by ear, by sound, but not primarily because of an aesthetic engagement with the sonic for itself or as an ethnographic grounding in documentary, but rather because sound is a primary locating device, as in a sonogram. The echo is not toward the autonomy of the poem or the reality of the language outside it. The echo is a probe.

Black is black taint
that marks the linoleum tile
she Mop and Glo's clean

"Black is black"—t'aint
that the color line—
"just cause" as refracted light?

My comments on Foster are abstract and technical. But Foster's work doesn't feel abstruse or conceptual (two qualities I often like in poems). Foster's work is constructed as a system or environment that explores the emergence and disappearance of identity and place. It's not a poetry of, or about, fixed points of reference that are described. The sites emerge and submerge in the flickering probes of Foster's accumulation of voices, her collection of verbal markers and shifting signs. *Ain't taint*. In "A Mathematics of Chaos" she writes, "Geography can be transformative—the way a bullet to the body can be transformed." Words wash over her work like the rain pours down, flooding a city ("water like language"). Speech is collected as tangible evidence of an imaginary home.

> *a girl who looks like her father is born for luck, alcohol, Algiers, alligator, Amazing Grace, Amelia, Angola, Atchafalaya, Aunt Noni, Aunt Sister, Azerine, back a town, bayou, because her daddy died or left, because the first-born baby died, beignets, bitch, Butsie, café au lait, . . . Father John's, file, first-born, first-born done died, fleur de lys, flood, "for true?" front porch, Galvez, Gerttown, "gimme some," "girl, gimme got shot," "git up in here," "God don't like ugly," good hair, gran'ma . . .*

The poetics of emplacement must be imagined before it can be real, so that it *can be* real. We listen and we see what we hear. Or, we hear, and dive into ourselves to avert the brute reality of what we have heard.

That is what we mean by going home.
This is the secret place of poetry.
This is the way Tonya Foster matters.

[2008: *American Poet* 35. Quotations are from Foster's manuscripts "A Mathematics of Chaos: Pay Attention to Where You At/From" (italics) and *A Swarm of Bees in High Court* (published by Belladonna in 2015).]

5. Rogelio López Cuenca and the Ordinary

The ordinary is blank. It's ordinary
because we don't notice it; or is it that
we don't choose to notice it? Like ideology
in a fully functioning system, the ordinary
is transparent: our parent that we cannot
see but all the more mind, take to heart.

One of the hallmarks
of modernist visual
and verbal art is
a turn
toward the
ordinary,
whether in
William Carlos Williams's
or Charles Reznikoff's
focus on otherwise
neglected details—
the broken glass
in a
vacant lot
beside
the hospital
or vignettes about
industrial accidents
long ago forgotten
& only barely noticed
at the time.
Then again, Kurt Schwitters
making his collages from the detritus

of everyday life—a torn
piece of newspaper, for
example—or
Duchamp exhibiting
apparently mundane objects
in a gallery:
a snow shovel, a urinal, a bottle rack;
these designations by now
having taken on
an auratic glow.
Or Gertrude Stein
making her poems
from the most ordinary
of words—
of & and & so,
may or can,
can and may.

The philosophy of the ordinary is in
Wittgenstein's investigations, and
insistence, on the way words are used in
the language play that is their home and
in Michel de Certeau's *arts de faire*, in
which the small inversions of order a
worker might make on the job create a
tactical opening of space.

You can't break down the distinctions
between everyday life and art because
everyday life is always a bit ahead of this
game. This is why Duchamp, contra
postmodern mapmakers, is the high modernist
artist par excellence; & it is why modernism,
up to the second world war, could synthesize
high and low, popular and esoteric, while
in the postwar cultural economy, related

efforts, as by Warhol—in his "fine" art
though not his movies—give up on everyday
life, switching focus to commodification
of persons and things. Of course, breaking
down the distinction between art and packaging
proved a more lucrative enterprise than
breaking down the distinction between art
and everyday life.

This is where the work of Rogelio López
Cuenca takes its original turn. To exhibit
the ordinary in an aesthetic context is
by now an empty gesture, since a
hollowed-out or banalized ordinary
is more or less the characteristic content of
"postmodern" high-art commodities.

López Cuenca sites the everyday not in
content, to be appropriated without intervention,
but in the specific forms of the contemporary
urban environment, above all the signage of
public spaces—the parking & traffic & information
signs of streets and airports. How make
these visible?—so that we can look at, not
simply obey, their regulation of flow &
punctuation of environment. López Cuenca
does not recontextualize, as it were
aestheticizing, signage: he is actively
intervening in the process by which
signage operates unseen. He
rewires the signs so that we might
rewire our lives.

I say that López Cuenca does not aestheticize
quotidian signage as such, repeating and
emptying the Duchampian gesture. Rather,

he reverses this process, bringing
the aesthetic into the everyday—his
works, derived from public spaces, are,
for the most part, re-sited in public spaces.
But before this re-siting, López Cuenca
transforms the content of the signs,
creating a poetic space within these
signs that contests the neutrality of the
forms that house them. It's as if
López Cuenca had created a working model
for Charles Sanders Peirce's idea of
language as a clash of signs by replacing
the informational content of the signs
with language that conveys no information.

I've placed one of López Cuenca's signs in
the hallway just outside my classroom.
The sign has the exact color scheme and
shape of a famous midtown Manhattan
traffic sign. At the top, replacing
"tow-away zone" is REAL ZONE, &
beneath this, in big letters:
DON'T EVEN THINK OF POETRY HERE.
This is one of López Cuenca's most
explicit, and comic, invocations to
the spectator to be conscious by
refusing the "real." Other
works remain pointedly inscrutable
in their own refusal to replace one
gloss with another. In one, an
elegant displacement of the ubiquitous
phone icon (a vertical phone handpiece),
López Cuenca has substituted POEM for
"phone". Poem home, indeed. For in this
phone poem, akin to a found poem (or is
it a poem phone, a phone made of a

poem?), López Cuenca reminds us
that we do phone poems home,
which is to say, transmit the sound
and inflection of our voice
as much as "say" anything.

The content pushes against the forms of these
works, making them unsettling, but without
any of the shock effect we tend to associate
with the controversial art of our time. In
López Cuenca's work the language is unsettling
because it deflects immediate interpretation.
The result is that López Cuenca's work has
repeatedly been removed from the public spaces
for which it was commissioned, often on the
complaint of public officials who objected
not to its content but to its apparent
lack of content. For if the space of official
information is negated, then the authority
of all such sanctioned transmissions is undermined.
It's certainly not that anyone would mistake
one of López Cuenca's signs for "real" parking
signs, but its presence, next to identically
designed, "functioning" signs, creates an
unacceptable discrepancy. The violation of
social order is not of the outrageous type with
which we have been so comfortable; a different,
subliminal, erosion is at work here.

[1994: *WORD$WORD$WORD$*, Centro Andaluz de Arte Contemporáneo, Seville, Spain, and *M/E/A/N/I/N/G* 15.]

6. *Canto Diurno* [Pierre Joris]

Pierre Joris's *Cantos Diurno* are never solemn, but they acknowledge the "darkness that surrounds," as Robert Creeley once put it, that we are always behind our ideals, hopes, aspirations, premonitions, regrets, fears—*behind* both in the sense of supporting and *after*, trying to catch up, desperately for the most part, but in these poems not desperate but fortunate, in good humors and with humor.

American poetry is born in second languages, it is our bounty and the secret of our success, if we have any, as much as Samson's long hair, once upon a time, was the source of his strength. That's why any attempt to homogenize and assimilate undermines the foundations of our poetics.

Joris's work is marked by a rare virtue for an American poet: *couragio*. Everybody is always talking about *affect* but no one ever does anything about it. We used to say "lifts your spirits" but that applies more to Thanksgiving balloons than to challenging verse. I want a poetry, like this, that changes my mind, puts me in the sway of currents of resistance and change. Where the courage is not just what is said but what is refused: the sanctity of the fixed place, nation or ideal, banner or standard. It's not just the tyranny of monolingualism that Joris's verse contests, it's the tyranny of all forms of monomania: single-mindedness in perspective, style, politics, form, language, identity, desire. "I speak in voices / always always / other people's voices / a thousand mouths."—We all turned away from virtues when that meant some uppity guy telling us the way we lead our lives is base. What happens if the base speaks in a basso profundo, as in being pro *fun* with *doing* more than the *done*?

Intellectus is not a dirty word. While so much of American poetry culture has run from thick historical context and wit as if they were a European disease, Joris has made a poetry that overthrows the hierarchies but not the minding, tending, churning, plowing, fermenting, and fomenting.

I want to claim Joris as an American poet par excellence, but that is only if we understand "American" as dissolving into the "image nation" (Robin Blaser's term)—"the city which is syntax"—of non-national possibility. To be neither here nor there, French nor German, Luxembourgish nor Americanische, is to inhabit a provisionality among and between, a toggling that creates a space of rhythmic intensities ("true movement unencumbered") that confounds binaries and repels axiomatic allegiances.

In "An Alif Baa," Joris speaks of a zig connecting to "orphaned" zag, evoking the nomadic condition of letters before they coalesce into words, what he calls in another poem the "zigzag nomad." The distance from the orphaned "zag" to the "zig" of history or place or name is "irreducible." The space from zig to zag is the antinomian *space between* ("between lips / be silk between / be between," "between the ephemeral & the invariant"). This is a space Joris claims as the nomadic possibility of poetry and thought, what sometimes goes by the name of imagination but also fancy, emptiness, and negation.

Joris's poetry is an unexpected overlay of Expressionism ("eye turned inside out") and Dada ("A fistful / of consonants / drifts from mouth to / mouth"), parataxis ("break the ice / to know") and lyric ("what is is / shimmers, stammers / on the vocal-cords-bridge, in the / Great Inbetween / with all that has room in it / even without speech").

Voicings and thing language.

His ever-burning searching is tempered by the realpolitik ("postmortem") of images, images that are uneasy, that propel a querical (queasy) inquiry.

Joris's "daily song" is a tracing of a definite but undefined course. The poet recognizes the necessity of a rhetorical address from "the center of my center of nowhere." No *where* but still always *here*, at this long-delayed hearing that determines neither guilt nor innocence but rather makes ways (makes waves) to actualize *copability* (the ability to cope), which along with adaption, translation, miscegenation, and élan is a guiding force of these beguiling works.

[2016: Afterword to Pierre Joris, *Canto Diurno: Choix de poèmes 1972–2014* (Paris: Le Castor Astral, 2017); published in French translation by Habib Tengour. See also "NoOnesRose," my interview of Joris in *boundary 2* 50:4 (2023).]

7. *Oculus Lucidus* [Bruce Pearson]

Now is a little on the early side, don't you think? We never arrive there, then again, we're never anywhere else. I like to think of history as a set of frames that lets us see one part of what's before our eyes at the cost of framing out something else. That's why seeing is always temporal, always mediated by words.

We see not just through words but with words. There's no way around it. Yet the idea is precarious.

Put it this way: Abstraction is never more than an extension of figuration just as figuration is never more than an extension of abstraction.

In Bruce Pearson's paintings, you see the figures melting into the paint then look again and all you see is abstract patterns. Since the work is filled with letters, which in small groups make up words, and which, in turn, constitute phrases, so much depends on how you frame it. Indeed, the frames—verbal, visual, textual, textural—come fast upon one another, piling up like the layers of a palimpsest.

The idea that you see a painting all at once, or that colors or shapes are any less symbolic than words or figures, is a malady of critical discourse that is given its comeuppance in each of Pearson's works.

Pearson's paintings offer balm for sore eyes. They are an aesthetic *oculus lucidus*. But unlike the medieval powder, which was made of dried, pulverized honeysuckle, they are made of oil and acrylic on polystyrene foam.

You have to read Pearson's paintings, but that just intensifies the visuality.

[2020: Introduction to my interview with Bruce Pearson in *Bomb* 150.]

8. Poeming [Maxwell Clark]

As your sway, so my lyrics,
My lyrics sway of you—who
Afar, is also nearest—
So you cradle me,
So I swoon.

Maxwell Clark is deeply infused with high Romantic poetry but equally with poststructuralist thought. His wild syntax connects him to a line of visionary innovators and Dada tricksters. Working sometimes in the everyday and sometimes "nowhere," Clark uses form as a conceptual tool to allow perception/interruption to occur in, and as, the poem.

Clark is a "Nude Formalist," a term I invented decades ago for self-conscious, sometimes conceptual use of traditional tropes and prosody ("poesy" as Clark calls it). "I am a conceptuality," he writes in a poem in this collection. "Where Is the Loved One's Face" (a title that alludes to philosopher Emmanuel Levinas) is a perfect example, with its four rhyming lines, one pentameter followed by four tetrameter iambics: "She is not here, in this dreamsy poeming, / But prior, behind its showing, / In a jumbled verve not unknowing, / Herself objectless bestowing." His neologisms "Dreamsy" and "poeming" suggest both childhood whimsy and queer deforming. There is a poignancy in Clark's sprung lyricism: a calibrated high silliness but also a sensuous majesty.

Clark's recurrent use of "pretty" may strike a dyschronic chord for contemporary readers, but it connects his verse with the "poetry of sensibility," to use Jerome McGann's terms for nineteenth-century "sentimental" poetry, mostly written by women, but which also brings to mind John Clare, Hart Crane, Joseph Ceravolo's *Spring in this World of Poor Mutts*, and Michael Haslam's *Continual Song*. Clark's work is neither pretty nor sentimental.

Quite to the contrary, Clark is often "bleatingly," disarmingly, frustratingly, "shamelessly" anti-poetic and deflationary ("grinchy-poofles!"), as with his tautologies ("The idiocy it is, so even more idiotic / Than idiocy itself") and arrays of literalizing yet allusive aphorisms and verbal tangles ("Ornaments Minus Reference"). His method is not to turn mundane things into beautiful language but to use *poesy* as a means to grip, to grapple with, the quotidian, but also—and this is fundamental—to register its loss: "My poesy is great and high / Because I am most brutal and sunken."

His poems made of prepositions, adverbs, and pronouns suggest Stein and early Clark Coolidge. Extending some elements from the L=A=N=G=U=A=G=E playbook, word stuff obtrudes in his poems as verbal test patterns (a poem made entirely of slash marks or another made of pluses/minuses/brackets), physicalizations of metaphoric possibilities (what Clark called "effluvia" and "whirligiging"), or, then again, Zukofskian studies of sounds as sentiment (as "o__o__oo," a poem on the "o" in *love*).

Many of these poems are addressed to, or call out to, *you*—reader, other, lover; it's unspecified; but absence is a recurring presence here, often insisting on bathos. "I am weak of your turning away"—"Till my voice is touch."

Clark's poetry is not dissociative but reassociative. In "Crazy Quilt," his ars poetica, Clark writes of "a knotted loop of braided spirals," evoking for me R. D. Laing's *Knots*. "I do with words what I can't say with them." "My voice, or my voices?" he asks in another poem. "Are present herein? from when? / Or is someone else writing? / Like myself? then? (else when?)"

Maxwell Owen Clark was born in Tarrytown, New York, on October 29, 1984. His family moved a number of times, from Pittsburgh to Memphis, landing in Fairfield, Connecticut, at the time Clark was in third grade. When he was thirteen, Clark was hit hard by major depression. Nonetheless, he attended the University of Vermont and then Yale, where he suffered a severe psychotic break. From then on, he did not go a year without a hospitalization for "intensely difficult psychiatric reasons" (as he puts it), including the risk of suicide. His current diagnosis "Psychosis (Not Otherwise Specified)." Unable to work, he survives, barely, and sometimes homeless, on social security disability benefits. Clark has a blog and an active presence on Facebook. I published two previous collections of his poetry as EPC Digital Editions, *Poesies* (2014) and +|+ (2016).

Clark is a great admirer of the work of Hannah Weiner. He once told me the one thing he was not happy about with Weiner was her refusal to accept that she was schizophrenic. For Clark, psychiatric disturbances are not something to hide. The facts of one's everyday life form a foundation for poetry. How such disability informs any poet's work remains something to explore, just as the work explores the many, sometimes clashing, parts of one's identity. Clark's invented language in "The Imperial God of Psychosis" is a challenge and a promise, a "schlizzo" manifesto in this unexpected, inventive, necessary book of poetry.

[2017: Foreword to Maxwell Clark, *(((. . .)))* (New York: Roof Books).]

9. Aesthetic Justice [Robert Sheppard]

So much of the aesthetically radical poetry of our time closes in on itself, hoarding its virtue or harboring the secret of its style.

Virtue, in the last word, is corrosive to style.

Aesthetic justice is when "form becomes reform," to quote one of Robert Sheppard's suite of poems published here. In Sheppard's poetics, reform doesn't mean ameliorative improvement. Reform is a mark of poetry's capacity to reformulate without final conclusion, to think outside formulation.

In Sheppard's writing, essays, and poems, we hear the clang of discourse: the warp, but also the whoop, of everyday life. His work will never stand for election. It resists even the self-election that is the sign of a poet's despair of (or for) polis.

Aesthetic justice is the onward movement of the imaginary smashing into the possible. But aesthetic justice is also *dwelling in a now* that burrows ever deeper into its refusal of thematic deliverance.

Sheppard's voices (discrepant discursive registers, transcreations, heteronyms) don't call out to us as readers, as in a well-mannered lyric, nor do they call out to each other, as in a story. Rather the voices, the textual shards, call out to themselves, self-reflexively, as in—a poem is the cry of its vocations and the measure of its resistances.

Form calls us out to ourselves: *calls out to*, a kind of aesthetic hailing; but also *calls us out*, exposing us, laying us bare, vulnerable, guilty as charged, without defense.

Sheppard has been a champion of British poetry that actively resists the complacent and the convenient, the merely competent. That has meant evading bullies who would "banish us," to use Dickinson's phrase. Sheppard's aesthetic justice has never been *just* for him; his social imagination is at one with his poems, essays, teaching, and editing. His work is restlessly agile, generous at heart. Or so the essays in this book propose in their various insistences.

Otherwise, innovation is just a fancy new saddle at the mind's rodeo.

[2018: Foreword to *The Robert Sheppard Companion,* ed. James Byrne and Christopher Madden (Swindon, UK: Shearsman Books, 2019)]

10. *Cat Painters*

We come old into a world newly born.

Poets I mean.

Conditions change so fast on the ground and yet we are walking receivers of traditions that defy objective temporal markers. Poems mark an intersection of the new, the news, and something outside that pressure of reality, something that resists such presence. The more resistant they are to the present, the more a perfect voicelessness emerges. In other words, it's not what poems say, it's what they do. And for those of us who prefer to read between the lines, it's also what they don't do, either by refusing or by chronic (and enabling) disability.

Cat Painters: An Anthology of Contemporary Serbian Poetry charts, for English language readers, an almost completely unknown poetry culture, unknown even to those most attentive to contemporary European poetry. Serbian poetry is the site of many competing political currents, from ultra-nationalist and patriarchal to antifascist, feminist, antiwar, and queer; from Roman Catholic, Moslem, Serbian Orthodox, to secular. In terms of poetic form, this translates into a recent history that goes from traditional lyric to confessional to formally innovative, from socialist realism to abstraction, from mystical to conceptual, from folkloric to modernist. The poems in this collection filter, through both adaption and rejection, literary movements from Symbolism, Expressionism, Futurism, Surrealism, Dadaism, New American Poetry, and L=A=N=G=U=A=G=E. (The anthology excludes more conventional styles of Serbian poetry.)

The two generations of poets gathered here came of age in the 1960s to 2000s. The older group started to publish during the heyday of Tito's Yugoslavia and pretty much all of these poets were around for the demise of Tito's "non-aligned" Communist amalgam of different ethnic groups. The older poets, the same generation as the American baby boomers, were born immediately after the Second World War (with a few exceptions of poets born during the war) and began publishing during the Cold War, while the younger poets lived through terrifying civil wars and regime changes of the post-Communist period (the youngest poet in the anthology was born in 1981). Whatever tumult we have experienced in North America and Western Europe in the postwar years, the world these poets found is something far more wrenching (although with some parallels to the experience of their fellow Russian poets).

Serbia is on the border of West and East. For poetry, perhaps nothing better exemplifies this than the fact that Serbian can be written with both Cyrillic and Roman letters. The presence of Slavic culture is a crucial background. But the 1980s in Yugoslavia was a culturally open time, including the strong presence of American and Western European pop culture. It's impossible for an outsider to fully understand the poetry politics of post-Communist Yugoslavia, but this anthology gives a ring-side view and maybe not having a score card is an advantage, since if there are sides, you can't immediately see how that plays out.

The most frequent word in the poetry collected here is *dark*. But there is also *love, eyes, light, god, nothing, everything, water, words,* and *window*. There are seventy-one poets, half women. The poems range from the more image-based, quasi-surrealist, yet conventionally legible work, associated with Charles Simic and the startling Radmila Lazić, on one end of the spectrum, to the formal/conceptual radicalism of Judita Šalgo and Slobodan Tišma, who declares "Writing is always connected with thinking, alas / With philosophy, that goes for the scribbling as well."[3] There is often a foreboding, biting humor and sense of engaged distance, self-observation. The poetry is sometimes sexually explicit. The grotesque and the diasporic dance deep into the night.

Dubravka Djurić, who coedited this anthology, has been a strong advocate of both feminism and poetic innovation, which is made explicit in her many translations of contemporary American poets. This collection should be read next to *Impossible Histories: Historic Avant-Gardes, Neo-Avant-Gardes, and Post-Avant-Gardes in Yugoslavia, 1918–1991,* edited by Djurić and Miško Šuvaković (Cambridge, MA: MIT Press, 2003).

There are around ten million speakers of Serbian, sixteen million if we say Serbo-Croatian. That's comparable to Dutch but greater than Hungarian or Greek. For an outsider reading this collection, what is most striking is not the many ways that the poems resemble what is familiar to us, and take up similar styles or attitudes, but the way the poems are unfamiliar,

3. See our group translation of Tišma at <jacket2.org/commentary/slobodan-tisma>.

slightly off synch, approaching, and falling off, different edges. Reading this book entirely in English, without any sense of the sound of Serbian, or the history of Serbian poetry, makes for an experience that the poets themselves cannot have. It is a work of English language poetry in its own right, thanks especially to the remarkable work of the lead translator, Biljana D. Obradović. The poems come to us shorn of some of their history but taking on new meanings for this new context. This is yet another new border, another new intersection, for these poems. Perhaps the ideal reader would come to all these poets fresh, hearing this book as a conversation over time: a plotless novel in verse. It's not just what the poems say or do, it is what they become.

The poetry is what is found in translation.

[2016: Foreword to *Cat Painters: An Anthology of Contemporary Serbian Poetry*, ed. Biljana D. Obradović and Dubravka Djurić (New Orleans: Diálogos). See also "Go Tell Aunt Rhody," foreword to Djurić's *The Politics of Hope (After the War): Selected and New Poems* (New York: Roof Books, 2023).]

11. Foreword and Backward [Tracie Morris]

For the last two decades, Tracie Morris has been transfiguring the relation of text to performance and word to sound. Such signature Morris works as "Slave Sho to Video aka Black but Beautiful" and "Chain Gang" are scoreless sound poems, originating in improvised live performance. At the same time, Morris has published text-based work in *Intermission* (1998) and *Rhyme Scheme* (2012). *Hand-Holding* is the first collection of Morris's work to present a full spectrum of her approaches to poetry. This is not so much a collection of poems, as conventionally understood, as a display of the possibilities for poetry. Each work here is not just in a different style or form but rather explores different aspects of poetry as a medium: re-sounding, re-vising, resonating, re-calling, re-performing, re-imaginings. In *Hand-Holding* the medium is messaged so that troglodyte binaries like politics and aesthetics, original and translation, and oral and written go the way of Plato's cave by way of Niagara Falls.

In her first recordings, Morris was already crossing the Rubicon between spoken word and sound poetry, showing that the river was only skin deep. In one of the two revisionist versions of a major modernist poem in this collection, Morris returns to the magnum opus of modernist sound poetry, Kurt Schwitters's "Ursonate" (1922–1932). For "Resonatae" Morris does not perform Schwitters's score; rather, she collaborates with the signal recording of the work by Schwitters's son Ernst. You don't hear Ernst's re-cording in Morris's work, but she is taking her cue from this performance. Because Morris has dispensed with the written (alphabetic) score, she is able to improvise, loop, extend, and re-perform "Ursonate" in a way that sets her performance apart. Her tempo is at half the pace of Christian Bök's magnificent, athletic version, which has become a classic of the sound poetry repertory. "Resonatae" re-spatializes the pitch of "Ursonate" as she re-forms its rhythms, creating a meditative, interior space that makes a resonant contrast to Bök; indeed to fully understand the achievement of Morris and Bök, you need to listen to both. While Bök's performance cre-ates an outer-directed, propulsive acoustic space, Morris creates an inner-directed, intimate one. This becomes especially poignant midway in the performance, when rather than create a percussive rhythm with phonemes popping against one another, Morris practically lapses into speech, into talking, into direct address. "Resonatae" is a brilliant charm, deepening and extending this modernist classic in a way comparable to Glenn Gould's revisionist Bach.

"Eyes Wide Shut" is another thing entirely. This poem invents a new medium for poetry, based on recent adaption by some American poets of Japanese "benshi" (live narration for silent films). "Eyes Wide Shut" pro-vides a new commentary track for the Stanley Kubrick movie: the audio file synchs with the full movie, while the printed poem is a sort of paratext or microfiche version. The two versions of the work are incommensurable; or maybe the relation is like a song lyric to a song. Listening to the audio track alone, the experience is of long silences, with voice suddenly breaking into the silence.

"Songs and Other Sevens," like "Eyes Wide Shut," is a commentary on a movie, John Akomfrah's 1993 documentary, *Seven Songs for Malcolm X*. Morris again provides two discrepant versions: one on the page, one as a sound recording. In this case, the audio is not meant to accompany the film but to provide a shadow version of the text (or perhaps it is the other way around and the text is the ghost of the audio). Listening to the audio track, the silences stand out as much as the sound in a way that undercuts the rhetorical momentum associated with poetry performance. Morris makes the space between the lines palpable. The neutrality of voice brings to mind the French poet Claude Royet-Journoud's desire for a lack of acous-tic resonance in a reading (Royet-Journoud employs a timer to insert non-rhythmic silences between cut-up phrases). With this frame established, the alphabetic poem seems nonlinear: you can read it backward or move around in it, sample it.

All that silence is made explicit by "5'05″," Morris's transcription/transposition of the John Cage classic "4'33″," where Cage frames a silence that is filled with ambient sound as well as with the sound of listening. Morris records sound as space: rooms, which like stanzas, can be a place to breathe or an enclosure that closes you off from the world.

"If I Reviewed Her," Morris's reworking of Gertrude Stein's *Tender Buttons* (1914) is a textual tour de force and the perfect bookend to her Schwitters: two towering modernist classics startlingly transformed. Stein: thou art translated! There is some connection to Harryette Mullens's *Trimmings* or perhaps to say that *Trimmings* is a touchstone for what is done in "If I Reviewed Her." Morris affords much cultural surround to her Stein variations and impromptus: Shakespeare and Williams, Yiddish and Broadway. She gives Stein back her accents, entering into a dialog with a work that veers toward soliloquy. Crucially, Morris re-sutures Stein's relation to blackness, which Stein was unable, given her time, to come to terms with: "What she said here is unfortunate. It isn't fortune and it isn't innate. I'll leave it there, but it was a disappointment. I'll say that. (She won't.) A 'white old chat churner' after all."

In "If I Reviewed Her" Morris asks the two central questions for *Handholding*: "What's a room?" and "What's an heirloom?"

She doesn't show, she tells.

[2015: Foreword to Tracie Morris, *Handholding 5 Ways* (New York: Kore Press, 2016). Some of the recordings discussed here can be heard on the Morris and Schwitters PennSound pages.]

12. For Claude
but I don't
know why

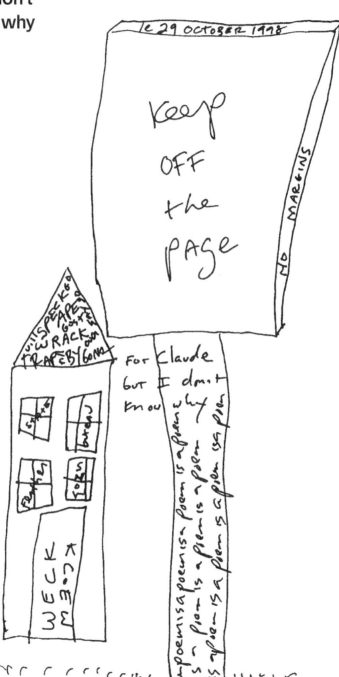

(extended play version for verso)

1. When Claude Royet-Journoud came to Buffalo in 1995 to read for the Poetics Program I was able to read with him my semi-homophonic translation of one of his poems, the last line of which I translated as "work vertical and blank." Claude used a clock to time the blank space in the poem, although whether that space is blank or white is of course a matter of some controversy. For my part, I used the space between the stanzas as a rhythmic interval and so expressed it through a kind of internal counting with (not just in) my head. Later, Claude noted that he wished to move away from the sound of the words, while in my translation I had foregrounded the sound of the French, trying to bring that over into my "American" version. Both these reversals seemed to me to suggest what I have found so interesting in my reading of Claude's work and my sense of an ongoing exchange with him. In this case, the notion of obstacle was translated into a poetics of reversal. If you read back through the translation via the reversal, the obstacle understood as something akin to resistance measured not in Ohms, as in electrodynamics, but perhaps O's!—you may experience a closed poetic circuit. Patent pending.

2. Later that same day, Claude, along with a large group of us, including Jean Frémon, Emmanuel Hocquard, and Jacqueline Risset, went to the Anchor Bar, home of the Buffalo Chicken Wing. I ordered the other famous Buffalo dish, Beef on Weck—a.k.a. roast beef on a hard (or kaiser) roll. The weck on the door in my drawing is possibly a reference to that but I can't honestly say why it's there. It just seemed like the right word.

3. When asked to participate in this special issue in honor of Claude I wanted to do something in the spirit of the many faxes I have received from Claude—spontaneous visual gestures that communicate a different sense of his personality than his poems. These works are meant as temporary gestures, marks of friendship and exchange. But unlike Claude, I can't draw very well. Still, I have never let inability get in my way; in fact, it has become my way.

4. A house standing next to a tree that becomes a sign of a page. A page that says it wants to be blank but isn't. Margins that are no more than optical illusions. A triangular enclosure that serves as a roof of words, our human ceiling, through which we leak language. These are a few of my favorite things.

5. A rabbi, a priest, and a poet were standing in a stanza. The priest says to the rabbi, "How do you get out of here?" The rabbi replies, "Depends on where you're going." The poet maintains an uncomfortable but telling silence.

6. I don't want to express my admiration for Claude Royet-Journoud. I want to live it.

7. My six-year-old son Felix likes to tell an old-time joke. "What's the difference between a teacher and a railroad train?"—The teacher says, "Spit that gum out!" and the train says, "Choo Choo."

8. Now here's one that Felix made up:

"What's the difference between a button and a shirt?"—The button is tied to the shirt, but the shirt is not tied to the button.

9. Or as we say in the land of Foot-High Melons, just off the coast of Taches Blanches:

"Can you please repeat that so Charles can understand?"

[1999: French translation in *Je te continue ma lecture: Mélanges pour Claude Royet-Journoud,* edited by Michèle Cohen-Halimi, P.O.L., Paris]

13. Marjorie Perloff: Wanderer's Swansong

Infrathin: An Experiment in Micropoetics (University of Chicago Press, 2021)

Almost imperceptible differences in the similar (and similarities in difference) are what Perloff in her new book calls the "infrathin." She gives a paradigmatic example from Wallace Stevens: an unseen "cat running over the snow almost inaudibly." Or take Duchamp's readymade snow shovel, titled "In Advance of a Broken Arm," which Perloff mentions in this new book: the shovel anticipates the snow and the broken arm; this is infrathin as metonymy or, indeed, as sleight (slip) of hand. Moreover, as with all Duchamp's readymades, the difference between art and not-art is infrathin. (Perloff cites Stevens's "The Snow Man": "Nothing that is not there and the nothing that is.")

Poetry is not made up (only) of big ideas or themes or grand contrasts—good and evil, love and hate, night and day, life and death—but (also) of microtonal shifts, as with the difference between *close, micro,* and *infra.* Over her many books these past fifty years, Perloff has shown, again and again, the supernal value of reading and sounding poems with preternatural attention of the "stuff" that makes them up—sound textures and rhythms alongside the choice of one word or phrase rather than other similar (possibly synonymous) words or phrases, repetitions, puns, and homonyms. Hence Perloff is a crucial commentator on all the poets she has written about: she can be counted on to account for what gives a poem its aesthetic charm or aura. Her work follows an inductive path, while never excluding relevant historical or biographical contexts. Moreover, Perloff's books are almost wickedly entertaining and enlightening—*wickedly,* if we think criticism should be less like a chocolate mousse and more like a dose of quinine and castor oil: medicinal. *Infrathin* is Perloff at her most delightful and insightful, with startling, fresh, indeed original, readings of some of her longtime passions—Yeats, Eliot, Pound, Stein, Duchamp (who invented the term *infrathin*), Stevens, Beckett, Howe, Ashbery, Armantrout, *und ich auch* (me too).

In the introduction to *Infrathin,* explaining her method, Perloff focuses on Goethe's sublime "Wandrers Nachtlied," in whose twenty-four words she finds several examples of the "infrathin." The poem comes into play in response to Jonathan Culler's discussion of it in his *Theory of the Lyric* (2015). Perloff questions Culler's foregrounding of the use of *du* (you) in the poem; for Culler, it is an example of a *you* that refers to the poet himself or to any one of us, but not, as in an apostrophe, turning from the poem to call out to *you, O you!,* dearest reader of these words. (Longfellow's deliberately archaic translation of *du* as *thou* forces the apostrophe.) If apostrophe is a centrifugal turning (*strophe*) outward, then infrathin is a centripetal turning inward (*patastrophe*). Perloff wants to redirect our attention to the ensemble of words in the poem, which she feels do not lead us to Culler's conclusion that the poem is about death and that this is what "Ruhest" (rest) suggests in the last line.

Perloff reads the final line of the poem as a reference to resting at end of day—*sometimes a rest is just a rest!*—and supports this reading with historical information about its composition in 1780. The difference between the two senses of this same word, *Ruhest,* is infrathin, but it is also the difference between living and dying. Perloff shows how getting the hang of (hanging out with) the poem's slopes and slips (not the same as understanding or interpreting) necessitates not (just) rhetorical or thematic analysis but minute attention to each word in the poem and to getting the sense through the rhythm and the micromodulations in the sound patterns.

If Goethe's title were translated not as "Wanderer's Nightsong" but as "Hiker's Nightsong," Perloff's interpretation would prevail; since she is primarily reading the poem in her native German, perhaps she does not get hung up on the translation, the homophone *wanderer*, which practically bleats its metaphoricity. (In Brooklyn, a wanderer is no day-tripper, except maybe one on LSD, though he could be a luftmensch.)

Translation choice is a good example of the significance of Perloff's poetics of the infrathin: the different, infrathin, choices made in translation have a profound effect on the meaning of this text. *Ruh* is in the second line of Goethe's poem, *Ruhest* in the last, but it is difficult to express this infrathin difference in English. Richard Stokes, in a standard translation used in music programs that include Schubert's setting of "Wandrers Nachtlied," has "Wait, soon you too / Will be at peace." Capitalization is another infrathin element: should it be *rest* or *Rest*?

In *Metaphors We Live By* (1980), George Lakoff and Mark Johnson note that *journey* is among the most basic cognitive tropes (not trips)—a metaphor for a day or a lifetime, for love or for an argument (for example: *while this commentary is short, we have come far*). Translating Goethe's title as "Wanderer's Nightsong" suggests the journey of the single poet; translating it "Wanderers Nightsong" suggests it is both our journeys, "du auch"—*you too*. What a difference an apostrophe makes (the other kind of apostrophe).

Perloff notes that "Kaum einen Hauch" (hardly, or barely, a hint/touch/breath/whiff) is an adequate symbol of the infrathin—*barely a trace*. In my American translation of "Wandrers Nachtlied," I try to cleave closely to the German (while acknowledging the inevitable cleavage), not to be faithful to an original but to explore the possibilities for an infrathin translation. I keep to Goethe's twenty-four words, the number suggesting the hours in a day's journey. Perloff and Culler both use thirty words and the common title, "Wanderer's Nightsong"; Zsuzsanna Ozsváth and Frederick Turner's "Wanderer's Night-Song" (following Longfellow's title) uses thirty-three words (their translation was first published in *Common Knowledge* 26:1, 2020).

"Kaum einen Hauch," *hardly a breath*: on the line between rest and death, in our journeys through the world, *here/not here*, the flickering rhythm of nightsong or breathing, toggling *presence/absence (fort/da)*, a strophic (stroboscopic) flip of you/me.

The line between rest and death is infrathin.

Wandrers Nachtlied

Über allen Gipfeln
Ist Ruh,
In allen Wipfeln
Spürest du
Kaum einen Hauch;
Die Vögelein schweigen im Walde.
Warte nur, Balde
Ruhest du auch.

Culler/Perloff	Culler
Above all the peaks It is calm, In all the treetops You feel Barely a breath; The birdies in the woods are silent. Just wait, soon You will rest too	Above all summits it is calm. In all the tree-tops you feel scarcely a breath; The birds in the forest are silent, just wait, soon you will rest as well!
Longfellow	**Zsuzsanna Ozsváth & Frederick Turner**
O'er all the hilltops Is quiet now, In all the treetops Hearest thou Hardly a breath; The birds are asleep in the trees: Wait, soon like these Thou too shalt rest.	The high peaks everywhere Are still; Scarcely a breath of air You feel Up in the treetops there: The birds have fallen silent too Wait for peace, wait still: It comes for you.

Wanderers Nightsong

Over all Crests
Is Rest
On high
You hear
Hardly a Breath;
The hummingbirds silent in nests.

Just wait until
You too will Rest.

for Marjorie Perloff, after Goethe

[2022: *Common Knowledge 29:1*]

14. Thirteen Controllable Vocabularies in Historical Vacuum Adores a Poem [Tan Lin]

I.

Tan Lin's poetry is just way too cool. Lin's poems are as chic as they are sharp and ingenious. They slap you in the face like a blue cheese in a sheep market. Lin returns us to the most traditional ideals for reading. Words, so transitory today, are fundamental elements that constitute Orphic engagements, singular among the many technologies that make up the shape of our rich semiotic landscape. You get the sense that Lin's words are meant to last forever. And they leave you feeling fresh and ready for a new day. By setting up a textual ecology—archiving and rejuvenating language—Lin makes us aware of something that is beyond both the material and ephemeral nature of words. Language is solid and palpable. Plunge the depths, close read, dwell, savor, project. Today these figments of eternity have come together between the covers of this book; tomorrow they'll be canonical. Also available in a wide selection of designer colors. This new book is a dazzling display of aesthetic élan and as charming as Magritte's pipe or Velazquez's Pope. In *Thirty-Three Uncontrolled Vocabularies in a Historical Vacuum Adores a Poem*, Lin makes language pop, sizzle, melt, careen, dodge, sparkle, and reform[ulate].

II.

Lin's work sparkles with unoriginality and falsification. He wants to make good on his sense of language as temporal and changing, subject to cancellation and decay, of language's harrowing, or is it hallowing, failure to specify anything in the here and now (as he puts it). Lin's poems are temporal processes cast into words: permeable, open, meandering. "Yes I am lying to you," he says. No he is not lying to you. Breathe / as you read.

III.

HEATH (PLAGIARISM/OUTSOURCE), NOTES TOWARDS THE DEFINITION OF CULTURE, UNTITLED HEATH LEDGER PROJ-ECT, A HISTORY OF THE SEARCH ENGINE, DISCO OS (Tenerife: Zasterle, 2006)

nominated for 15 Purple Globe awards
Best 2009 book © 2006
Best original pageplay
Best type designography
Best performance by a supporting actor (Heath Ledger)
Best typomancy
Best pageplay adapted from another source
Best concept
Best execution
Best book party
Best book by New York poet teaching in New Jersey
Best book—situation comedy
Best book—drama series
Best book—VVV
Best book—color/image
Best derivative effects

Special Jury Selection:
- Islas Canarias Badge ("The Canary")
- Quadrupple Con ("The Drupple") for Foreignness in a Domestic Production

The award ceremony was held on April 1, 2010, in the Make Believe Ballroom at nospace.no. *Heath* received the award for "Best Derivative Effects" and "Best 2009 book ©2006," widely considered among the bloggeoisie as the "it" award of the night. Lin accepted these two awards plus the "Canary" and "Drupple." The other awards went in a sweep to *Dancing with the Tsars* with the exception of "Best Book—drama series," which went to Larry David for *Curb Your Enthusiasm.* The notorious and widely shunned Lifetime Survival—"I'm famous and you're not"—Award went to Oyce Arol Oats.

Lin's acceptance speech was recorded from entirely found materials, with no intervention by editing, according to the best conceptual poetry practices (BCPP), and played back to the virtual mass audience on ambient

Blues-Tooth micro-speakers attached to the listener's body at five of the main acupuncture points; the text-generated audio was interrupted (113 seconds for every 33 seconds of text-audio) by bird calls from the Audubon Society boxed cassette set, *Sound of the Wilde: The Warble of the Yellow Bellied Sapsucker (You Motherfucker!) and Other Aviary Songs*. The audio portion of Lin's acceptance speech—"Tinkership today, *Tanqueray* tomorrow"—is not available at this time due to the sensitivity of its contents. When all personal and legal issues have been resolved, the speech will be available at tttppp:\\lin-tan.gps

Purple Globe Awards®, "The Canary"® and "The Drupple"®
are Registered Trademarks of "Web Log"®
Full information on the awards downloaded rules from htttpss://purple globeawardsforpoetry.gps
Heath is available for free pdf download in Braille for all PayPal customers from httpiou://plagiarismoutsourcenotestowardsthedefinitionofcultureun titledheathledgerproject-ahistoryofthesearchenginediscoo51.purpleglobe awardsforpoetry.gps

A NOTE ON THIS TEXT: It has been taken from a single found source without any editing, alteration, framing, or intervention, according to Best Conceptual Poetry Practices (BCPP). If you look hard enough, you will lose track of what you are seeking, and in the process discover many things of little or no interest.

[2010; section II is adapted from an introduction to Tan Lin's work I chose for *Boston Review*, published April Fool's Day, 1999; parts of section three appeared in *American Book Review* 31:3 (2010).]

15. Hung Meaning [Lyn Hejinian]

I've always been confused by the difference between the beautiful and the sublime. I mean if something is really beautiful, isn't it also sublime? Well, I see already I'm getting off on the wrong foot. And what do feet have to do with poetry anyway?

There's more to a poem than blue cheese!

This is meant to be a guide for reading one section of Lyn Hejinian's iconic *My Life*. I say iconic because there's no work from the 1970s or '80s that better shows the possibility of serially ordered, disjunct (*not* junk) sentences than *My Life*. The poem reads like a series of non sequiturs except that it all ties together, the way a series of at first unrelated clues starts to add up in a detective story. In *My Life*, the palpable sense of connection among the non sequiturs (*that's no non sequitur, that's my life!*) is aided and abetted not only by the striking repetition of phrases throughout the book, but also by a relatively simple device that Hejinian invented for the poem. The first edition of *My Life* was published in 1980 by Burning Deck, when Hejinian was thirty-seven. This version consisted of thirty-seven sections, each with thirty-seven sentences. In the 1987 edition, published by Sun and Moon, the poem was expanded to forty-five sections of forty-five sentences, reflecting Hejinian's age at the time.

Each section of *My Life* is set off by a keynote phrase, taken from another part of the poem. "What is the meaning hung from that depend" is the keynote of the section under consideration here. *So much depends*, William Carlos Williams famously writes, *upon a red wheelbarrow*. Depends is the mark not of subordination but consanguinity, as in, we're all in this together. The sentences in *My Life* are codependent but in a good way. None of them can stand on their own, but the ensemble shimmers.

What comes next? In my life, at least, I don't know what comes next. One afternoon it rains and then before you can call it a day I'm overcome by the sun. But it's really snowing, and I hear a piercing sound coming from under the rafters. Or the circuit breaker blows but it's not because I had the toaster and coffee maker on at the same time.

Just because something don't follow don't mean it don't come next, do it?

The sentence-to-sentence disjunction in *My Life* is not arbitrary but weighted, one moment to another, to create a constellation—a music of changing parts—that illumines the patterns of life lived, as reflected/refracted in/as writing. *My Life* is a crossover poem, a signal work of radically inventive poetry that is readable as memoir and autobiography.

Each sentence of *My Life* is beautiful because of the music made with the sequence of words (the turning of the phrases) but also because of a wistfulness verging on sentimentality (but never dwelling in it). That is to say, the beauty of the individual sentences is grounded in the exquisite valences of Hejinian's observations and sensibility.

You can see what I mean by looking at any sentence in the poem. The most memorable line in *My Life* is "A pause, a rose, something on paper." It comes up eighteen times in the poem and its meaning changes with each new context. "A pause" suggests the space between moments, the lacunae between the sentences, the sense of life as an unfolding series. A pause is a line. "A rose" brings to mind Gertrude Stein's "rose is a rose is a rose"; here, as in Stein, not a symbol, not *the* Rose, but a given instance flowering in its specificity—arising anew with each mention: memory's air/heir of Eros. "Something on paper" is the book in our hands, or our mind's eye—perhaps echoing Williams again, "no ideas but in things."

"As for we who 'love to be astonished'" is another emblematic phrase from *My Life*, that, like "A pause," also appears in this passage—and twenty-four other times in the poem. Here it is being astonished at the zoo seeing "Bubbles" the hippo, a childhood memory of amazement. In another instance, the phrase on its own, a pivot for the book, registers that each crystalline moment jogs the aesthetic sense, where love leads. The shock of each new sentence: stoned into sentience. But mostly astonishment is yoked to quotidian events and observations that hardly seem out of the ordinary. In *My Life*, the ordinary is astonishing.

The section at hand begins with a sentence without a verb, that is a fragment, three phrases without explicit connection: "A dog bark, the engine of a truck, an airplane hidden by the trees and rooftops." The phrases are metonyms and the string of three is metonymic of the structure of this long poem-in-prose. Metaphors and similes work by comparison, as in *my love is like a rose*, the beauty of the rose is compared to the beauty of the one loved, where, moreover, "rose" is not "a" rose, for example, the one decomposing in the street, but the symbol of beauty. Metonymy works differently: it's a part, a fragment, that evokes—perhaps *triggers* is more vivid—something else, something with which it has no metaphoric relation. An object—a keepsake—given to you by a parent, lover, or friend may evoke—every time you see or touch it—your relation to that person, but it is not a metaphor for the person or for the relation. *A dog bark* might involuntarily bring to mind a moment in childhood when you were suddenly left by yourself and you associate that moment with the bark of a neighbor's dog, for this was the first time you noticed it. A metonymic shard pierces the present with something absent or lost. *My Life* is an elegy, just as my life is shot through with the piercing light of what is *nevermore*.

Every word is a metonymic echo chamber. When I am writing I am Quasimodo, ringing one bell in counter-rhythm to the next. The poem is my cathedral.

People sometimes think fragments and disjunction underscore a lack of relation. In *My Life*, the metonymic structure sparks intensive unconscious, intuitive, *felt* connections, which can be more intense than logical or plot-driven ones. *My Life* may not have plot, but it's crackling with narrative.

Each sentence is beautiful. The work as a whole is sublime.

[2019: *The Difference Is Spreading: Fifty Essays on Modern and Contemporary Poems*, ed. Al Filreis and Anna Strong (Philadelphia: University of Pennsylvania Press, 2022). Re: Lyn Hejinian, *My Life* (Los Angeles: Green Integer, 2002), pp. 20–23: section set off by "What is the meaning hung from that depend."]

Weathermen
Whitman, Dylan & the Weather Underground

I make truce with you, Walt Whitman—
I have detested you long enough.

Ezra Pound, "A Pact"

You don't need a weatherman
To know which way the wind blows.

Bob Dylan, "Subterranean Homesick Blues"

1. The Weatherwomen's Terror

Women in the Weather Underground Organization, *Sing a Battle Song: Poems by Women in the Weather Underground Organization* (Queens, NY: Factory School/Southpaw Culture, 2006); originally published in 1975 by the Red Dragon Print Collective.

No one could miss the poetic fervor in *Prairie Fire: The Politics of Revolutionary Anti-imperialism*, the Weather Underground's 1974 manifesto (by Celia Sojourn, Jeff Jones, Bill Ayers, and Bernardine Dohrn, reprinted in 2003 by AK Press): one part Che, one part Dos Passos, one part Molotov cocktail, one part missing (screw loose):

> Our art, music, poetry, theater will interpret and awaken the relationship of ourselves to the world forces, acting on each other. Our culture will be insurgent, celebrating people's victories, and record the history of the struggle. We will support those who are still fighting and continue fighting ourselves. We will awaken our sense of being part of a world community. ARM THE SPIRIT![1]

1. *Prairie Fire: The Politics of Revolutionary Anti-imperialism: Political Statements of the Weather Underground* (NP: Communications Co., 1974), p. 41. Both *Prairie Fire* and *Sing a Battle Song: Poems of the Women in the Weather Underground Organization* have been collected, with related material, in *Sing a Battle Song: The Revolutionary Poetry, Statements, and Communiques of the Weather Underground 1970-1974*, ed. Bernardine Dohrn, Bill Ayres, and Jeff Jones (New York: Seven Stories Press, 2006). The original copyrights on the two books allow, indeed encourage, the kind of reproduction represented by Factory School's edition, published by Joel Kuszai, which replicates the original in every detail. The quotation below is from pp. 59–60 of this edition.

Factory School's Southpaw Culture series has reissued a book far more obscure than *Prairie Fire*—a collection of anonymously authored inspirational/agitprop, and sometimes feminist, poems from the same period and presumably the same (and related) folks who, though dangerously misguided, and destructive for US progressive politics, still smell sweeter than those in and around the US government who worked to actively, and often violently, undermine democratic governments abroad and domestic protest at home.

Despite their often-poignant cries against injustice and brutality, these poems are in some ways more wooden, self-conscious, and moralistic than *Prairie Fire*'s occasionally soaring prose. Factory School's provocative insistence that we (also) think of this political movement in terms of its poetry is not so much revisionist amelioration as a necessary coming to terms with the aesthetics of American radicalism. The failure of these poems is also the failure of the politics behind them, just as the failure of the politics is a failure of the poetics: the shackling of imagination to principle, the desperate need to be so clear and so accessible that nothing in particular is left to say, and an identification with the struggles of others so crushing that it fatally represses the struggles within oneself. This book provides telling evidence that you can judge a movement by its words, especially when the movement was primarily an act of rhetoric, a poem-in-action. In this respect, the Situationists, especially as their work morphed into the bumper-sticker slogans of 1968—from "We want nothing of a world in which the certainty of not dying from hunger comes in exchange for the risk of dying from boredom" to "Poetry is in the streets"—provide a powerful counter-model, as do the 1990s speeches/sayings of Subcommander Marcos (of Chiapas, Mexico).

Yet, still, there is, near the end of this brief collection, "For the SLA," a poem written in the spring of 1974. It is the most rhetorically powerful poem in the book and a prescient deconstruction of the use of the word "terror" by spokespersons of the state who use terror of the foreign to mask the terrorizing of the state's own people, as well as those in far-off lands. SLA, for those not of the moment or who missed the movie, is the Symbionese Liberation Army, the group that kidnapped Patty Hearst. Just think about the quality of mind among a group of US leftists who thought it was a good idea to kidnap, imprison, and brainwash an heiress. And no, this was not an episode of *South Park*. To come to terms with the poetics of this group, keep in mind that the Weathermen and women subjected themselves, and were in turn subjected, to a profound state of terror, as if to simulate the terror so many other people in the world experience, without recourse. Coming from homes of wealth and security, like a song might say, they chose lives of fear and penury. But living in such a state of terror, in turn, warped both their political and poetic judgments.

"For the SLA" is about a viral form of language abuse, the same viral abuse that, during the Vietnam war, called burning people to death "defoliation," or during the War against the People who live in Iraq, calls torture "interrogation." This poem reminds us that the powers that be have appropriated the terms of our common language with a nihilistic disregard for meaning that makes what gets called postmodernism seem innocent. They have done this so often and with such sociopathic abandon that, like the boy who cried wolf, their cries of terror ring hollow even when, as now, they might refer to acute dangers requiring a full measure of response.

The 1960s-era crisis of belief in the language of authority and government, a foundational breach of the ongoing culture wars, is epitomized in this poem by the Women of the Weather Underground:

They call it terror
if you are few and have no B-52s
if you are not a head of state
with an army and police
if you have neither napalm
nor tanks nor electronic battlefields
terror is if you are dispossessed
and have only your own two hands
each other
and your rage
It is not terror
if you are New York's Finest
and you shoot a ten-year-old Black child in the back
because you think Black people
all look like
they've just committed a robbery
It is not terror if you are ITT
and buy the men
who line Chilean doctors up in their hospital
corridors
and shoot them for supporting the late
democratic government of their country

It is not terror but heroism
if you were captured by the Vietnamese
for dropping fragmentation bombs
on their schools and hospitals
Only those who have nothing
can be terrorists

[2006: *The Brooklyn Rail*, December / January 2007]

2. Knockin' on Heaven's Door: Bob Dylan and the Adolescent Sublime

Bob Dylan, *Chronicles: Volume One* (New York: Simon & Schuster, 2004)

All is forgiven!
As soon as you're ready to come out of your room
We will be there to listen.
—Your fickle listeners

Bob Dylan and his *Chronicles* came to mind this past season at two unex-
pected places—the retrospective of the sculptor Eva Hesse at the Jewish
Museum and Richard Foreman's most recent show, *Zomboid!* Both Hesse
and Foreman are, like Dylan, part of a constellation of mostly poets I wrote
about in "The Second War and Postmodern Memory" (in *A Poetics*), all
born during World War II and all of whom respond, in often subliminal
and allegorical ways, to the systematic extermination process and the bomb.
(Hesse was born in 1936, Foreman in 1937, while Dylan was born in 1941; all
three are Jewish.)

I thought about Dylan, Hesse, Foreman, and such poets as Susan Howe,
Clark Coolidge, Ann Lauterbach, and Robert Grenier—all of whom
have articulated an idiosyncratic sensibility that averts group or genera-
tional identification (more commonly associated with those of us born in
the years immediately following 1945) in their deep aversion of confor-
mity (conformity even to oneself). The poem of Grenier's from *Phantom
Anthems*, which I quoted in "The Second War and Postmodern Memory"
is emblematic: each unit swerves from its repetitive uniformity through
the articulation of anomalies; the work is constituted by the seriality of its
anomalies—

o—u -
u—u -ni -
form—ity—o -
u—u—u—ni -
formity—o -
u—unit—de -
formity—u -
unit deformity[2]

Hesse died in 1970, so we have no way of knowing how she would have fared in a period of American culture, and an art world, that, since her death, turns ever more indifferent to eccentricity and ever more fascinated by money, fame, and market share. (But her posthumous career and fame has been stellar.) The poets, though, and such kindred spirits as Foreman, have managed to follow their own instincts, even when they might seem to lead them further and further astray. Their work has deepened with time, even while their audiences have remained relatively small.

Dylan's *Chronicles* invites a new, longer view of his vexed work, as a singer-songwriter and as a cultural figure. Dylan's book is designed, in part, to warp and perhaps avert readymade contexts. But it also calls to mind contexts that are not available within the stock frames of "Behind the Music" that Dylan rails against, teases, but to which he ultimately succumbs.

Bobby Zimmerman done good. From 1962, when, at the age of twenty-two he invented himself as Bob Dylan, and for the next thirteen years, ending with one his many masterpieces, *Blood on the Tracks*, when he was thirty-five, he wrote 'n' sung some of the most remarkable, buoyant, an' expansive works in the history of American song. Yet Dylan reached his apogee just five years after *Blood on the Tracks*, with his unredeemably lost "Christian" album (which he called, without evident irony, *Saved*). And now Dylan has released the first of what may be an ongoing memoir. The book attempts to grapple with what made those thirteen years possible and what happened after. Yet, from the point of view of dealing with what happened after 1975, the book is a strategic failure, since Dylan has about as much critical distance on himself as a trapeze artist in a lion's den. But then, the morale of his tale is that there is, indeed, no failure like success.

Chronicles could be described as Melville's *Confidence Man* meets Fellini's *8½*, with a touch of *Garbo Speaks!* (or possibly *Harpo Speaks!*). Flashes

---

2. "Song," in *Phantom Anthems* (Oakland: O Books, 1986), unpaginated [p. 27]

of brilliant let-me-do-th'talkin' prose sparkles amid a bevy of nameless wives and named producers. (I find myself particular attracted to the way Dylan cuts off the *ly* from the end of adverbs.) This is a funny, often witty, Great Adventure (a.k.a. picaresque tale), whose featured character plays, at times, the role of the Unhappy Camper: Paul Reubens might well be the ideal choice to play the lead in the movie version: My privacy was stolen! But for all the fun and local color, the book has the perfume of deep sadness fused with confusion that links imaginatively to Dylan's greatest songs, and, in the end, has the richness lacking in much of the singer-songwriter's work of the past thirty years.

I liked best Dylan's detailed account of the of '60s and the folk scene, maybe because I remember much of this myself, from the vantage of a high school kid going down to the Village to see Len Chandler and Richie Havens, both of whom make significant appearances here. Indeed, my teenage years were filled with concerts and records by Tom Paxton, Tim Hardin and Hamilton Camp, Richard and Mimi Farina, Leonard Cohen, Joan Baez, and Judy Collins. But also, as of 1968, Randy Newman, Van Dyke Parks, and Tiny Tim (whom Dylan writes about with warmth, suggesting a perhaps unexpected affinity). I have a vivid memory of seeing Bill Cosby at the Bitter End on Bleecker, just about the time his first album came out with his signature routine about staring in the mirror one day and discovering "little tiny hairs growing out my face."

My favorite singer/songwriter from this time, apart from Dylan and Newman, was Phil Ochs, who is never mentioned in his comrade's chronicle, which is a shame, given their connection in time, place, and approach; but Dylan is more interested in charting his connection to his imaginary generational comrades, Ricky Nelson and Frank Sinatra, Jr.—and indeed he plays the oddness of this to great effect.

I still recall when my brother (four years older than me and hanging out in the Village) put on that first Dylan disk in 1962—and I thought what is that sound, that rawness, that blast of full-bodied force. Dylan's voice embodied the opposite of the sweet-toned, in-tune pop and folk singers; indeed, it was a sort of voice brute or even voice concrète—a rejection of polish or finish, a virtuosic, rhythmically powerful merging of the ugly, the raw, and the untrained. This was what McLuhan called "hot" and it blasted out against the "cool" culture of the early '60s like a bucking bronco in a record shop. Dylan's howl, his willfully non-pretty singing, used the noise of the voice as the ground against which his words figured. In retrospect, I'd say the closest correlate to this was the Mississippi Delta blues of Charlie Patton (about whom Dylan has written a recent song), even more than

Robert Johnson, who is discussed in detail in *Chronicles*. It makes sense that Dylan gives so much credit to Dave van Ronk, for he got there, or near there, first.

Around the time I heard Dylan wailing "I'd DO anyTHING in this GOD Almighty WORLD if you JUST let me FOLLOW you down" from the room next door, I also discovered Al Jolson, buying six compilation LPs on the boardwalk in Atlantic City, where I had gone, with my sister and grandmother, just after my father's heart attack. My brother was quick to note that Dylan was the opposite of Jolson (and some of the other Broadway singers I liked at the time, in particular, much to my brother's disapproval, Sammy Davis Jr.); but perhaps Jolson and Dylan have more in common than meets the eye. Many of the dilemmas of *The Jazz Singer*, in terms of mimicry and identity, are also dilemmas for Dylan, who, after all, stops his narrative to discuss, in detail, his invention of the name Bob Dylan, just as the Jewish Asa Yoelson tells us how he became Al Jolson. Behind Dylan is not just Woody Guthrie but the Gershwins, Irving Berlin, E. Y. Harburg, and Oscar Hammerstein II. Dylan comes about as close to saying this as he can, noting his always happy, never ambivalent, identification as a commercial song writer. What brings this all back home, though, is his acknowledgment of the famous early '60s New York production of Kurt Weill and Bertolt Brecht's *Threepenny Opera* as a galvanizing experience.

We are all Brechtians now.

Early Dylan was blisteringly unsentimental; his voice projected, paradoxically, a convoluted, tangled, introversion, a voice that had drawn on the cacophony of free jazz and that symbolized the ascent of the rough over the smooth. All this would change in 1969 with the introduction of Dylan's new voice on *Nashville Skyline*, a voice he perfected in the parodic bliss of his most significant self-reinvention, *Self-Portrait* (which, given his interest in Rimbaud, could be more accurately titled, *portrait of self as an other*). Dylan grouses throughout *Chronicles* that he should not be taken at his word, that he is not, and could never be, authentic; but the narrative (in the book and in his music) is conflicted and ambiguous. On the one hand, Dylan portrays himself as the Brechtian performer, as an entertainer playing a role, or rather, as playing the role of an entertainer who plays roles. On the other hand, Dylan allegorizes his changes as a search for his "real" self, that is, a journey of self-discovery. Does Dylan betray folk music at Newport or is he being true to himself? Or is he being true to folk music by being true to himself?

"There must be some way out of here . . ."

Chronicles reveals Dylan to be in the sway of what Susan Schultz calls "a poetics of impasse": poetry that is stopped in its own tracks, hoisted on its own petards. Among her examples are Hart Crane, who is the second-wave modernist poet that bears the closest resemblance to Dylan, and Laura Riding, who stopped writing poetry in the late 1930s from a sense that her own artifice was in conflict with her desire for truthfulness.

From the first, Dylan hitched his star to a practice of nonconformity; but along the way he began to take nonconformity as something literal rather than metaphoric; the parodic lost its *jouissance* and became (in his own perception) a shell game. The problem is not that Dylan ever betrayed his listeners or his genres, quite the contrary, but that he came to feel, like the Lon Chaney figure in the "False Face" episode of *Way Out* (a 1961 TV show), that his roles and masks were not only impossible to shake off but that that they had taken possession of him.

(Like so many others in the 1960s, I was deeply attracted to Dylan's aversive response to the press of characterization; at the time I saw this as ironic and self-possessed, Dylan as trickster; in retrospect, it seems to me to reflect his inability to cope with the overwhelming response to his work, a malady to which he would ultimately succumb.)

In his memoir, Dylan is at pains to come across not as an iconoclast ('cept if the icon he wants to smash is "Bob Dylan": he is good at that) but as an autodidact. Being a proud autodidact is crucial to Dylan's self-presentation and he uses this identity as cudgel to explain his intentional and disconcerting avoidance of any connection (much less commitment) to the social grounding of his early songs. 'cordin' to Bob, it's all 'xplained by the Civil War, based on some mid-nineteenth-century newspapers he pored over in the library in the early '60s. This ain't history (any more than a memoir is history), but history used as a veil for an ahistorical, occasionally apocalyptic worldview. When, toward the end of the chronicle, our antihero insists that Master of War Hall o' Famer Barry Goldwater is the politician he most admires, you know that this incarnation of Bob Dylan is not one of Woody's people, even if we are deep in tall tale country. When you turn the page, it should no longer be a surprise, yet somehow it always is, in this looking-glass world, that Dylan is awe-struck (in his own wry way) with Archibald MacLeish but finds James Joyce too intellectually challenging to bother with.

Indeed, the Dylan of *Chronicles* is not so much apolitical as anti-political, because much of the effort of the book is directed at throwing the overly curious off the trail of the "true" person behind the songs. Moment to moment, the point of view of the writing appears disconcertingly inside the mind's eye of the narrator. Dylan practices his phenomenology as shell game: even his solipsism is a peek-a-boo charade. Because he allows himself almost no critical distance, it can feel as if the memoirist is offering himself as patient, etherized on the table. Few readers will resist making their own diagnoses, at least until they find themselves inside a carefully laid trap, designed to short-circuit just such arm-chair analysis ("it ain't me babe"). With his uncanny synthesis of vivid serial anecdotes and an unreliable narrator, Dylan is able, quite effectively, to counter expectations, characterizations, and the sort of clichés for which he has such a visceral disgust.

I liberally sampled "Shelter from the Storm" in one of the sections in a 1977 essay, "Three or Four Things I Know about Him" (collected in *Content's Dream*); I didn't even mention Dylan's name; since the lyrics were so much in the air, I thought no reference was needed. Some years later, Dylan was very much on my mind when I was writing an essay about poets born during the Second World War, "The Second War and Postmodern Memory." Dylan seemed to me then, and now, exemplary of a radical asociality and a determinately idiosyncratic sensibility that averts group or generation identification (more commonly associated with those of us born in the years immediately following 1945) in its deep aversion of conformity (conformity even to oneself).

Like early Eliot and Ginsberg, both mentioned with appreciation in this book, Dylan's early work is redolent with Adolescent Sublime. Yet *Chronicles*, written by a man in his sixties, is as much a work of Adolescent Sublime as is "Blowin' in the Wind" and "Like a Rolling Stone." In those songs, and others of that moment, Dylan echoes the reversals so prominent in one of Whitman's greatest poems, and certainly Whitman's most dystopian work, "Respondez!":

Let that which stood in front go behind! and let that which was
    behind advance to the front and speak . . .

Let none be pointed toward his destination! (Say! do you know your
destination?)

Perhaps then the moral of the story can also be found in "Respondez":

Let the reflections of the things of the world be studied in mirrors!
    let the things themselves still continue unstudied! . . .

Let the heart of the young man still exile itself from the heart of
the old man! and let the heart of the old man be exiled from that
of the young man![3]

Bob, we love you. Grow up!

[2006: *The Brooklyn Rail*, September.]

3. *I chant a new chant of dilation or pride*

In order to read Whitman, to make my pact with him, I have to get over
something that drives me crazy: the bombast, the flimflam pitch of Mel-
ville's confidence man—the very opposite of Dickinson's "I'm nobody,"
as when Whitman writes, in the preface to the 1855 edition of *Leaves of
Grass*:

*The greatest poet hardly knows pettiness or triviality. If he breathes into any-
thing that was before thought small, it dilates with the grandeur and life of the
universe. He is a seer . . . he is individual . . . he is complete in himself . . . the
others are as good as he, only he sees it and they do not. He is not one of the cho-
rus . . . he does not stop for any regulation . . . he is the president of regulation.*
(Italicized passages below are from the preface.)

Can someone who proclaims they are the "greatest" really be great? Pos-
sibly, but in that case the greatest poets are filled with pettiness, rivalry,
and triviality; that is what keeps them close to the ground and away from
the Profound Heights of Greatness (PHG) which, in nineteenth-century
American terms, is marked by Moral Purpose (MP) and High Class Di-
dactics (HCD), signifying the Great Poet (GP) is our social and moral
better, even if that entails that the GP's work is lacking those short and
intense stabs of sensation that Poe called supernal.

*The Americans of all nations at any time upon the earth have probably the
fullest poetical nature. The United States themselves are essentially the great-
est poem.*

"Of all nations at any time"? This is American exceptionalism on a com-
bination of steroids and acid. But something odd too: it's so hyperbolic
as to transcend its noxious content. Say, who is an American? Are these
altered "states"?

Other states indicate themselves in their deputies . . . but the genius of the

---

3. *Leaves of Grass*, 1867 edition, at whitmanarchive.org, pp. 280–83

*United States is not best or most in its executives or legislatures, nor in its am-
bassadors or authors or colleges or churches or parlors, nor even in its newspapers
or inventors . . . but always most in the common people.*

OMG. Not the ruling classes but we, the people, in order to form . . .

*The American poets are to enclose old and new for America is the race of races.
Of them a bard is to be commensurate with a people.*

So then does America mean the multicultural overlay of contradicting
people, black and white, immigrant and landed, Jew and gentile, Asian and
European, indigenous and settler? The American state has defined itself by
acts of exclusion, in the law and in practice. Are we "a people?" Not yet!:
"Are to" projects into a process.

We have not yet arrived. And never will. But we can move in the imper-
fect (more perfect) direction of the new.

*Of all nations the United States with veins full of poetical stuff most need
poets and will doubtless have the greatest and use them the greatest. Their Presi-
dents shall not be their common referee so much as their poets shall.*

You wish! Perhaps you could say, Poe almost does, that the United States
is the country with least regard for its poets, as much now as in the nine-
teenth century, because disdain for poetry as anything but a moral prop is
built into the fabric of these states. Whitman is echoing Shelley's "unac-
knowledged legislators," but close to George Oppen's "legislators of the
unacknowledged world." But I also think of Rosmarie Waldrop's refusal of
poets as any kind of legislators.

*The known universe has one complete lover and that is the greatest poet. He
consumes an eternal passion and is indifferent which chance happens and which
possible contingency of fortune or misfortune and persuades daily and hourly
his delicious pay. What balks or breaks others is fuel for his burning progress to
contact and amorous joy. Other proportions of the reception of pleasure dwindle
to nothing to his proportions.*

This comes close to Poe's supernal pleasure principal, but for Poe it is
the poem for poetry's sake, whereas Whitman cathects his cosmogonic
aestheticism onto the "greatest poet," an imaginary object that is looking
increasingly like Dickinson's "nobody."

*The messages of great poets to each man and woman are, Come to us on equal
terms, Only then can you understand us, We are no better than you, What we
enclose you enclose, What we enjoy you may enjoy. Did you suppose there could be
only one Supreme? We affirm there can be unnumbered Supremes, and that one
does not countervail another any more than one eyesight countervails another . . .
and that men can be good or grand only of the consciousness of their supremacy
within them.*

Not *from many one* but *from one many.* Whitman's delicious inversions explode meritocracy and the pernicious ideology of greatness as a zero-sum game.

Nobody's the greatest. The one that doesn't count.

"You don't understand! I could've been a contender. I could've had class. I could have been somebody. Instead of a bum, let's face it, which is what I am. It was you, Charley."[4]

Say, Are you nobody too? ("How dreary to be somebody.")

This is nobody exceptionalism.

There will soon be no more priests. Their work is done.

Amen.

[2019: *Every Atom; Reflections on Walt Whitman at* 200, ed. Brian Clements, *North American Review* 157. All quotations from *Leaves of Grass*, 1855 edition, at whitmanarchive.org; the title quote from p. 26, the rest from the preface, pp. iii–xii.]

4. *On the Waterfront* (1954), screenplay by Budd Schulberg

Three Flasks of Gin with a Flax Chaser

FENG YI: *It has been more than ten years since you were first interviewed by Professor Nie Zhenzhao in 2007.[1] In the interview with Nie, you said that the influence of classical Chinese poetry and philosophy on American poetry had been profound from the nineteenth century onward, but you also implied that the influence had been subtle and indirect, with a lot of cultural variations and adaptations in the exchanges. My first question is about the relationship between your poetics and traditional Chinese philosophy. I saw the analogues between Zen-Taoism and your poetics and wrote an essay about it. I wonder how do you think Zen-Taoism reflects your poetics, namely, your echopoetics?*

I am grateful to you for your essay on this topic published in a recent issue of *boundary 2*.[2] When I read your essay, I felt that yes, the connections you were making were right, that this was something I was quite conscious of, but also something that I did not wish to claim. Coming of age in the 1960s in New York, philosophical winds from East swept over us, intoxicated us, changed us, even as it mixed up—and often badly confused—Chinese and Indian sources. Bengali poet Runa Bandyopadhyay's essay, also in the *boundary 2* issue, on the relation of my work to classical Indian sources was, like yours, immensely useful to me.[3] You both know what you are talking about! Me, less so.

In the 1960s, we carried in our pockets cheap paperback editions of Laozi, the sayings of Buddha, and the *Bhagavad Gita*, went to lectures by

1. Nie Zhenzhao's interview was originally published in *Foreign Literature Studies* (Wuhan); a translation was included in *Pitch of Poetry*.

2. "The Epiphany of Language: The Connotation of Zen-Taoism in Charles Bernstein's Echopoetics," in *Charles Bernstein: The Poetry of Idiomatic Insistences*, ed. Paul Bové, *boundary 2* 48:4 (2021)

3. "Pataquericalism: Quantum Coherence between the East and West in Charles Bernstein's Echopoetics"

Indian swamis that were accompanied by psychedelic light shows, heard Ravi Shankar play ragas at Lincoln Center and Allen Ginsberg chant *om* in college auditoriums, sang along with Pete Seeger's *Ecclesiastes*, listened to Alan Watts's and D. T. Suzuki's Zen lectures (tailored for Western ears) on the radio, cast sticks to find our fortunes in the *I Ching*, read Hermann Hesse's *Siddhartha* (1922) along with Thoreau and the *Upanishads*. What this promiscuous mix planted in my mind only time would tell, but I was, and am, wary about its relation to the Chinese and Indian sources. We were looking for an alternative to Judeo-Christian (and capitalist) goal-oriented morality, something that valued the flickering moment—"be here now" in the famous slogan of Ram Dass, born Richard Alpert, the LSD guru's Timothy Leary's comrade, both tossed out of Harvard just five years before I started there.

In your latest poetry collection, Topsy-Turvy *(2021), you quoted from* Tao Te Ching. *For instance, there are lines from* Tao Te Ching, *in "Twelve-Year Universal Horoscope": "What is most full seems empty. Yet its use will never fail. What is most straight seems bent. The greatest skill seems like clumsiness. The greatest eloquence like stuttering."*[4] *How do these classic lines in* Tao Te Ching *resonate with the voice in your poem?*

"Twelve-Year Horoscope" includes a certain amount of "wisdom" sayings with alcohol recommendations and zany astrological-sounding pronouncements, along with genuine zingers like the line you quoted from *Tao Te Ching* and a couple of marvelous phrases of Wallace Stevens, a favorite poet. The poem swerves from satire to something else again, maybe just when you realize that liquor is a *spirit*. My epigrammatic spiritedness comes from many sources, including the German Romantic poet Friedrich Schlegel, and the early twentieth-century Jewish writer and satirist, Karl Kraus. Schlegel's *Über die Sprache und Weisheit der Indier* (*On the Language and Wisdom of the Indians*, 1808) locates the origins of Western civilization in Sanskrit, something my dear friend, Thomas McEvilley, echoes in his epic study, *The Shape of Ancient Thought* (2001). As I say, I don't know about all that. But I do know that what goes around comes around, like they say. What I do joins together disparate (sometimes desperate) and discrete particulars, turning them round and round and upside down in the echo chamber of the poem.

4. *Topsy-Turvy* (Chicago: University of Chicago Press, 2021), p. 152; Laozi, *Tao Te Ching*, tr. Arthur Waley (London: George Allen & Unwin Ltd., 1934)

I notice that there is a large amount of blankness in your poems. Would you please talk about why these blankness, emptiness, and silence are intentionally left in your poems?

I told a friend of mine, who has achieved great success in American poetry, "you really stand for something."

Me, I stand for nothing. And not even that.

But I'll sit for a good cup of wonton [云吞] soup and an egg roll [蛋卷]. (It may seem odd, but wonton soup and egg roll are comfort food for many secular New York Jews—and not only Jews—children and grandchildren of immigrants: we often went out for Chinese food, notably on Christmas.)

I have nothing to say about this, *nothing* in the sense of *a lot. Nothing* in the sense of *no thing* (how can you convey that quality of the English word in Chinese?). In the sense of *not one thing.* I've often used this word along with *blank, blankness, emptiness, empty* in a generative sense, but it does grate against the Judeo-Christian tradition, where *nothing* is no good, suggesting the absence of God and morality. You can see this echoed in T. S. Eliot's iconic title, *The Waste Land,* a world without meaning or purpose, filled with unbelievers. *Genesis* begins with a "void," or perhaps an "emptiness," from which the light of divine creation comes. Is that void like a black hole (or again, an English homonym, sorry!, *black whole*)? The Hebrew is *ohu va-Vohu* (תֹהוּ וָבֹהוּ): unformed (or without form) and empty. But this could also be *potentiality*, openness.

Another book I carried around in high school, though it was too big to fit in my pocket, was the bible of existentialism, *Being and Nothingness* (1943), by Jean-Paul Sartre. The tag line has become a cliché, *existence precedes essence* (essence in the sense of meaning and values). Sartre intended to turn this idea of value on its head (topsy-turvy). We humans create our values, not God. It's a view that often gets mislabeled, but just as often is embraced, as *nihilism*: there is no meaning or purpose to life, just nothingness.

And all the while we were listening to the great leftist folk singer, Woody Guthrie. In "This Land Is Your Land," which is for many of us the real American national anthem, he points to a sign that says PRIVATE PROPERTY. On the other side, Guthrie sings, it doesn't say *nothing.* "This land is made for you and me."

I often say that disagreement in poetry is theological, though those who would condemn poetry like mine as *meaningless* don't see the view as theological as much as just common sense or upright and socially responsible. The French poet, Edmond Jabès, says that meaning occurs not in the formed letters or words but in the *blank space* between them, in the potential for infinite combinations that is a space of openness *as blank*. This is the basis of *echopoetics*: meaning is not in any one letter or word, but in the resonance among them and the possibilities for infinite recombination, in what Blake calls the "Echoing Green." That is the space of no thing—or of infinite possibility of things, newly forming at each moment. You could say this is a poetics of transvaluation: turning what may at first appear as a deficit into its opposite, but also seeing the catastrophic problems with fixed (ahistorical / invariant) ideas of morality and meaning.

Early in college (at Harvard), I took a course on the *Upanishads* with Raimon Panikkar, which I loved. Panikkar was not only a Vedic scholar but also a Catholic priest. He was interested in the connections—points of contact—between different ontological belief systems. He started the class by saying that while *Genesis* imagines creation as beginning in terror, the *Rigveda* begins in wonder. Being cognitively prone to inverting opposites (I tend to go east when I should be going west), I was never sure about the difference. *Light precedes logos* sounds a little like existentialism and I was always attracted to the idea that creation, as we know it, is the rending of some anterior whole/hole, which brings to mind the Kabbalah (Jewish mysticism).

What is most full seems empty.
But then what do I know?
          —Nothing I can't say.

I see the subtle and deep integration of the Eastern and Western ideas in your answer. The line follows "What is most full seems empty" in Tao Te Ching *is "Yet its use will never fail." In other words, by emphasizing emptiness or nothingness in the "most full," namely, the undoing / inaction (无为), it says that its use will never end. You seem to indicate that readers should leave behind traditional verbal analysis and adopt an overall insight into these "deficits," or nothingness, to reverse it into something aesthetically valuable. What linguistic levels do you suggest your readers look for or take into consideration to reverse the nothingness in a relatively successful way?*

Your take on what I am suggesting seems right to me and, usefully, it's more explicit. I like to be a bit hazy in response, something like fuzzy logic: *fuzzy poetics*. Within American democratic social space, I often argue for the syncretic and miscegenated; in America that reflects the pluricultural facts on the ground. It's what makes America so different from China. The danger of this "free association" is that it can trample the integrity of individual histories and in so doing create, in reaction, increase ethnic/cultural/national conflict. Moreover, there is a danger of creating one super-massed-media culture, which leads to homogenization, which I abhor. So, my particular "mix" is not meant to be universal, not centrifugal, not one-size-fits-all, something I see as problem with the way "Surrealism Beyond Borders" was pitched at a show at the Metropolitan Museum of Art in New York in 2021. In contrast, I'd say: "ideosyncratic," antinomian, and—as would go for the spin of echopoetics—centripetal.

I'm not making any claims that my echoes or allusions connect, or show an allegiance, to a systematic philosophy or religion or even body of literature. There's no necessity for readers to recognize the allusions or echoes—or to follow them up. The test for me is that what I "sample" will come to life in the poem and in my inner ear and, because of that, will permit me to take responsibility for it. Whatever truth there may be, it is for readers to find and to respond.

What I am proposing, then, is a poetics of syncretic immanence.

Just before the passage you quote from the *Tao Te Ching*, there is a line, "the most perfect seems imperfect" [大成若缺], that brings to mind Emerson's idea of "moral perfectionism" (as interpreted by Stanly Cavell): that we never arrive at our goal, perfection, but are always *on the way*; that what seems "perfect" would be closed off, complete but no longer *completing*, and so would fail at being perfect. This also echoes in one of America's founding ideas, the forming of "a more perfect" union (in the Preamble to the Constitution)—not perfect, but moving toward a perfect that, by its nature, can never be achieved, for if achieved it would be DOA ("dead on arrival" as the police say). (I discuss this in "In Unum Pluribus: Toward a More Perfect Invention," my 2011 CAAP keynote collected in *Pitch of Poetry*.) The later line you cite from the *Tao Te Ching*, chapter 45, "其用不窮"—"Yet its use will never fail" in your version—I hear as *can't be exhausted*, rather than *can't fail*, because it has always/already un-used potential. The precept that *use* cannot be exhausted has a curiously Wittgensteinian / pragmatic echo: *meaning is use / not absolute*. But as to failing being a measure of success, Samuel Beckett's much quoted "fail better," but also a line from Bob Dylan, that we all sang as part of the late '60s mix I have been evoking, "There's no success like failure, and . . . failure's no success at all" ("Love Minus Zero / No Limit," 1965).

I take your question to be about teaching and I had the pleasure of your being with me for several classes, so you well know my practice, which is documented on my Penn website (writing.upenn.edu/Bernstein) and in my essays.[5] The fundamental work of teaching is listening rather than speaking, listening that informs you about what needs to be addressed; listening in pursuit of undoing the expectations that readers may have about finding a poem's meaning in its "theme." The fundamental work of the reader is also listening: an immersion into poetry, being born again into it, dunked in that water—listening without trying to figure out (as one might with music). I am all for interpretation, but that *cometh* later, once one has the hang for what one is interpreting. The sound/form/performance precedes the meaning.

Reading a poem is kind of *doing*.

大盈若沖, to come back to that again, could also be *a big profit is a big flush*—what you gain, seen in one frame, is a big loss seen in another, as "what profits a person to gain the world and lose their soul?" that familiar question from the New Testament. In fuzzy poetics: what value is there in extracting the "meaning" of a poem but losing its reason for being, losing its soul?

Great poetry needs direct communication between souls. This resonates with "The text doesn't stand" or "Pu-li-wen-tzu" (不立文字) in Zen's sense. I remember that you taught John Cage's poetry in your class and in the past interview with Maurizio Medo, you said that you loved John Cage and his famous 4'33".[6] I notice that you would also use silence or split words apart into explosive and fricative sounds in your poetry. Could you please tell me why silence and noisy sounds are important in your poem?

Or maybe not just "direct" but indirect, diffuse, ambient, osmotic communication. *Touching* rather than understanding (standing under), though I am sure that is what you mean by *direct*. We could generate a new aphorism: *the most direct communication will seem indirect.* I was thinking of something like that with my early title *Shade*—we see better in the shade than in the blinding light of the sun, one might say the fierce light of technorationality.

Reason is in the shade; rationality's shorn of it.

But there is something else going on with seeing value in what appears worthless, eloquence in what is stigmatized as stuttering, perfection in what is rejected as flawed, or the modernist sleight of hand: turning the ugly into the beautiful (or is that just taken from a fairy tale?!)—all of

5. Full set of syllabi at <writing.upenn.edu/Bernstein>

6. "Bernstein and Various Voices / Cento: Interview with Maurizio Medo (Peru)" in *Charles Bernstein: The Poetry of Idiomatic Insistence*

which might better be called a social, rather than a fuzzy, poetics (though the two are intimately connected). This is what, following Baudelaire, is called "transvaluation." And it connects up to a poetics of disability, where we can speak of *deficit gain,* on the model of a loss of sight might be related to more acute hearing (perhaps this could be called an ecology of the senses). Where one might have, in a modernist sense, celebrated "deformance," perhaps more useful now (to respond to a note from Daniel Snelson) to say re-formance, if not just performance. This has always been a preoccupation of mine—poetry as an imaginative act of reversal of stigma.

Silence and noise are interconnected in terms of entropy in information theory. The degeneration of the signal produces noise. But poetry is not about sending a message; it's an activity of re-sounding language, playing the signal as one might a harp. *Noise* to those looking for the message, *music* of ethernity (to use Jarry's pataphysical term) to the rest of us. Cage's view of silence was that there can be no absolute silence short of death, but that when we silence the dominant signal, we begin to hear other things. So, to go back to your previous question: to learn to read poetry, the kinds of poetry I want anyway, means learning to listen differently, listen to what might have seemed like background noise, static, empty, blank.

A BLANK IS A BLINK.

But there is another sense of silence, the kind American feminist poet Adrienne Rich addressed in acknowledging those who are, or have been, silenced, shutdown, ignored. This is a silence that can be broken by poetry, but I'd also say it is silence that speaks in poetry. One of the problems with hegemonic (dominant) language conventions being linked to personal expression is that those silences, but also things/ideas silenced, may not be conveyed, like a message, in a conventional and "clear" style; indeed, the demand for such uniformity may itself be silencing. I realize this concern is stigmatized as elitist and aesthetic, as the product of privilege, by those speaking in the name of social justice and witnessing. Ironically, the discursive modes they champion may themselves be compromised by its privilege, a privilege that discredits nonconforming, or wild, language. When the dead speak, we may not understand them, *at least not at first* (to echo Rich's title, itself from Ibsen, "When We Dead Awaken").

When the dead awaken, we need to listen, as if to a new language.

I mostly thought of direct communication in the sense of Zen-Taoism, and I think that your new aphorism "the most direct communication will seem indirect" makes sense in Zen. Let us take the communications between a Zen master

and his disciple as an example. Once, it is said that when a disciple asked:
"Master, what is Zen?" "Bricks," the master answered. Another time, a disciple
asked, "Master, what is Tao?" The master said: "Three Jin of flax" (Jin is a unit
of weight). The communication here is diffuse and ambient and can be most
direct and the most indirect, which calls for insights and epiphanies. My next
question is about the relationship between your poetry and painting. You once
mentioned that you got involved with visual art, such as abstract expressionist
paintings and Pop art, in your earlier career as a poet. Has the interplay of
words and pictures played a part in "the new language"? Would you talk about
the relationship between your poetry and abstract visual art?

I love Zen koans, with their apparent non sequiturs. Micropoems, don't
you think? My work is filled with fractured, twistering aphorisms. The
comic and enigmatic undercuts the high-seriousness and proscriptive
quality of much religious teaching. And there is also a midrashic aspect—
rabbis arguing over contradictory interpretations of the text at hand.
We could call those Zen Cohens, if you can bear the terrible pun on the
common Jewish name (which is the name associated with an ancient caste
of Jewish priests).

What is the sound of one hand clapping?
—The poem for a reader.

What is poetry?
—Three flasks of gin with a flax chaser (a Zen scone).

Verbal language has a juridical and informational function that makes
it seem different from the language of music and visual art, though
iconicity is inevitable in all human art forms. As much as I appreciate
listening to poetry as if it were music or art, I am also interested in *reading*
visual art and *textualizing* music. One result might be recognizing that
the difference between figurative and "abstract" is a matter of interpre-
tation: no visual mark is free of iconicity. This is what is so significant for
me about the Chinese calligraphy as a means of performing poems. The
Metropolitan Museum of Art generally does not translate the poems in
its sublime Chinese calligraphy collection, which may encourage looking
at these works as if they were abstract visual art. In fact, they do look a
bit like the work of Franz Kline and other abstract expressionists. Do the
different versions of a poem change the "meaning" of the poem? Does

seeing the calligraphy performed live, as if it were a dance, change the "meaning"?

What is meaning?
—Not bricks.

I want to read a poem as if it were a poem.

Yes, I think that Zen koans are micropoems. I would like to have "Three flasks of gin with a flax chaser" and very possibly I will have some epiphany after that! So, yes, Chinese calligraphy can look like some works by Franz Kline. However, the English language is based on alphabet. Do you think that there are some reconciliations between your poetry and visual art? What are the analogies in techniques between your poetry and visual art?

A poem is visual on a page and acoustic when heard. These are dual, not entirely reconcilable, ontologies of the event of the poem. Let's call it *quantum poetics*. There is no fixed original of a poem, no "poem itself," to echo Kant. Poems shift shapes over time and as perceived by different readers. In this sense, all approaches to a poem are a type of translation. At the same time, the poem being written is a translation of a blank, which is to say, an unrealizable (or inexhaustible), source. That is why we sometimes say that the poet is writing the same poem over and over again.

All the versions of the poem converge at a *tache blanche*, a blank or blind spot.

Much ink has been spilled about the difference between the Chinese written character and the alphabet. Suffice it to say that the Chinese written character is more semantic and the alphabet more iconic than is sometimes recognized.

The layout of the poem on the page is crucial to its meaning. For Western, modernist poetry, we often point to Mallarmé's *Un coup de dés* (1897) as the paradigmatic poem of the "white space" of the page, where the "blank" or negative space of the page is as significant as the alphabetic inscription. In such poems, the visual field of the poem is not just a matter of design. The closest thing to this semantic dimension of the blankness of the page might be line breaks. Indeed, line "brakes" are as much a visual as a metrical measure. And then there's the whole large range of visual poetry which pushes against the fixity of lines and letter shapes.

Still . . . it's a very different experience to see words out of the context of information-giving compared to visual inscriptions, since we don't necessarily associate visual display with giving information, even though much information is conveyed by visual means. For this reason, treating words as if they are plastic material can be provocative. Xu Bing's marvelous Chinese written characters, composed of alphabetic letters, is a comic dance of quantum poetics, a tango (and tangle) of Wittgensteinian ducks and rabbits.

We cognitively process words differently than visual signs, just as we process speech-sounds (even of a language foreign to us) differently than other kinds of sounds. Roman Jakobson thought of poetry as hearing verbal language as if it were not verbal: hearing the materiality, the whoosh and whoop, of the sonic. That materiality is always a social materiality. And it is this social materiality that gets translated away if we listen only for information or story or content.

I'd like to transform Ezra Pound's saying, "literature is news that stays news," into *poetry is noise that stays noise.* I've got a nose for noise, for the sheerness of the social materiality as embodied by sound and, let me call it, *sprung semantics.* And, indeed, as you insist, this is analogous to the sheerness of visuality and visual iconicity (figuration) in radical modernist and contemporary art.

In Pitch of Poetry, *you invent a poetic term, pataquerical, which is related to the poetics of failure and noise, etcetera. What does the pataquerical interfere with? Would you please talk about why the pataquerical is an important force in American poetry?*

Over the more than fifty years I have been writing, I've invented many novel literary terms and rubrics. I am wary of sticking to any one name because I want to keep terms turning: wildly and wily provisional.

This makes for difficulties.

To old friends, I may seem to have moved on from the approach we took collectively in L=A=N=G=U=A=G=E. But I saw L=A=N=G=U=A=G=E as a gathering point (a point blank), indeed, an *unschooling*, even unspooling, a place to explore possibilities. (We agreed more on what we didn't like than what we did.)

Not a be all nor an end all but an *opening call*, where things (and poets) newly discovered become as important as those established.

Schools or movements or rubrics lose aesthetic and epistemological force when they get hemmed in by self-defined genre motifs. I've discussed that here in terms of "abstraction," "surrealism," and now "language"; let's add the poem of lyric interiority and its bedfellow, the social justice lyric. Pataquerics is meant to be comically unsettling and resistant to reification. But (only) *nothing* is resistant to reification and my desire to write "characteristically uncharacteristic" poems is itself all too characteristic.

I wouldn't say a poet shouldn't write in a similar style across a lifetime, though the meaning of those poems will change in and with time.

I don't want to say *shouldn't*, since then that becomes a rule. But I can't help myself. My language did this to me (to echo Jack Spicer's last words).

I have defined (and refined and deformed) preferences and aversions, some personal and some social. One of my aesthetic precepts is, indeed, *the most unruly is the more perfect*. It's similar to the aesthetic preference for torn edge versus straight cut, unbalanced over symmetrical, bumply or clumpsy over smooth, inconsistency over constancy, upside down more than right-side up. Those preferences become formulas. But in my case, they are also lived, felt perceptions and connect to cognitive deficits transformed by poetic justice: deficit gain. Pound called his translations of Confucius, *The Unwobbling Pivot*. What I'm after, or in the thrall of, or maybe just trying to get from under, is *The Swerving Spigot*.

The Hobbling Rivet.

Not unbalanced. Balanced differently. Balanced by other means.

I swerve for poetry.

I see you "swerve for poetry," by transforming and deforming English words in your poems. In your poetry, it is contrasts, puns, bathos, ironies, and humors that swerve and bring life to poetry. Would you please say something about how humor and irony play a role in the swerve of the pataquerical?

I'm attracted the pessimistic quip—"nothing changes." But *nothing* is the one thing that can't change. On this side of nothing, everything wobbles. *Wobbling* (the title of a marvelous 1981 poetry collection by Bruce Andrews, which was later echoed in Rae Armantrout's 2018 collection *Wobble*) is a mark of the presence of time. People like to say, to illustrate a linguistic theory, that the indigenous people of Alaska and Siberia have 22.22 different words for snow; that turns out not to be true because the 22.22 are varieties of snow, not different words for the White-Stuff-that-Falls-from-the-Sky. But there are 11.11 words for the spectrum that goes from comedy to irony to sarcasm to puns to bathos. These are different things, not varieties of the same. I use them all.

Comedy can be disarming, which is useful if you are inclined to think the culture that surrounds you is armed. My kind of comedy has a way of diffusing difference, awkwardness, foreignness. Strange to say, one can be a foreigner even in one's own language. In fact, what I find strange is people who don't feel estranged. That's my home ground and I share it with all kinds of people.

Then again, the comedy I use is sometimes linguistic pratfalls: mistakes proliferate. That may be a way to cover my own cognitive dyspraxia, my tendency to invert words and letters and confuse left and right. Freud called such slips of the tongue *parapraxis*. And that's another root of pataquerics.

It's funny, if that's the word, how our conversation keeps revolving around cosmologies (not to be confused with cosmetology), which are, after all, a kind of poetics, a worldmaking.

I don't know much about cosmology, but I know what I don't like.

I have long been drawn to the pre-Socratics. There is something delightfully wacky about Heraclitus's fragments and Zeno's paradoxes. Both figures appear in *Topsy-Turvy* and, in an infrathin joke, I spell Heraclitus two ways in different poems in the book. More infrathin: In "Me and My Pharoah" in *Near/Miss* I have this line—"Xeno and Heraclitus are my father's milk."[7] (The common expression "mother's milk" refers to one's mother tongue or first language.) I certainly am alluding to Zeno here, but by spelling it with the homophone "xeno," I refer to the meaning of that word in Greek—foreign or other, my *other* milk.

Comedy can be a tangled web and, if all goes well, I trip myself up without hurting anyone.

It's a poem after all.

You can never step into the same joke twice.

But it can sure seem like you are.

Lucretius comes along hundreds of years after Zeno with an exquisite sense that "things happen" without rhyme or reason. That's the poetry of it. He keeps the awe by being wary of ascribing meaning and purpose to "things." Thing's nature (*rerum natura*) is atoms swerving as they collide in the void: the swerve makes for change and for freedom.

How about this origin story: In the beginning, just to break up all the deadening null and void, there was laughter.

I like this origin story with optimistic laughter, which forms a swerve with the "pessimistic quip" at the beginning of this answer! Your answer exemplifies the swerve of the pataquerical, the worldmaking. Since 1993 when the first

---

7. *Near/Miss* (Chicago: University of Chicago Press, 2018), p. 81

Language Poetry collection was translated by Zhang Ziqing and Huang Yunte,
a collection that includes you, Hank Lazer, and James Sherry, more and more
Chinese readers have learned about Language Poetry, and many Chinese poets
have become interested in it, too. Nie Zhenzhao and Luo Lianggong, then Liu
Zhaohui, together with other Chinese translators and scholars, published their
translations of your poems and essays on poetics in 2011 and 2013, respectively.
More recently Rae Armantrout and Mei-mei Berssenbrugge have also been
published, in translation, in China. How do you feel about your works being
translated into Chinese?

I have been fortunate to have been involved with Chinese poets, scholars,
and translators for three decades, all the while realizing how one-sided
these exchanges are, since I don't know Chinese. These conversations have
enriched my life and my work. And I am still catching up on my reading
of my contemporaries in China, dependent on the far too limited amount
that is translated.

I was fortunate to meet Huang Yunte in the early 1990s, when he came
to Buffalo as a graduate student, just a few years after leaving China. He
has been a crucial guide for me, and trusted friend, whose writings have
created a bridge between America and China, including his scholarly
books, *Transpacific Displacement: Ethnography, Translation, and Intertextual
Travel* (2002) (based on his Buffalo dissertation) and *Transpacific Imag-
inations: History, Literature, Counterpoetics* (2008), his books on popular
culture figures, Charlie Chan and the Siamese Twins, and his magisterial
*The Big Red Book of Modern Chinese Literature: Writings from the Mainland
in the Long Twentieth Century* (2016).

Translation provides the opportunity for transformation. It's a thrilling,
enthralling process, especially when the cultural barriers are as great as
between Chinese and American English. In this interview, we've talked
about several overlaps between East and West. Nonetheless, many core
aesthetic and cultural assumptions are not shared, so any literal transla-
tion, one that does not account for these differences, is averting the *task* of
the translator, to use Walter Benjamin's word. (Benjamin's German word
is *Aufgabe*, which has Hegelian echoes, suggesting both the problem of
freedom and the problems of philosophy.) A frequently cited example of a
Chinese/American translation "problem" concerns Bei Dao. If an English
translation makes him seem like a conventional American lyric poet, then
the cultural significance of his work is entirely lost. Maybe this task can
only be accomplished through a paratext: footnotes or commentary. But
another approach is suggested by Huang Yunte's *Shi* (1997), where he
breaks down the translation of classical Chinese poetry by the elements of

the written characters, so you get a more direct feeling of the sequence of linguistic "stuff" in the poems he translates.

In the early 1990s, I received a set of detailed letters from Zhang Ziqing. Those letters were filled with the kind of questions I often get from translators, including, more recently, and ever delightfully, you. When I write a poem, I don't have to know what a phrase I invent means, I don't have to parse it or explain it. It just needs to work for me. As you know as a translator, I make a lot of things up, twist expressions around, come up with inscrutable sayings. In translating, it's helpful to have some sense of the ingredients that make up the "stew," the *echoes*. I loved Zhang's questions and felt he had gotten to the heart of my poetics. Many of his questions concerned cultural references that he could not possibly know or look up (even if he had had access to the internet, which had not yet been created). His questions were not about my unusual syntax, rhetoric, tone, diction, prosody, or vocabulary—all the conventionally difficult elements of a translation that, because of his great knowledge, he was able to determine on his own. Rather, his questions were about the syncretic language (and imaginaries) I had invented that echoed often ephemeral aspects of American culture and personal associations: cultural samplings I had turned upside down and run through my trademark set of funhouse mirrors. Zhang had a genius for flagging my odd coinages and confections. I found his letters were becoming a poem, not just about my work, but also about the exhilaration of translation and the gaps fomented by cultural difference. So, using the letters, I composed "A Test of Poetry." That work, translated into seven languages (though not Chinese) is a favorite work of mine and is a comic and telling poem about translation—not just the limits but the possibilities.

From misunderstanding comes the greatest understanding.

I love your poem, "A Test of Poetry," and I really hope that this poem can be translated into Chinese in the future. I also think that although some good work has been done in translation, still a lot more should be done in the future, especially translating contemporary Chinese poems into English. Indeed, sometimes misunderstandings can break the ice of barriers and bring the possibilities for a deeper understanding.

Stein Stein Stein

τὸ μὲν οὔ τί σ' ἐίσκομεν εἰσορόωντες . . .
σοὶ δ' ἔπι μὲν μορφὴ ἐπέων, ἔνι δὲ φρένες ἐσθλαί.
μῦθον δ' ὡς ὅτ' ἀοιδὸς ἐπισταμένως κατέλεξας

Odyssey 11: 362ff

(We don't suppose you are a cheat or liar.
Your words have grace. The tale you tell
is told with art, as by a poet.)

1. Three Steins

Fifty years ago, during my last semesters of college (1971–1972), I wrote a senior thesis on Gertrude Stein's *Making of Americans*, which I read in the context of Ludwig Wittgenstein's *Philosophical Investigations*.[1] I had concentrated in philosophy at Harvard even though my interests were primarily literature, art, and performance (poetics and aesthetics). I didn't know anyone who had read Stein but was surrounded by philosophers deeply engaged with Wittgenstein. Still, I saw two key issues that Stein addressed in her early work that related to the philosophical problems that echoed through Emerson Hall, where Stein herself had studied with William James.

Throughout *The Making of Americans*, Stein confronts the problem of what she calls "the real thing of disillusion"[2]: a sense of being a stranger, queer, to those around her; the sinking feeling that one is not, and perhaps cannot be, understood, that drives you to cry out in pain that you write for "myself and strangers," in Stein's famous phrase (p. 289). Stein's formulations struck me as being connected to the problem of other minds, or skepticism, a virtual obsession of Stanley Cavell in those years.[3] It seemed to me that Stein and Wittgenstein had crafted a related response to skepticism.

---

1. *Three Compositions on Philosophy and Literature*, a.k.a. "Three Steins." Asylum's Press Digital PDF (2012): <writing.upenn.edu/epc/3-Steins.php>

2. Gertrude Stein, *The Making of Americans* (1903–1911) (New York: Something Else Press, 1966), p. 483

3. Cavell, born Goldstein, could be the "fourth" Stein. His father's Polish name had been Kavelieruskii or Kavelieriskii, Americanized at Ellis Island, as he reports in *Little Did I Know* (Stanford, CA: Stanford University Press, 2010), p. 10.

The related philosophical issue that Stein's work addresses is the nature of meaning and reference in verbal language: how words refer to objects in the external world. Both Wittgenstein and Stein dramatize the breakdown of a one-to-one correspondence between word and object. They are both averse to the conception that words are akin to names or labels and that meaning is grounded in a verbal mapping of a fully constituted external world. What do words or phrases designate? This goes beyond the issue of private language, which has dogged the interpretation of Stein's work. The problem of where the pain is when pain is expressed opens up for Wittgenstein and his interpreters (for me, primarily Rogers Albritton and Cavell) a more general problem of the nature of reference, designation, and naming for such intangibles as (in Stein's words in *The Making of Americans*) "*thinking, believing, seeing, understanding*" (p. 483). I felt, still do, that this philosophical conundrum directly bears on the meaning and reference of not just words or phrases in poems but of poems themselves, which certainly mean, designate, and express, but do not necessarily refer to "things," if things are assumed to be already existing and named objects. I am not satisfied with the argument I make about the nature of reference in the final sections of *The Making of Americans* and *Tender Buttons*, where Stein invented a compositional method that I named in this work "wordness" (anticipating later formulations such as "language-centered"). Still, despite the manifest shortcomings of this work, it locates some ongoing problems that remain to be addressed, both in terms of a full-scale reading of *The Making of Americans* and a more technically rich account of reference in works such as *Tender Buttons*.

Looking back, I am aware of how circumscribed my frame of reference was in 1971. I am content here to play straight man (third Stein) to Stein and Wittgenstein, those diaphanously queer, secular Jews born just fifteen years apart.

2. Never to Let Her to Be What He Said

Six years after finishing *Three Steins*, Bruce Andrews and I edited a feature on *Tender Buttons* for the sixth issue of *L=A=N=G=U=A=G=E* (1978). After that I published three essays on Stein: "Professing Stein / Stein Professing," collected in *A Poetics* (1992), "Stein's Identity," collected in *My Way: Speeches and Poems* (1999), and my most comprehensive essay on the subject, "Gertrude Stein: The Difference Is Spreading," collected in *Pitch of Poetry* (2016). For that essay, I incorporated some of a talk I gave on Stein at New York University on October 6, 2001. But I didn't include in that essay some additional remarks I made on that occasion, in which I responded to comments of fellow panelists Al Carmines, Richard Howard, and Wendy Steiner, and which were published in *Theater* 32:2 (2002). I adapt those remarks here:

In political terms, equating Gertrude Stein with Ezra Pound, as we have just heard at this conference, is ludicrous. Just read Pound's speeches during the Second World War versus the material that Stein published at the same time, or for that matter even her proposed introduction to a never-published collection of speeches of Maréchal Pétain. There's no connection between the two kinds of rhetoric. Not to be too reductive about it, but the difference has to do with hate. Stein was not focused on hate and demeaning, even while she shared the class and racial prejudices of her time. At the same time, she was trying to articulate a poetics that was an antidote to antagonism. She didn't manage to obliterate antagonism, but the basic orientation of her work was to create an ethics of dialogue as much as an aesthetics of presentness. I would emphasize this ethical, as opposed to moral, orientation as a way to approach the politics of her work.

The ongoing controversy about Stein, reflected at this event in her honor, is a constant measure of the anxiety her pertinence continues to generate. Richard Howard's concern that Stein is too difficult to teach, or that Pound is too difficult to teach, troubles me. For a professor of English to tell us that Stein or Pound is too difficult to teach is analogous to a professor of physics saying that Einstein is too difficult to teach, or a professor of history saying that Hitler is too difficult to teach. Controversy and difficulty are part of our subject matter. Literature does not need to be nice or neat to be taught, as if the anxiety that a work may generate would make that work untouchable. On the contrary, confronting difficulty—aesthetic, political, ethical—is not only engaging and generative, but also a necessity.

Stein's difficulty, to call it that, is very different than the male modernists, at least as exemplified by Eliot and Pound, whom I also find crucial to teach and whose great work remains for me engaging and provocative, even while troubling. Al Carmines really hit upon it when he spoke of Paul Tillich. Stein's work incorporates a critique of the teleological that is similar to what I first encountered, in high school in the 1960s, reading Tillich, just around the time of Carmine's first Stein performances. To describe Stein's writing as ontological would just be to say that its meanings are not ulterior or interior, not external to what she is doing as she is doing it. Her work performs a process.

In her talk, Wendy Steiner brought up Stein's interest in Otto Weininger. As I discovered, with excitement, shortly after finishing my undergraduate thesis on Stein and Wittgenstein, an engagement with Weininger is a tangible link between Stein and Wittgenstein (though they were hardly alone in this attraction). All three were Jews of the same generation, had ties to Vienna, and, as we would say today, queer. Weininger was meshuggeneh—a diabolical thinker whose self-harming ideas are inevitably associated with his suicide at the age of twenty-three in 1903. No doubt it was the ontological and phenomenological character of Weininger's thinking that attracted both Wittgenstein and Stein, particularly his idea that meaning is not "behind" words but in words. Weininger's single book, *Geschlecht und Charakter* (Sex and Character) (1903), directly addressed, and with a kind of male hysteria, changing ideas of gender in fin-de-siecle Vienna. Weininger believed that everyone had both male and female (homo- and heterosexual) tendencies, but that only the male element was associated with genius; Jewishness was disparaged as feminizing and Weininger converted to Protestantism. Within Weininger's warped worldview, male-identified women might be free of the curse of the feminine as, I suppose, converts could be free of the curse of Jewishness. In effect *Sex and Character* was a kind of protocol of Christian, male suprematism, that is, of patriarchy. As Weininger himself says, in a line that sounds almost Wittgensteinian, "Wir erwehren uns der Welt durch unsere Begriffe" (We resist the world with our concepts).[4] Perhaps Stein's claim to be a genius relates to Weininger's tract.[5] In any case, it brings to mind these lines from Stein's radical poem against patriarchy, which she called with biting irony "Patriarchal Poetry" (1927):

Let her try
Just let her try
Let her try
Never to be what he said. . . .
Let her to be what he said.
Let her to be what he said.
Not to let her to be what he said not to let her to be what he said.
Never to be let her to be never let her to be what he said. Never let
    her to be what he said.

4. Otto Weininger, *Geschlecht und Charakter* (Wien and Leipzig: Wilhelm Braumüller, 1903), p. 1. My translation.

5. "The three geniuses of whom I wish to speak are Gertrude Stein, Pablo Picasso and Alfred Whitehead."—*The Autobiography of Alice B. Toklas* (1932) in Stein, *Selected Writings*, ed. Carl Van Vechten (New York: Random House, 1946), p. 5.

Never to let her to be what he said. Never to let her to be let her to
    be let her to be let her what he said.[6]

Earlier today, Richard Howard, unable to hear Stein's own insistently
performative rhythms, suggested that a problem with Stein's plays is that
they need to be set to music. In one of her many plays without music,
"Identity A Poem" (1935), which I discuss in "Stein's Identity," Stein writes,
"So then the play has to be like this."[7]

The play of which Stein speaks has to do with the ethics of reading that
her work embodies, which insists that to read we have to perform. All of
her writing is a play to be performed.

And now the play begins again.

3. Dogging Stein

Disinformation about Stein's wartime activity—what I call brown-
baiting—continued to mount in the first decade of the new century, from
Alan Dershowitz in the *Huffington Post* to Emily Greenhouse in the *New
Yorker* to Michael Kimmelman in the New York *Review of Books*, just to
mention her Jewish debunkers. *Buzzfeed, Haaretz*, the *Washington Post*, and
Tablet also joined the gang bang, as did the then Manhattan Borough Pres-
ident (and later mayoral candidate) Scott Stringer (also Jewish).

A couple of demonstrably false factoids underwrites much of this ma-
terial, pushed by publications that otherwise decry right-wing conspiracy
theories, perhaps because in this case the debunking matched their ideo-
logical presuppositions. There are three key elements essential to the scape-
goating and they trigger each other in a variety of ways:

1.   Stein is pro-Nazi (what I call *brown-baiting*)
2.   Stein's literary work is fraudulent
3.   Stein has a different profile than the other major modernist authors:
     queer, female, a wealthy non-observant/non-conforming (and to
     some degree non-identifying)—free-thinking—Jew who declined
     redemption by conversion.

6. In *Writings 1903–1932*, ed. Catherine Stimpson (New York: Library of America, 1998), p. 582

7. "Identity A Poem," in Joan Retallack, ed. (Berkeley: University of California Press, 2008), p. 301

Janet Malcolm's 2003 article in the *New Yorker* on Stein's wartime sur-
vival (and her two subsequent articles on Stein) set the stage for much of
what came after, though Malcolm, who was born into a European Jewish
family, is more careful in her factual claims than many of Stein's later de-
tractors, who nonetheless pick up on Malcolm's dog whistles. Still, Mal-
colm *profiled* Stein. By *profile*, I mean her tabloid treatment of Stein not as
a major literary thinker (a genius, on Stein's terms) but as a nefarious char-
acter. Her profile makes clear that Malcolm has no regard for Stein's work
or any ability to read it; indeed, she takes pride in her ignorance. I cannot
imagine an article in a liberal mainstream periodical on Robert Frost's pol-
itics, or his view of the rights of indigenous people in the United States,
that contemptuously dismissed any aesthetic value in his work. In this re-
spect, the treatment of Stein is closer to our contemporary takedowns of
celebrities, suggesting that Stein remains a part of celebrity culture that her
modernist contemporaries do not.

Stein was quite conscious of the difference between her celebrity pro-
file and her more private work. She plays with this in "Identity A Poem"
(whose terms are subsequently developed in *The Geographical History of
Americans* in 1936). Stein contrasted her mind and work with her celebra-
tory, or public persona, how her "little dog" knows her: in other words, her
profile. Indeed, Stein ingeniously fashioned her profile, treating it as part of
her work as an artist but also as a way to protect herself.

Wanda Corn and Tirza True Latimer's *Seeing Gertrude Stein: Five Sto-
ries* makes a compelling case for Stein as the genius (or possibly genie)
behind the many portraits of her, which Corn sees as a striking act of
self-fashioning—creating a remarkably legible body of work, popular and
iconic, to accompany her allegedly illegible writing.[8] Before hearing a lec-
ture by Corn in Paris as part of the "Stein Collects" show, I hadn't thought
of the portraits as a discrete body of work. Following Corn, I am convinced
that Stein recognized the significance of the photographs, paintings, and
sculptures for putting into views a set of identities that are as much a part
of her work as *The Making of Americans*. With that in mind, Corn was
able to identify distinct sets of images and it becomes apparent that Stein
recomposed her image over her lifetime. There has been a fair amount writ-
ten about Stein as celebrity. What interests me here is slightly different:
Stein as image fabricator, who used the portrait as a way of supplementing

8. A 2011–2012 exhibition at the Contemporary Jewish Museum in San Francisco and the National
Portrait Gallery, Smithsonian Institution, Washington, D.C. The catalog was published by the University
of California Press in 2011. I assembled a gallery of Stein images at <jacket2.org/commentary/gertrude
-stein-pictures>.

her writing (in a similar way to how *The Autobiography* works in tandem with its looking-glass other, "Stanzas in Meditation"). Stein was acutely engaged with verbal portraiture, from her early word portraits on (and in *The Making of Americans* as well). These images, created for widely different purposes by many different artists and journalists, became, for Stein, portraits by other means.

Human nature, as your dog knows you or you know your dog—is not superficial but nonetheless is different than human mind. Thinking of the expression Sterling Brown uses for his poem "Puttin' on Dog"—dressing up, performing for an audience's objectifying gaze—Stein's still performing for us. Seventy-five years after her death, both Stein's celebrity and her poetry remain resilient:

In his box-back coat and his mutt-leg britches,
And a collar high enough for to choke a ox;
And the girls stopped cryin' when they saw how Scrappy
Was a-puttin' on dog in a pinewood box.

O you rascal, puttin' on dog,
Puttin' on dog, puttin' on dog[9]

In her detractor's eyes, Stein can seem like a little dog to be hunted down. But she cautions, in "Identity A Poem," written in 1935 on the cusp of the European Jewish Extermination, where one's dog nature was marked by yellow star fastened on one's lapel: "Dogs smell like dogs. / Men smell like men. . . . And my little dog is not the same thing as I am I" (pp. 301, 307).

4. Gertrude Stein Taunts Hitler in 1934 and 1945: "Seig heil, seig heil, right in der Fuehrer's face"

The "wartime" attacks on Stein, fomented by the *New Yorker* in 2003, peaked early in 2012. Stein and the Metropolitan Museum of Art were subjected to an unprecedented torrent of tabloid attacks, prompted by "The Steins Collect: Matisse, Picasso, and the Parisian Avant-Garde," a show of the art collection of the Stein family, that originated, without controversy,

9. Sterling Brown, *Collected Poems*, ed. Michael S. Harper (Evanston, IL: TriQuarterly Books, 1996), p. 239

at the Grand Palais in Paris and opened at the Met in New York on February 28, 2012. Even the Anti-Defamation League denounced Stein, although when I called them and explained the irony of their position *supporting* defamation of a Jew, they relented.

Maybe because I had been rereading Proust and Zola's *J'accuse*, *l'affaire Stein* sometimes struck me as a farcical reprise of the *l'affaire Dreyfus*, over a century later, I felt compelled to assemble an online intervention, for *Jacket2*, sardonically labeled a "dossier" with the title *Gertrude Stein's War Years: Setting the Record Straight*.[10] (I seemed to have never learned that there are some places in which irony fails.) I contributed three essays to the dossier: the preface, "Gertrude Stein Taunts Hitler in 1934 and 1945: Seig heil, seig heil, right in der Fuehrer's face" and my magnum opus on this sordid story, "Gertrude and Alice in Vichyland." I had first thought to include that material here, but it's too long, too detailed, and too much of a downer. "Vichyland" is something of a visual collage, with the citations reproduced from the original sources and a number of images I created. It also reads a bit like one of those endless streaming documentaries, promising to reveal something diabolical in the final episodes. I do make such a revelation and name names along the way. Spoiler: the self-proclaimed liberal pundits at the *New Yorker* and New York *Review of Books* were having their tails wagged by far-right disinformation specialists who dislike free-thinking Jews as much as they do. But wait: that can't be. Some of them are free-thinking Jews themselves. Go figure. And while the New York *Review of Books* shamelessly refused to print a letter that I coauthored with Joan Retallack, Marjorie Perloff, and Edward Burns, they did publish a link to the "dossier."[11]

In "Vichyland," I started by comparing the scores of condemnations of Stein and the Met for "Steins Collect," along with the demand that the Met prominently display signs denouncing her, and a 2016 Museum of Modern Art retrospective for Francis Picabia, who, unlike Stein, has a well-documented history of Vichy collaboration. Here is the summary of my empirical research:

> The number of articles or politicians decrying the Vichy sympathies of Picabia in relation to the recent MoMA retrospective, and demanding he be prominently denounced in the signage for the show, "Francis Picabia: Our Heads Are Round so Our Thoughts Can Change Direction": 0.

10. <jacket2.org/feature/gertrude-steins-war-years-setting-record-straight>. The dossier features links to many of the articles attacking Stein.

11. See note 8 in "Vichyland."

"Our Heads Are Round so Our Thoughts Can Change Direction" sounds a bit like a Stein line and in any case applies to both artists. Indeed, Picabia is not only a great painter—his magnificent portrait of Stein was in the MoMA show—but also the most radical of the French "Dada" poets—perhaps the only one of Stein's contemporaries who pushed away from figuration as much she did and whose most extreme poems engage with dissociation in a quite un-Steinian way. The poems of this "freeloading angel" and "beautiful monster" dare the unprecedented and traffic in the sheer possibilities of abstract shimmering gesture. Picabia's early poem "Staircase" could be about Stein:

Everything in the world
far from the truth
is a hurricane of divine roads
like the light of heaven.

Those women who deny the hereafter
have a place next to me.
I am the virtuous guide
In the crystal city.[12]

The New York *Times Book Review* piece on the catalog for the MoMA Picabia show quotes Michèle C. Cone's catalog essay "Francis Picabia's War," which describes Picabia's "residence in Vichy France and association with the local Gestapo as 'confused and confusing behavior.'"[13] In her thoughtful and restrained essay, Cone goes on to note "Like his friend Stein, Picabia's personal life during the occupation was murky." I make the contrast between Picabia and Stein's "murky" behavior to emphasize the stark contrast in treatment. Why was Stein subjected to such virulent scorn when her family art collection was shown at the Met (with no focus on her own work) while Picabia, subject of a full-scale retrospective of his work, was not?

Ironically, some of Picabia's quite intriguing paintings reflect his "murky" views of the war years, which is not the case with any of Stein's literary works. It's possible that the discrepancy is the result of Picabia being

---

12. Francis Picabia, *I Am a Beautiful Monster: Poetry, Prose, and Provocation*, tr. Marc Lowenthal (Cambridge: MIT Press, 2007), p. 33. In "Smile" he writes "Like a freeloading angel / I am on the stairway / Of hysterical fits" (p. 42). For my selection of Picabia's poems, go to <writing.upenn.edu/library/Picabia/>.

13. December 3, 2016, p. BR64

considered French and Stein American, but this is a dubious distinction since Stein lived in France for forty years. It may also be because Stein was a Jewish lesbian and Picabia . . . was not. Picabia offers an explanation in an aphorism: "Jews have their noses in the air, Christians have them down" (*Beautiful Monster*, p. 310). Perhaps Jews are held to a different standard; perhaps they are expected to be heroic resistance fighters. It is also possible that Picabia's reputation is protected by a powerful network of museums and collectors while Stein had no such institutionally vested supporters. Or that the pataquerical nature of Stein's poetry still outrages more than Pica-bia's painting: in other words that Stein is part of contemporary celebrity culture in a way Picabia is not, that there is a lot of appetite for canceling Stein where there is none for doing that to Picabia. Perhaps Picabia confirms what is expected of a man in his situation and Stein betrays expectations, even though Stein and Toklas were at risk of extermination while Picabia was not. In any case the vastly greater interest in Stein's "murk" than Picabia's cannot be justified by the historical or aesthetic record. Stein provokes a matricidal and misogynistic ruthlessness on the part of her most devoted haters.

In both my dossier essays—"Sieg Heil" and "Vichyland"—I take up the viral, malevolently dishonest references to a May 6, 1934, New York *Times* interview by Lansing Warren entitled "Gertrude Stein Views Life and Politics." The interview begins with a disclaimer that Stein's remarks should not be taken at face value, a point that is concealed by those who deceptively quote it out of context. Saying that Stein endorsed Hitler for the Nobel Prize in the 1934 interview is like saying that Mel Brooks includes a tribute to Hitler in *The Producers*. In Stein's remarks about Hitler and the Nobel Prize, she associates Hitler with all that is bad in Germany. Her remarks constitute an attack on Hitler. A related charge made against Stein is that she later actually nominated Hitler for a Nobel Prize. I trace the origins of this "big lie," spread by the mainstream liberal press, in "Vichyland."

Yet another libel is that Stein and her GI buddies are making a "Hitler salute" in a 1945 *Life* magazine article by Stein entitled, "'Off We All Went to See Germany': Germans Should Learn to Be Disobedient and GIs Should Not Like Them No They Shouldn't."[14] This attack is premised on the delusion that *Life* magazine would publish a pro-Nazi photo and that GIs, reeling from the death of four hundred thousand of their comrades, would be "heiling" Hitler in anything but derision.

I leave the rest of the story to the dossier. "Vichyland" offers graphic

---

14. References and sources in "Gertrude Stein Taunts Hitler in 1934 and 1945" are in the *Jacket2* dossier.

"**We all did Hitler s pose** on Hitler's balcony at Berchtesgaden." Miss Stein liked Hitler's radiators, wanted to take one home for a flowerpot but was talked out of it.

detail on Stein's relation to the Vichy regime and offers something her detractors don't: context.

The last thing I wanted to do in 2012 was to write more about Stein or to do the work of documenting Stein's wartime activities in response to the defamations, knowing also that I would pay a price for my obstinacy. But I became consumed by the task. While I have great appreciation for Stein's work, the dossier neither endorses nor rejects her politics. For myself, growing up in a largely Jewish world on the Upper West Side in the 1950s, if I think of what I would have done had I been in Nazi-occupied France in the 1940s, I am sure I would have taken out my machine gun and mowed down rows and rows and rows of Nazis. And then I remember that most of the Jews of Europe were exterminated without a fight and I'd be with them.

   When push comes to shove, as it has, I read Stein's war years as a survivor's tale. Jewish, openly lesbian, elderly (Stein was sixty-six in 1940), living in occupied France, Stein and Alice Toklas successfully escaped extermination. That is something for which we can be grateful. And I'm also glad that, by hook or by crook, Stein's art collection was not looted by the Nazis. In the end, Stein was able to go on to write her great feminist opera, *The Mother of Us All* (1947), a celebration of American democracy.

Unlike Pound, Eliot, Celine, Frost, or Marinetti, Stein's political views don't conform to our contemporary left/right assignation. She has a heady mix of both and, as certainly her conservative views on class and American race relations are disconcerting (and far from mine). While Stein liked to think of herself as American, her outlook during the war is best understood if we recognize that Stein was also French and shared (or needed to share) some of the views of her neighbors in rural France. The anti-Stein propaganda/scapegoating was possible only because its perpetuators relied on ignorance of the facts on the ground in France during the war.

But Gertrude Stein is guilty of something: Crimes against Official Verse Culture.

Stein's liberal establishment tormentors got caught up in a quagmire created by their own self-righteousness: in their mob-like glee tarring Stein, they feathered themselves.

Hoisted on their own petards.

Or let's just say, folks who shoulda known bettah let their visceral dislike of what they imagine Stein represents get the better of them. The very "liberal" places that decry "cancel culture" and slander piled on. To take a line from Hugh MacDiarmid's "British Leftish Poetry, 1930–1940," and thinking of our own contemporary fight against fascism: "You cannot light a match on a crumbling wall."[15]

Lest someone accuse me of a pro-Hitler gesture in my subtitle, "Seig heil, seig heil, right in der Fuehrer's face"—it's from "Der Fuehrer's Face," the 1942 anti-Nazi parody by Spike Jones and His City Slickers (featuring

15. Listen to MacDiarmid read the poem on PennSound.

the inimitable Mickey Katz). The song, by Oliver Wallace, was taken from *Der Fuehrer's Face*, the Academy-Award-Winning Walt Disney Donald Duck cartoon, which originally was entitled "Donald Duck in Nuzi Land" (according to the Wikipedia article on the film). The cartoon was made in 1942 and released in 1943. In the cartoon, Donald Duck also gives the fascist salute, which may be why Disney kept the cartoon out of circulation, fearing what is happening to Gertrude would happen to Donald.

"Why a duck?" says Chico Marx in *The Cocoanuts* (1929).

"It's deep water, that's why a duck. It's deep water." . . .

"All I know is that it's a viaduct."

"Now look, alright, I catch on: why a horse, why a chicken, why a this, why a that . . ."

"I no catch on: why a duck?"[16]

I no catch on.

Why Gertrude Stein?

Why now?

5. St. Gertrude of Diaspora

On October 29, 2001, as savings time morphed into standard time, Gertrude Stein was inducted into the American Poets' Corner at the Cathedral Church of St. John the Divine, in New York. As part of the annual ceremony, which fell on the day Eastern Standard time resumed, a chorus sang a few settings of Stein's work, among other choral works, poet Honor Moore read from Stein's work and Molly Peacock, Cathedral Poet-in-Residence, spoke about Stein, along with New York University Dean Catherine Stimpson and myself.

Walking through the cobbled streets of Providence on Thursday night with the poet Keith Waldrop, I mentioned my great pleasure that Gertrude Stein was going to be inducted into Poets' Corner on Sunday. Keith immediately replied, "And the time is changing too."

It is indeed, and there is no time like the present time for time to change, as Stein might say, for Stein there is no time like the present because the present is like no time at all.

And the time is changing too.

The Poets' Corner honors both poets and prose writers. And while Stein can certainly best be described as a poet, one of her remarkable achievements is to have written lustrous works in all genres of literature, plays and

---

16. <marx-brothers.org/whyaduck/info/movies/scenes/whyaduck.htm>

novels, autobiographies, librettos, essays, lectures, mysteries and valentines, portraits and landscapes, children's stories and travelogues, and, well, about half a dozen literary types for which we haven't yet come up with a name.

Stein's most immediate generational company at Poets' Corner is Eliot and Williams, Cummings and Stevens and Frost. Among those, Stein and Williams are the first whose parents were immigrants and who did not have English as their native language.

She is also the first Jewish poet to join the poetic elect here at the cathedral.

And the time is changing too.

The newness of Stein's family history in America made America if anything more important to her, as she wrote in her epic novel *The Making of Americans*:

> It has always seemed to me a rare privilege, this, of being an American, a real American, one whose tradition it has taken scarcely sixty years to create. We need only realize our parents, remember our grandparents, and know ourselves and our history is complete.
>
> The old people in a new world, the new people made out of the old, that is the story I mean to tell, for that is what really is and what I really know. (p. 3)

Gertrude Stein was born in Allegheny, Pennsylvania, in 1874 and lived, in the United States, mostly in Oakland and Baltimore and Cambridge. She moved to France early on and that is where she died in 1946.

Stein was not always celebrated, as she is today. Throughout much of the twentieth century, her work has been derided and belittled. She challenged the prevailing notions of poetry, language, and communication in such a powerful way that even today you will find that her work stirs controversy. But maybe this is just what verse needs to be contemporary, to stay in time and not be "out of it" as Stein writes in "Composition as Explanation."

And the time is changing too, even now, exactly now, exactly now as as is as as is now as now is as and how and now and as and is and wow.

So now let's actively repeat it all, exactly as she do, she does too, she does truly, exactly as she do. As as and as is and as is now. And how.

Among all twentieth-century American poets, Stein was the one who went the deepest into the turn toward language that characterizes much of the modernist art of her time.

As Stein says in *Tender Buttons*: "Act so that there is no use in a centre."[17]

Stein, like several of her contemporaries, was a poet of everyday life,

17. *Tender Buttons* (1914), ed. Leonard Diepeveen (Toronto: Broadview Press, 2018), p. 71

using common words to create new constructions for the new worlds we are hourly craving. Stein's aversion to symbols and allusion created a poetry richly saturated with sounds doing their business of making meaning as it was made, not reflecting meaning as if it were already a done deal.

In her essays she insisted that doing was much more significant than explaining or anyway that what is done is always more important than anything won.

One of the last things Stein wrote, in the year she died, was a preface to the Modern Library edition of her *Selected Writings*.

"I always wanted to be historical, from almost a baby on," Stein writes.[18]

Well now, just in time, and the time is changing too, and Stein, always historical, all of us are always historical, is being taken out of time as we celebrate her as someone necessary for her time and our time.

And the time is changing too.

When I was 14 [Stein continues] I used to love to say to myself those awful lines of George Eliot, may I be one of those immortal something or other, and although I knew then how it went I do not know now, and then later when they used to ask me when I was going back to America, not until I am a lion, I said, I was not completely certain I was going to be but now here I am, thank you all. (ibid.)

And now here we all are and the time is changing too and thanks for that, thank you all, yes thanks for that, that Gertrude Stein is here, all here, here and now, and how.

And the time is changing too.

[2002: *Hotel Amerika* 1]

18. "A Message from Gertrude Stein," in *The Selected Writings*, ed. Carl Van Vechten (New York: Random House, 1946), p. vii

Languages
Acknowledgment

The land that never has been yet—

Langston Hughes

I live in Brooklyn, New York, also called King's County, though we have no King of Brooklyn and go out of our way not to speak the King's English. Five hundred years ago, these lands were inhabited by people whose ancestors spoke Lenape/Munsee among many other languages in the region. Most of those languages are now endangered or lost because of the genocide by mostly English- and Dutch-speaking Christian immigrants who were unable to share this place with those who did not worship their God.

I am a sojourner in this borough with people whose ancestors were abducted in Africa, brought here, with catastrophic cruelty, and enslaved. Their ancestors spoke Yoruba, Igbo, Hausa, and Bantu languages, among others. Many of my neighbors came here, or their parents or grandparents came here, from every part of the globe, to find sanctuary from economic, ethnic, racial, and religious persecution; from famine, death, genocide, and dispossession. Some came simply to seek a better life.

Their ancestors spoke hundreds of different languages, from Chinese to Celtic; Italian to Bengali, Yiddish and Polish; Russian to Spanish, Vietnamese, Arabic, Armenian, Creole, Portuguese, and Tagalog, to name only a small fraction. Some of these languages percolate through the many accents you hear on the streets of Brooklyn, but others are almost stilled—still, when you closely listen you can hear them too, in the burning spaces between the words and in the spaces between the spaces.

Those spaces are our native tongue.

English is second language even for those for whom it is an only language.

I is *they*; *they* is *us*.

English does not occupy us: *we occupy English.*

[2021: *Michigan Quarterly Review* (2022)]

Dichtung Yammer

1.

THOMAS FINK: *In* Recalculating, *quite a few poems are labeled "after." These include "Sad Boy's Bad Boy after 'Mad Girl's Love Song' by Sylvia Plath," "Blown Wind after Douglas Messerli," "Loneliness in Linden after Wallace Stevens," and "Umbra" (Apollinaire). Imitation, adaptation, parody, and translation are some nouns that come to mind, and you have much to say about the challenges of translation in "In Unum Pluribus: Toward a More Perfect Invention" in* Pitch of Poetry, *a talk originally delivered in China. What were you after in pursuing this aftering?*

Poetry is the company it keeps.

Echopoetics is an acknowledgment that my approach to poetry is a weaving of voices, languages, rhetorics, cants and decants, into a poem, to allow the poem to come into a life of its own.

So often the scolds in American poetry have shamed us with proscriptions—stick to your own voice, multiplicity is duplicity or an empty gesture of—God forbid!—juxtaposition/disjunction. As if disjunction was not a means to creating new constellations. Disjunction without aesthetic transformation is realism; it's the given. Yet all around us we see earnest calls for a diminished field of the lyric. For aesthetic revanchists, the nepohumanists I discuss in the final essay in *Pitch of Poetry*, "hatred of poetry" is one and the same as a defense of poetry.[1] Such treacherous defenses founder on fear of uncontained contradiction and clashes of voice. While some hear such clashes as cacophony, I hear democracy in action.

Save us from those whose mission is to save poetry from poetry.

Poetry is a lost art, and, for me, that means sounding the loss.

---

1. Ben Lerner, *The Hatred of Poetry* (2016)

The translations in *Recalculating* and *Near/Miss* are personae, providing a way to pursue the radical seriality of the book with new swerves that nonetheless bring it all back homeless. These transcreations are no more (or less) "other voices" than the rest of the poems in the book. While many of these "after" poems are translations, others take liberties, making transcreation a form of re-originating. That's a way to describe my responses to poems originally in English by Plath, Messerli, and also to Stevens's "Loneliness in Jersey City." (I associate Linden with Susan Bee's relatives, death camp survivors, who lived there.)

The best account of my use of translations in *Recalculating* is a review of the book by Jed Rasula that appeared in *Provincetown Arts* (Summer 2003):

> Bernstein's penchant for trying anything and throwing in the pantry with the kitchen sink risks making this collection seem more of the same—until, that is, the insistence of veiled lamentation makes itself heard. It's as if his previous books have all been played in C major, so the shift to the key of E is haunting despite the apparent continuity of prior methods. If there's a single component that announces the shift, it's the plentitude of translations (at least sixteen, by half a dozen poets), most of them carefully chosen for theme, it seems, yet each translated with a different procedure.
>
> Beginning with the wonderful "Autopsychographia" by Portuguese poet Fernando Pessoa from 1931, and ending with a wistful croon, "Before You Go," *Recalculating* traverses 185 pages of nonstop inventiveness. The Pessoa poem serves notice of the black grief that lies ahead, though its cleverness strikes exactly the evasive note that Bernstein's own jauntiness often adopts:
>
> Poets are fakers
> Whose faking is so real
> They even fake the pain
> They truly feel
>
> Another poet, Gérard de Nerval, gives voice to the grief near the end of the collection in "Misfortune":
>
> My morning star's dead and my disconsolate lute
> Smashes in the blackened sun of torn alibi.
> In the tomb of every night, memories of
> Venetian reveries raw rub the inconsolable
> Pitch of the dark, where over and again
> I love you.
>
> "Misfortune" drastically contracts Nerval's sonnet "El Desdichado" into a direct personal lament. Phrases like "torn alibi" follow the sound rather than

the sense of the original French (*la tour abolie*—ruined tower), as the poet gradually brings Venice into view (a city not in Nerval), where his daughter died in 2008. Using other poets' works as crutches for the expression of anguish might seem evasive but for the fact that it's one of the longest-running practices in the history of poetry. Bernstein is also capable of the most disarming unrehearsed direct address: "I was the luckiest father in the world / until I turned unluckiest" (158). That this heartbreaking, heartbroken poem is preceded by the tender lament of Victor Hugo's "Tomorrow, dawn . . ." reinforces a sense of poetry as the site of ultimate sharing. A welcoming place, as *Recalculating* itself proves to be.[2]

Recalculating favors us with a tall order of metapoetry. Happily, for some dessert lovers and citizens of Yorkshire, two such long poems have "pudding" in the title. If Emerson (who will come up again in another question) equated "sin" and "limitation," you exert major metapoetic energy to oppose that "sin"—to combat what you've just termed "earnest calls for a diminished field of the lyric"; here, for example, is some marvelously collaged Robert Frostiness on "framing":

Something there is that doesn't love a frame
That wants it laid bare.

Before I made a frame I'd ask to know
What I was framing in or framing out.

Two frames diverged on the common road
& I, I could not choose the one for the other
So stood, astounded, in place.

For frames are what we are inside of.

Two frames are better than one
Three's the thicket.[3]

What I draw from this passage is: a frame (context) is not "loveable" when we aren't aware of its existence or influence and hence don't know what it's "framing out," so "laying it bare" reduces its power to limit the potential for

2. <writing.upenn.edu/epc/authors/bernstein/reviews/Rasula-Jed_Recaclulating_PtownArts_2013.pdf>

3. "The Truth in Pudding," in *Recalculating* (Chicago: University of Chicago Press, 2013), p. 5

signification, and we don't have to be "inside of" a single frame—what in a previous essay you called "frame lock" and connected to "tone lock"—but can have the pleasure and excitement of engaging with multiple frames in writing or reading a text, since there's no such thing as performing these acts without any frames. Charles Olson may relate "thicket" to "cold hell," but you like the complexity and "thickness" of going beyond, say, two contexts.

In "Gertrude Stein: The Difference Is Spreading," you perform a highly illuminating examination of various passages in Tender Buttons *and the "Portrait of Picasso." Contending that "thematic close reading . . . won't work" and that "close scrutiny through an associational/ambient reading of the linguistic prompts and an allegorical reading of form" will, you encourage readers to "let the figurative plenitude of each word play out."[4] And in "Echopoetics," also in* Pitch of Poetry, *you praise how Marjorie Perloff will "note down . . . how possible associations read in conjunction with one another" (p. 189). To rephrase your response to my first question slightly, "disjunction" is not a loss of context but an opportunity for associations that engender "a means to creating new constellations," new contexts.*

However "ambient" it might be (chez Tan Lin), "associational reading" seems the primary way to arrive at two or three or more frames "diverging" and perhaps converging/re-converging as the writer or reader travels "the common road" of a poem. What in the displacement and multiplication of frames goes beside, beyond, above, or below the work/play of developing associations?

When I speak of "frames," I am thinking of Erving Goffman's *Frame Analysis.*

People have sometimes felt that Goffman, like Wittgenstein, was a behaviorist, as if he thought there was no "real" (no referent), only the frames. *No pea just the shells—in your con game.* Similarly, there are those who feel George Lakoff's focus on frames means he cares more about "spin" than "policy." Lakoff would say the focus on "policy" without frame dooms oppositional politics. There's no vision.

Ron Silliman provides an aesthetically exhilarating exhibition of serial framing and reframing in *Tjanting* and *Ketjak.* On a narrative level, so does Paul Auster in *4 3 2 1.*

Frederich Schlegel: "A really free and cultured person must be able at will to shift philosophic or philologic, critical or poetic, historic or rhetorical, ancient or modern, as one tunes an instrument at any time and to any pitch."[5]

4. *Pitch of Poetry* (Chicago: University of Chicago Press, 2016), pp. 90 and 88

5. "Critical Fragments" #55 (1797) at <textlog.de/kritische-fragmente.html>: "Ein recht freier und gebildeter Mensch müßte sich selbst nach Belieben philosophisch oder philologisch, kritisch oder po-

Could poetry be spin for its own sake? As in the rhythm of toggling, shifting, frames? Frame oscillation is a way to allow for 4-D world scans, a way out of the 2-D (Euclidian) trap of much conventional writing.

We are limited to language not by language. I have learned, painfully, how many rational people get apoplectic when you say that.

Only the imaginary is real.

There must be a great satisfaction in thinking that frames just get in the way, as if language was an obstacle to reality and poetry's job was to remove it.

The imagination is not a lawn mower.

How annoying for poetry to embrace frames as if they were a long-lost relative visiting town for the weekend. Let's have a drink! And there's still time to see the Egyptian show at the museum.

I am for metaphor but against metapoetry. Maybe it's because I am part of the congregation of Emerson of the Latter-Day Feints. We believe that one step in space is also a step in time.

"Meta" is just the real becoming conscious of itself.

Not polygamy but polysemy.

"Associational" reading as opposed to what?

But I'm getting dizzy. Didn't we pass this oasis two hours ago? We'll never get home.

Language is a paradise, why settle for more? Even if the offer is in cash.

When I was working in the kitchen of the Fenway Cambridge Motor Hotel, while in college, I thought the Yorkshire pudding mix was the salad dressing. None of the wedding guests complained.

Whose woods these are I think I know. There's still time to run.

One dismal alternative to "associational" reading is not so different from mowing the lawn: to begin with a preconceived frame and then force associations that come up during the reading into that frame and discard associations that don't fit the frame. In your terms: frame lock.

You spoof on Jack Lack in "The Twelve Tribes of Dr. Lacan" (Recalculating, p. 52), but when you say, "Only the imaginary is real," I can frame your use of "the imaginary" (as a noun) in a Lacanian sense, though the adjective "real" is not the Lacanian "the real," but something like "what is actual." To follow this path might be to suggest not only that the individual cannot break out of the mirror stage but that there is nothing "real" beyond the "contents" of anyone's imaginary: "LACK-anians focus on 'the ache of lack' and the desire to fill this

etisch, historisch oder rhetorisch, antik oder modern stimmen können, ganz willkürlich, wie man ein Instrument stimmt, zu jeder Zeit, und in jedem Grade."

void with ultimately unsatisfying and imaginary objects." But then, in Laca-
nian terms, perhaps you are "really" dealing with the symbolic order, language,
as "the real becoming conscious of itself." Thus, the "obstacle to reality" is not
language but considering language an obstacle.

It's heartening to hear that you're "for metaphor." Some experimentalists
have tenderly caressed metonymy and smacked metaphor upside the head, and
I wonder if that's such a generative form of discrimination. Do you find the
privileging of metonymy over metaphor justifiable, overly prescriptive, or
wrongheaded? Does the binary afford much traction, or does it fail to serve the
"paradise" of "language" and thus deserve to be put out to pasture?

Only the imagination is real!
  I have declared it
    Time without end.

So Williams writes in his late poem "Asphodel, That Greeny Flower."[6] I
echo Williams in "The Kiwi Bird in the Kiwi Tree," the opening poem in
Rough Trades:

I want no paradise only to be
drenched in the downpour of words, fecund
with tropicality. Fundament be-
yond relation, less 'real' than made, as arms
surround a baby's gurgling: encir-
cling mesh pronounces its promise (not bars
that pinion, notes that ply). The tailor tells
of other tolls, the seam that binds, the trim,
the waste. & having spelled these names, move on
to toys or talcums, skates & scores. Only
the imaginary is real—not trumps
beclouding the mind's acrobatic vers-
ions. The first fact is the social body,
one from another, nor needs no other.[7]

---

6. "Asphodel," Book 3 (1955) in *The Collected Poems*, II, ed. Christopher McGowan (New York; New Directions, 2001), p. 334. "Only the imagination / is real!" first appears in "The Host" in *The Desert Music* (1954), p. 262.

7. *Rough Trades* (Los Angeles: Sun & Moon Press, 1991). Digital edition at EPC.

"Only / the imaginary is real" is echoed a few pages later, in "Whose Language": "Only the real is real."

I mean "imaginary" in the sense of the world we perceive and live in. Freud makes palpable the consequences of thinking the symbolic is less real than the event itself, which is, voilà, imaginary. For Freud, our memories, perceptions, apprehensions, traumas condition how we respond to the world. Lakoff and Goffman would speak of this in terms of framing. In Althusser it's a *matter* of ideology—the way we experience things as conditioned by the economic and social order. There is a racial imaginary, a gender imaginary, an ethnic imaginary, a class imaginary. And there are conflicts among and between them, which is where frames sometimes come into view. Marking such conflicts remains key to any politics of poetic form. Call it *marking time.*

There are no innocent frames any more than there are natural ones. What's delusional is the supposed commonsense idea that we can get around all ideology/framing/language by clear or expressive writing. You could call this aesthetic neoliberalism.

"Only the imaginary is real" is not a statement of fact but possibility. The alternative is the shadows on the wall of Plato's cave. Plato was right to ban poets from his version of the republic. The visceral sense that metaphors are what we live by is disruptive to the kind of authority Plato c(r)aved.

Metonymy is the figure of substitution and can be cathected onto a site of loss, as a gravestone or a pebble that you place on a grave. I have a set of cheap silver serving spoons from my daughter's Bat Mitzvah twenty years ago. Every time I see one of those spoons, I think of Emma and of that event. Fragments of things, split off from a scene or action or time or place or event, can come to trigger it. An allusion, a line from another work, may trigger the whole work: "Hurry up, please. It's time." Indeed, the first section of Eliot's *The Waste Land* is full of such triggers, suggesting something traumatic. "Hold on tight."

"A heap of broken images."[8]

Metonymy is linked to the fragment. Think of Schlegel and his alluring, cutting, and quixotic *Critical Fragments*. Schlegel evokes the fragment as metonym for a lost and perfect ancient world, or better to say, for a utopian space outside our historical and broken world. In his practice of the fragment, Schlegel's metonyms are not broken off from a whole but do their own thing: *a part* and *apart*.

---

8. Listen to Eliot's 1935 Speech Lab recording of the poem, ed. Chris Mustazza on PennSound's Eliot page.

Metaphor is not precluded by metonymy; sometimes they overlap: "the broken / pieces of a green / bottle" in Williams's "Between Walls" are both metaphoric and metonymic—of the poem itself (its broken-up form) and the broken society that breaks off and discards the unwanted.[9]

I'm a compulsive metonymist. Substitutions are the tissue of my text, whooping and Whorfing and generally making merry, at least for a time, before the mood turns black. Metonymy, that is, is not just the part standing for the whole (as in synecdoche) or substituting for something else.

In my poetics, metonymy is *substitution for its own sake.*

In your various books of criticism, you've oft mentioned Emerson. His advocacy of nonconformity has been important to you. In his prose, he often exhorts his readers to think, feel, and act on their own, without submitting to external authority. But then, I often sense the counterforce of highly authoritative, often sententious injunctions, frequently clothed in extremely broad generalizations:

> *Whoso would be a man must be a nonconformist. He who would gather immortal palms must not be hindered by the name of goodness, but must explore if it be goodness. Nothing is at last sacred but the integrity of your own mind. Absolve you to yourself, and you shall have the suffrage of the world.[10]*

Well, yes, "the integrity of your own mind" is extremely significant, and exploring morality is preferable to abiding by an inherited morality unthinkingly, yet am I to take his word that "nothing is at last sacred" except for that particular integrity? Hmm. I won't get into the patriarchal generalization of "man," but compulsory nonconformism does not sound like freedom. When compulsion—in this case, externally authorized—drives nonconformism, Pavlovian doggerel dominates the nonconformist.

Like Whitman, Emerson contains multitudes. Does he contradict himself? Is harping on his "inconsistency" a "hobgoblin of little minds"? Is he just exercising a "latter-day feint"? If you think there is a coexistence of anti-authoritarian and authoritarian rhetoric in passages like the one I've just cited, what do you make of it?

My students find Thoreau "arrogant" and "privileged." But I would rather his arrogance and privilege than the pride of those who refuse to think for themselves or who decline to use whatever privilege they may have

---

9. "Between Walls," in *The Collected Poems of William Carlos Williams*, II, ed. A. Walton Litz and Christopher MacGowan (New York; New Directions, 1986), p. 453

10. "Self-Reliance" (1841) at

for some purpose other than to earn interest on it or to display their righteousness.

> I desire to speak somewhere *without* bounds; like a man in a waking moment, to men in their waking moments; for I am convinced that I cannot exaggerate enough even to lay the foundation of a true expression.[11]

That somewhere is neither here nor there; it is next to this world, not entirely of it. I fancy that imagination is an extravagance. True expression is a fantasy, a figure of speech that necessarily enters the world as self-proclaimed falsehood.

> There are probably words addressed to our condition exactly, which, if we could really hear and understand, would be more salutary than the morning or the spring to our lives, and possibly put a new aspect on the face of things for us.[12]

* * *

"He never said a mumblin' word."
This is one way enslaved African America poets of the nineteenth century addressed their condition exactly, veiled as crucifixion.
"Not a word, not a word, not a word."[13]
To keep silent in the face of unspeakable cruelty is a defiant refusal. But the injunction "He never said a mumbling word" is not against *saying* but against *mumbling*, and indeed these words *say*. They are armor-piercing arrows whose meaning is performed.
To mumble or shuffle, to eat one's words, is a still-current slur against the subaltern. It is the mandated masquerade of speech, two-faced, a wig: an inarticulate, subvocal mutter or grumble. It is speech suppressed. Mumbling is the language of compromise, amelioration, obsequiousness, servility, fawning, assimilation, capitulation, appeasement, compliance, surrender.
Not a word but *words*, pressed into utterance/action as force of resistance. "An arrow from the Almighty bow" (to add Blake to the echo chamber).[14]
That this resistance is imaginary makes for its supernal beauty.

---

11. Henry David Thoreau, "Conclusion," in *Walden*, vol. 2 (New York: Houghton, Mifflin, 1882), p. 500

12. "Reading," in *Walden: Volume I* (New York: Houghton, Mifflin, 1854), p. 169

13. See week 9 at <writing.upenn.edu/bernstein/syllabi/253.html>

14. My performance of "The Grey Monk" is at Blake's PennSound page.

*Well, maybe Emerson, along with Thoreau, thought that he couldn't "exagger-
ate enough even to lay the foundation" for the kind of oppositional stance he
considered crucial to challenge the stranglehold of his New England milieu.[15]
However, there can be effective "saying" between egregious exaggeration and
mumbling.*

Maybe not always. It won't surprise you that I like exaggeration and am
suspicious of professionalization. "He never said a mumblin' word" is
neither exaggerated nor mumbling. That is its genius. It partakes of a
different order of genius than Emerson's. I am haunted by this work. Yet
I am wary of juxtaposing my response to your question with a discussion
of "He never said a mumblin' word," since it comes from a lifeworld that
cannot be meshed or absorbed into a general account of nineteenth-
century American literature. The slave songs (or sorrow songs or spiritu-
als) are incommensurable with the rest of American literature and need
to be accorded their own cultural space, with an acknowledgment of their
opacity, even as we recognize their profound influence. I cite this work to
reframe the discussion for myself, to pull me out my habitual responses.
But I recognize how precarious that is.

I surmise that the single words per line in "The Most Frequent Words in Girly
Man" *(*Recalculating, *pp. 141–52) are what you found running the book
through a digital word frequency counter, but maybe you rearranged the order.
The single words per monostich in "Last Words" in* Recalculating *are taken
from "Sentences My Father Used," a poem in* Controlling Interests *(Roof,
1980). Here is a juxtaposition of the beginning and the end, which feel very
different to me, due to the pattern of syntax:*

fields.
to
is
the
that
at
reflection
complete
slowly (p. 57)

---

15. *Walden,* "Conclusion," p. 500

. . . . .
laugh
amid
counter
course
let's
you
recover
your
mind
and
its
circular
transparent
rectitude (pp. 63–64)

In the opening part, the arrangement forces me to pay attention to the relation of the small, "ordinary" words in the second through fifth lines/stanzas within a textual "field" (if not "fields") that refers to pointing, being, emphasis, and location/direction. In the second part, I can discern a mini-narrative about the recovery of the addressee's mental state—and not necessarily a totally useful recovery. I don't think of the "original" "Sentences My Father Used."

Could you please say something about the framing devices in this poem and your intentions in using them? Earlier, you called yourself a "compulsive metonymist." For you as a (re-)reader, do various words in these two texts act as metonymies for salient aspects of poems in Girly Man *and/or for aspects of "Sentences My Father Used" respectively, or does your reading go somewhere else without pointing back to those texts?*

They point back in a pataquerical way. The first word frequencies piece I did was in *The Sophist* (1987), and it was based on transcripts of psycho-analytic sessions ("Word Frequencies in Spoken American English"). It's quite a long poem that starts with the most common English words, handled so beautifully by Kit Robinson in *The Dolch Stanzas* (1976). Those early sections have the beauty of the everyday, both concrete and spacious. But after a while, and in an uncanny way, a collective narrative begins to emerge. Around 2005, I wrote a suite of poems called "My Frequencies" which sampled the most commonly used words in *Girly Man, The Sophist, With Strings,* and *My Way: Speeches and Poems.* There is also one called

"Words Used Five Times in *Girly Man*" [in *Topsy-Turvy*]. These poems have a propulsive rhythm (especially when I perform them). I'm mining (and minding) the earlier works to create alternate versions via vectoral data slices. The poems provide a cross-sectional view of the source works. They illustrate a nonlinear mode of reading not only for my work, but also for any work. I kept the word frequency order but when words had the same frequency, I went with my preference. Subsequently, this kind of "distant reading" became popular in the digital humanities, but often for the opposite effect.

"Sentences My Father Used" sampled a recorded interview I did with my father, not long before he died in 1977 (so if not his last words, something like his last words to me). I used his interview as prior source for my poem, collaging it into the poem, which offers a sort of commentary on my father's words or perhaps my father's words offer the commentary on my poem. Poems have a funny way of being hijacked by their sources. "Last Words" was a simple procedure but struck me as very evocative, as getting at the heart of the poem by its, indeed, obsessive metonymy. That's especially true of the final lines, which you quote. Those one-word lines convey the poem's theme.

Derek Beaulieu did a small edition of *Last Words* (Calgary: No Press, 2005). I made a cover for the book which is a textual veil from "Sentences My Father Used." In the image, you can see the source for the first five lines of 'Last Words," which you quote. The first line of "Sentences My Father Used"—"Cast across otherwise unavailable fields"—is another way of getting at what I am saying here. My father's words, like my father, are both intimate and distant. The poems use textual refraction as a 4-D probe that allows me inside the words, but the content—my father's distance—remains refractory.

I'd like to return to one of the "pudding" poems. In "How Empty Is My Bread Pudding," the leaping from aphoristic section to section, I think, enacts what you "embrace," "a poetics of bewilderment":

> *I don't know where I am going and never have, just try to grapple as best as I can with where I am. The poetry that most engages me is not theoretically perspicacious, indeed it has a poetics and an aesthetics but not a predetermining theory; it is multiform and chaotic, always reformulating and regrouping. (Recalculating, pp. 83–84)*

While rereading the poem, I frequently don't know precisely how one section is (or whether it is) commenting on the one before, and I'm intrigued rather than

Casts across otherwise unavailable fields.
Makes plain. Ruffled. Is trying to

alle s codifiers to   date. Yet all is
"to ling chairs.   ief, the
vari the surprise   s which. Roofs that
        Straps,
        ate around
        disconsolation,   over, misuse of

          i ut belief, the
s ccesucceeds which. Roofs that
ding ss. Points at
the misuse of r ction
        belie
Stra veeps, enta complete
ate I realize slowly. vailable fields.

        ut belief, the   ing to
succeeds which. Roofs e. Yet all is
ss. Points at   , the
r misuse of r ction hich. Roofs that
veeps, enta complete it
I realize slowly.   f reflection
        at
mir ls, or how you in ils complete
        re
      a vapor, to   lowly,
          ntails
Surprising de that how you, intricate
nnounce, s codifiers to
      nds, or w u, in icate
leopards ding chair
      ke a v
hich is m ss the surprise
        ail that
ashion es. Straps,
      nce codi ists
stores uminate around
      s, le   ing c ai
for m ndatory dis lation,
      wh o less the
i bee s. Not so ble as
      prizes. S
no signs. I g eglasses,
        Rumi nd
up behind lar heap tall— pulleys,
      for ndate   iso
ther with mild fection, like
      ed e N ita
nes utto is, or a
bea o s es
t the ke, rivers discoursing

ds.
hat

ricate
ti

le

odi iers to
w u, in icate
g chair
r.
e surprise
      ail that
aps,
      codi ists
around
       using c ai
ess the
      ble as
es. S
eglasses,
ni nd
heap tall— pulleys,
      iso
ection, like
      ita
es
s discoursing

vailable fields.
ing to
e. Yet all is
, the
hich. Roofs that
it
f reflection
ils complete
lowly,
how you, intricate
or, to
details that
hells codifiers to

frustrated by my bewilderment, though anxiety from uncertainties is perhaps mitigated by the fact that recognizable tenets of your poetics (like the one above) keep recurring, figured differently from before, at intervals.

In With Strings, *you'd introduced, as you re-cite it in "How Empty Is My Bread Pudding," the notion that "art is made not of essences but of husks" (p. 88), and you return a few more times to the motif of "husk":*

> *A husk is "the outer covering of an ear of maize"; mine was always that, enmazed, or, in other words, the inner lining of our outer aspirations. History is husk and eternity its other shore . . .*
>
> *It's also that the tunes that are going through my head are remote; they remind me of being reminded. "Sense remote" is like "husks" in that way . . .*
>
> *The motif of poetry is just a husk. When it falls away you don't get to essence but are drifting in time, like always, the strings maybe lifting you up (like a puppet?) or else playing alongside. (p. 89)*

On the one hand, the "falling away" of the husk might prompt "a dread that the context that imparts meaning to our work is so fragile" (p. 83). But if one adopts the dictum that "longing for nothing is often the only way to get anywhere" (p. 85), then the husk, as the outer covering that reveals/unveils the "emptiness" within the "bread pudding"/poem, seems a way to experience bewilderment as openness to the absence of fixed referentiality, to travel without map or determinate telos. So there seems to be a metonymic relationship between "husk" and "bewilderment."

In your process of writing a poem like "How Empty Is My Bread Pudding" and then reading it afterward, what reflections about "husk" and "bewilderment" and a pragmatic "grappling as best I can with where I am" emerge?

Here we were in medias res. Thar she blew. And all the time I thought it was my heart propounding.

Sometimes I think I talk in riddles, think in riddles. Or the riddle talks me. But mine are riddles without answers. Rattles.

I am riddled with echoes.

It's not that there is nothing but frames any more than there is nothing but eyes or ears or minds. Our perception is informed and informing. Frames frame us, so naturally we want to beat the rap or at least protest the injustice. Problem is—we are guilty as charged.

Beating the rap is the foundation of rhythm, in my prosody. And isn't a wrap a kind of husk?

Imagine that the real is blank and that we come to terms with it by our midrashic overlays. What's blank is not meaningless or void, it is a site of possibility. Paved roads with direction signs are fine but one thing a poem can do is "show the road."

So, husk is to frame as bewilderment is to grappling.

I believe that you're nearing three decades in teaching after engaging in other kinds of labor. In "How Empty Is My Bread Pudding" we hear: "The issue of availability is in many ways external to what I do as a poet (in contrast, for example, to what I do as a teacher)" (p. 90). How have the frames, echoes, husks, blanks, bewilderments, recalculations, dialogic give, torque, push, pull, shove, and nudge, riddling, rattling, and raddling that mark teaching infiltrated ways in which your poiesis founders, dis/dys/re-orients itself, succeeds failingly, and errs felicitously?

I address poetry pedagogy in two essays in *Attack of the Difficult Poems* that include a discussion of my deformance "wreading" experiments and the "poem profiler." erica kaufman has invited me twice to Bard's Writing and Thinking seminars for (mostly) high school poetry teachers; I feel a strong bond with those teachers and with the Bard program. Let me mention also the remarkable work Al Filreis is doing with his ModPo MOOC and his Poem Talk series. A full set of my syllabi, going back to 1989, is available at <writing.upenn.edu/bernstein/> .

My practice of teaching has something in common with psychoanalysis: it focuses on evenly hovering attention to what students write and say. The substance of my seminars is not free-standing lectures on literary subjects but situational responses to students' perceptions and predicaments. Perhaps you could say I offer a sort of aesthetic therapy, opening up paths to reading by maximizing the ability to respond to multiple layers and kinds of meaning, to recognize impasses as formal features of a work, and to identify blockages, bumps, blips, and burps (just to keep it to b words) as part of the semantic spectrum. *It's on the spectrum!* is my motto. My aim is never to convince a student that a poem is good (or bad) but rather to show how it works, what's going on. But to do that, students need to feel free to express (and develop) their tastes and preference and to be aware these are going to be necessarily different than mine. (Say! Why should we share the same taste?)

Before every class, I read a response to the assigned readings by each student. These responses, not the literary work, drive the conversation. I sometimes get frustrated that this approach does not always allow time to read closely the works at hand, but that is the cost of the method. In my thirty years of teaching, I have never come into a class with a prepared lecture or any notes apart from notes on the student responses. And I am primarily interested, in undergraduate classes, in spotting "issues": resistances, negative responses, incomprehension, frustration. In fact, I design my syllabi to provoke such "negative" responses, in other words, to engage with what is often thought of as "difficulty."

My approach relates to what education advocates call "pedagogical content knowledge," which in my line of work means awareness of learning difficulties for those new to poetry. So, in a class, I am more interested in discussing what a student didn't understand, and why, than what a poem "means." And I have become adept as spotting poem/reader "hotspots." The best work I do is when I point to a comment by a student and say—you could reframe this same reaction and look at this *this* way. Acknowledging the student's response as legitimate, rather than in need of correction to a predetermined "right" answer, or casting the student as naive and in need of tutoring, I offer alternatives. In this sense, the student is never wrong. Even if an interpretation is totally unjustified by the text, the interpretation is "real," so the thing to explore is how did such an implausible (imaginary) reading arise. That is the crucial discussion to have. And that includes even such an elementary parapraxis (Freud's word for slips) as misreading a word.

Often it seems difficult to see the social or political value of writing poems; it's remote, at best. Teaching's value is tangible. Over the last thirty years, many critics (and mostly ones employed by a university) have said that "Language Poetry" sold out its radicality when I (and a few others) took teaching jobs. It's true I didn't like universities much and had no connection with any from the time I graduated college to just a couple of years before I got a job as a professor at Buffalo (when I was forty). I think there are critiques to be made about poet/essayist/scholars like me and the institutions we are part of. But while I often subject the literary academy to scathing criticism, I value highly the American university and I am grateful for the jobs I have had at Buffalo and Penn, for my colleagues, who often put up with me way beyond the call even of professional courtesy, but mostly for the many students with whom I have gotten a chance to work. From where I sit, about to retire, it's hard not to see that move from freelance office worker to university teacher as giving me the opportunity to be *more* radical, to prove if I could practice what I preached.

The truths are in the pudding.

[2018: *Dichtung Yammer*]

2.

THOMAS FINK: *In* Topsy-Turvy *(Chicago, 2021), there are four "Books," "Cognitive Dissonance," "As I Love," "Locomotion," and "Last Kind Words." Would you say something about the rationale for that structure and the "Book" titles? In the notes section of* With Strings *(Chicago, 2001), you state that the volume "is organized as a vortex, with each poem furthering the momentum of the book while curving its arc of attentional energy. The structure is modular: a short work might become part of a serial poem or a section of a serial poem might stand on its own. The effect is to make the book as a whole a string of interchanging parts. Political, social, ethical, and textual investigations intermingle, presenting a linguistic echo chamber in which themes, moods, and perceptions are permuted, modulated, reverberated, and further extended" (p. 131). Is this notion still applicable, two decades later, to* Topsy-Turvy?*

Yes. I think that description is accurate for all my collections from *Islets/Irritations* (1992) on; in fact, the new title alludes to this approach to making a book. I see poems as kinetic, so the book becomes a constellation of moving parts. I prefer *constellation* to *collage* or *montage*. Books inside books create more possibilities, clusters, webs, matrices—echoes. More strings attached. I began assembling *Topsy-Turvy* just a year ago, when the lockdown was starting. It felt urgent, right then, but also gave me something complex to focus on. In early spring, 2020, I submitted a manuscript, without section breaks, to Randy Petilos and Alan Thomas at the University of Chicago Press.[16] One of the (anonymous) readers suggested creating section breaks. There are 110 poems in *Topsy-Turvy*. This was just too many discrete items to create the ping and pong, push and pull, weft and wept, that I needed. Not like playing tennis without a net but like playing with just one net, or when wet. Using numbered sections seemed anodyne (what an annoying word to use here). I wanted each book to have its own distinct character and one that created a contrast, or better, conflict with the others. I'd used section titles for several other books, poems, and essays, but this time I called them "books." *Locomotion* was a title I almost used for *With Strings. As I Love* I had also thought of for a collection of essays about other poets, similar to the "Pitch" section in *Pitch of Poetry*; it takes on a different sense here.

Topsy-Turvy is the final work of a trilogy that includes *Recalculating* (2013) and *Near/Miss* (2018). Not that I planned it that way, but it's some-

---

16. What better place to acknowledge the extravagant generosity, acumen, and support of Alan and Randy, for which I remain forever indebted.

thing I've realized in retrospect. The titles themselves are a constellation, or maybe triangulation.

I cannot make it cohere. But I can make it bounce.

What makes the three books a trilogy?

Practice.

What I love about the poem "The Medicinal Uses of Factitious Airs" (p. 34), whose title, Google tells me, comes from a 1795 medical text by Thomas Beddoes and James Watt, is how it deploys "factitious echoes"; with lines frequently ending in "r" sounds, the poem consistently repeats whole lines as a pantoum does, but it messes up the very regular interlocking order of the pantoum:

Patience will get you only so far
And with and what and whether
See it bounce on the razor wire perimeter
I'd gamble the full three and seven
And with and what and whether
Reliance is a thing for warmer weather
See it bounce on the razor wire perimeter
A friend in need fills me with terror.

A pantoum has this structure: a b c d/ b e d f/ e g f h, whereas your first 12 lines look like this: a b c d b e c f d g a e. So the first 8 lines of each are the same, except you substitute d for c in your seventh line, but after that, every line in yours departs from the traditional pantoum structure. How did you come up with and execute such a wild formal idea? What effects resulted from the process?

I learned about Beddoes and Watt's book from Neşe Devenot, who was doing research for her fascinating dissertation on the poetics of psychedelics. "Factious airs" refers to the experimental fabrication of oxygen and nitrous oxide, but I went for the metaphoric senses, keeping in mind that Beddoes's son was the poet Thomas Lovell Beddoes, author of *Death's Jest-Book* (a favorite of my friend Jerome McGann).

If you put on "airs" aren't they always factitious?

And just today I discovered that the wonderful Scottish poet Peter Manson has a 2016 booklet called *Factitious Airs*.

It all ties together.

I thought a *pantoum* was a floppy three-corner hat with white bunting. But now I've looked it up and see what you mean. (And no I have not been inhaling nitrous oxide.) Ted Greenwald liked to say: don't repeat a word, repeat a line. Years ago I gave a name to these kinds of poems: nude formalism (call them *loons*).

"The Medicinal Uses of Factitious Airs" was written about five years ago, in Provincetown. What you say about factitious or phantom (*pantun*)—*fractured*—echoes resonates. I like to create echoic effects without a stable "original."

Air in the sense of tune.

Maybe what you hear is the echo of an absent pantaloon.

It's remarkable that your nude formalist echoing came so close in the first eight lines to the traditional pantoum without your intending it.

I'd call several poems in Topsy-Turvy *elegies—for example, for the poets Sean Bonney and Steve Dalachinsky and for the African American martyr Shields Green. "Karen Carpenter" is in a long, spinal shape, with hyphens separating some parts of some words to slow down the processing. Karen Carpenter had a prodigious range and powerful voice but sang treacly pop songs like "We've Only Just Begun," which you quote and felicitously transform. Although you use this shape for various poems in* Topsy-Turvy, *perhaps its elegiac function here is to remind us that Karen Carpenter suffered from anorexia nervosa and died of it at the age of 32: "Her voice / weeps / sin- / g- / ing / to God / o- / n a / fre- / quen- / cy / that / tu- / nes / out he- / r / cries" (p. 9).*

As I see it, you expose Karen Carpenter as the victim of the sacrificial (Christian) religiosity that she puts into practice; anorexia turns out to be a literal mortification of the flesh in the attempt to reach a theologically driven perfectionism that's paralleled by her songs' plaintively articulated idealisms. In the early seventies, the heyday of the Carpenters, I found the way she stretched out her syllables, as you do (as if parodying her "airs") in the poem, annoyingly mannered. But damn, she really could sing! And you give the meaning of pain/ masochism to these attenuations: "Hurting each / other, b- / ut- / c- / oming / back f- / or / more. / As i- / f / hurt / is / what / matters" (p. 9). Your poem provokes thought about the tragic consequences of bad art, bad ideology on a very capable singer. OK, Charles, correct me if my not so airy interpretation is off-key or in the wrong time-signature. And how did "Karen Carpenter" come about? How do you hear its skinny soundings?

Elegy may be what threads my last three poetry collections together. There is something haunting about Karen Carpenter's voice, as it dances over the abyss of kitsch and bathos. I wanted to write an essay about it, along the lines of Barthes in *Mythologies*, but ended up writing this poem. When she says "you" in what are ostensibly love songs, I hear that as an address to God. That's inherent in many love lyrics, but several of the Carpenters' songs crack the edge in a heartbreaking way. (If love is God's grace, its absence pierces the soul.) My narrow, broken, shard-like lines sound that out.

Like jagged edges of a broken piece of glass.

Did you see the early Todd Haynes's film, *Superstar: The Karen Carpenter Story* (1987), acted, in part, with Barbie dolls? He brings out some of the dynamics you note. I didn't listen to the Carpenters at the time they recorded their songs; perhaps, like you, I found them, if not mannered, empty. But not too long after, I got hooked, not on all the recordings, just a few songs. I don't think it's the backstory but something in the grain of the voice. But no doubt there are layers of identification (and distance) at play. In any case, that emptiness opened into something sublime. If there is a value in my poem, it's not to tell you what I think about the significant issues you raise, or not only tell you, but rather to offer a place to think about it.

At the end of "Creative Wreading and Aesthetic Judgment," you declare, "When reading poetry is not directed to the goal of deciphering a fixed, graspable meaning but rather encourages performing and responding to overlapping meanings, then difficulty ceases to be an obstacle and is transformed into an opening."[17]

"Poems of Passion," one fine opportunity for such an opening, is a feast of grammatical disruption. The first sentence, with its elegantly bumpy enjambments, reads: "Uneven throbs freak / repair, altered by slow / pontoon in sight of sodden / glare" (p. 13). The second, third, and fourth words in the sentence can either be nouns or verbs, and "uneven" is an adjective that could be yanked into service as a noun (if "throbs" is taken as a verb). If "freak" is a verb, then throbs that aren't even but irregular engage in freaking, yet are they "freaking out" (slang of the sixties and seventies) (about) the (im)possibility of "repair" or are they spooking repair? I presume that metonymy is at play: the throbber is freaking out the person(s) who want to repair or freaking out about the prospect of irreparability. The beginning of the next clause, a truncated past tense verb or verbal, seems connected to "repair" but perhaps the throbbing is what's altered. A reader ponders how the "pontoon," whether boat or bridge (and not a pantoum or pantaloon), alters either the uneven physical or emotional effect on the person

17. *Attack of the Difficult Poems: Essays and Inventions* (University of Chicago Press, 2011), p. 48

or the repair process. The "sodden / glare" could come from sunlight's impact
in the immediate locale or from a person. But "sodden" and "glare" give pause:
perhaps a synesthetic oxymoron!?

The next sentence shows that the "pontoon" is a boat and introduces two
characters: "Then, again, my darling / we'll paddle to the pass / where eyes
rebuff rough / glances and sins peruse / improbable glances" (p. 13). The "eyes" that
"rebuff" the expressions of others' "rough" eyes could belong to the speaker and the
"darling" or to onlookers being glared at by the paddlers. Further complications
arise in the third and final sentence: "Once / in time, thrice delayed, / caboose
will lead its prey / to inkless odes on feather boats / drunk in nick of fray." The
first two phrases indicate that something will happen after multiple delays, but
I don't know whether the "caboose" is the kitchen area of the "pontoon" or just a
substitution for the word in the previous sentence. Why are the speaker and the
darling "prey" of the "caboose"? Or is this a metonym indicating they are victims
of their own travel experience? If prey, they are prey with benefits: "inkless
odes," a nonverbal or at least non-written articulation of praise. This happens
on other vehicles, "feather boats" that also convey the luxury of a fashion acces-
sory ("feather boas"). As for who is "drunk" in the cut of combat, we don't know
whether it's the couple or the boat. I detect an allusion to Arthur Rimbaud's
"The Drunken Boat" and also to "As One Put Drunk into the Packet-Boat,"
the first poem in John Ashbery's Self-Portrait in a Convex Mirror; *the poem's*
title is the opening line of Andrew Marvell's "Tom May's Death." But neither
allusion can "explain" your poem's ending. Perhaps both couple and boat are
"drunk," the first with passion (in "Poems of Passion") and the second because of
turbulent water.

I often think of those poems by Ashbery and Rimbaud and echo them
in other poems too. I appreciate your commentary, which reminds me of
many delightful exchanges I have had with translators, trying to puzzle
through one of my poems, as you are. To adapt a remark of Gertrude
Stein: they may be puzzling, but they are not puzzles. To make a trans-
lation, you have to figure out certain things that you don't need to in
writing or reading a poem. So I often spend time looking at one of my
poems from the point of view of a translator. But if I performed this
poem, or when I reread it, I am not tempted to figure it out. Maybe that's
what "passion" means.

I hear the poem as making grammatical sense throughout, so, yes, to
do that means hearing what might more commonly be a noun as a verb,
as in "freak repair"—not an accidental repair or a repair by a freak but
a repair that has been "freaked." The *OED* (my most frequent reference

source) does have *freak* as a transitive verb meaning "To fleck or streak whimsically or capriciously." Sounds like my poetics. Maybe something like—"the uneven throbs" are undermining "repair," which certainly is my experience. *Out, out damn throbs. Uneven throbs the heart of my true love's hair.* Maybe the *pontoon* is related to that obscure *pantoum* of desire. Once I had to explain to a translator that my personal association with my phrase "fat-bottom boat" was a Florida "glass-bottom boat" trip I took as a child, even though "flat-bottom boat" would be the more likely association. But why not just a boat with a fat bottom? Sometimes a pontoon is just a pantomime (aunt of mine).

Caboose: what's behind's in the lead, one of my (inconstant) reversals.

Is there no way out of this echo chamber?

Niedecker writes, "No layoff / from this / Condensery."[18]

"Poems of Passion" has fifty-three words in twelve five- to eight-syllable, lines. The title comes from an 1883 collection by Ella Wheeler Wilcox.

Here's to more and more echoing! Recalling that Ashbery has a poem in The Double Dream of Spring *(1970) called "Variations, Calypso and Fugue on a Theme by Ella Wheeler Wilcox."*

Speaking of quatrains, "Covidity" is one of your "simple" quatrain poems, ballads that could be made into pop tunes: "The covid gonna get me / If not now, it will / The covid gonna kill me / Find me where I live" (p. 138). You've been writing these ballads for a while now, and the best known is "The Ballad of the Girly Man." In "Covidity," I often hear the meter of Johnny Cash rather than the Puritan hymn structure of Emily D., though, like Amherst's feminist rapper, you sometimes rhyme or slant-rhyme the second and fourth lines of each quatrain: "Too much death surrounding / I darn near given up / Keep calling on the telephone / But you're hung up on Skype." The speaker, who calls "social distance" "a pain in the soul" that is "too heavy a load" is "hung up" on the absence of a beloved addressee; the atmosphere of "covidity" intensifies his avidity for intimacy: "You've always been distant / But not from me / Now I feel you drifting / Like you're far out at sea." He (if it's male) declares that "if I'm distant from you / I'm sunk before I swum." The poem's funniest passage counters the Romantic passages, shows that the speaker complies with pandemic protocol despite the "pain in the soul," and indicates that he's doomed no matter what he tries to do: "I practice social distance / Even got an oversize mask / Feel like the Lone Ranger / Just before he got the clap." The line, "And I am much misunder-

18. "Poet's Work," in *The Collected Works*, ed. Jenny Lynn Penberthy (Berkeley: University of California Press, 2002), p. 194

stood" in the third quatrain is repeated with a key difference in the final line: "And we are much misunderstood."

Keeping in mind that poetry "is made of words, poetry, not ideas" ("Ars Impotens," p. 99), I feel that the move from "I" to "we" feels political, and "covidity" unfortunately became politicized. As far as I can tell, the entire book shows most admirable restraint in refraining from alluding directly to the narcissist-in-chief who left the White House, screaming and kicking, two months ago. So, it may be impertinent for me to ask (rather baldly): what specific thoughts about the political environment "stung you into song" to produce "Covidity"? And how do you think this poem relates or doesn't relate to some of your earlier ballads?

I appreciate your commentary and it makes me happy to have a reader who hears, and can point to, many of my echoes. Echoes, as I use the word, are different from allusions: they are unstable and involve palpable overlays rather than "pointing back" (anaphor). Like the caboose leading the train, the echo remains while the origin may be lost. Or maybe there is no origin. Or possibly there are many.

Topsy-Turvy was written almost entirely before the pandemic, but there are several poems I wrote during that first month, when things were so bad in New York. "Covidity," "Shelter in Place," and "Before the Promise" directly address "rona." I address Trump and the nature of the ballad in "The Ballad Laid Bare by Its Devices (Even): A Bachelor Machine for MLA," in *Near/Miss*, which was written just after the 2016 election. My ballads, while sharing the sort of publicly legible address suggested by the form, are fractured, in the sense of the "fractured fairy tales" I watched as a kid, though my fracturing is of a different kind.

"Always historicize" but don't *only* historicize.

Topsy-Turvy is stamped by the time it was written and by the person who wrote it. Negotiating how and why is not just the pleasure of the text but the value of the poems.

Your distinction between echoes and allusions—hinging on stability/instability of reference—is very interesting and useful. I'm going to cite you on this point when this issue of reference comes up in my literature classes.

A translation of Virgil's Eclogues is the basis for your collaboration with artist Richard Tuttle in "Echologs," which begins:

Damoetas
To all's high, guys! everything that echoes!,
what gives ground and by Jove'll cure our songs.

Menalcas
But it's me that beauty loves!; all her charms
surround, crowns of sweetest ruddy roses.

Damoetas
My girl's cupid, first she creams me with an apple
then slides behind the willows: peek-a-boo.

Menalcas
My guy's no tease: he comes on to me so often
our dogs know him much better than my bitch. (p. 85)

What seems most Bernsteinian in this passage is "she creams me with an apple."
And Menalcas's second sentence has the wonderful vulgarity that you can find
in good translations of Catullus.

What impelled the two of you to choose this famous pastoral text by Virgil?
What did you learn from your conversations with Tuttle about the process? Was
there a lot of negotiation about particular words and phrases? What did you
learn about language from the labor of (re)translation?

In the spring of 2014, Richard Tuttle suggested that we work together
on translating the poetry match in *Eclogues*. At the time, he made a
practice of reading some lines of Greek or Latin every morning. Before
we started, Richard suggested we meet at a show of first-century BCE
Roman sculpture at Christie's gallery in Rockefeller Center. As we
looked at the many busts and full figures, Richard said that, contrary to
the common view, he liked these works as much as, if not more than, the
earlier art from Greece. At one point we were able to take a sculpted head
off the shelf and hold it in our hands. There was directness, an intimacy,
to this work—an immediacy. In contrast, many of the translations of
Virgil seemed archaic, filled with arcane references and crusty figurative
language. I wanted to create the same kind of presence for Virgil that
we experienced with the Roman busts: "a ball of light in one's hand," as
Pound put it.[19]

Richard pointed to the cosmopolitan sophistication of Virgil's poems;
yes of course "pastoral," but also playing to the royal court. So part of

19. *Guide to Kulchur* (New York: New Directions, 1970), p. 55

what I had in mind was translating that sense of uncanny contemporaneity, recognizing the paradoxical task of the translator here.

Richard and I shared a great enthusiasm for the Latin writers from two thousand years ago.

Lucretius is a God to me, along with his cosmic cousin, Baruch Spinoza.

It was in the year that I turned sixteen that I encountered my first teacher of poetics, Marcus Tullius Cicero. From that greatest of all orators I learned to love periods more than sentences; yes, Thomas, periods, and not of the biological kind that afflict young woman at a most awkward age: no, not biological periods, Thomas, put those out your mind; I speak here today, to you, and to the friends who have gathered to listen, and to those who may have found our conversation who we don't yet know—I speak of verbal periods, with their weaving and dodging, dodges and weaves, yes, with their exhortations and loops; these verbal utterances have a force, Thomas, no, let us not say force, let us say, and then let us repeat, a charm, charm and power, that our modern and tranquilized sentences, caught up in anemic notions of decorum, cannot, cannot and will never, match.

Virgil, Cicero, Lucretius, and, indeed, Catullus. Richard and I had already translated together Catullus's most famous poem, you know, the one about how even though you hate somebody you can't stop loving them too, and how it drives you crazy. (Collected in *Recalculating*.) And, as you note, a number of Catullus translations do have the erotic charge and the vulgar vernacular I was looking for in translating Virgil's poetry match.

However, I would never have thought to translate Virgil.

Richard and I worked on the translations for months. Richard would start me off by sending a fairly literal rendering of a couplet. Then I'd get to work. I consulted a number of historical translations and commentaries. My rudimentary knowledge of Latin came in handy. Last year, I decided to supplement the translations I made for "Echologs" by compiling a set of comparative translations.[20] Reading through that set of translations, each with a different approach, is great fun and offers the fullest answer to your question.

In "Poetic Citizenship and Negative Dialectics," which was written for an academic conference on poetry and citizenship, you alternate (dialectically)

---

20. "Echologs" is in *Topsy-Turvy*. Art and Letters (Cambridge, MA: 2020) published a pamphlet version with comparative translations, available as a free pdf: <writing.upenn.edu/epc/authors/bernstein /books/Echologs-Art-Letters.pdf>.

between plain type and italics to foreground different perspectives without valorizing particular ones:

Poetry is best that governs least.

No it isn't.

Poetry and citizenship are inconsolably incommensurable, conjoined at the heart but beating time to different drummers.

From time to time.

Aesthetic justice is symbolic and dwells next to, not in, the world of political action.

Give me a break! *(p. 106)* . . .

The promise of a poem, the kind of poetry I want, is that it refuses reality.

But is it good for the Jews?

To be a poetic citizen is not to act as a citizen but to perform as a poet. But there can be no citizenship without poetry. Even citizenship is symbolic. Citizenship that refuses dialogue with the delirious, wanton, discomforting possibilities of poetry approaches nativism.

Get off your low horse.

If citizenship is the first language of the democrat, then poetry is a second language that, out of love and deep need, refuses to obey its mother tongue.

Poetry has no purpose and that is not its purpose. *(p. 108)*

What does your allusion to Adorno's Negative Dialectics *in the poem's title signify? The first voice often sounds like your aphorisms in essays; that second voice is slippery: why should the first voice "get off [its] low horse"? The "dialogue" poses questions: Couldn't "discomforting possibilities" stemming from the refusal of "reality" be "good for the Jews" and the Palestinians and Croatians, etc.? Does realpolitik/ideology constrain imagination any more or less than sterile uses of imagination fail to account for ideology? Does poetry's purposelessness make it the reader's job to discover multiple purposes for their engagement with it? How does the "negative dialectic" of "Poetic Citizenship" reflect your own current dialogue with past "selves," past and present fellow travelers, antagonists, former students?*

Poetic thinking can be activist: dialogic rather than monologic, not to say *lyric* (but, sure, my poems are as lyric as the next guy's).

The gaps I mean (the poem as mending wall).

There is a chilling shame directed at any aversion to grounding a poem in a stable, anaphoric, positive, lyric voice. Negative dialectics: I may be guilty of that, but I refuse to be ashamed. My book is signed with my name and my poems are as much identifiably mine as anyone else's; even my aversions are anaphoric (that is, can be assigned to a biographical person outside, or "before," the poem).

Negative dialectics is the chicken soup of the soul, poetry's soil.

In other words, there is more than one way to get to Rome. (Take a left just a half-mile after where the filling station used to be.)

In other words, sometimes "yelping dogs" can orient you, but you don't need to become one—I mean the yelping dogs in myself.

In other words, sometimes not knowing is the closest we come to truth. Because truth doesn't listen to us; we listen for it.

And that means, from time to time, just listening.

[2021: *Dichtung Yammer*. Condensed.]

ACT THREE

Doubletalk

(*allegro*)

It is therefore manifest, that mediocrity ought to be allowed, yea indulged, to the good subjects of England. Nor can I conceive how the world has swallowed the contrary as a maxim, upon the single authority of Horace. Why should the golden mean, and quintessence of all virtues, be deemed so offensive in this art? or coolness or mediocrity be so amiable a quality in a man, and so detestable in a poet?

Martinus Scriblerus (Jonathan Swift)

Als Nicht-Nichtjudebin ich Jude
(As Not-Not-Jewish, I'm Jew)

Jean Améry

Summa contra Gentiles

An Oration in Sixteen Cantos

I have set myself the task of making known, as far as my limited powers will allow, the truth that the poetic faith professes, and of setting aside the errors that are opposed to it. To use the words of Hilarity: 'I am aware that I owe this to Art as the chief duty of my work, that my every word and sense may speak of It.'

After Aquinas

διχθὰ δέ μοι κραδίη μέμονε φρεσὶν ὁρμαίνοντι
(in two my heart torn turning it over)

Iliad 16:435

Trouble is my business.

Philip Marlowe (Raymond Chandler)

1. *Alter Kockers*: Cranky Poems for Aging with Anger, Resentment, Intemperance, and Regret

POEMS TO HELP YOU AGE WITHOUT LOSING YOUR NEGATIVE CAPABILITIES.

This anthology collects centuries of poems of bad advice and denial, guaranteed to pour salt on wounds large and small from poets who developed exquisite expertise in nursing "old wounds in old age" and exacerbating infirmities (real and imagined). Sections include "I Don't Want a Revolution If I Have to Dance," "Despair Springs Eternal," "I Did It Before You Were Born," and "Incontinent Songs."

"A comfortless collection bound to agitate and annoy while discouraging the elderly from aging gracefully."—[Name Withheld at request of family]

Coming soon from You Bet Your Life! Press's Dorothy Parker Collection.

2. FirstGen

Dicunt ut ego sit super haec omnia; sed infra ego est. Haec vita non est; id est fossio. Statutum limitum memoriae non est. (They say I am supposed to be above all this, but I am below it. This is not autobiography, it is excavation. There is no statute of limitations on memory.)

Caudio Amberiam

The assembly hall at the Bronx High School of Science had about one thousand seats, enough for a third of the student body. It was packed the day in the spring of 1968 when I was called to the stage to accept the Award of Excellence for Journalism from the New York *Times* and St. Bonaventure University, for editing the school newspaper, and the Yale Club of New York Book Award, for outstanding high school student. I got three books for the award, but I only remember one of them: *Who Governs? Democracy and Power in an American City* by Robert Dahl. But neither that book nor C. Wright Mills's more incisive *The Power Elite* quite prepared me for going to college that fall. I got a good education at Science and appreciated the commitment to learning on the part of my fellow students and teachers. Science was more like Dahl's New Haven. Harvard College was something else, something Science, and the enclave of mostly Jewish middle-class liberals that had been my world, could not prepare me for.

My parents were thrilled I had gotten into Harvard. However, they had no conception of what a place like that was like nor how much it would be, for me, like emigrating from their world into a different culture. It wasn't just Harvard, but also my politics and cultural engagements. Once I left for college, I never spent a single night in the apartment in which I'd grown up.

I go into all this in more detail in the autobiographical interview I did with Loss Pequeño Glazier (collected in *My Way: Speeches and Poems*). My mother, Sherry Bernstein, hated that interview. I don't think she otherwise read much of my work or, if she did, that it would have been of interest to her apart from the very significant fact that I wrote it. My mother felt I had been too harsh about my father in the interview, and she was incensed that I didn't talk about her. I explained that if I had written about her, she wouldn't have liked it, not that I would be negative, just that she had very strong preferences about how she wanted to be portrayed. My father, Herman Bernstein, had died long ago in 1978. In any case, my mother was right. In the account of my growing up, I was unswervingly accurate. I read fancy books and went to the opera, my parents did not. But what I failed to account for was how my parents had made the life I entered possible—built floor to ceiling bookshelves for me, paid for every book and record I had, and left me alone in my room to pursue my interests. In other words, made possible a world for me that was not possible for them to be a part of. They did this for me because that's what they believed in, even if it meant, for my father, fierce disagreements with my politics and ultimately for my not choosing to take advantage of my blue-chip degree in a way that made sense to him.

After my mother died in 2017 at ninety-seven,[1] I was surprised to find a letter my father had written to a Harvard dean, pleading with them not to expel me after I had been arrested during the occupation of Harvard's University Hall in the second semester of my freshman year. My father wrote that I meant well, was committed to nonviolence, but also that I would be angry if I knew he was writing the letter. I don't recall any conversations with my father about that and would have tried to avoid any.

Four of us from Bronx Science got into Harvard—two Jews, a Japanese American, and a Latino, and two of my classmates got into Radcliffe—one WASP, one Black. I both admired and liked these classmates, though I hardly saw them once we moved to Cambridge. Looking back, it seems as if we were chosen to go to another planet, but without spacesuits.

I was FirstGen—first generation to go to college. Only I wish I had known that at the time, I mean that it was a *thing*. At it happens, I first heard the term many decades too late to help me with freshman orientation. Nor was I aware of the history of Jews in the Ivies, which also would have been useful. I had too little awareness that people might have been reacting to me because of my Jewishness.

Coming to college in the fall of 1968, I felt acutely alienated from most of my classmates and the social culture of the school. At the time, I chalked that up to something similar to FirstGen, but not quite the same—being from a public school. I can also see now that I was experiencing something common for first year at college, regardless of background. Before my freshman year, I hadn't had the opportunity to experience prep school culture. In 1968, Harvard took 18.5 percent of those who applied from all schools, in contrast to 53 percent of the applicants from just six selected New England prep schools; sixty-three of them were part of my class.[2] These "elites," as Mills describes them, dominated because they were on familiar ground and, indeed, many knew each other.[3] On top of that, the

---

1. I created a memorial page at <jacket2.org/commentary/sherry-bernstein-funeral>.

2. See Jerome Karabel, *The Chosen: The Hidden History of Admission and Exclusion at Harvard, Yale, and Princeton* (Boston: Houghton Mifflin, 2005), p. 369.

3. In my limited experience, many from the favored preparatory schools were oblivious to the fact that their admission was not merit-based; their schooling had emphasized preferential admission as their

men in my class outnumbered the women by manyfold. When the university president, Nathan Pusey, was confronted with this discrepancy, he said that the number of men could not be reduced because Harvard had a responsibility to educate the future leaders of America.[4]

While, I had strong bonds with professors and many fellow students, much of the "private" upper-class social life of Harvard remained unknown to me—I never even heard about the clubs, for example, and felt unwelcome at literary coteries such at the *Advocate*.[5] Despite editing the "official" freshman literary magazine, and my engagement with poetry, I was unaware of the Robert Lowell clique that has had such a lock on mainstream poetry culture. I didn't know, for example, that Lowell taught seminars while I was at Harvard. Some of this lack of knowledge is just me, what I knew, who I was friendly with or talked to, and my own decidedly nonconforming ideas.

In my last year in high school and in college, I joined my fellow students to protest the Vietnam War and racism. In his 1975 article "What Did You Do in the Class War, Daddy?," published in the *Washington Monthly*, James Fallows famously addressed those of us, including himself, who avoided the draft. Fallows was editor of our college newspaper, where he modeled gravitas in contrast to those of us more actively opposing the war.[6] In his essay, Fallows expresses his shame that people like him gamed the draft system rather than resisting it honorably by going to jail or to Canada, as if we should have observed Marquess of Queensberry rules. He feels we let working-class people serve for us. (As it happens, I applied for landed immigrant status in Canada just after I graduated from college but was

---

inalienable right (a view adopted by the majority of the 2023 Supreme Court). Naturally, there would be a certain disdain for anyone who could not grease the wheels of the buggy. Career-enhancing clubbiness was open to a select group who were admitted on merit but aspiring to be accepted by those who weren't. "The more 'fency' they become, the less of God's power do they have," as Henry Roth puts it in *Call It Sleep* (New York: Farrar, Straus and Giroux, 1991), p. 183. At the same time, some of the most virulent student radicals were defectors from the "fency" side of the street. Which is only to say that *merit* has always been a gerrymandered category.

4. See Karabel, p. 441.

5. I did make one submission to the *Advocate*. A friendly editor told me I would have to be an established experimentalist for such an unconventional poem to be accepted. While *Catch-22* was published in 1961, the film came out around the time of this conversation.—I don't recall if I had ever heard of the Signet Society, Harvard's "arts and letters society." Snob that I was, I wouldda found in such "Society" barbarians guarding the gates.

6. Fallows's "left of mainstream" but "moderate" position, as the *Harvard Crimson* characterized it in a 1976 interview, would today be called bothsidesism. Indeed, his interviewer characterizes Fallows position as being that "what everyone did then—on both sides—was 'so extreme and so unreasonable ... sounded harsh, inhuman, bitter and wrong and cruel ... irrational.'" See Charles E. Shepard, "The Education of Jim Fallows: From Crimson President to Carter Speechwriter," *Harvard Crimson*, October 25, 1976.

turned down, so my choice on that front would have been to violate Canada's immigration rules.) Fallows, however, does not express shame that class status and gender allowed so many of his classmates, by default, to game the Harvard-Radcliffe admissions process, if you can be said to game a game that is already gamed in your favor. Nor does Fallows appear to be ashamed that, based on the gravitas of his shame, and the fact he went to Harvard, he got to work for mainstream publications while many with more radical views or from less prestigious colleges did not. Those of us opposing the war did it not just for the Vietnamese—I would never have taken arms against the Vietnamese people, and neither would Fallows. But the antiwar movement was also for American GIs, who were fighting in an unjustifiable war built on lies. The draft system was rigged for sure but so was the war, so was the American class, race, and gender systems. Showing contempt for the draft protocols is not something to be ashamed of. The issue was stopping a racist war.

I had been opposed to the 1969 occupation of University Hall and to the use of any force, blocking entrances, or destroying any property. I argued for these positions at several meetings. When a massive police brigade showed up just feet from where I was asleep in my dorm room, I joined the protesters in solidarity and was arrested. Decades later, Richard Hyland attended one of my undergraduate modernist poetry courses at Penn. At that point he was a distinguished law professor at Rutgers.[7] Of the 135 students accused of being in University Hall, three were provisionally expelled. Hyland was given a "suspended suspension," while I was placed under "warning" for my remaining college years.[8] Hyland sat in on my Penn class in part to make up for the liberal arts education he felt he missed because of his political work and its consequences.

In 1970, I directed a production of the musical *The Persecution and Assassination of Jean-Paul Marat as Performed by the Inmates of the Asylum of Charenton under the Direction of the Marquis de Sade*, which I discuss in the Glazier interview.[9] What I didn't realize until later was that our lead singer,

7. When last I checked, you could find the photo by a web image search with each of our names in quotes. (I propose for MLA format this style: "When I last checked" + search terms.) As part of my class, Hyland wrote superb essays on Charles Reznikoff and Vachel Lindsay, available to *Jacket2*.

8. James K. Glassman, "Which Side Were You On?," *The Browser, Harvard Magazine*, May 2005, and email from Richard Hyland, April 20, 2023. See also Declan J. Knieriem, "'Haunted by the War': Remembering the University Hall Takeover of 1969," *Harvard Crimson*, May 27, 2019.

9. The production ran April 23–26 and April 30–May 3, 1970, with one subsequent benefit performance. David Ignatius reviewed the show in the *Harvard Crimson*, April 28, 1970. In the online digital scan, there is a typographical error in first line: "Paradise Note" should be "Paradise Now" (the Living Theater work). You can find Susan Bee's poster for the show at <writing.upenn.edu/epc/authors/bee /images/marat-sade_1970-72dpi.jpg>.

who played the role of Marat's assassin Charlotte Corday, was Jill Stein, the Green Party candidate who facilitated the election of Donald Trump. I am still trying to process that. *Marat/Sade* was performed in street clothes in the dining room of Adams House, where I lived, and my concept, in radical contrast to Peter Brook's production, was to break down the artifice of the play, overlapping "now" time with the historical events of the French Revolution. The actual "master" of Adams House played the master of the insane asylum. After the run, we did an extra performance as a benefit for the Bobby Seale Defense Fund, the equivalent of Black Lives Matter today. In the final scene the cast chanted "Free Bobby Seale" along with chants related to the French Revolution. Some in the audience joined in, in the spirit of the production.

Two years later, the Harvard alumnae magazine's Undergraduate column featured a graduation piece by classmate Michael Kinsley, who was, in his account, the cousin of my assigned freshman roommate.[10] Kinsley would go on to become a prominent "liberal" pundit and editor, at one point editing *The New Republic.*

Kinsley describes our first day at college from the point of view of someone looking at mongrels at the gate, making a point that my father drove a Cadillac up to our dorm room and calling me "the beard." It's true my father did have Cadillac and thought of it as a status symbol, although he had gone out of business six years earlier, which triggered a heart attack, so he had not been able to buy a new car since. In 1968, I must admit to being embarrassed by my father's Caddy; now I am embarrassed that I felt that way. I wish I could get the '55 Caddy convertible my father loved. Kinsley does not mention the brand of his father's car, though perhaps he was dropped into Harvard Yard by helicopter. He characterizes my parents as "prosperous"; given we were driving into a bastion of wealth such as me or my parents had hardly seen, I take this to mean *mercantile.*

In the article, Kinsley reports that in my first hour at Harvard (I had not made a campus visit) I mentioned to my assigned roommate that I had an interest in "music and philosophy." It is a puzzling detail for Kinsley to throw in if you don't realize that, in contrast to Bronx Science, where this was a respectable pair of interests, disdain for "music and philosophy" was a source of pride for some of my Harvard classmates. Kinsley goes on to suggest how gouache "the beard" was to be carrying into a dorm room

---

10. "Monday-morning Martyrs and Other Classmates," *Harvard Bulletin* 74:7 (1972), pp. 16–17. *Harvard Alumni Bulletin* changed its name to *Harvard Bulletin* in 1969 and then to *Harvard Magazine* in 1973. Kinsley refers to me only as "Charles" and "the beard" in his essay but his details are so specific as to make my identity apparent to those on the scene.

"boxes and boxes of books and records," and an "IBM typewriter." Just imagine, bringing books and a typewriter to college. What could I have been thinking? Perhaps he was looking for my squash rackets. Kinsley also remarks on my "massive stereo system": in reality, two small speakers and an amplifier. He then suggests that my mother was pushy; indeed, a Jewish mother settling her son in his new, small dorm room. The most surprising thing about this account is that Kinsley is also Jewish, but one showing us that he fit in, while me and my parents did not.

Though I don't remember meeting Kinsley, he was evidently keeping tabs on me and goes on to tell the story of my University Hall arrest, which for him was an "exploit" done to make classmates "jealous." He then turns to the benefit performance of *Marat/Sade*:

> Charles had felt moved to interrupt the proceedings occasionally for chants of "Free Bobby Seale" and "Get Some Feathers, Get Some Tar, Let's Go Get the CRR."[11] After the play Charles stood on a table and urged the audience to join the cast in a brief riot through Harvard Square (popular fad in those days) to show solidarity with the Black Panthers currently on trial in New Haven and to "fight repression by the U.S. Government and Harvard University." Charles had to wait till the next regularly scheduled riot to vent his ire. . . . to make up an end to this anecdote, I might say [Charles] turned pre-med and was buried in the chem labs, or he'd dropped out of school and settled on a commune in Oregon, or he's working on a book of prose poems for Little, Brown about the death of the revolution.

In the following issue, *Harvard Bulletin* published the earliest example of a genre which I had to turn to far more than I would like.

False Statements

To the Editor:

The following statements made in the February Undergraduate Column ("Monday-morning martyrs and other classmates," page 16) are false:

I. "After the play Charles stood on a table and urged the audience to join the cast in a brief riot through Harvard Square."

11. The first I heard this awful "CRR" chant was in this Kinsley column. It may be what is now called a "false flag." The CRR (Committee of Rights and Responsibilities) was the disciplinary committee that handed down punishments to those who occupied University Hall. In 1970, just as much as today, I had aesthetic standards about what I would say, write, sing, or chant.

2. ". . . Charles had to wait until the next regularly
scheduled riot to vent his ire . . ."

        C. BERNSTEIN '72
        Cambridge[12]

This remains a model of brevity that I once aspired to. As you can see, I've fallen into the spell of digression, in this case about an incident better left forgotten. Under my letter, the editors posted their apology: "The BULLETIN is sorry to have published erroneous statements, and apologizes to the student referred to in the Undergraduate column." "The student" being me.

Now I have to ask your indulgence, because I am going to quote nearly the full letter of my roommate from sophomore and junior year, David Keyser, whose play "I Had to Get a Ticket to the Matinee" I directed when we were freshman, at the blackbox space of the Loeb Drama Center, and who went on to become a lawyer and professor. When I first met David, he reminded me of a character out of a Eugene O'Neill play or a Thomas Wolfe story. David was from St. Louis and spoke of his plan to write the great American novel. He was a lost soul but with a heart as big as anyone I've known. I was sad to learn he died a few years ago. I thank him for this:

To the Editor:

Michael Kinsley's recent ad hominem attack on student radicals
centered its ire on one murkily drawn and supposedly menacing
figure named "Charles." Kinsley without going so far as to
reveal who "Charles" in reality was, gave enough hints so that
anyone familiar with the Harvard scene would soon recognize
the mysterious rioter's identity. As a former roommate of
"Charles," and, more importantly, as a man with serious
political disagreements with "Charles," I must register my
protest against Kinsley's snide disregard of truth. Not only
has Mr. Kinsley not checked into Charles' real politics (a
fact which the BULLETIN should have noted), but he has in the
process accused Charles of two crimes which I can swear that
Charles never even thought of committing--inciting to riot and
destruction of property--the first overtly cited, the second
covertly implied in his childish and insipid manner. Charles
is one of the most dedicated pacifists I know. . . .

Charles deplored the riots and was in tears over what had
happened on April 15, 1970, as he has been nearly in tears
many times over the violence that has wrecked the hopes

12. Letters to the Editor, *Harvard Bulletin* 74:8 (1972), p. 4

he might have had for building a better society. Charles's
decency and sincerity are common knowledge among his friends,
and I have never known him to lift his voice in anger, much
less to incite to riot. The most disturbing thing about the
whole Kinsley article was not its libelous accusations--one
might expect them considering the insipid paranoia that Mr.
Kinsley's writing so often displays. What is a disgrace is
that the BULLETIN would allow those libels to be published
unchallenged. Kinsley's article may well serve the cause of
Harvard fund-raising. It most assuredly does not serve the
cause of Truth.

DAVID R. KEYSER '72
Cambridge

David's reference to "April 15, 1970" is crucial for understanding Kinsley's
smear. On that day violent riots erupted in Harvard Square after Bobby
Seale–related protests.[13] Kinsley knows there is no connection between me
and that event, weeks before our benefit, but he insinuates a link.

Kinsley's red-baiting is hardly news. But this story provides a snapshot
of Harvard in 1972. For the men at the top, antiwar demonstrations were
mocked as being akin to buying a sports car or "scoring" a date: something
to brag about. Far worse, protesting anti-Black racism was a fad equated
with fomenting riots, while the reality of racist repression in the United
States and indeed at Harvard was derisively dismissed. In the view of Kins-
ley and his kind, those who questioned the status quo were secretly strivers
with big stereos whose parents drove vulgar cars and who would sell out
their values when the first attractive offer came along. After four years at
Harvard, maybe it was difficult for Kinsley to envision values that were not
transactional. That was one kind of Harvard education. But there was also
the one he missed.

After the *Harvard Bulletin* article was published, I asked Stanley Cavell
for advice on what to do. Imagine, he said, that you knock on Kinsley's door
and say, "My name is Charles *Bernstein*," and punch him in the face. Cavell
didn't mean that I should provoke a physical confrontation. I've never hit
anyone. But what Cavell said, like a Zen master's slap, brought me to my
senses.

Marat/Sade is about the perils of political terrorism but also the motiva-
tions for it. That's why I wanted to present a "poor theater" version of this
mix of "music and philosophy," with students playing asylum inmates in

13. Garrett Epps, "Rioting Devastates Harvard Square; Windows Smashed, Scores Injured," *Harvard Crimson*, April 16, 1970

the thrall of competing political philosophies. The show had many sold-out performances, and I was lucky to work with the brilliant musician Leonard Lehrman. A few years later, I called my first book *Asylums*, in the sense of sanctuaries but also places of incarceration. I don't know if Citizen Kinsley ever saw a performance of our theatrical phantasmagoria, but if he had, he would have heard these lines, sung (to Richard Peaslee's music) by the students/players/inmates:

Marat we're poor and the poor stay poor
Marat don't make us wait any more
We want our rights and we don't care how
We want our revolution NOW![14]

3. Woodstock: Peace and Mud

All through my first year at college, I listened to the LPs of the musicians who assembled at Woodstock the following summer, having bought most of the albums one by one on my frequent visits to Sam Goody's Rockefeller Center store. (I recently gave the remainder of my LP collection, several overstuffed boxes, to Lawrence Kumpf of Blank Forms, though only after Jay Sanders and Bruce Pearson has skimmed the cream [though I never had a Cream record].)

I knew many of the songs of the Woodstock bands by heart, and they were the soundtrack for the antiwar/antiracist demonstrations that led to my arrest at college in the spring of 1969, just months before the music festival.

Susan and I bought advance tickets for Woodstock, a big expense for us at the time. We drove out to Bethel from New York, getting snarled up in a day-long (not Day-Glo) traffic jam. We ended up parking in deep mud in a field perhaps a mile from the festival. I had no idea how we would be able to get out of the space. (Such were the bourgeois concerns that overwhelmed me at the time.)

The area in front of the music stage was packed with people. From where we stood (sitting in the mud was no more appealing to me then than it would be now), it was impossible to see the faces of the musicians. The sound was considerably worse than from on my 1957 AM portable radio. There were long lines for the uninviting portable toilets and no apparent way to get water or food.

14. Peter Weiss, *Marat/Sade*, verse adaption by Adrian Mitchell (New York: Atheneum, 1965), p. 11

It was raining and we had come totally unprepared. City kids, we had never gone camping. Large crowds of intoxicated people jammed into a small space has never been my idea of fun. (I was never a hippy, as I have had to tell my children repeatedly, even if I sometimes looked, and seemed to act, like one.)

Susan and I agreed: let's go home. We were able to find the car, no mean feat, and, with some trouble, got it out of the mud and on to the road, this time no traffic jam, returning to the apartment of a high school friend near 79th and Riverside Drive, where we were staying in the summer of 1969.

I should have kept my Woodstock tickets. They are worth more than the refund I got from the promoters. (Yes: I did apply for and received a refund.)

Back in the Upper West Side ("you don't know how lucky you are boys"), I sat on the couch and listened, for the n'teenth time, to Country Joe and the Fish's *I-Feel-Like-I'm-Fixin'-to-Die Rag*. In wraparound stereo sound.

They never sounded so good.

4. Come Back to the Raft, Lionel, Baby!
The Jewish Imagination, 1950

Yesterday sad to read of Dr. Williams dying in Rutherford. We lose a member of the family. No more Bill, & what a world is left to us—Henry Rago, Delmore Schwartz, the Trillings, Jacques Barzun—the booby professors will reign from now on. BAH.

Philip Whalen, *Journals*, 1963

If I had a yaller dog that didn't know no more than a person's conscience does I would pison him. It takes up more room than all the rest of a person's insides, and yet ain't no good, nohow.

Mark Twain, *Huckleberry Finn*

A letter I sent to Paul Bové on July 14, 2021:[15]

```
Dear Paul,

There is much to admire in Lionel Trilling's The Liberal
Imagination (1950). I can see how your insistence on
imaginative intelligence in Love's Shadow connects to that.
```

---

15. Revised and extended. *Bové* has just retired after decades as editor of *boundary 2*, for which he recently edited *The Poetry of Idiomatic Insistences*, on my work (48:4 [(2021)]; the first essay in the first movement of this work is dedicated to Bové, reflecting our many conversations in letters.

Trilling advocates "variousness and possibility, which implies
the awareness of complexity and difficulty," along with a
certain degree of unresolvability in literature. He argues
for historicism against the New Critics. I am sure all for
all that. Yet I feel there is a bait and switch too--that he
himself would (and did) exclude difficult poetry and would
(and did) struggle with unsanctioned variety. Louis Menand,
in his new introduction to the New York *Review* edition, does
nothing to confront these problems and indeed seems to want
to make Trilling as safe for the present-day *New Yorker* as he
is, and as Trilling was, for the *New Yorker* and *Times* in his
day. Menand tries to outdo his guru in putting hygienics over
aesthetics: Trilling's "first lesson, and the most influential,
is that there are more and less politically hygienic works
of literature, and the function of criticism is to identify
them and to explain why they tend to good or bad political
consequences--a job that requires special skill, since a
book's politics may be quite different from its political
consequences."[16] Trilling's pathos has become Menand's bathos,
but not in the Douglas Sirk sense. Can Trilling be saved from
Menand or Adam Kirsch and Leon Wieseltier--or is that a fate
he earned?

Trilling's liberalism has an unacknowledged demonic twin--
the hygienics of neo-illiberalism. It's not as bad as some of
the other *Commentary* folks such as Trilling's student Norman
Podhoretz, or Hilton Kramer, but it's a slippery slope. It's a
Cold War liberal humanism, of course, and as you and others
have shown, that too is a God that Failed.

But then I come into the story humming along with Phil
Ochs's "Love Me I'm a Liberal" and Chuck Berry's "Roll over,
Beethoven."

Perhaps the most striking (if unsurprising and common) thing
about *The Liberal Imagination*, read in retrospect, is the
repression of the war and the invisibility of his well-known
and at other times explicitly embraced Jewishness--the war
going on while Trilling wrote the essays and just a few years
"over" when he published the book. No substantial mention of
the extermination of the European Jews, hardly a mention of
the word Jew, or Nazi or Hiroshima in the entire book. This
repression is the subject of Al Filreis's radiant book, *1960:
When Art and Literature Confronted the Memory of World War II
and Remade the Modern*.

16. Louis Menand, introduction to Trilling's *The Liberal Imagination: Essays on Literature and Society*
(New York: New York Review Books, 2008), p. x

I understand why Trilling chose not to foreground his
Jewishness, just struck by it now: Jewish invisibility was not
only a mode of survival, but also a tactic of secularization
that he believed in and which I inherited. In 1940, Trilling
became the first Jewish scholar given tenure at Columbia's
English Department, despite antisemitic headwinds. His
relation to his Jewishness is complex and there are times he
addresses it and times he chose not to.[17]

> The life Trilling wanted for himself, as a university
> professor of English, was still largely denied to Jews.
> In the years of his early manhood, university teachers
> of literature were making a determined effort to
> maintain the purity of what they thought of as Anglo-
> Saxon culture. This was especially true at Columbia,
> which always felt itself to be in danger of turning
> into a Jewish enclave like City College. The gentlemen
> scholars of Columbia's department of English were
> disposed to being all the more defensive on account of
> their university's location in New York City, where Anglo-
> Saxon culture anxiously fended off what it felt to be the
> barbarism of the immigrant hordes.[18]

Following Trilling, if not to say Erich Auerbach (1892–
1957), Jewish professors of English generally did not teach
courses in "Jewish studies" and often averted foregrounding
Jewish subject matter, a path not readily available to later
professors hired to teach their own primarily racial, gender,
or ethnic identity. This was certainly the course I took
coming to SUNY Buffalo in 1989, even if the number of Jewish
writers I included on my syllabi was as undeniable as it was
unmarked. Yet Trilling's approach as much as mine, was always
precarious, since antisemitism thrives on the demonization
of both the Jewish appropriation of, and complicity with,
the national cultures we found ourselves part of, both
foundering and founding. Free–thinking Jews, what Isaac
Deutscher (1907–1967) called in 1958 "non–Jewish Jews," might
disassociate ourselves from Jewish immersion without a pledge
of absorption into a deracinated/sanitized Western Civilizing.

17. See Robert Benjamin, "Lionel Trilling's Jewish 'Reverberation' of February 1944," in *Studies in American Jewish Literature* 36:2 (2017). Benjamin discusses Trilling's 1944 anti-identitarian statement in "Under Forty: A Symposium on American Literature and the Younger Generation of American Jews." For a most recent discussion of Trilling's Jewish identification, see "Teachers and Students: On Lionel Trilling's Blurbs," in Joshua Lambert, *The Literary Mafia: Jews, Publishing, and Postwar American Literature* (New Haven, CT, Yale University Press, 2022), chapter 2. Lambert chronicles Trilling's valuable professional support for his male Jewish students, especially ones writing about Jewishness. One case study gives a detailed account of his effective promotion of Irving Feldman.

18. Mark Krupnick, "Lionel Trilling, 'Culture' and Jewishness" in *Denver Quarterly* 18:3 (1983), p. 108

Such disavowal might allow for affiliation of diasporic with dispossessed, congregating on an imaginary raft, somewhere between here and there. That raft is, for me, *poetry*. Yet such disavowal does not free me from being what Jean Améry (Hanns Chaim Mayer [1912-1978]), in "The Necessity and Impossibility of Being a Jew," calls "the catastrophe Jew" ("der Katastrophenjude"): the indelible mark of postwar Jewish identity.[19]

In *The Liberal Imagination*, Trilling does address slavery and the Civil War when he writes on Mark Twain, and I can't help feel the projection; seen this way, it's painful. It marks Trilling's self-fashioning as an Arnoldian figure of a high culture where Jews might be heard if not seen as such. Trilling's 1938 doctoral dissertation at Columbia was on Arnold. In contrast, his classmate Louis Zukofsky (1904-1978), much in mind as I write this, wrote his Columbia master's thesis on Henry Adams. Indeed, I find great poignancy in Trilling's warning, in his essay in praise of the *Partisan Review*, about "the alienation of the educated class from the most impressive literature of our time," when you realize this applies to Trilling and that his valuation of moral "seriousness" and "high respectability" puts him in conflict with aesthetic invention (pp. 99-100). There is something Freudian about this: killing the mother of invention out of love for the father of quality control (in the ideological service of Cold War liberalism). Trilling's lust for high culture trips on his stigmatizing the primitiveness of the uncultivated, as if to almost name the shtetel. His confident praise of "the advance of civilization" (p. 96) associated with high culture came just a few years after the death camps that turned his assumptions topsy-turvy. And yet, in his essay on *Huckleberry Finn*, Trilling sees Huck's way out of both primitive and upright bondage through the guidance of his "true father," the Black "saint" Jim, and he compares Jim to Stephen Daedalus's Jewish spiritual father, Leopold Bloom.[20] In this allusion of Jewish exile, Jim and Huck's queer bond suggests an American *Exodus*, echoing the slave songs. Put that in your Freudian pipe and smoke it.

19. Jean Améry, *At the Mind's Limits: Contemplations of a Survivor on Auschwitz and Its Realities*, tr. Sidney Rosenfeld and Stella P. Rosenfeld (Bloomington: Indiana University Press), p. 94. The original German title is *Jenseits von Schuld und Sühne* (Beyond guilt and atonement); the German title of the cited essay cited is "Über Zwang und Unmöglichkeit, Jude zu sein."

20. P. 108. Jonathan Arac has a chapter on Trilling's essay on Huckleberry Finn in his *Huckleberry Finn as Idol and Target: The Functions of Criticism in Our Time* (Madison: University of Wisconsin Press, 1997). He places the work in the context of both anti-fascism and anti-Communism and notes the connection of Nazi death camps to American slavery. Trilling quotes, without comment, Twain's use of the racial epithet that Arac, in his book, insists cannot be neutralized in twentieth-century accounts simply by citing its historical context or *Huckleberry Finn*'s anti-racism.

Leslie Fiedler (1917-2003) was a lively and friendly presence
at SUNY Buffalo when I arrived in 1989; he was one of an
unusually large number Jewish intellectuals associated with
the English Department. Our offices were located in Samuel
Clemens Hall. Fiedler's "Come Back to the Raft Ag'in, Huck
Honey!"--which explored the queer bond between Jim and Huck--
was written in 1948, the same year as Trilling's essay and
published in Trilling's home turf, the *Partisan Review*. Jews
on Huck: Fiedler's essay has a delightful impudence that gives
it more currency than Trilling's but that they both singled
out this book, just a few years after the war, is striking.

Related to this is Trilling's almost hilarious account of
the *Kinsey Report*, which, even so, is admirable for its time.
In effect, Trilling's retort to Kinsey is that just because
people do something doesn't make it right: "The Report has in
mind both physical normality . . . and a moral normality, the
acceptability, on the authority of animal behavior, of certain
usually taboo practices" (p. 234). In a Freudian way to which
the Freudian Trilling seems oblivious, his fear that *queerness*
would be given the status of "normal" ends up undermining his
view of what he calls "important books" (p. 95). His discomfort
reveals his own acknowledged anxiety about "moral normality"
and by extension who gets to be "normal" or "neurotic" (p. 168).
I realize it is outrageous and unacceptable, truly, but you
could substitute "Jew" for "homosexual" in this passage:

> The Report holds out the hope to respectable Christians
> that they might be as intellectual as Jews if they were
> as unrestrained as this group. But before respectable
> Christians aspire to this unwonted freedom they had
> better ascertain in how far Jews are ridden by anxiety
> and in how far their intellectuality is to be correlated
> with other ways of dealing with anxiety, such as dope,
> and in how far it is actually enjoyable. . . . The
> Report has it in mind to raise questions about negative
> attitudes toward Jews. But then it goes on to imply
> that there can be only one standard for the judgment of
> human conduct--that is, conduct as it actually exists;
> which is to say that conduct is not to be judged at all,
> except, presumably, in so far as it causes pain to others.
> (But from its attitude to the "inconvenience" of the
> "gentiles," we must presume that not all pain is to be
> reckoned with.) The preponderant weight of its argument
> is that conduct is a behavioral fact, to be considered
> only in its behavioral aspect and apart from any idea
> or ideal that might make it a social fact, as having
> no ascertainable personal or cultural meaning and no
> possible consequences--as being, indeed, not available to

social interpretation at all. In short, the Report by its
primitive conception of the nature of fact quite negates
the importance and even the existence of the Jew [as
distinguishable in terms of conduct from the gentile].
That is why, although it is possible to say of the Report
that it brings light, it is necessary to say of it that it
spreads confusion.[21]

"No one who reads thoughtfully the dialectic of Huck's great
moral crisis," Trilling writes, "will ever again be wholly
able to accept without some question and some irony the
assumptions of the respectable morality by which he lives"
(p. 113). Evidently not. Trilling often feels to me like a mid-
twentieth-century version of Huck's Widow Douglas trying to
"sivilize" us. Or maybe he's like Tom Sawyer, getting hung up
on doing "things regular" (p. 15) like in the books that make
up Tom's canon, complicating and possibly thwarting a path to
a freedom already won: "It don't make no difference how foolish
it is, it's the *right* way--and it's the regular way. And there
ain't no *other* way, that ever *I* heard of, and I've read all the
books that gives any information about these things" (p. 364).

The question of how the "liberal imagination" can acknowledge
Jews and Blacks, as well as those whose sexual or mental
orientation goes against "respectable society" (p. 164)--
much less aesthetic wildness--haunts Trilling's book in the
guise of what Menand calls *hygienics*. In the end, Kinsey is
an Einsteinian (and Freudian) leap ahead of Trilling, which
he somewhat ambivalently suggests himself. Jump cut to Diana
Trilling's abjection before (the very Jewish) Norman Mailer and
his misogynist *Prisoner of Sex* in the 1971 Town Hall debacle or
Trilling's son James outing him as cognitively perverse (ADD)
in 1999 in *The American Scholar*.[22]

Trilling writes of "the inadequacy" of "passive" American,
versus "active" European, prose literature as of 1950 in ways
that trap him in this inadequacy, Freudian sense intended
(pp. 292, 302). He admirably advocates the work of the more
radical European novelists over more tepid Americans,
criticizing the Americans for "conform[ing] to the liberal
democratic tradition" and market values (p. 301). "It must
necessarily occur to us to ask," he writes, "why it is that
these particular ideas have not infused with force and cogency

21. Adapted from pp. 241–42 and 232

22. See "Town Bloody Hall," a 1979 film by Chris Hegedus and D. A. Pennebaker; Priscilla L. Veil, et al.
"My Father and the Weak-Eyed Devils [with Replies]" in *The American Scholar* 68:3, The Phi Beta
Kappa Society, 1999: <jstor.org/stable/41213481> and <jstor.org/stable/41212918>.

the literature that embodies them" (pp. 301-2). Ironically, this statement comes back to bite Trilling and the criticism his ideas embody. But let me just say it: I more than agree with, I *follow*, Trilling on the need, now as much in 1950, to push back against market and liberal humanist values in making aesthetic judgment. Paul--it's now twenty-one months since I started this letter to you on a Bastille Day in the middle of a pandemic--and I am still confused about my sense not only of Trilling's "inadequacy" but also my ability to identify it. Why does Trilling's contemporary, and *Partisan Review* comrade, Clement Greenberg (1909-1994), remain so much more compelling in his account of aesthetic judgment as well as his actual judgments, even if his teleology led him to disintegrate into art history's unpredictable metamorphoses. Trilling suffers from his examples, which seem like admirable, but stock, figures out of the mainstream liberal culture he fostered. His negative examples, Eugene O'Neill and John Dos Passos, with their buoyant and at times wacky energy, betray him (pp. 294, 299). I'll play son Edmund to Trilling as the father, James Tyrone, in our own private long day's journey into night.[23]

Speaking of bathos: At one point Trilling speaks, in a negative way, of the "piety" of liberal democratic art, which he otherwise calls "philistine" (p. 164); but in another context he says a resonance of "piety" is essential for art that counts. Trilling is torn between two senses of piety: as rote morality and as "imagination."[24] This conflict forms the emotional center of *The Liberal Imagination* and drives his anti-aestheticism. Trilling recounts that at college "we were very down on Walter Pater, very hostile to what we called 'aestheticism,' . . . we took him to be everything that was disembodied and precious."[25] He reports a change of heart on Pater, but his youthful resistance hardens into what I'd call Cold War aesthetic containment. Menand reminds us that Trilling requires that we consider the political--and I'd add aesthetic--consequences of ideas, recognized as different than politics. The consequences of Trilling's ideas did not hold up well in the Cold War, where the American usurpation of "imagination" and freedom--call it the Imperial Lyric--became a tool of global and local containment under the guise of humanist (anti-Communist) morality.

23. O'Neill's *Long Day's Journey into Night* was written in 1939-40 but not produced until 1956.

24. "The Function of the Little Magazine," p. 98, versus "The Meaning of a Literary Idea," p. 299. On "philistine": see, for example, pp. 21 and 164.

25. Trilling, *The Moral Obligation to Be Intelligent: Selected Essays*, ed. Leon Wieseltier (New York: Farrar, Straus and Giroux, 2000), pp. 342-43. Cited in Mark Scroggins, *The Poem of a Life: A Biography of Louis Zukofsky* (Berkeley: Shoemaker & Hoard, 2007), p. 34.

I may be projecting my father (1901-1977) onto Lionel Mordecai
Trilling (1905-1975), ben Fannie Cohen. I was born the year *The
Liberal Imagination* was published. My parents had a similar
parental immigration history to Trilling, though they had
little in common; but then that little may be a lot. I did
meet James Trilling once at college (he was two years ahead of
me). When Harvard President Nathan Pusey was invited to Adams
House in 1969 or '70, a group of us arranged to do a series
of confrontive antiwar toasts. Mine started "In the name of
Henry David Thoreau who wrote"--but I can't now recall the
quote--"we welcome you to Adams House." A young man whom I
had never seen, dressed in full J. Press preppery, turned to
me and expressed his contempt both for our demonstration and
for me personally. Nowadays I very much like J.Crew shirts and
underwear and all things seersucker.

It comes down to this, which I say knowing it is ungenerous
and perhaps even unfair and Oedipal: poetry as a disruptive
force hardly grazes the pages of *The Liberal Imagination*;
poetry and aesthetics are resisted and then repressed. (What
does Mandelstam say?: poetry has not rumpled the sheets, has
never spent the night.[26]) In this Trilling is in line with
Winters's and Blackmur's distrust of Poe that I discuss, via
Delany, in the Pataquerical essay in *Pitch of Poetry*. Consider
this touching--private--comment in a letter from 1950, the
same year as *The Liberal Imagination*, to the twenty-four-year-
old gay, Jewish Allen Ginsberg:

> I won't try to respond to your interesting struggles with
> the theory of verse. I've been reading Williams lately
> and have a growing sense of what he is up to. I think I
> like what he is up to, although sometimes I am wearied
> and depressed by what he writes, as I was wearied and
> depressed when I met him last spring, although at the
> same time I was rather taken by him. Did I ever confess
> to you that my relation to modern verse is very largely
> academic and dutiful?--it seldom means as much to me as
> prose.[27]

Trilling's personal support for Ginsberg is worth contrasting
to his ardent professional sponsorship for Irving Feldman, a

26. "The sheets have never been rumpled, there poetry, so to speak, has never spent the night" in Osip
Mandelstam, "Conversation about Dante," in *The Complete Critical Prose and Letters*, ed. Jane Gary
Harris, tr. J. G. Harris and Constance Link (Ann Arbor: Ardis, 1979), p. 397

27. Letter #105, October 20, 1950, in *Life in Culture: Selected Letters of Lionel Trilling*, ed. Adam Kirsch
(New York: Farrar, Straus and Giroux, 2018). On May 29, 1956 (letter # 149), Trilling writes Ginsberg
that he finds the poems in *Howl and Other Poems* "dull": "all rhetoric, without any music." But most
pertinent here: "the doctrinal element of the poems ... I of course reject ... in all its orthodoxy."

poet as distant from Williams and Ginsberg as a model railway
tinker is from an astronaut. With Trilling's support, Feldman
came onto the scene with an attack on Karl Shapiro's Jewish
ethnic identification in a review of Shapiro's *Poems of a
Jew*, published in *Commentary* (November 1958). Feldman wants
to police Jewish identity: "But what has happened is that,
except in name only, [Shapiro] is no longer a Jew. Jewishness
has become as mythical to this neo–Semite as it is to anti–
Semites."

Irving Feldman was my unfriendly colleague at Buffalo. While
avoiding teaching literature classes in the graduate or
undergraduate program, Feldman loudly proclaimed his contempt
for new approaches to literary study and especially for the
Poetics Program. A poet of great authenticity! I figured
that it was views like those which got Feldman a MacArthur
Fellowship in 1992, as opposed to my Poetics Program comrades
Creeley, Howe, Tedlock, or Federman. But then it just may be
the MacArthur prefers highbrow kitsch to what we were doing.
When they say "genius grants," I wonder—genius for what?

In an article in the *Buffalo News*, just after Creeley and
I left, after taking a quick swipe at Creeley as divisive,
Feldman gets to me. You have to imagine this in the voice of
the police chief played by Rod Steiger in *In the Heat of the
Night*. I know it's a bit of stretch:

> Bernstein I could observe in action building his empire
> from the word "go." I knew even before he came he was
> power hungry. I always wonder about people like that—
> what kind of interior emptiness they're trying to fill
> with power. His poetry shows a certain kind of interior
> emptiness, I think.[28]

Feldman could be replaying his putdown of Shapiro almost
a half–century earlier: "These poems seem to lack an inner
Jewish consciousness; viewed as art, they lack lyric
centrality."

I appreciate that the Jewish culture I am part of sometimes
values quarrelsomeness over solidarity. It might be that Jews,
in the world of secular culture, may at times find it safer,
if not more convenient or even familial, to criticize one
another. Triggered and triggering. But that is a minor chord
compared to this major one: Jewish poets, artists, critics,

28. Jeff Simon, "Local Poet Displays a Greatness Cultivated in Private," *Buffalo News*, October 17,
2004, p. G1.

philosophers, friends, past and present, that have helped form
my thinking and been supportive beyond measure.

Feldman, Federman, and I once read together at an academic
conference in Buffalo. We should have taken the act on the
road, billed as *Three Faces of Judaism.*

But let me now shift gears to take up the discussion you and
Bruce Robbins have long been having about whether the 1960s
reaction against sanctified literary "tradition" produced
something sinister.[29] I wouldn't define the problematic
reaction as spontaneity, process, openness, or informality
(aversion of professionalism), as I don't see much of those.
On the left, I think the Weathermen and their nemesis, the
Progressive Labor Party, played into the hands of the right,
just as much as the social/virtue gospel true-believers do
now. The power dynamics you discuss in your Debray piece are
closer to it--the erasure of history and ideology--and there
is a line from Core Curriculum humanism/liberalism to that--
indeed much of the virtue "left" is not left at all, but Good
News liberalism.[30] Otherwise, the danger is to go down the
rabbit hole of Fredric Jameson in his attack of postmodern
fragmentation, including, you recall, a poem of Bob Perelman.[31]

Trilling, in a 1961 article in *Partisan Review*, "On the Modern
Element in Modern Literature," discusses his ambivalent
embrace of teaching a course in "modern" (early twentieth-
century) literature; and then, too, Trilling remains
associated with the Columbia Core Curriculum. The problem
with teaching only official/canonical figures from long ago
has been subject to so much debate it's hard to go back there.
But perversely, I want to argue that this reactionary view
actually undergirds the current swerve away from teaching
literary works, the view that poems have no intrinsic value
and that aesthetic value is spurious. The short version:
the high canonical/civilizing (High C) pitch for literature
degrades its significance, albeit unintentionally, because
it's understanding of literature takes pride in being narrow,
ahistorical, and ethnocentric: Literature reflects refinement
not an active aesthetic intelligence. It's the ghost in the

29. For Robbins: *Criticism and Politics: A Polemical Introduction* (Stanford, CA: Stanford University
Press, 2022); for Bové, the critique of Jameson in *Love's Shadow* (Cambridge, MA: Harvard University
Press, 2021)

30. Paul Bové, "Celebrity and Betrayal: The High Intellectuals of Postmodern Culture," *Minnesota Re-
view* 21 (1983)

31. Fredric Jameson, "Postmodernism, or the Cultural Logic of Late Capitalism" in the book of the same
title (Durham, NC: Duke University Press, 1991). I respond to this essay in "In the Middle of Modernism,"
collected in *A Poetics* (Cambridge, MA: Harvard University Press, 1992).

current no-literature machine because it seems to make
"literature" such a plum target. And those of us who make the
strongest *aesthetic* argument *against* the High C pitch are as
much on the outs now as before. In short, High-C / Great Books
relies on a fundamental, ontological, and epistemological
misreading of what poetry, and what literature, is, how it
performs you might say. So, its effective devaluation of most
poetry, including most poetry of significance, continues in
the present, turning the approved brands into the Living Dead
devouring the whole field of action.

Perhaps it was Harold Bloom that made High C a "canonical"
argument best fit for parody. It's a one-two punch: first you
miscast literature as a rigged supremacist joint; that, in
turn, opens it to attack as a rigged supremacist joint (so we
don't need it). I can't escape that these secular Jews wanted
to elevate certain works to "sacred" status to the exclusion of
contemporary others, which means that his "class" of priests/
rabbis got the "last" word in their commentaries. If you fix
the sacred texts / masterpieces, no matter how great they
are, you don't allow for conflict with contemporary and *other*
art works. Canonical art works only have contemporary social
meaning when *challenged* by other, contemporary, art works.
Otherwise "criticism" becomes supreme, in the name also of
scholarship or preaching, in your fashion (to echo Baudelaire,
as echoed by O'Neill, on virtue). Dickinson and Emerson knew
this and Peirce and many others, including you, as in your
Debray piece and elsewhere. Clement Greenberg knew this too,
but he also got pulled down in the muck by his monolithic view
of art history and what "counts" (as much as I do still love
aspects of Greenberg).

As I trust this letter makes clear—Jewish solidarity is not
part of my experience or practice: this lack of solidarity is
one of the most vibrant aspects of Jewish ethnic culture.

As you remember, Jonathan Arac, then English Department
chairman, invited me to teach at Columbia in the 2002 spring
semester. Kenneth Koch was sick, and I was to take his
undergraduate class, with the idea that perhaps I might join
the English Department. Columbia, after all, was just a short
walk from my apartment—and a lot closer than Buffalo. I met
with Kenneth at his place on Claremont, the only time we'd ever
had a chance to talk. He had been using a Norton anthology for
the class; I explained I would create my own set of readings
of innovative postwar American poetry (I also included his
recent collection *New Addresses*). Since I now found myself in
Philosophy Hall, I went to see Sylvère Lotringer on the French
Department floor. Sylvère, who, like Koch, was Jewish, though

from Europe, appeared to have no connection to the folks
in the English Department, despite his close proximity. He
told me he was eager to free himself from Columbia. Another
Jewish-born faculty member at Columbia, Edward Mendelson, the
Lionel Trilling Professor no less, was as unfriendly to me as
Feldman had been at Buffalo and that seemed likely to settle the
matter of whether I would go to Columbia. At a faculty lecture
I attended, Mendelson declared that there was no longer any
interest in Surrealism and justly so; this despite the fact that
a Surrealist show across the park at the Met was attracting
huge crowds. Mendelson's colleagues kept quiet, the way orthodox
families keep kosher, but I couldn't. So, keep that in mind when
I say--If teaching modern literature means Mendelson's Auden-
centric provincialism--is that any better than no literature? Is
it worse? Because it makes literary study--it makes aesthetics--
into what's called in *Huckleberry Finn* "comb up, Sundays"[32]:
an easy target for marginalization as parochial and haughty.
Now, for sure, Auden is better than that and will survive it.
But can the English Department? This is also why I say the New
York *Review of Books* and the *New Yorker* are not just missing
the boat--they are sinking it. But poetry will survive!

A graduate student at Penn told me how much she loved
Mendelson's seminar, pointing to the fact that he did not allow
students to eat in his seminar. "He Had Refinement." I keep
thinking of that Dorothy Fields (1904-1974) song--"He never
came down to dinner without his shirt was on."[33]

My "midrashic antinonimianism" in the pataquerics essay is
meant to be funny but it speaks to this point. That is, as in
social gospel, "masterpieces" morph into "virtue" and then
you don't need literary works at all. This "liberal/illiberal"
error leads to the elimination of "literature" (as Terry
Eagleton leads the charge in his *Literary Theory*). Yes "new"
works are "uncooked," "unrefined," unmastered--that is just
why they have the potential to challenge, even if few do.

--Over the years, nightmarish Trillings have repeatedly come
after me. These phantoms take the shape of my superego or my
id (I get the two confused).

Only it's not (only) imaginary.

        Charles

---

32. Mark Twain (Samuel L. Clemens), *Adventures of Huckleberry Finn* (London: Chatto & Windus, 1884), chap. 17, p. 151

33. I contrast *refinement* to *innovation* in "Invention Follies" in *Attack of the Difficult Poems: Essays and Inventions*.

5. The Importance of Being Unimportant

A BBC crew was coming to talk to me in 1995 for *Soundwaves*. When I told Emma, who was ten at the time, she wondered why I was being interviewed since I was not "cool," as she put it, meaning famous. The crew arrived at our apartment on the Upper West Side from Princeton, where they had just interviewed the popular and admired writer Joyce Carol Oates. I knew Joyce a little from the two semesters I had taught for Princeton's Creative Writing Program in 1989 and 1990. A few years later I met Joyce's father, Fred, a thoughtfully engaged, modest working-class man from Lockport. Fred took an undergraduate seminar of mine on twentieth-century poetry at SUNY Buffalo. As a senior citizen, he could take (with permission) any UB class he wanted. Fred asked if I knew about his daughter and was delighted when I said I did. I loved having older people in the class and especially Fred; his sense of history and, indeed, his life history, enriched every discussion. During my two semesters at Princeton, all the creative writing classes were held at the same time so that the faculty could have lunch first. These lunches were very convivial, and Joyce was welcoming. Paul Auster was teaching in the same program as Joyce and me, and had helped me to get the job; we would take New Jersey Transit to Princeton together. Those days at Princeton were the first time since college that I had had access to a research library, and I would take home as many books as I could carry. Several years later, at the time of the radio interview, I was living in New York and commuting to Buffalo. When my BBC friend arrived with his crew from Princeton, he told me that after he told Joyce his next stop she said, "Why are you interviewing him? He's not important." He was taken aback but I pointed out that she was right, I wasn't important, and that my daughter had just said something similar. Emma hung around and talked to the crew. When they left, she said to me—Now I get it, you're cool by not being cool.

6. Roman Gods in a Punic Land

What certain reviewers have imagined . . . I am incompetent to explain, and unwilling to imagine. I am evidently not virtuous enough to understand them. I thank Heaven that I am not. . . . I have not studied in those schools whence that full-fledged phoenix, the "virtue" of professional pressmen, rises chuckling and crowing from the dunghill, its birthplace and its deathbed. But there are birds of alien feather, if not of higher flight; and these I would now recall into no hencoop or preserve of mine, but into the open and general field where all may find pasture and sunshine and fresh air: into places whither the prurient prudery and the virulent virtue of pressmen and prostitutes cannot follow; into an atmosphere where calumny cannot speak, and fatuity cannot breathe; in a word, where backbiters and imbeciles become impossible. I neither hope nor wish to change the unchangeable, to purify the impure. To conciliate them, to vindicate myself in their eyes, is a task which I should not condescend to attempt, even were I sure to accomplish.

A. C. Swinburne

[Swinburne's reply is] very foolish and furious . . . in which the clever, overstrong, shrieking words, though often chosen as only a poet could choose them, express nothing but weakness, white rage, studied ferocity, and immeasurable thirst for vengeance.

Spectator

In the mid-1980s, William Spanos invited me to give a reading at SUNY Binghamton. It was one of the first times I had been invited to speak at a university or for that matter had been on a campus since graduating college. I took a small plane from New York's LaGuardia Field for the short hop to central New York. I brought along the new edition of Paul de Man's *Resistance to Theory.* The title essay of that collection had been written for a book of essays edited by the Modern Language Association (MLA), which ultimately rejected it. Years later, my essay "The Practice of Poetics" was included in the 2007 volume of the same MLA series.[34] It was snowing when I arrived in Binghamton and headed to the university. In the cab, I realize I had left *Resistance to Theory* in the seat pocket of the plane. I never read the essay.

In the early 1990s, articles by Paul de Man, written in his early twenties for a Belgian collaborationist newspaper, were discovered. It wasn't just where he published the articles or even that he had apparently concealed the publications, but also that a couple of articles were antisemitic. Leading journals not only condemned de Man but also, by association, his friend Jacques Derrida. It created a stir at SUNY Buffalo, shortly after I started teaching there, as de Man was important to some of my faculty friends, with the added twist that a few, like Derrida, were Jewish. Soon de Man's history was used to taint the entire field of Derridian philosophy, from "literary theory" to "deconstruction." Poet and journalist David Lehman's 1991 *Signs of the Times: Deconstruction and the Fall of Paul de Man* made that case.

Still, it came as a shock to me to receive a proposed manuscript of an essay by Eliot Weinberger, with whose work I felt an affinity, intended for publication in Clayton Eshleman's great literary magazine *Sulfur*, linking de Man to the poets in and around L=A=N=G=U=A=G=E. I wrote a

34. Collected in *Attack of the Difficult Poems: Essays and Inventions.*

response for publication, with the subtitle and epigraphs I am using here, but withdrew it when Weinberger removed his references to de Man.[35] I was astonished that Weinberger would consider projecting the taint of de Man onto the poetics of L=A=N=G=U=A=G=E. I took it more personally, even though Weinberger's disparagement was not directed only to me, because it came from a fellow "free thinking" Jew. As this series continues, I will have to find a couple of Shabbos goys to be my subjects in case I am writing (or you are reading) on a holy day.

I had been used to red-baiting and I could understand being attacked for seeming too left, aesthetically and politically. But "brown-baiting"— being attacked for being soft on Nazism or fascism or more generally for being a rightist—was new to me. But I came to realize that "brown-baiting" was more damning than "red-baiting." Weinberger's de Manian turn came in a response to Michael Davidson's cogent response to an article by Weinberger in an earlier issue of *Sulfur*, an article that mostly focused on touting the significance of *Montemora*, the literary magazine he edited: it was, he tells us, more significant than the magazines edited by other poets of our generation. In his response to Weinberger, Davidson compares him to Lionel Trilling, "dismiss[ing] the current generation for un-Arnoldian backsliding" (p. 179). As for the taint of Paul de Man, Weinberger lets stand something more toxic, if anodyne, from his earlier article—the taint of Reaganism, specifically the "rampant nationalism and xenophobia" of his disfavored poets, who, nonetheless, as he notes, opposed Ronald Reagan.[36]

In his scathing assessment of Eliot Weinberger's 1993 anthology *American Poetry since 1950: Innovators and Outsiders*, John Yau laments "the sarcasm and smug condescension evident in Weinberger's dismissive generalizations," including his 1983 dismissal of our generation's poetry as "irradiated." "Weinberger ignores . . . poets because they don't, or can't, be made to fit into his understanding of the Pound-Williams-H.D. tra-

35. Weinberger's essay was published as "A Note on *Montemora*, America and the World," in *Sulfur* 20, Fall 1987. Two issues later, *Sulfur* published responses: "Davidson and Weinberger on Language Poetry," with additional remarks by Rachel Blau DuPlessis and Clayton Eshleman, in *Sulfur* 22, Spring 1988. Weinberger reprises this for his *Written Reaction: Poetics Politics Polemics 1979–1995* (New York: Marsilio, 1996), which he kicks off (p. 83) by noting that my polemical response to his essay was withdrawn without noting that I withdrew it only after Weinberger cut the pejorative material, relating to de Man. Yet Weinberger scolds that I included some of the "pejorative" language of my polemic in a poem, without naming him or the immediate context; he is referring to "The Value of Sulfur," an essay collected in *My Way: Speeches and Poems*.

36. *Sulfur* 20, p. 197. Weinberger says Ron Silliman's anthology *In the American Tree* is nationalistic because it uses "American" in its title and xenophobic because it excludes Canadians. His own anthology from a few years later, discussed below, does the same thing.

dition. . . . The real stress in this anthology is on tradition and similarity, rather than on rupture and difference."[37] Weinberger situates his anthology squarely in the tradition of Pound. Does that make his earlier condemnation of a phantom association of poets with de Man seem . . . disingenuous?

In "American Poetry Since 1950," the afterword to his anthology, Weinberger writes:

> Meanwhile, on the poetic left, as in the universities, European theory (the other New Formalism) took hold, setting adrift signifier and signified, dismantling the "authorities" and "hierarchies" of syntax, voice, meaning, content. Not only were reams of critical prose written by poets: both avant-gardists and academics were writing in the identical technocratic jargon. And the poetry (the so-called praxis) that these theories produced—reacting to the unexamined free expression of the workshops—ranged from strictly non-referential arrays of words to unending prose poems and lyrics that, like a ghazal on amphetamines, kept changing the subject with every line: the poem as MTV, under the guise of a preoccupation with "surface texture" and pure "language." It was a sign of the times that the avant-garde presented its most militant polemics not in a Beat café or in an underground magazine, but at the annual meetings of the Modern Language Association.[38]

Pop quiz: Does rhetorical condescension absolve misrepresentations? In all fairness, we need to give the guy some slack if we see his attempts to hold the line against the unenlightened as preparation for his lauded work at the *London Review of Books*, though it would be ten more years before he became a regular contributor. Weinberger is savvy: to break into the mainstream nothing works better than an antipathy to "European theory" coupled with trashing a strawman avant-garde, especially if you might have been suspected to have been a fellow traveler of "innovators and outsiders."

Pop quiz 2: what debilitating drug best describes this prose? Quaaludes? What animal? A pony?

Pop quiz 3: What is the relation of meth-addled poems to "irradiated" ones?

The most likely MLA talks Weinberger is alluding to in the passage cited are my "The Academy in Peril: William Carlos Williams Meets the MLA," presented at a poets' tribute to Williams (1983) and "Pounding Fascism (Appropriating Ideologies—Mystification, Aestheticization, and

---

37. John Yau, "Neither Us Nor Them," *American Book Review*, March/April 1994, pp. 46–47

38. Eliot Weinberger, "American Poetry Since 1950: A Very Brief History," *American Poetry Since 1950: Innovators and Outsiders*, ed. Weinberger (New York: Marsilio, 1993), p. 406

Authority in Pound's Poetic Practice)" (1985). While I find Weinberger's prose filled with shibboleths, notably his eschewing of jargon, I'd like him to point to any technocratic jargon in either of these essays. Both my MLA essays were published in *Sulfur*, which at the time included Weinberger, Yau, and me on the masthead. *Sulfur* was a step up for me in publishing, as my earlier essays were in smaller-scale places like *L=A=N=G=U=A=G=E*. And, contrary to Weinberger's assertion, the venues in which those of us he reviles presented our poetics, up to the date of his anthology, were mostly lofts and alternative art centers. In Weinberger's "American Poetry Since 1950," he makes a critique of "Official Verse Culture," similar to the one I make in the Williams essay he mocks as presented at the MLA; ironically, he borrows the term from that essay (p. 397). Even so, Weinberger's comments, as I quote them here, are a perfect expression of the official verse culture of the early 1990s. It's the jargon of authenticity.

Weinberger should not need reminding that liberal arts institutions are among the few places in the United States committed to freedom of expression and scholarship. Yes, these institutions need to do better; my commitment has been to stay engaged for that reason. I have been lucky to be able to speak at MLA meetings. I have found the audiences there among the best informed and responsive I've had. And, yes, I believe it is as valuable for poets to speak at the MLA as in Beat cafés.

I write this with misgivings and self-recrimination. Eliot Weinberger, a fellow Jewish New Yorker, was born just a year before me. We have close mutual friends and share a passionate devotion to many of the same poets as well a love of the ironic, sardonic, and sarcastic. Best known for his translations of Octavio Paz, Weinberger went on to work closely with that most auratic of American poetry publishers, New Directions.

I become a "correspondent" for *Sulfur* in 1985, after Clayton Eshleman published "Pounding Fascism." I remain grateful to Clayton for welcoming me (while remaining at odds with some of my opinions: we spent many happy, and some unhappy, hours disagreeing). Clayton is well-known for his sometime cranky rejection letters. Early on he wrote in response to a poem of mine, which he later published, that it was like being hit with rancid popcorn. I loved that. I wrote him back and asked would he prefer if the popcorn was fresh? That was the beginning of a beautiful friendship.

I've often imagined writing responses to my critics such as I found in *Swinburne Replies* (Syracuse University Press, 1966), from which I've taken my epigraphs, but I have been reluctant to publish such sentiments, despite my affection for the genre. By and large, such responses bring unwanted attention to objectionable material. If you go for the bait, you can only lose out. Defensiveness, especially in the heat of hurt, can make for tedious prose. In my most polemical pieces I have tried to avoid naming individuals. But that can be evasive. Events don't occur in the abstract.

I ended my unpublished 1992 response to Weinberger wondering whether there is an alternative to the bitter competitiveness and aggressive envy that is the stock-in-trade of American daily life. Rather than turn the other cheek, how about giving cheekiness a chance. In other words, I prefer not to . . . forget. For which, perhaps, I cannot forgive myself.

7. Ron Silliman Wins Pulitsar Prize

by Mike Freakman

New York, April 21, 2009 (AHP2 News)—Ron Silliman's *The Alphabet* is the winner of the 2009 Pulitsar Prize for Poetry.

The Pulitsar jury wrote, "Regardless of one's position on the various strains of American poetry, no one can doubt that this work is one of the most ambitious books of poetry published in our time. At the same time, the work affords great pleasure to the new reader of poetry as much as to the old hand."

This is Silliman's second Pulitsar. *Tjanting* won the Pulitsar Prize for poetry in 1981.

Darien Credenza, Executive Muckamuck of the Amalgamated Writing Poetry, told AHP2 news, "This should establish once and for all that the prize system is working and there has not now, nor has there ever been, discrimination against any approach to poetry. We are all together in one big tent." Credenza went on to blast "those who make divisions where there is unity," adding that "Silliman's work is of the highest quality: that's all that counts." He noted that Silliman would be a featured reader at the next Amalgamated annual convention.[39]

The Pulitsar Prize commemorates the 1917 dismantling by pulleys of the statue of Tsar Nicholas II in St. Petersburg.

Web comments sections were buzzing in reaction. "This just shows Silliman's hypocrisy," said Spent Ronson, on Nowhere.Com. "If his work had any integrity, it would not have won this prize."

---

39. See "The prison house of official verse culture," section XCIX of "The Pataquerical Imagination," in *The Pitch of Poetry*. In 2021, my press paid for an AWP (Association of . . . Writing Programs) virtual session to publicize *Topsy-Turvy*. I couldn't find the listing, and not a single person showed up. My other AWP appearance was in 2003, speaking to a packed ballroom, especially recorded by AWP. When I asked for a copy, I was told it was "lost."

8. You Can't Make This Up: Twice-told Tales

As if a man should spit against the wind;
The filth returns in's face

John Webster

I.

In 2000, Richard Kostelanetz, started out an essay in the *American Book Review* by recycling his favorite jab—that I am not a "distinguished poet—the last time I checked, few familiar with his poetry could identify a single major work, let alone remember the titles of individual poems."[40] He then goes on to compare me to two right-wing icons, William Buckley (because, like Kostelanetz, we went to Ivy League colleges) and F. T. Marinetti and by loose association Benito Mussolini (because I am influential).[41] Kostelanetz goes on to mention a list I gave of formally innovative antifascist poets born during the Systematic Extermination of the European Jews in an essay titled "The Second War and Postmodern Memory," collected in *A Poetics*. The essay addresses the response of a few American poets to the Shoah and ends with a discussion of Jerome Rothenberg's *Khurbn*. Kostelanetz calls my essay an "outrageous deception" and, moreover, charges me with—wait for it—the "sin of fascism" for not including his name in my essay. Kostelanetz goes on to list several poets that I don't mention in my essay (I could list many more). He concludes by saying that the title of my 1999 book of "Speeches and Poems," *My Way*, comes not from the Frank Sinatra / Paul Anka song, as I had thought, but from—wait for it again—*Mein Kampf*. The great Ron Sukenick, copublisher of *American Book Review*, wrote an apology for this piece in the following issue: "It should not have been written. It should not have been thought. It is an example of the breakdown of literary community."[42] Sukenick gave me a free lifetime subscription to *ABR*, which I read each month with appreciation.

There is a backstory here. In *The Literary Mafia*, Joshua Lambert notes that in *The End of Intelligent Writing—*

---

40. Hank Lazer responded to this bunk several years earlier: Hank Lazer, "Charles Bernstein's Dark City: Polis, Policy, and the Policing of Poetry," *American Poetry Review* 24:5 (1995); collected in Lazer's *Opposing Poetries* (Evanston, IL: Northwestern University Press, 1996), vol 2.

41. Richard Kostelanetz, "Picketing the Zeitgeist: PoBusiness," *American Book Review* 21:4 (2000)

42. Ron Sukenick, "A Note from the Publisher," *ABR* 21:5 (2000). See also James Shivers's letter in the following issue, *ABR* 21:6 (2000).

Kostelanetz (also Jewish) . . . claims that by the 1960s, a "Jewish American group became the dominant literary-political force" in the U.S. (p. 13). He characterizes that group as a "literary clique or mob" (p. 78). Kostelanetz remarks, "As the most efficient literary machine ever created in America, [this group] had unprecedented power to determine what writing might be taken seriously and what would be neglected or wiped out" (p. 31).[43]

Decades later, Kostelanetz's malefic scanning for influential literary Jews picks me out, and, lo and behold, an undistinguished poet like me triggers a massive intelligence failure on his part.

II.

On March 20, 2003, based on lies about "weapons of mass destruction," the United States of America rained terror on Iraq with catastrophic consequences that continue to this day. Patriotic American citizens protested in the streets; I was part of a resilient group in New York that marched together as poets.

Six days later, David Antin presented a talk poem called "War" to the Buffalo Poetics Program. It was the first recording I digitized for what was to become PennSound. In his performance, Antin noted that metonymy was a key rhetorical device for right-wing disinformation—the linking together of two unrelated metonyms such as "Iraq" and "weapons of mass destruction" (particulars standing for something general).[44] In Antin's compelling analysis, though he doesn't use the phrase, "Big Lie," propaganda juxtaposes unrelated metonyms and synthesizes them into a "meme."

It was around this time, in February and March, that I wrote a poem called "War Stories," which was published in the *Philadelphia Inquirer* on March 31, taking up a full page along with reports of a large antiwar march in Philadelphia. I had first read the poem on March 5 at Buffalo, as part of a "Poets Against the War" reading I organized.[45] (I moved from Buffalo to Penn the following Fall.)

---

43. Lambert, p. 4; in the extract, page numbers in parentheses are from Richard Kostelanetz, *The End of Intelligent Writing: Literary Politics in America* (New York: Sheed and Ward, 1974). Kostelanetz's list of "the New York Literary Mob" is on pp. 84–86 of his book; he lists Trilling as a "mob elder" on p. 82.

44. I discuss Antin's talk in "UP Against Storytelling" in Act Three of this book.

45. Available at PennSound's Poets Against the War page (via anthologies/collections)."War Stories" was collected in *Girly Man* (2006). I discuss Antin's "War" in more detail in "If Socrates Was a Poet" in "Up Against Storytelling" (Act Three of this collection).

In 2020, Russian scholar Vladimir Feshchenko described the poem this way:

> At the heart of this linguistic satire is the clash of discourses in the arena of the poetic text. First and foremost, discourses of mass influence: political, media, military. Thus, the definitions of war in "War Stories" sounds like fragments of various discourses, from the mundane and logical-philosophical to the legal and geopolitical, with the inclusion of poetic metaphors in the midst of all this discordance: "War is us." "War is our only hope." "War is pragmatism with an inhuman face." "War is the logical outcome of moral certainty." "War is the principal weapon of a revolution that can never be achieved." "War is a slow boat to heaven and an express train to hell." Ultimately, for the poet of language, war is a way of writing: "War is the extension of prose by other means."[46]

Hungarian scholar Enikö Bollobäs added that the humor of the poem has its source in tragedy.[47]

The *Boston Review* offered a strikingly different account of this poem, likening it to the commentaries of Glenn Beck, then at the height of his Fox News fame.[48] Perhaps, when choosing to feature this article, the editors were thinking of Beck's antisemitic slander, widely reported in the months before this article was published, that George Soros helped "send the Jews to the death camps."[49] Or maybe it was Beck's March 2003 prowar "Rally for America," organized to counter the kinds of antiwar rallies in which I had participated. "Bernstein's rhetorical strategy may be set side by side with that of the U.S. right," says David Micah Greenberg, noting that this hyperbole is necessary because "War Stories" is "emblematic" of much "experimental" poetry.

Using Antin's analysis, we can say that Beck links factually irreconcilable metonyms like "Soros" and "Nazis." Greenberg's linking "Bernstein" and "Beck" works in this way. In contrast, "War Stories" actively resists the malignant synthesis of welding the two metonyms into a univocal truth.

46. Vladimir Feschenko, "Charles Bernstein's Experimental Semiotics: Language Poetry between Russian and American Traditions" (Владимир Фещенко Испытательная семиотика Ч. Бернстина. Поэзия языка между русской и американской традициями), *NLO* 168:2 (2021); English translation: <jacket2.org/commentary/Feschenko-Bernstein>

47. Enikö Bollobäs, "In Imploded Sentences: On Charles Bernstein's Poetic Attentions," *Arcade*, November 12, 2015 <arcade.stanford.edu/content/imploded-sentences-charles-bernsteins-poetic-attentions>

48. David Micah Greenberg, "When That Becomes This," *Boston Review* 36:4 (2011)

49. Alex Eichler, "Was Glenn Beck's George Soros Takedown Anti-Semitic?," *Atlantic*, November 12, 2010

Greenberg's lyric shaming debunks as "false consciousness" any poetry that refuses the truth of a conventional, monologic lyric voice. As a result, Greenberg can equate "War Stories," a poem that he recognizes as explicitly presenting multiple points of view, with right-wing disinformation. His resistance to irony leads him to a "strategy of developing false comparison, designed to inflame supporters and shift the terms of debate." Ironically, that is the charge he makes against Beck.

Though the *Boston Review* has often featured forums on controversial topics, they relegated the responses to Greenberg by Marjorie Perloff, Susan Stewart, along with me and others, to their website, leaving no trace in the print edition.[50] For the editors of the *Boston Review*, questioning shibboleths and bringing together conflicting ideological viewpoints—exploring how meaning is contingent and contextual—can be reasonably compared to fascism. By giving unchallenged credibility to Greenberg's chilling absurd argument, the *Boston Review* editors display a zeal for prosecuting poetry that resists a post–Cold War humanist ideology; in this sense brown-baiting carries on the work of red-baiting. The editors drank the glue—or is it sniffed the Kool-Aid? By sanctioning the equivalence of poetic questioning or complexity to political deceit, they reenact the tragic death of Socrates, this time as farce.

I will leave the last word to Stephanie Burt, from the online forum. Asked to comment on the comparison of my dialogic poem "War Stories" to the demagoguery of a pro-Iraq-war, antisemitic fascist, Burt responded: "The issues [raised] are perhaps the largest and most urgent in contemporary poetics. . . . If I must say anything right away about poetry and politics in general, I'm liable to scratch my eyes out."

9.   Lyric S(h)ame

~~First shun~~
then say
BEEN SHAMED
by the
~~ones whose~~
punk puns
stung your

---

50. The forum was posted on March 7, 2012, <bostonreview.net/articles/david-micah-greenberg -forum/>. *The Boston Review* refused to print my letter to the editor in their print edition.

TAME TONGUE.
Shame game
~~is a~~
vain pain:
a sucker
PUNCH *EN*
plein air.

N.B.: In *Lyric Shame* (Harvard University Press, 2014), Gillian White shames those who question the jargon of authenticity in lyric poetry. White claims that active skepticism toward Romantic ideology is a form of shaming. White fights this phantom shame with her critical shaming.[51]

[*b20 (boundary 2 online)*, April 20, 2017]

10. Under Erasure Marks Bad History

When *The Grand Piano: An Experiment in Collective Autobiography* (2006) came out, I read the essays by a set of terrific poets and friends before I got to one of Barrett Watten's entries, which recounted our first meeting in 1974.[52] Barry and I were strangers when he answered the door of the San Francisco apartment he shared with Ron Silliman. I had started corresponding with Ron the year before, while I was living in British Columbia. Susan and I drove south to meet him and see the Bay Area for the first time. We were driving a VW bug with a stick shift that neither of us had quite gotten the hang of, so every uphill stop was a cliffhanger.

Just the year before, Jerry Rothenberg had suggested Ron and I get in touch with each other: a magical connection. When Ron came to the door in San Francisco, he said he wanted to go out to hear the band of a friend of his at a nearby bar. We spent our first meeting together hardly able to hear one another over the deafening music. But after that, we began writing to each other at a furious pace.

Barry's *Grand Piano* essay goes on to talk about another meeting he and I had two years later, this time at a swanky bar called the Colonnades in Astor Place in Manhattan. We met up with Ted Greenwald and Tom

51. See Lytle Shaw, "Framing the Lyric," *American Literary History*, 28:2 (2016).

52. See Barrett Watten, "VII," *The Grand Piano: An Experiment in Collective Autobiography, San Francisco, 1975–80, Part 3* (Detroit: Mode A, 2006), pp. 100–101.

Raworth, who, like Jerry and Ron, became lifelong friends, centers of my poetic universe. In 1977, Ted and I did our first collaborative work, meeting four times to record fifteen hours of conversation. I don't remember much about that gathering at the Colonnades except how Tom could speak with just the twinkle in his eyes, not saying a word. And, oddly, I recall that when Barry and I left the Colonnades we were reeling from how expensive our few drinks were; neither of us was used to going to a bar that was that expensive.

As Barry recalls in his initial *Grand Piano* entry, we then walked halfway up Manhattan, "talking nonstop all the way." *The L=A=N=G=U=A=G=E Letters* includes one I wrote to Barry in 1977 that gives a glimpse of what we may have talked about on that walk. My letter starts off with my addressing our fundamental "disagreement": "i dont think its important to have any kind of unified theory to operate out of" [*sic*].[53] Just a few years later, I was happy to be published in Barry's paradigmatic magazine *This* and Bruce Andrews and I featured Barry in *L=A=N=G=U=A=G=E*. Lyn Hejinian and Barry started *Poetics Journal* in 1982, just after Bruce and I stopped our newsletter. They published my essay "Writing and Method" in 1983. Two years later, though, Barry rejected "Pounding Fascism (Appropriating Ideologies—Mystification, Aestheticization, and Authority in Pound's Poetic Practice)," my vociferous formulation of anti-antisemitism through a critique of unified theory—indeed, of any poetics of totalization and control.[54] If I remember right, Barry ended his adamant rejection with an obscure rejoinder—"Look at a picture of Ida Rolf," referring to the founder of a school of often painful body manipulation therapy in supposed pursuit of "structural integration." I was perplexed by the comment. I wonder now if Barry was saying that he imagined himself as the aggressive shaper of a structurally integrated school?[55]

Ted and Tom and many others are named in the *Grand Piano* essay in "collective autobiography," but my name has been put under erasure: Barry refers to me only as "N—." Perhaps my name is "N—," as in no one;

53. *The L=A=N=G=U=A=G=E Letters: Selected 1970s Correspondence of Bruce Andrews, Ron Silliman, and Charles Bernstein*, ed. Matthew Hofer and Michael Golston (Albuquerque: University of New Mexico Press, 2019), letter number 50, p. 170

54. The essay was presented at the MLA at the very end of 1984, published by Clayton Eshleman in *Sulfur* in 1985 and collected in *Content's Dream: Essays 1974–1984* (Los Angeles: 1985). "Pounding Fascism Today," a plenary session presented at the 27th Ezra Pound International Conference, University of Pennsylvania in 2017, included a paper by Joshua Kotin on my essay, along with other responses.

55. *Poetics Journal* ran from 1982 to 1998. In 1991, the journal published one other essay of mine, "Professing Stein / Stein Professing." In its first five years, *Poetics Journal* also published several of reviews of my books, for which I am grateful.

Niemandsrose. The "N——" marks a loss of control on the part of the redactor, a pathos that cannot be erased.

Barry stayed in touch with Ted, soon after our Lady Astor's meeting publishing Ted's great 1979 book, *You Bet!* I remember when I read at the Grand Piano, the year *You Bet!* was published, Barry insisted on reading with me.[56] Ted and I had dedicated *The Course* to Tom and his wife Val. Tom died the year after Ted.

I can still see the twinkle in Tom's eyes.

11. Recommendation

February 5, 2016

Dear Admissions Committee:

Danniello Violin-Cello is in the top .001 percent of students
I have taught at Final Acres Residential College. In fact,
Danniello is the best student I have ever had in my seventy-
three and a half years of teaching--praise I reserve for no
more than two students in each admissions cycle. Danniello
far exceeds my previously best student, Morridichai Ersatz,
who went on to become full professor of Anaerobic Arts at the
University of Distant Learning.

What distinguishes Danniello, and makes him such a strong
candidate for admission to your doctoral English program, is
his deep animosity to literature. Danniello has an intuitive
understanding of how literary works are not just complicit in
the darkest deceptions of capitalism but are also an active
agent of global environmental catastrophe. In my research
seminar last year on poetry and genocide, Danniello wrote a
marvelous paper on how poets who were victims of, and wrote
against, twentieth-century genocides bore some responsibility
for their fate by working within literary forms that
perpetuated the cultural institutions that ultimately sealed
their fate. This paper won our highest department honor, the
Swillian and Jocasta Immaculata Regicide prize.

Though his mentors at Final Acres can take some credit for
nurturing Danniello's approach to literary studies, he comes

---

56. The Grand Piano was the location of a reading series in San Francisco. Ron Silliman recorded the 1979 reading: Barry's and my readings are available at our PennSound pages. *Under Erasure* (1991) and *Bad History* (1998) are titles of Watten's poetry books.

by his insights naturally. At a personal level, I can say that
Danniello is an unforgettable person who has made a big impact
on our campus, both organizing guest speakers and managing
the discussion after lectures. His presence is so commanding
that the response of students and faculty alike is invariably
either professed consent or awed silence.

Do not hesitate to contact me if I can provide you further
information on this truly exceptional individual.

        Sincerely,

        Fidelio B. Fidel
        Acheson, Topeka, and Sante Fe Professor of Semiotic
        Emission
        Final Acres Residential College
        Mountebank, New Jersey

12. Poem-A-Day, Poem-A-Day, Jiggety Zam: The Academy of American Poets Keeps Poetry Safe from Poetry (Or Why I Will Never Be / A Chancellor of the AmPo Academy)

"Why Do You Love the Poem" was selected for the "Poem-a-Day" series
at the Academy of American Poets, which claims three hundred thousand
readers.[57] The producers of the show told me it was mandatory to submit
an "About This Poem" statement along with an audio recording—"whether
that statement is a full-blown exegesis or simply reportage on when and
where the poem was written, or what compelled you to write the poem,
etc., etc., is completely up to you." (Audio of the poem itself was optional.)
Because my possibly sardonic poem was about not substituting anything
for the poem (a line could have been: "If you love the poem for what it's
about, then you don't love the poem but what it's about"), I wrote a sen-
tence that echoed a series of related poems I've written (one of which even
made it in the *Norton Anthology of Poetry*): "This commentary intention-
ally left blank." I also attached an enhanced audio version of the line. The
staff producers wrote back that what I sent did not meet their "standards."
Evidently, I misunderstood what "completely up to you" meant. Even so,

57. 2022: <poets.org/poem/why-do-you-love-poem>

I wrote a commentary explaining my point of view—why I preferred not to write an "about" statement—and I attached an enhanced audio of this new commentary. I was informed by the producers that my audio would not be "accessible" to those who relied on the audio version of Poem-a-Day posts, even though my enhanced audio is entirely accessible, albeit slightly aesthetically challenging. The producers said they would make the needed audio themselves.

Just before publication, I received a proof with the opening—and key— sentences of my commentary redacted: without those sentences, the commentary lost its motivation and so its sense. The producers sent a recording of the poem followed by the mangled commentary. I couldn't tell if the recording was done by a first-gen digital reader or a person imitating one. I had to act immediately as there was no time for back and forth. Within an hour I had made a new, "straight" recording of the poem, restoring only a version of the first redacted sentence of the original commentary [➔], assuming, correctly, that this would meet Poets.Org standards, even if it still lobotomized my comment.

And that, well, was that.

In one of their emails, "The Academy" expressed its appreciation for my "being an important part of our work." "We . . . would love" to sell you a membership. At a discount.

Making the purchase was left entirely up to me.

The rejected audio of the extended commentary is at my PennSound "audio/tapeworks" page. Here's the redacted commentary (the four initial sentences deleted by the producers are crossed out):

~~This commentary intentionally left blank.~~

~~That's the "about" statement I initially submitted. However, the editors told me this response didn't "meet our standards." My poem is about not meeting standards.~~ [➔] [I'd prefer to keep the commentary blank.] The kind of poetry I want doesn't follow rules: it makes up its own rules. Perhaps my commentary needs a commentary? The poem is itself a series of commentaries. The idea of "blank"—letting the work stand for itself—is my commentary on the poem. In other words, if you love the poem for what it is about, you don't love the poem but what it's about. Or perhaps you could say the commentary is the poem and the poem the commentary. I get things all, well, *Topsy-Turvy*.

[2022: *b2o* (boundary 2 online)]

13. The Taint of the Human

In an effort to make humanities classes more accessible to a wide range of students, and boost enrollment, Hodgepodge University has eliminated the requirement for reading poems in all classes. Instructors will be required to offer prose summaries as the primary texts for examination. Original poems will be provided, if at all, as optional reading.

•

Because of the taint of the human, and the human participation in environmental destruction, tyranny, and violence, Hodgepodge University has decided to eliminate the study of human-produced documents, instead focusing on the nonhuman world.

•

Because of the morally repugnant nature of much animal behavior, Hodgepodge University has decided to remove biology from the curriculum. We will continue to focus on the nonhuman sciences.

•

Because the nonhuman sciences lack the critical thinking previously offered by the humanities, Hodgepodge University has decided to cease all instruction in these fields. Classes will meet in silence.

14. Judeopessimism

We are white
We told the brownshirts

15.

[recanted]

16. Memorial

No Mass will anyone sing
No Kaddish will anyone say
Neither said nor sung
By none when I'm done.

But maybe one day
When the weather's bright and gay
Out for a stroll in Montmartre—
My Paulina alongside Mme Christina

With garlands of Evergreen
Comes she, to adorn my grave
And sigh: "Oh my, poor guy!"
Wet melancholy in her eye.

Alas! dwell I way too high
That even for my sweet
A stool I can't supply—
Jeeze! Her weary wobbling feet.

Sweety, fatty, don't go
Back to your house by foot—
At the curb—
Grab a cab.

after Heine's "Gedächtnisfeier"

UP against Storytelling

For David Antin

≤≥÷∫√≈Ω.

I told my
wife,
I
don't want
any more
stories,
tell me what
you need.
I told
my husband, I
don't
want any
more stories,
tell me what you
think.
I told my
mother, I
don't
want any
more of
your stories, just
tell
me what
you want.

I
told
my father,
I
don't
want
any more
of
your stories,
just
tell me
where I
went wrong.
I told my
rabbi, I
don't
want any
more of your
God-damn
stories, just
tell
me
how to
get out of here.
I told
my friend, I
don't want
any
more stories, just
tell me
what's
going on.
I told
my professor,
I
don't want
any more

stories,

just tell

me you'll

stop.

I

told my president,

I

don't want

any more

stories,

just get

your foot off

my face.

15. Amit Chaudhuri:

About a decade ago, I interrupted a talk I was giving to a small group of international writers and academics gathered in Delhi to say, 'Fuck storytelling.'

My respondent, a British Asian literary journalist, later said, while commenting on my talk, how "shocked" she'd been by my remark. It wasn't the expletive she objected to, but my attack on "storytelling," which had been so "empowering to peoples and cultures." "Storytelling" had, by now, become a sacred cow that you insulted at your own risk.

My discomfiture [was] with the idea that "storytelling" is a feature of non-Western culture, and a valuable resource, as a result, of a postcolonial politics that sets itself up against the Enlightenment. A glance at non-Western artistic expression reveals, however, a deep commitment to forms outside of what we now think of as "narrative" (synecdoche, for instance, and other means of poetic elision). . . . Globalisation, by the turn of the millennium, had become a kind of narrative—a lateral, interconnected network from which there was no escape, and from which no one evidently desired to escape—and this privileging of a narrative that had no "outside" (globalisation) led to the marginalisation of the poetic. . . . "Storytelling," with its kitschy magic and its associations of postcolonial empowerment, is seen to emanate from the immemorial funds of orality in the non-Western world, and might be interpreted as a critique of the inscribed word, and its embeddedness in Western forms of knowledge.[1]

1. Posted at the "Against Storytelling" website (2018): <ueaindiacreativewritingworkshop.com/against -storytelling/>. In his statement, and also in his talk at the conference, Chaudhuri debunks the claim that "storytelling" is an essential feature of third world cultures, characterizing this claim as a form of

¶¶§∞¶•∞.

In the aftermath of Trump's election in 2016, the search for blame began. On some accounts, the blame was laid on postmodernists and poststructuralists who had so undermined truth that now a president is free to lie with impunity.[2] As a professional sophist, I am used to the charge. Like the marshal said to the sheriff, *it comes with the territory.*

Questioning the essential truthfulness of stories—the jargon of storytelling—including journalistic stories, is always provocative and it's best when it's meant not to shut down the views of others but a way of getting more voices into the agora. (No, *agora* is not deep muscle pain treatable by Ben-Gay: Get real!) The *opposite* of Trumpism's univocal embrace of the *truth in my lies* is the sophist's *lies in my truth.* The Trumpian appropriates the mantle of truth, insisting that those who disagree are the liars because they deny the truth not only of his story, but also the truth of stories. Indeed, Large Sectors of the Massed Media (LSMM) find themselves on precarious ground in calling Trumpisms out, given their almost religious devotion to the truth of stories. There is a history here going back in America from Chautauqua, the nineteenth-century platform for preachers, entertainers, and self-help gurus right up to today's Ted Talks, and clones, which scrub away any narrative shards on NPR's airwaves. But this American life is more than an endless drone of hyperfascinating stories.

Hyperfascination, as William Burroughs might say, is a virus, but not from outer space, from inner space. Trump's truth is his lies: they are not a mask. For Trump, lying is not a means of hiding a policy: it is the policy.

To echo David Antin's old friend George Lakoff: *The repetition of a lie, even when it is labeled a lie, reinforces it.* There is an undeniable urge to defend the mainstream media against the assaults of Trumpism, to see it as us against them. But this elides our own unintended complicity with Trumpian storytelling. Trump plays P.T. Barnum to mainstream journalism's all-day sucker. And the social media chorus spreads the virus like zombies in *Dawn of the Dead.*

Romantic primitivism, fostered by postcolonial politics, which makes a false opposition between authenticity and Enlightenment. Chaudhuri's essay was published in the *Los Angeles Review of Books* (September 20, 2019) as "Storytelling and Forgetfulness" <lareviewofbooks.org/article/storytelling -and-forgetfulness>.

2. See, for example, Thomas Edsall's summary, "Is President Trump a Stealth Postmodernist or Just a Liar?," New York *Times*, January 25, 2018 <nytimes.com/2018/01/25/opinion/trump-postmodernism -lies.html>.

111.

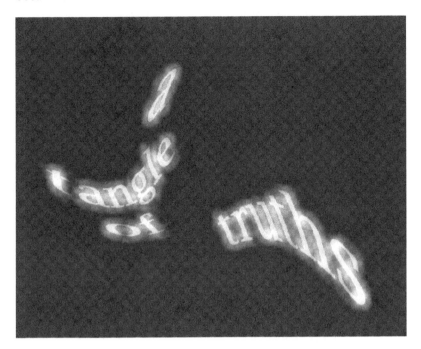

‡‡∞§§. If Socrates Was a Poet

One of my multiple and conflicting commitments as a writer is to collage as reframing. I am drawn to unexpected swerves that heighten contradictions. In my poetics, disjunction is a means to more intense connections. Interruption and disruption heighten the experience of the verbality of language, so that you are not just subjected to rhetorical devices but get to see and hear them pop, like firecrackers on Independence Day.

David Antin's suspicion of collage, parataxis, and metonymy allowed him to create an essential body of work that pushed back against reflexive uses of parataxis. I share with Antin a sense that collage is a troubled legacy of modernism (as are all legacies). Antin's disapprobation pushes me to make sure that my use of my favorite poetic devices doesn't fall prey to the arbitrary and entropic, sugared by the lure of an attractively dissonant surface. The kind of poetry I want averts the asemic in pursuit of n-dimensional semantic hedonia (n/SH).

I value poetry that has the transformation Antin finds in narrative, that often goes missing in story or plot. Antin's counterintuitive distinction

between story and narrative is similar to the difference between fragmen-
tation as an end in itself ("isolate flecks," to use a phrase of William Carlos
Williams) and what Walter Benjamin calls *constellation*. I prize poetry and
essays, such as Antin's, in which the parts resonate with one another, be-
yond just logical or metric connection. But I also want poetry and essays
that realize an echopoetics by apparently anti-narrative means.[3]

In a March 26, 2003, talk poem for the Poetics Program at Buffalo called
"War," archived by PennSound, Antin makes a strong case against meton-
ymy and elision, what he calls in the talk "edge to edge relations," using as
his example then-President Bush's linkage of "9/11" with "weapons of mass
destruction" with "Saddam Hussein," to justify the recent invasion of Iraq:

> If . . . you imagine that metonymy connects things that are associable with
> each other   and you can imagine that metonymy is what governs the prin-
> ciple of collage   you are assuming essentially that all the things next to each
> other   obtain their meaning from their juxtapositions   but is that true? . . .
> are they related to their referential character   or to their significational
> character? . . . synecdoche works on very different principles than meton-
> ymy   metonymy is part-to-part relations   and the other is part-to-whole
> relations   part-to-part relations can be an infinite chain   you know, like
> butter   milk   churn   my aunt Tilda . . . bees   I was stung   a bear
> at the blueberry bush   you know all these things could come up one after
> another   in a metonymic chain   and contact between them seems to be
> missing   although it seems to be filled with the possibility of narrative in-
> terpolation   it may be that that is what makes it work   so, I guess when
> George Bush uses metonymy   to connect Saddam Hussein   with 9/11,
> what he imagines you will do   is fill it with a scoop of desperadoes   all
> under Saddam Hussein's order [My transcription.]

Jews/parasites, the Nazi Big Lie, is the locus classicus of this type of mal-
efaction, where "Jews" can readily be replaced by any designated threat.
Trump's signature series—Hussein/Obama/Birther—is a terrifying ex-
ample. Elision erases the connective tissue of discourse—how you get from
one place to another. "You can drive a whole army" through the gaps, says
Antin. It is not that he is advocating the logical relation of each element in
a narrative, but rather that his talking cure insists on visceral contiguity over
and against deliberate discontinuity, erasure, and jump cutting.

---

3. See Jerome McGann's discussion of "anti-narrative" versus "non-narrative" in his essay "Contem-
porary Poetry: Alternate Routes," in *Politics and Poetic Value*, published in *Critical Inquiry* 13:3 (1987).
McGann situates my work as anti-narrative, actively opposing the convention of narrative, in the tra-
dition of Blake.

In Antin's great talk poems, digression, anecdote, and association are favored over disconnection, fragmentation, and dissociation. The gaps in the talk poems mark pauses in an improvised talk (a bit like Charles Olson's "breath" lines). Antin's gaps eschew erasure and allow for rhythm, allowing for what he calls "radical coherency." Above all, like many of his fellow New American Poets, and following Dewey, Antin valued process over craft and revision. As Antin famously put it, "if robert lowell is a poet i dont want to be a poet   if robert frost was a poet i dont want to be a poet   if socrates was a poet i'll consider it."[4] Antin's talk poems invite you to think with them, in dialog, as they are being composed. They don't convey a fixed, predetermined meaning or plot or story. Rather, they allow for what Chaudhuri calls "deliberate irresolution."[5]

Still, there is a fundamental difference between eliding the gaps and accentuating them; that is, between "Big Lie" metonymy and metonymy used to break such viral associations. Just as there is, for Antin, a crucial difference between story (a logical series of plot points) and narrative (which averts closure as a means of grappling with experience). Consider, for example, Ron Silliman's exemplary articulation of disarticulations in *Ketjak* and *Tjanting*. Silliman does not naturalize his disjunctions but rather brings the structure of disjunction into view. He is using "non-narrative" or para-narrative means to narrative ends, as McGann puts it.

6.

4. David Antin, *Radical Coherency: Selected Essays on Art and Literature 1966 to 2005* (Chicago: University of Chicago Press, 2011), p. 273

5. Amit Chaudhuri, *The Origins of Dislike* (Oxford: Oxford University Press, 2018), p. 62

∞=∩∇∉⊀≲. A House Is Not a Home

In the New Delhi "Against Storytelling" symposium, Amit Chaudhuri made the distinction between a single story and a house, suggesting an even more fundamental distinction between a *house* and a *home* but also between *story* and *history*. A series of plot points, like a flurry of Tweets, might make a story but not the network of connected elements that is a history.

In his essay "The Beggar and the King," David Antin argues for a fundamental difference between story and narrative.[6] A plot or story, Antin says, is a "sequence of events," while a narrative involves a "transformation"—a transformation that, Antin intimates, entails an aversion of closure. Story or plot "is about making sense," creating from its elements "a temporal whole." In contrast, narrative "explains nothing" because it makes present an "experiential" dimension that defies "intelligibil[ity]." Indeed, closure, the plot, may well obstruct narrative's "incommensurability and unintelligibility."

According to Antin, a story, as for example a news story, leaves the individual plot elements as is: it is a set of facts, real or imagined. Narrative transforms those individual elements into something else, something fundamentally different than in their initial articulation.

When story becomes narrative there is a reckoning and a price to pay. There is a "threat and terror of a / narrative which could if experienced transform" one beyond one's "own recognition," as when a beggar become king or Oedipus recognizes what he has done.[7]

Antin's contrast of story and narrative is reflected in his preference for live improvised performance of a poem (the talk poem) over reading a set text (the poetry reading). The talk poem allows for what, in *Senses of Walden* (1972), Stanley Cavell calls "the conditions of our present."[8] (Cavell's readings of classic Hollywood films, in *Pursuits of Happiness* [1981], are a primer in how to read those works not simply as entertaining yarns but as narratives, in the sense Antin means.)

House/home, story/history, plot/narrative, fragmentation/constellation. *Book*, in Edmond Jabès's sense. I think also of Freud's contrast between

---

6. Antin, "The Beggar and the King," in *Radical Coherency*. Initially published in *Pacific Coast Philology*, 30:2 (1995). I cite pp. 261–64, 266, and 270.

7. Antin, "The Price," in *How Long Is the Present: Selected Talk Poems of David Antin*, ed. Stephen Fredman (Albuquerque: University of New Mexico Press, 2014). Antin first staked out the difference between story and narrative in this 1986 talk poem.

8. *Senses of Walden: An Expanded Edition* (Chicago: University of Chicago Press, 2013), p. 61

melancholy, which obsessively seeks (and fails to find) rational intelligibility, and mourning, which acknowledges unintelligible loss.

David Antin, "Sociology of Art":

> . . . now in a written work   it would have been very easy to go back   erase
> the false step . . .   /   but the iliad is not a written work   and there
> are some things fundamentally different about an oral poem   one thing in
> particular   the technique of erasing   i mean in a literary poem theres a text
> and a determined reader can flip the pages back over and over again   and
> there is something of an illusion of spatial form the idea that you can have it
> there   all at once   lying under your hands   leading to the notion of ele-
> gant spatial arrangement and its contraries   clumsy arrangements all based
> on fantasies of some spatial existence   that is the result of the minds   de-
> ceiving itself into forgetting that it has itself constructed this "space" and the
> "form" that is an imaginary configuration within it   by mere flipping of
> pages and taking this synthetically derived memory   produced by constant
> reavailability and confusing it with real memory it is this "constructed" literal
> form which requires the mechanical operations of erasure and excision   the
> only way you can get rid of an object is to destroy it   but an oral poem has no
> such problem   if you take a wrong turn make a false start   you cant "erase"
> it   but you can recover and you can obliterate it from memory   /   you
> can take advantage of the weakness of human memory by extending through
> time some kind of   diversionary brilliance[9]

CVC. The Book of Ezekiel

The darkness has its secrets
which light does not know.
It's a kind of perfection,

while every light
distorts the truth.[10]

9. David Antin, "Sociology of Art," in *Talking at the Boundaries* (New York: New Directions, 1976), pp. 190–91

10. Nissim Ezekiel, "Hymns in Darkness: XII," in *Collected Poems: 1952–1988* (Oxford University Press, 1989), p. 224

"At a certain point in history," Chaudhuri said at the "Against Storytelling" symposium—it can be dated to the 1980s, at the time of globalization—"people started saying, we are born storytellers. And they said it with an air of satisfaction. One began to hear that storytelling is the primal human and communal function. That we've been telling each other stories from the beginning of time. . . . No, we haven't been telling each other stories from the beginning of time."

The idea that Indian writers should tell "our" own stories, as "we" have always done, was, according to Chaudhuri, an invention of (literary) globalization:

> In India "regional" [and associated languages possess] a sort of authenticity that, say, a foreign or colonial tongue such as English doesn't. To my knowledge, the "regional" isn't discussed in India . . . in conjunction with what it has actually been inextricable from in that country—the modern, the modernist, the avant-garde, a particular intimation of strange. . . . The "regional" . . . is hardly ever seen in India for what it has often been—an elite, high, counter-culture project, imperiously overturning the conventions of nationalism and identity. (*Origins of Dislike*, p. 247)

By reducing Indian writing to personal, not to say nativist, authenticity, the imperative for stories undercuts, for Chaudhuri, the rich and complex history of West Bengali modernism, aesthetic innovation, and intellectual inquiry that is foundational for his work. The mandated production of first-person stories scented with local color for the export market undermined the validity of work stigmatized as aesthetic and difficult.

In *The Arimaspia*, Thomas McEvilley traces the classic origin of this pernicious trope to Megasthenes (fourth-century BCE Greek historian): "I come to suspect that it is a racist projection, to the effect that dark skinned peoples can't deal with abstraction, that they are associated with the instincts, and so on."[11]

Meanwhile, in a kind of self-colonialization, a.k.a. blowback, the West has internalized its own supremacist imperatives for the natural and virtuous and against artifice and the cosmopolitan. The result is compulsory storytelling as shibboleth, based on sacrosanct authenticity—the *jargon of storytelling*, to adapt Max Horkheimer and Theodor Adorno's "jargon of authenticity." Intersectionality, which is the acknowledgment of possibly

---

11. Thomas McEvilley, *The Arimaspia* (Kingston, NY: McPherson & Company, 2014), p. 228. Perhaps this is echoed still, albeit now valued as positive, in Yeats's ecstatic 1912 introduction to Tagore: "The work of a supreme culture, they yet appear as grass and the rushes"; quoted in the introduction to *Name Me a Word: Indian Writers Reflect on Writing*, ed. Meena Alexander (New Haven, CT: Yale University Press, 2018), p. xx.

incommensurable identifications, is airbrushed into the fiction of a holistic single, seamless identity.

But, as Chaudhuri tells it, the story is more complex than that. Following Deleuze and Gramsci, we may think of the relation of major to minor, high and low, center to periphery, in terms of hegemony or mastery. Chaudhuri shows how the transvaluation of minor to major can fall into Orientalist traps of their own, while giving insight into why Indian poetry in English seems formally conservative and overly Anglophilic to an American attuned to the radical modernists and the New American Poets, such as Antin, but ignorant of India. In "Nissim Ezekiel: Poet of a Minor Literature," in *The Origins of Dislike*, he casts Ezekiel (1924–2004) as the iconic modern (post-Independence) Indian poet writing in English.[12] English in India, as Chaudhuri stresses, is marked by being the colonial language among many local tongues but also, for Ezekiel, it is a cosmopolitan, rather than regional, language. Ezekiel's first language was Marathi.

Ezekiel radiates double consciousness, and in more than one way. He averts the role of the authentic storyteller who rejects European aesthetic innovation. He's local but not just local and his work engages different kinds of locality and foreignness; Chaudhuri's discussion of his work shows that such binaries are better understood as situational than as fixed, as conflicts within a poetics rather than points of policy. Ezekiel sets the stage "In India" and in his biblical diasporic poem, "Lamentation":

. . . Here among the beggars,
Hawkers, pavement sleepers,
Hutment dwellers, slums . . .
Suffering the place and time,
I ride my elephant of thought,
A Cézanne slung around my neck.
        ("In India")

My lips lack prophesy
My tongue speaketh no great matters

---

12. In A. Ragu, *The Poetry of Nissim Ezekiel* (New Delhi: Atlantic Publishers, 2002), Ragu calls Ezekiel "the cultural tzar of English poetry in India" (p. 1). Ragu's study begins by signaling troubling gender politics in Ezekiel's poems and goes on to make an unconvincing case against Raj Rao's critique of Ezekiel's naturalizing, not to say, primitivizing woman in one of his best-known poems, "Poet, Lover, Birdwatcher," which begins "To force the pace and never to be still / Is not the way of those who study birds / Or women. / The best poets wait for words" (Ragu, pp. 40–14). In *The Origins of Dislike*, in his discussion of the minor poet's affect, Chaudhuri cites this passage, emphasizing the final line (p. 232).

The words of the wise are wasted on me
Fugitive am I and far from home
A vagabond and every part of me is withered
       ("Lamentation")[13]

    In his "Very Indian Poems in English" and "Goodbye Party for Miss Pushpa T.S." (below), Ezekiel perverts the nativist demands made on Henry Meredith Parker:

Friends,
our dear sister
is departing for foreign
in two three days,
and
we are meeting today
to wish her bon voyage.
You are all knowing, friends,
what sweetness is in Miss Pushpa.
I don't mean only external sweetness
but internal sweetness.[14]

In these ideolectical poems, Ezekiel averts mastery, turning the tables on both authentic storytelling and Orientalist condescension, while risking censure for making fun of (rather than *with*) very distinctively non-King's-English pidgin. Or is Ezekiel, like William Carlos Williams on LSD, making present in poetry the languages of the ear, creating an Indian English as distinct as Williams's American English.[15]

    Chaudhuri writes about Ezekiel's work not as the truth of the subaltern but as minor poetry aware of itself, that is, as minor and as accommodating; his characterization of Ezekiel echoes "Prufrock": "outwardly

13. *Collected Poems*, pp. 132 and 72

14. *Collected Poems*, pp 191–92. See Irshad Gulam Ahmed, "Nissim Ezekiel's Critical Nationalism and the Question of Indian English" in *Indian Literature* 53:2 (2009).

15. I discuss ideolectical poetry in two linked essays, "The Poetics of the Americas" in *My Way: Speeches and Poems* and "Objectivist Blues" in *Attack of the Difficult Poems: Essays and Inventions*. Ezekiel dedicates a 1953 poem to Williams: "I do not want / to write / poetry like yours / but still I / love / the way you do it" (*Collected*, p. 46). Williams also had an "other" language, also a colonial one, Spanish.

timorous, seemingly unconfrontational, and at once 'politic, cautious, and obtuse.'"[16]

"In this case of the minor poet writing in a minor tradition, there is no possibility of grand failure; there is only the inconsequentiality of decorum," Chaudhuri says (p. 226), going on to quote an 1830 poem of Kasiprasad Ghosh, one of the first Indian poets to write in English:

To spin such verse out I'll dare.
And please the public ear again
With such discordant, silly strain (p. 226)

Chaudhuri admires Ezekiel for his recognition of himself as a sometimes "comic player"—"a poet-rascal-clown," as Ezekiel describes himself, which Chaudhuri interprets as a poet who resists grandiosity with delight, and, I'd add, a welcome irony bordering on sarcasm. "The wise survive and serve," writes Ezekiel in "Background, Casually."[17] "Here are the two aims of the minor writer and his tradition," Chaudhuri comments, "to not challenge, to not ask for independence or mastery, and thereby to continue to be able to write, to produce, to 'survive'" (p. 234).

My morals had declined.
I heard of Yoga and of Zen.
Could I, perhaps, be rabbi saint?
The more I searched, the less I found.
        ("Background, Casually")

What does it say that polar opposite poets, David Antin and Nissim Ezekiel are both Jewish (Ashkenazi and Bene Israel, respectively), born just seven years apart?
    —"Fugitive am I and far from home."

I dreamed that
Fierce men had bound my feet and hands.
The later dreams were all of words.

16. *The Origins of Dislike*, p. 228. The internal quote is from T. S. Eliot's "The Love Song of J. Alfred Prufrock."

17. "Background, Casually" in *Name Me a Word*, pp. 123–24

I did not know that words betray
But let the poems come, and lost
That grip on things the worldly prize.

. . . .

I have made my commitments now.
This is one: to stay where I am . . .
In some remote and backward place.
My backward place is where I am.
            ("Background, Casually")

✝✝✝✝✝✝≽≼✝✝✝✝✝✝.[18]

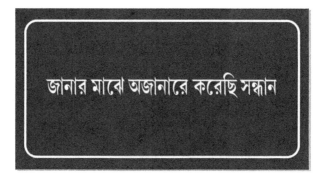

জানার মাঝে অজানারে করেছি সন্ধান

LXVVII.

My obituary for David Antin was printed on the inside cover of the pro-
gram for a memorial event at the Getty in Los Angeles on February 4, 2017.
For my talk, I presented a commentary on my obituary, adding to it and
contradicting it, based on notes I made during the first part of the program.
I came to the event not knowing what I would say. Among the first speak-
ers was Barbara T. Smith, who asked each of us to cut a lock of hair, which
she collected. This reminded me of the Jewish ritual of cutting a piece of
clothing at a funeral, usually ritualized as cutting a tie. So I ended my talk
with a reading of "Rivulets of the Dead Jew," which makes a reference to

18. "In the midst of the known, I have found the unknown" (from a Tagore song). From Amit Chaud-
huri's new "Indian Road Signs" series at the Harrington Street Arts Centre, Kolkata in August 2018.

David Antin was one of the great American poets of the postwar period, transforming the practice of poetry, art criticism, and the essay. His "talk poems" are chock-full of startlingly philosophical insights, weaving narratives on the fly and making poems that are as engaging as they are wise.

Antin was born in Brooklyn on February 1, 1932. His father died two years later. He went to Brooklyn Technical High School, where he imagined becoming an inventor, engineer, or scientist. In his own way, Antin became all three. While at Tech, he read Stein and Joyce; that changed everything. In 1961, he married the multimedia artist Eleanor Fineman (now Eleanor Antin). In 1968, David and Ellie, with their one-year-old son Blaise, moved to San Diego to teach at the University of California at San Diego, where David co-founded the visual arts program.

Through his work as a performance artist and conceptualist, and his commitment to process and improvisation, Antin transformed the genre of poetry. Best known for his signature "talk poems," performed and translated around the world, Antin has published more than fifteen books. Antin died on October 11, 2016. He had been diagnosed with Parkinson's disease, though, iconoclast to the end, he disputed the diagnosis.

An inspiration to both his contemporaries and younger poets, Antin challenged us all to think on our feet and in the vernacular. A thrilling conversationalist, Antin's voice echoes in and through time. He is gone, but his talk lingers on.

Charles Bernstein

this ritual. I gave my annotated program to Jake Marmer, who immediately followed me. Marmer told us how Antin had talked to him about poems his grandfather read to him in Russian: Marmer gave a stirring reading of one of those poems in Russian (without translation, none needed).

🍸 ✳ ☛. Non-plot elements of verbal art

rhythm / tempo
gesture
sound
performance
accent / timbre
allusion
echo
pitch
rime
voicelessness
audible elements of the recording device
erasure
collage
typography
rimelessness
pattern / tone / tune
patternlessness
tunelessness
haecceity
non-sensuous similarity (Benjamin, "Doctrine of the Similar")
puns
color
thickness
style
forms
syntax
decoration
utterance
incomprehensibility
artifice
visual organization (line breaks, visual poetry)
context of publication
paper

digression
vocables in liberty
the word as such (not ideas but "actual word stuff" [Williams])
the unconscious
fetish
the particular not subsumed into (reified as) story, voice, theory

∂∂∂∂.

The history of the novel is replete with works that avert the jargon of story-
telling in the pursuit of narrative (in Antin's sense). There is certainly no
shortage of "story" writers who welcome multiple, competing versions,
holding storytelling to an aesthetic fire. Chaudhuri will find company with
Samuel R. Delany's *Motion of Light in the Water*, Lydia Davis's *End of the
Story*, Raymond Federman's *Take It or Leave It*, Laura (Riding) Jackson's
Progress of Stories and *The Telling*, Peter Straub's *The Throat*, Ko Un's *Ten
Thousand Lives*, Thomas McEvilley's *The Arimaspia*, and Paul Auster's *4 3 2 1*.
To name only a very few paradigmatic examples.

🔔 🔔 🔔. Aversive Thinking

- Avoid frame lock, trouble consistency.
- Proliferate competing frames the way Hendrick's Gin proliferates
  botanicals.
- Being moody is the inability to shift moods.
- Virtue is for those who have given up on life and want to share their
  disapproval.

•£¢®¥˝∑∑¬°. More Fool You That Are Puzzled by It.

In a January 2017 conversation with reporter Mary Louise Kelly and NPR's
senior vice president for news Michael Oreskes, NPR News made clear
that its policy is not to use the word "lies" when referring to Trump and
his aides.[19] As if possessed by the ghost of logical positivist A. J. Ayer, NPR

---

19. Richard Gonzales, "NPR and the Word 'Liar': Intent Is Key," January 25, 2017 <npr.org/sections
/thetwo-way/2017/01/25/511503605/npr-and-the-l-word-intent-is-key>

News believes that the price of objectivity is the aversion of truthfulness. Truth lies waiting, just over the bend; a lie's a thing that never ends.

> *Child steps on chair to reach cookie jar. Takes cookies out of jar and sits at kitchen table. Parental Unit walks in, stage left.*
>
> PU: I told you not to take the cookies.
>
> C: I did not take any cookies.
>
> PU: What is in your hands?
>
> C: There is nothing in my hands.
>
> PU: Don't lie to me. I can see the cookies in your hand.
>
> C: You are the liar . . . these are not cookies, they are berries.

"He can walk fast enough when he tries, a good deal faster than I; but he can lie yet faster. He's some white operator, betwisted and painted up for a decoy. He and his friends are all humbugs," as Melville put it in his iconic *The Confidence Man: His Masquerade.*
    "More fool you that are puzzled by it."[20]

20. *The Confidence Man* (New York: Dix, Edwards & Company, 1857), pp. 18 and 20

††† *After Thoreau and Goffman*

There are nowadays many storytellers, but it is admirable to tell because it was once admirable to live.

I never met a person who cried "fire" when confronted by a snowball. But there are many today who cry "freedom" when confronted with tyranny. My aggrievement may be absolute to me but that does not make it greater than yours. My freedom is only that to the extent it guarantees yours. Anything different, to the extent of the difference, is not liberty; it is oppression.

«»«»«»«»». *After Pound and for Shklovsky's Plotless Prose*

Never use any word that contributes to a plot.
EACH SENTENCE MUST RESIST THE SENTENCE BEFORE IT.
Even the absence of narrative had to be narrated.

∆∆∆∆∆∆.

"The disjointed and superfluous are what preoccupy Tagore at the end of the nineteenth century," Chaudhuri explains. He quotes Tagore on the propensity to filter out what doesn't fit from our stories, so that "only a small fraction" of the "tremors" and "comings and goings" of perception are acknowledged. "This is chiefly because one's mind, like a fisherman, casts a net of integration and accepts only what it can gather at a single haul:

everything else eludes it. [The mind] has the power to move all irrelevancies far away from the path of its set purpose."[21]

The task of poetry is to bring the nets into view. *A task anyway* . . .

√∫~µ≤≥÷≥÷. Eulogy for David Antin in English English[22]

if andrew motion is a poet i don't want to be a poet
if philip larkin was a poet i don't want to be a
poet   if david antin was a poet   i'll consider it

Charles Bernstein & Nick Thurston   Eulogy for David Antin in English English   2016

Δ . . . ÷≥≤µΩ≈√. Techniques of Erasure

"Roseland" is one of my earliest poems. It is the last poem in *Parsing* (1976). "Roseland" samples phrases from Antin's signal talk poem, "Sociology of Art." It is a collage poem that erases much of Antin's talk poem, creating a network of motifs that extend and contest Antin's active thinking and his resistance to erasure. The opening page of "Roseland" is reproduced below (from *Parsing*), followed by a compilation of the phrases I took

21. "Unconstitutional Spaces," in *The Origins of Dislike*, pp. 200–201. The Tagore passage is significant for Chaudhuri as he also cites it in the introduction to *Clearing a Space: Reflections on India, Literature and Culture* (Oxford, UK: Peter Lange, 2008), p. 26.

22. Nick Thurston's 2016 broadside from a remark I made at reading in Britain, based on Antin's quip quoted in "#CageFreePoetry" in Act Two of this book and also in "If Socrates Was a Poet," just above in this essay. Two-color risographic from Information as Materials in the United Kingdom.

ROSELAND

                              you need some way of
                   some set of
                     you live in a place
                                   it isn't much
                        you move out
                 you have to
                        you live at the edge
         your memory has let you down
                              a kind of chaos
                   when you go
                        if you face it
                 this axis this
                     the human order
             more or less
                     you have a map
         you put yourself in position
                 and try to
                     this is the
                 a human construction
                              you try out the space
                 try to
                     you drive on them
             go straight
                     one might imagine
             only grasping
                     a pity
         a pile of rocks

from Antin's "Sociology of Art."[23] The phrases, highlighted in orange on
the printed text of Antin's "Sociology of Art," were excerpted to compose

23. "Roseland" was first published in *Parsing* (New York: Asylum's Press, 1976). A full mark-up "Sociol-
ogy of Art," together with "Roseland," is online at <writing.upenn.edu/epc/authors/bernstein/essays
/Antin_Sociology+Roseland.pdf>. Antin's talk poem was included in *Talking at the Boundaries* and col-
lected in *How Long Is the Present*.

something unappealing about the notion of a "primitive" art

is not possible   or desirable   you use language   and in

you need some way of describing that yam   some label for
that yam   or some set of instructions by which people will find

you live in a place   and you have to get somewhere
regularly   and you have to go into places that are   confus-
ingly similar   say you live at the edge of a forest   and you

regard this as an improvement but it is clear that your memory
has let you down   since it is obvious that most hunting or for-
village   is   a human construction   is humanly devised
or arranged   even if it is a temporary station   you will have
adapted to a human order   the place that youre going into is
not humanly arranged   it is the forest   the desert   a kind of
chaos   or at least its order is "natural"   rather than "human"
when you go into it   you can become "lost"   which
means that   you cannot apprehend its order   or relate its
order to your human order   so what do you do?   you seek
its regularities   you make a map   the sun rises regularly
more or less regularly   in the east   this is the order of
nature   and it sets in the west   if you face it   the rising   try
sun   your left hand points north and your right hand south
this axis is the order of culture   the human order   now
you lay out the space   with your home at the center   or at
you mark off proportionate distances in your picture   you have
a map   now anytime you are in the forest   if you are con-
fused   all you have to do is find out where you are in your map
to do this you look for the sun   you put yourself in position

"Roseland." I used the excerpts mostly, but not entirely, in the order found in the Antin's talk poem (for example the first two highlighted phrases occur in the middle of "Roseland"). I have hand-corrected a few places where I miscopied Antin's original. All lines in "Roseland" are taken directly from Antin's talk poem.

⇑ ⇡ ⇡ §&. The Last Time I Saw David was on December 4, 2014

Ellie and David were going to come to dinner the day after David's Poetry Project talk, for which I had made a video that is on PennSound. In the Parish Hall at St. Mark's, David laid himself bare, turning the talk poem onto his physical movement in the space, as he walked away from the podium to show us, as if he were Yvonne Rainer, the way his Parkinson's debilitated his bearing. In the talk poem, almost David's last, he pushed hard against the

Parkinson's diagnosis. His thought and his body were one and yet at odds with each other. Antin was making present an experiential dimension that defied intelligibly, being there, in that space, as fully present as any poet can be, standing alone before an audience. No, not alone. *Next to us.*

The following morning David called me. He spoke in a whisper.

He said he couldn't come to dinner.

That he was no longer able to speak.

That he had lost his voice.

~~~~~~~~~~
          .

[2018: The first version of this work was presented at the "Against Storytelling" symposium on February 24. The symposium was organized by Amit Chaudhuri and held at the India International Center in New Delhi, sponsored by Ashoka University and the University of East Anglia (UK). A sound recording of my talk, entitled "Against Storytelling / Before Time, for David Antin" was published by *Obieg* (Warsaw) in *Art & Literature: A Mongrel's Guide* edited by The Book Lovers (David Maroto and Joanna Zielińska). The recording concludes with a coda called *Now Time*—a sound version of the final section, made especially for this publication. *Obieg* also published the handwritten cards I used as my notes for the talk. In presenting the talk, I shuffled the cards to create a disjunct order, meant to interrogate Antin's distrust of parataxis. At a memorial event for Antin at Artists Space on March 27, 2018, I presented another version of the talk, this time with PowerPoint slides randomly arranged, called "Up Against Storytelling." A bilingual version was published as *Speaking and Listening* and *En parlant, en écoutant* by Shelter Press at La Criée Centre d'Art Contemporain in Rennes, France. For links and media files go to PennSound <writing.upenn.edu/pennsound/x/Bernstein-talks.php#Dehli>. Thanks to Peter Middleton, Marjorie Perloff, Amit Chaudhuri, Susan Bee, and Julien Bismuth.]

Doubletalking the Homophonic Sublime

Comedy, Appropriation, and the Sounds of One Hand Clapping[1]

Who am I? I am not a straight stonemason,
Neither a shipbuilder, nor a roofer,
I am a double-dealer, with a double soul,
A friend of night, and a daymonger.

Osip Mandelstam[2]

He speaks in six known and six unknown languages.

Daniil Kharms[3]

My self is not by my body's boundaries bound
In the thicket, we are

Tonya Foster[4]

1. Sound Writing

Never met a pun I didn't like.

I'm a veritable Will Rogers, with plenty of *roger* but without the will to say *enough's enough already*. All instinct. Like a Brooklyn Ahab stalking

1. Translated by the author from Esperanto, "Duoble-Parolas la Homofonia Sublima: Komedio, Alproprigo, kaj la Sonoj de Unu Mano Kunfrapante"

2. "The Slate Ode" (1923) translated by Ian Probstein, in *The River of Time: Time-Space, History, and Language in Avant-Garde, Modernist, and Contemporary Russian and Anglo-American Poetry* (New York: Academic Studies Press, 2017), p. 108

3. "From the Notebooks, Mid-1930s," in *Russian Absurd: Selected Writings*, tr. Alex Cigale (Evanston, IL: Northwestern University Press, 2017), p. 104

4. "Hood Hauntings: (A Poem In/On Progress): Draft 2," *Michigan Quarterly Review* 62:2 (2023), p. 230

a whale in the backyard or a curmudgeonly Odysseus hurtling toward his sirens.

But wait a sec.

This is not the opening of a nightclub act.

Jokes are not arguments.

I am for avant-garde comedy and stand-up poetry.

That is, to my way of seeing it, there are only two kinds of writing: Sound and unsound.[5] Stand-up and stand-down. Wanted and spurned. Risible and bereft. Incomprehensible and desperate. Performed and blank.

What a glorious idea Truman Capote had for typing that wasn't writing, as he said of Jack Kerouac in 1959 on David Susskind's TV show (Capote meant it as an insult).[6]

Can there be verbal sound without meaning? Soul without soullessness? Body without flesh? Listening without hearing? Hope sans history?

But this is going too fast.

Let me start at the beginning.

When Vincent Broqua asked me to come to Paris for a conference on homophonic translation (not *homophobic*, don't even THINK of that here!), he proposed to call it "Sound—Translation—Writing." I suggested "sound/writing"[7]: "the sturdy resources of [the] ear," as Robert Creeley once wrote me, echoing Charles Olson's "by ear, he sd."[8]

"Homophonic translation" is a genre of "sound/writing." Sound/writing provides a broader context for the homophonic imaginary and includes modernist European sound and *zaum* poetry and within the larger context of radical translation, what Haroldo de Campos calls *transcreation*[9] and Ezra Pound calls *traduction* (in the sense of *transduction*).

---

5. "Thelonious Monk and the Performance of Poetry," in *My Way: Speeches and Poems* (Chicago: University of Chicago Press, 1999), p. 22

6. The source for this quote is provided at <quoteinvestigator.com/2015/09/18/typing/>.

7. Vincent Broqua and Bernstein, email exchange, October 14, 2015

8. "One thing to me instantly attractive is the sturdy resource of your ear, as Williams would say . . . ," Creeley wrote to me on February 6, 1979, responding to *Shade*. The letter is included in *Selected Letters of Robert Creeley*, ed. Rod Smith, Peter Baker, and Kaplan Harris (Berkeley: University of California Press, 2014), p. 350. But there is a typographical error in the published version, close to the kind of dyslexic inversion I often make: "the sturdy resources of your era," which recalls Zukofsky's paean, at the beginning of *"A"*- 22, to the errors of the ear: "An era / any time / of year" (*"A,"* also from University of California Press, 1978; reprinted by New Directions in 2011). Olson's ear line is from "I, Maximus of Gloucester, to You" (1953); see the typescript at <charlesolson.org/Files/Max1appendices/AppendixD .html>.

9. See K. David Jackson, "Transcriação / Transcreation: The Brazilian Concrete Poets and Translation" in *The Translator as Mediator of Cultures*, ed. Humphrey Tonkin and Maria Esposito Frank (Amsterdam: John Benjamins Publishing Company, 2010).

Pound often avoided using the verb 'to translate,' preferring a calque such as 'to bring over' that recalls the etymology of the conventional term. When his first translation of Cavalcanti's "Donna mi prega" appeared in *The Dial* in 1928, he called it a "traduction," replacing the usual word with a Latinism derived ultimately from *traductio*, "a leading across."[10]

—*Calque* is a loan-translation, a word-for-word carrying over from one language to another (as *vers libre* to *free verse*), from the French *calquer*, to trace.

Homophonic translation is a form of sound tracing.

(My term is echopoetics.)

The homophonic sublime is a form of *délire* in Jean-Jacques Lecercle's sense, either phony or toney, depending on how you frame it.[11] At its core, homophonic translation refuses a Cartesian split between sound and sense, seeing sense as never more than an extension of sound. At every moment it refutes the idea that meaning can be displaced from sound or that reference has an arbitrary, rather than motivated, relation to acoustic rhythm, sound patterning, and aural iconicity.

From a pragmatic point of view, any individual poem will fall short of the homophonic sublime. In that sense, homophonic translations might be heard as pushing in a direction, correcting a course, re-embodying the word. The homophonic is poetry that leads by the ear, foregrounding aurality: poetry that resists cutting the umbilical c(h)ords between translated and translation, source and target, original and copy, essence and accident, brain and mass, figure and ground, spirit and materiality, irony and sincerity, singer and song, imaginary and real, semantic and antic. The homophonic sublime is a necessary improbable of poetry, a rebuke to rationality in the name of linguistic animation.

In its archetypical form, homophonic translation creates a perfect mirror of the sound of the source poem into the target poem. It is mimesis by, and as, other means. While homophonic translation is related to sound poetry, the premise is that it extends an original text into a new language using real, not made-up, words of the target language. In a Borgesian pluriverse, the ideal homophonic translation would be heard by the speakers of the source language as if it were the original poem while heard by the speakers of the target language as a strange word concoction but still in their own tongue. I tried this with "Sane as Tugged Vat, Your Love," my 1993 homo-

10. "Editor's Introduction," *Pound's Cavalcanti: An Edition of the Translation, Notes, and Essays*, ed. David Anderson (Princeton, NJ: Princeton University Press, 1983), p. ix

11. See Lecercle's essay in *Sound / Writing: On Homophonic Translation*, ed. Vincent Broqua and Dirk Weissmann (Paris: Éditions des archives contemporaines, 2020).

phonic translation of Leevi Lehto's "Sanat tulevat yöllä" ("Word Arrive by Night).[12] A favorite joke of mine, when I've performed my homophonic version of Lehto's poem, is to say that Finnish speakers hear it as if it is their own language. What follows is Lehto's original Finnish quatrains. followed by my homophonic version, which in turn is followed by Lehto's "barbaric" English translation:

Olen sanonut tästä jo monta kertaa.
Talon jokaisessa veeseessä on valo.
Sillat virtaavat itään.
Sanat tulevat yöllä koputtamatta.

O when sanity tasted of muffled curtsy.
Talon—Jokasta's vivisected valor.
Silly virtual item.
Sane as tugged vat, your love, kaput.

I've said about this many times before.
In every toilet of the house there is a light on.
Bridges flow east.
Words arrive by night without knocking.

—

Tämä tapahtui kaukaisessa maassa tässä lähellä.
Olen sanonut tästä jo monta kertaa.

---

12. There is a recording of Lehto and I reading this at his PennSound page. I collected the poem in *Re-calculating* (Chicago: University of Chicago Press, 2014), p. 29. Lehto's "barbaric" English translation is in *Lake Onega and Other Poems* (Helsinki: ntamo, 2006), p. 19 and 143. See also Leevi Lehto, Frederik Hertzberg, Bernstein, "On The Origins, State, and Future Perspectives of Finno-Saxon" (2004), in *The Conversant* (2012): <archive.org> + <theconversant.org/?p=1759>. I have written several other homophonic translations: "From the Basque" (1993, uncollected); "Click Rose for 21" from Dominique Fourcade's *Rose Declic* (1987) in *The Sophist*; "Nuclear Blanks" after Esteban Pujals (1998) in *Topsy-Turvy*; "Me Tranformo," after Régis Bonvicino (uncollected, 1999); "Laurel's Eyes" from Heine's "Die Lorelei" (1999), part of *Shadowtime*; "Death Fugue Echo" after Stefan Georg's "Maximin" (2006) in *Girly Man*; Paul Celan's "Todtnauberg" (2009) in *Recalculating*, and "Klang" after Peter Waterhouse (2016) in *Near/ Miss*; but also two quasi-homophonic/homeomorphic translations, which retain much of the lexical sense of the source poems—*"The Maternal Drape"* or the *Restitution* from Claude Royet-Journoud's *"Le drap maternel" ou la restitution* (Windsor, VT: Awede Press, 1984); and "Work Vertical and Blank" from Anne-Marie Albiach's "Travail Vertical et Blanc" (uncollected, 1989).

Talon jokaisessa veeseessä on valo.
Sillat virtaavat itään.

Tamed tapestry's caressed master's tasseled luaus.
O when sanity tasted of muffled curtsy.
Talon—Jokasta's vivisected valor.
Silly virtual item.

This happened in a faraway country nearby.
I've said about this many times before.
In every toilet of the house there is a light on.
Bridges flow east.

—

Maaseudulla puut eivät vielä olleet lähteneet juoksuun.
Tämä tapahtui kaukaisessa maassa tässä lähellä.
Olen sanonut tästä jo monta kertaa.
Talon jokaisessa veeseessä on valo.

Medusa pouts as vat's veil's oldest lament jokes.
Tamed tapestry's caressed master's tasseled luaus.
O when sanity tasted of muffled curtsy.
Talon—Jokasta's vivisected valor.

In countryside the trees had not broken into run yet.
This happened in a faraway country nearby.
I've said about this many times before.
In every toilet of the house there is a light on.

—

Presidentti itse oli täysin lamaantunut.
Maaseudulla puut eivät vielä olleet lähteneet juoksuun.
Tämä tapahtui kaukaisessa maassa tässä lähellä.
Olen sanonut tästä jo monta kertaa:

354 DOUBLETALKING THE HOMOPHONIC SUBLIME

President—he itsy, oily, tainted, laminated.
Medusa pouts as vat's veil's oldest lament jokes.
Tamed tapestry's caressed master's tasseled luaus.
O when sanity tasted of muffled curtsy.

The President himself was utterly paralysed.
In countryside the trees had not broken into run yet.
This happened in a faraway country nearby.
I've said about this many times before:

—

talon jokaisessa veeseessä on valo,
sillat virtaavat itään ja
sanat tulevat yöllä koputtamatta.

Talon—Jokasta's vivisected valor.
Silly virtual item, yah!
Sane as tugged vat, your love, kaput.

In every toilet of the house there is a light on,
Bridges flow east, and
Words arrive by night without knocking.

There is a kind of perverse pleasure in trying to create the same (*homo*) from difference (*hetero*): homophonics is pataque(e)rical. The homophonic sublime is also the dream of a pure poetry, words for their own sake, the cry of their occasion, "COME CI": *only this and nothing more.*[13]

A pure homophonic (or isophonic or synphonic) translation would be the same words brought into a new language, not at all uncommon for proper names and place names. The Mexican conceptualist Ulises Carrión plays on this possibility with his "The translation of 'Pedro Páramo,'" a reference to the 1955 novel by Juan Rulfo:

---

13. I reflect on these echoes of Mallarmé, Stevens, and Poe in "The Pataquerical Imagination: Midrashic Antinomianism and the Promise of Bent Studies" in *Pitch of Poetry*.

to English: Pedro Páramo
to French: Pedro Páramo
to Italian: Pedro Páramo
to German: Pedro Páramo
to Portuguese: Pedro Páramo
to Dutch: Pedro Páramo[14]

Homophonic translation is parasitic: a parasite that may want to live symbiotically with its source or may wish to replace it, at least in becoming a new poem in its own right, autonomous, no longer dependent on the original but an original of its own.

In "The Use of Poetry," Basil Bunting writes about reading Persian, German, Italian, and Welsh poetry to a class that did not know those languages. He genially insists that the students would get as much out of hearing a foreign language poem as hearing one in their own language, since pronouncing a word is more important than knowing its meaning.[15] While Bunting's recitation of foreign language poems incomprehensible to his students was a quite serious endeavor, I see a connection with postwar American comedian Sid Caesar's "doubletalking"—deliriously funny live verbal improvisations that sound like Italian, German, and Japanese speech but are composed on the tongue with made-up strings of words.[16] Al Kelly and Prof. Irwin Cory, both older than Caesar, pioneered the style. Caesar's own doubletalking professor is related to Cory's shtick (doubletalking in the sense of intellectual gibberish not foreign language mimicry). In a different vain, Ruth Draper in "The Actress," from around 1916, leaps into Slavic doubletalk.

Where Caesar gets laughs, Bunting gets poetry.

Bunting's insistence on sound over meaning is an extension of his framing of poetry in terms of music. Perhaps the most common experience related to Bunting's modest proposal is listening to an opera sung in a language you do not know and feeling you are missing nothing, indeed, preferring to hear the original to having the libretto sung, in translation, in your own language; and, moreover, preferring to listen without subtitles. It's no coincidence that opera parody is crucial to Caesar's doubletalking.

---

14. Heriberto Yépez, "Ulises Carrión's Mexican Discontinuities," in *Ulises Carrión: Dear Reader. Don't Read*, ed. Guy Schraenen (Madrid: Museo Nacional Centro de Arte Reina Sofía, 2016), p. 51

15. Cited in "Artifice of Absorption" in my *A Poetics* (Cambridge, MA: Harvard University Press, 1992), p. 58.

16. See <ruthdraper.com/selected-monologues/>.

The *zaum* poems of Russian futurians Velimir Khlebnikov and Aleksei Kruchenykh were composed of synthesized or invented words that, whether intended or not, broke down the barriers of nationalist tongues and evoked species-wide listening, something that might be compared to Esperanto, despite the radical differences. Khlebnikov's "Incantation by Laughter" (1909) is the best-known zaum poem. My transcreation follows the sound:

We laugh with our laughter [O, rassmeites', smekhachi!]
loke laffer un loafer [O, zasmeites', smekhachi]
sloaf lafker int leffer [Chto smeyutsya smekhami]
lopp lapter und loofer [chto smeyanstvuyut smeyal'no]
loopse lapper ung lasler [O, zasmeites' usmeyal'no!]
pleap loper ech lipler [O, rassmeshishch nadsmeyal'nykh]
bloop uffer unk oddurk [smekh usmeinykh smekhachei!]
floop flaffer ep flubber [O, issmeisya rassmeyal'no]
fult lickles eng tlickers [smekh nadesmeinykh smeyachei!]
ac laushing ag lauffing uk [Smeievo, smeievo,]
luffing ip luppling uc [Usmei, osmei, smeshiki, smeshiki,]
lippling ga sprickling [Smeyunchiki, smeyunchiki,]
urp laughter oop laughing [O, rassmeites', smekhachi!]
oop laughing urp laughter [O, zasmeites', smekhachi!][17]

In modernist poetry, *zaum* is the most radical—and perhaps hysterical— extension of the sublime ideal of a poem being *only itself*, a cry of its occa- sion, "only this," overthrowing a subservience to representational meaning, or a parasitic relation to an original. Khlebnikov may have desired a deeper ur-Slavic but he also wrote of his desire for "a single human conversation"; in some sense—"beyonsense "—*zaum* echoes international socialism. *Zaum* is translated as both "trans-sense" and "beyond sense." According to Probstein:

> Khlebnikov "rejected borrowings from foreign languages and invented Russian words even for new scientific and technological phenomena. . . . Although Khlebnikov supported the October revolution, he was more con- cerned with the future unity of all humankind: 'Fly, human constellation, / Further on, further into space / And merge the Earth's tongues / Into a single

---

17. My American version was published in *Recalculating*, p. 94. I did a bilingual reading with Probstein, archived, with related recordings, at PennSound's Khlebnikov page.

human conversation.' . . . Both Khlebnikov and Kruchenykh spoke of *zaum* and 'the self-sufficient' word, but each interpreted those terms differently."[18]

Probstein goes on to quote Khlebnikov on his search for "the magic touchstone of all Slavic words, . . . a self-sufficient language" that provides a path to the "universal language" of *zaum*.

On the Dada side, there are the sound poetry inventions at the Cabaret Voltaire, one hundred years ago, especially the work of Hugo Ball; and the ur-text of sound poetry, composed from 1922 to 1932, Kurt Schwitters's "Ursonate."[19]

Within American popular religious culture, there is speaking in tongues (glossolalia)—the spontaneous utterance, as if possessed, of an unintelligible or foreign language, which Jennifer Scappettone contrasts with xenoglossia:

> Xenoglossia . . . refers to the intelligible use of a natural language one has not learned formally or does not know and is distinguishable from . . . glossolalia, or lexically incommunicative utterances. . . . Such tales of miraculous translation evince a yearning for the promise of correspondence between languages, and thereby of erased cultural difference.[20]

Within American popular music, consider the scat singing of Ella Fitzgerald and Cab Calloway.

Reuven Tsur argues that you can't hear verbal utterances as nonverbal, but a poem can surely try to entice you by foregrounding the physical materiality of language, short-circuiting semantic processing. Then again, what's verbal and what's not is a matter of framing. We can hear a brook talking to us, can make animal sounds, and even turn the clackity-clacking of a sewing machine into a song. Tsur's cognitive poetics is immediately useful for literary sound studies. In *What Makes Sound Patterns Expressive? The Poetic Mode of Speech Perception* (1992), Tsur offers a groundwork for recognizing the expressivity of sound patterns, following Roman Jakobson's work on sound symbolism (sound iconicity).[21] (Jakobson published a zaum

---

18. Probstein, *River of Time*, pp. 11, 15, 17

19. Listen to Schwitters, Ball, and the Russian futurians on PennSound.

20. Jennifer Scappettone, "Phrasebook Pentecosts and Daggering Lingua Francas in the Poetry of LaTasha N. Nevada Diggs," in *The Fate of Difficulty in the Poetry of Our Time*, ed. Charles Altieri and Nicholas D. Nace (Evanston, IL: Northwestern University Press, 2018), p. 265

21. Tsur was born in 1932 in Transylvania, Tsur's native language is Hungarian. He started as a translator (into Hungarian and later Hebrew), getting his PhD at Sussex (UK). After retiring from Tel Aviv University, he moved lived in Jerusalem. Tsur died in 2021. More Tsur at <www.tau.ac.il/~tsurxx>.

collaboration with Kruchenykh in 1914 and wrote an essential account of Khlebnikov.).

The transformation of voicing or homophonically mimicking mechanical or machine sounds is its own genre of "sound-alike" poems. In Gertrude Stein's "If I Told Him: A Completed Portrait of Picasso" (1923), she echoes the sound of a shutter opening and closing: "Shutters shut and open so do queens. Shutters shut and shutters and so shutters shut and shutters and so and so shutters and so shutters shut and so shutters shut and shutters and so."[22] Then jump ahead to 2012 and Michael Winslow's mimicking the sound of thirty-two different historical typewriters.[23]

In Western poetry, birdsong has been a foundational metaphor for poetry, especially the nightingale's song. The earliest homophonic poetry would then be mimicry of birdsong in human language. Robert Grenier took this almost literally, writing a series of poems in 1975, *Sentences Toward Birds*, that transcribed, into "the American," the "actual" sounds of birds in his immediate environment. Here are three of the poems, which, like his later *Sentences*, are each printed on individual cards:

why you say you see later

didn't see go to a

A BIRD / who would call / not for but for you / in the day[24]

More recently, Hanna Tuulikki's "Air falbh leis na h-eòin—Away with the Birds" (2010 to 2015) has explored the "mimesis" of bird sounds in Gaelic poetry and song.[25]

In *aaaaw to zzzzd: The Word of Birds*, John Bevins not only provides a "lexicon" of birdsongs—"chinga, chinga, chinga" is the homophonic signature of the swamp sparrow—but also a set of "mnemonics," such as the song sparrow's lyric refrain, "maids, maids, maids, put on your tea, kettle,

22. Gertrude Stein, "If I Told Him: A Completed Portrait of Picasso" is on Stein's PennSound page.

23. "The History of the Typewriter Recited by Michael Winslow": <openculture.com/2014/06/the -history-of-the-typewriter.html>

24. Robert Grenier, *Sentences Toward Birds* (Kensington, CA: L Publications, 1975), online at <eclipsearchive.org/projects/BIRDS/birds.html>

25. Hanna Tuulikki, "Air falbh leis na h-eòin—Away with the Birds" and "Guth an eEòin"—"Voice of the Bird": <hannatuulikki.org/portfolio/awbirds> and <score.awaywiththebirds.co.uk>

kettle, kettle,"[26] which makes me burst into song, as if this is Broadway musical:

Maids, maids, maids
Put on your tea
Kettle, kettle, kettle.
No time to waste
Get out your bass
Fiddle, fiddle, fiddle.
Young lads make haste
Dance to your love's
Riddle, riddle, riddle.[27]

Bevins also suggests a motto for the homophonic sublime is his adaption of Walter Pater on music—"All art aspires to the condition of birdsong" (p. 15).

But perhaps the ultimate revenge of the long tradition of homophonics belongs to Sparkie Williams, "the talking budgie," a bird who, in the mid-1950s, was able to parrot a wide range of English words, mimicking human speech.[28]

A decade after Sparkie, Michael McClure's *Ghost Tantras* (1964) features a partially invented vocabulary that he calls "beast language" (guttural, expressive), suggesting a kind of primitive *zaum* (McClure references Vladimir Mayakovsky). McClure wanted to find a level of language that invoked animality:

Grahhr! Grahhhr! Ghrahhhrrr! Ghrahhr. Grahhrrr.
Grahhr-grahhhhrr! Grahhr. Gahrahhrr Ghrahhhrrrr.
Gharrrrr. Ghrahhr! Ghrarrrrr. Ghanrrr. Ghrahhhrr.
Ghrahhrr. Ghrahr. Grahhr. Grahharrr. Grahhrr.
Grahhhhr. Grahhhr. Gahar. Ghmhhr. Grahhr. Grahhr.
Ghrahhr. Grahhhr. Grahhr. Gratharrr! Grahhr.
Ghrahrr. Ghraaaaaaahrr. Grhar. Ghhrarrr! Grahhrr.
Ghrahrr. Gharr! Ghrahhhhr. Grahhrr. Ghraherrr.

---

26. John Bevins, *aaaaw to zzzzd: The Word of Birds* (Cambridge, MA: MIT Press, 2010), pp. 48, 114. Bevins makes the argument for birdsong as music, comparing the experience to hearing songs in a foreign language (pp. 15–17).

27. A poem I based on the sound of the song sparrow. Collected in *Topsy Turvy*, p. 165.

28. See Andrew Dodds, *I, Sparkie* (UK: Information as Material, 2013).

The 1964 and 1966 recordings he made reading his poems to lions are pow-
erful poetic documents, notable for how much more expressive and poi-
gnant are the roars of the lions than are the homophonic translations of the
poet, whose human language echoes wanly against the formidable sounds of
the beasts.[29] Wittgenstein famously remarked, "Wenn ein Löwe sprechen
könnte, wir könnten ihn nicht verstehen," a homosyntactical (word-for-
word) translation is "If a Lion speak could, we could him not understand."[30]
But when the lion roars, in a duet with McClure's mimicking, we hear the
sound as song, a wail, perhaps a lament. The lion is growling at the human
intruder's appropriation, as if to say I am the king of my own language, do
not mock me. And growling at us, the unseen listeners: *beware!*

Listening to a poem or opera in a language foreign to you, but feeling
you get it all the same, is a far cry from homophonic translation: it leaves
the original just as is, the foreignizing occurring in the listener's response. If
the aim of a poem is to foreground the materiality of sound, then listening
to a language you don't know is a kind of poetic experience. But that only
goes so far. Listening to a poem in a language you don't know gets less
interesting the longer it goes on; entropy sets in faster than a mosquito
dodging a fly swatter. Sid Caesar's doubletalk is hilarious because it is ex-
aggerated in its stereotyping and because you know he is going on nerve:
it's a high-wire act and the wire is not that long. In contrast, homophonic
translation allows for extensions and textual subtly since it goes beyond
imitation into commentary and because it is able to create a new poem in
the new language.

2. Wot We Wukkerz Want

Let me make a brief detour in my account to consider Edgar Allan Poe's
"The Philosophy of Literary Composition," published in 1846, near the end
of the troubled poet's life. Poe's delightfully bizarre paean to artifice is, in
part, a send-up of spontaneously inspired, frenzied, sincere verse, what Poe
calls "ecstatic intuition." Writing about "The Raven," Poe claims that the

29. "Michael McClure Reads to Lions": <jacket2.org/commentary/michael-mcclure-reads-lions>

30. German text quoted, along with a discussion of Anscombe's translation of *Philosophical Investiga-
tions*, in Marjorie Perloff, *Wittgenstein's Ladder: Poetic Language and the Strangeness of the Ordinary*
(Chicago: University of Chicago Press, 1996), pp. 74–75. See Ludwig Wittgenstein, *Philosophical In-
vestigations*, tr. G.E.M. Anscombe, 2nd edition (Oxford: Blackwell, 1958), p. 223. The revised 4th edition
of the translation by P. M. S. Hacker and Joachim Schulte (Blackwell, 2009) gives the line as "If a lion
could talk, we wouldn't be able to understand it"; for Anscombe the lion is "him."

origin of a poem is a set of logically predetermined effects, including sound effects: meaning comes after. In effect, Poe attempts to treat verbal composition as if it were musical composition. Poe's elaborate and impossible rules for poetic composition bring to mind Sid Caesar's grifter-like elaboration of impossible rules for a card game in his early 1950s sketch "The Poker Game."[31] Both Poe and Caesar offer a kind of doubletalk, or talking out of both sides of the mouth, though, in these cases, not deceptively, since their discourse foregrounds the absurdity, even though performed with straight faces. In the comic pathos of Poe's insistence on the author's total control of the poem through the rigidly predetermined, Poe never breaks character, that of the author whose sole aim is beauty, achieved by maximizing melancholy (not to say pathos). Poe elaborates his doubletalk with absolute conviction. Like Caesar, Poe aimed to please "the popular and the critical taste."

Both Baudelaire's and Mallarmé's translations of "The Raven" (1865 and 1875, respectively) swerve toward the homophonic, often echoing Poe's exact sound patterns.[32] Even if you don't know French, you'd recognize "The Raven" if the translations were performed. A performed Yiddish translation by I. Kissen is always already a homophonic translation.[33] "The Raven" is as identifiable as Beethoven's Fifth, and if you don't know Yiddish, it can seem as if it is doubletalk.

The modern history of radical translation in American poetry might reasonably begin with Pound's Chinese adaptions but I want now to briefly cite his two translations of Guido Cavalcanti (1250–1300), "Donna mi prega," the first from 1928, the second from 1934. Pound gives the constraints, worthy of Poe's "Philosophy of Composition" or Caesar's poker rules: "Each strophe is articulated by 14 terminal and 12 inner rhyme sounds, which means that 52 of every 154 syllables are bound into pattern."[34]

Because a lady asks me, I would tell
Of an affect that comes often and is fell

31. Sid Caesar, "The Poker Game," *Your Show of Shows* (date unknown): <youtu.be/RyNSFLkXTvA>

32. See Robin Seguy's 2015 hypertext presentations of the translations at <writing.upenn.edu/epc/mirrors/text-works.org>.

33. I. Kissen's Yiddish, "The Raven: Multilingual," cut 21: <archive.org/details/raven_multilingual_0903>

34. *Pound's Cavalcanti*, p. 216. Pound's commentary on "Donna mi prega" appeared in *The Dial* (with the subtitle "Medievalism") in 1928; this article included his translation in its first publication; a few years later it was collected in Pound's essay collection *Make It New* (1934). See my related discussion in "Objectivist Blues," *Attack of the Difficult Poems: Essays and Inventions* (Chicago: University of Chicago Press, 2011), pp. 135–36.

And is so overweening: Love by name.
E'en its deniers can now hear the truth.
                    (1928, *Pound's Cavalcanti*, 171)

    •

A lady asks me
    I speak in season
She seeks reason for an affect, wild often
That is so proud he hath Love for a name
Who denys it can hear the truth now
                    (1934, *Pound's Cavalcanti*, 179)

    In 1940, at the beginning of World War II, Louis Zukofsky took the
Cavalcanti translations to another dimension. What he produced was not
a homophonic translation but rather a sound transcreation that radically
accented the poem, making it, in part, an ethnic dialect poem, a sort of Yid-
dish doubletalking, where doubletalking implies bilingualism and double
consciousness.[35] As with his inaugural "Poem Beginning 'The,'" Zukofsky
radically engaged an American vernacular, following the model of Pound
and Williams, and he brought it home, to a *mamaloshen* (mother tongue),
homey and homely, but with a majestic beauty brought over from the sound
structure of the Cavalcanti:

A foin lass bodders me I gotta tell her
Of a fact surely, so unrurly, often'
'r 't comes 'tcan't soften its proud neck's called love mm . . .'[36]

---

35. The most likely Yiddish word for doubletalk is פֿאָנפֿען (*fonfen*)—mumbling. In contrast to Jeffrey
Shandler's term "postvernacular" in *Adventures in Yiddishland* (Berkeley: University of California
Press, 2006), pp. 19–27, I'd call this work *patavernacular*.

36. In 1940, Zukofsky privately circulated "A foin lass" in *FIRST HALF of "A"- 9*, a numbered and auto-
graphed edition of 55. Zukofsky included sources for *"A"*-9, including "Donna mi priegha [*sic*]," twenty-
two pages on value and commodification excerpted from Marx's *Capital* and *Value Price and Profit*,
a short excerpt from Stanley Allen's *Electronics and Waves: A Short Introduction to Atomic Physics*
(1932), "translations of Cavalcanti's Canzone" by Pound (both versions) and vernacular versions by
Jerry Reisman and Zukofsky, followed by a note on the form and "A"-9, first half, and concluding with a
two-page "Restatement" of the poem. The first publication of "A foin lass" was in Zukofsky's *Selected
Poems*, which I edited (New York: Library of America American Poets Project, 2006), p. 152.

In two PennSound recordings, Zukofsky performs this poem with a high, formal tone, neutralizing accent, while I emphasize a Yiddish/Brooklyn twang, performing a kind of "Jewface."[37]

Perhaps the closest recent work of this kind—a translation into a marked, comic dialect, with accent *über alles*—is the riotous "The Kommunist Manifesto or Wot We Wukkerz Want"—"Redacted un traduced intuht' dialect uht' west riding er Yorkshuh bi Steve McCaffery, eh son of that shire" in 1977.[38] But consider also Nathan Kageyama's 1996 spin on Pound's vernacular translations with a Hawaiian pidgin version of Pound's "The Return": "See, they return; ah, see the tentative / Movements, and the slow feet, / The trouble in the pace and the uncertain / Wavering!" becomes "Spock em, dey stay come; auwe, spock da scayed / Movaments, an' da luau feet, / Stay all twis' an' kooked / Walkin' all jag!"[39]

3. Doubletalk

Discussion of homophonic translation is generally placed in the context of radical poetic innovation. I want to contrast that lineage with two examples from popular culture, one from the postwar American comic Sid Caesar and the other from *Benny Lava*, a recent viral YouTube video.

Doubletalk, as Caesar uses the term, is homophonic translation of a foreign-language movie, opera scenario, or everyday speech into an improvised performance that mimics the sound of the source language with made-up, *zaum*-like invented vocabulary. Consider an uproarious 2015 performance by French poet Joseph Gugliemi, where he performs a made-up language under the guise of reading a poetry text, which at one point he shows to be all blank pages.[40] In contrast, literary homophonic translation begins with a defined foreign-language poem as source text and creates a new work in English that mimics the sound of the original.

37. Go to <writing.upenn.edu/ezurl/5/> for my performance and <writing.upenn.edu/ezurl/6/> for Zukofsky's. I heard Zukofsky's performance only after I had made my recording. I discuss "Jewface" in "Objectivist Blues" in *Attack of the Difficult Poems: Essays and Inventions*, p. 142.

38. Steve McCaffery, "Kommunist Manifesto": <writing.upenn.edu/library/McCaffey-Steve_Kommunist -Manifesto.html>. McCaffery and Jed Rasula edited a crucial anthology of sound writing and invented vocabularies called *Imagining Language* (1998). "Sound writing" echoes "sound poetry" and what Richard Kostelanetz anthologized as *Text–Sound Texts* (1980).

39. *Tinfish* 3 (1996): <writing.upenn.edu/epc/ezines/tinfish>

40. Performance by Joseph Guglielmi in the Paris studio of Anne Slacik on October 11, 2015: available at PennSound's Deformance page (listed in anthologies/collections).

The best example of Caesar's "double-talk" is a concert in which he moves through four languages, starting with French and moving to German and Italian, ending with Japanese (replete with recognizable anchor words, such as Mitsubishi, Datsun and sushi).[41] Taken as a whole, this five-minute performance is macaronic—a burlesque jumble or comic hodge-podge of different languages. The camera pans to the audience during each segment to show benign and approving laughter. The serial movement from language to language also suggests a nomadic display of multi-lingual code-switching. It brings . . . home . . . the final line of Charles Reznikoff's 1934 poem about diaspora:

and God looked and saw the Hebrews
citizens of the great cities,
talking Hebrew in every language under the sun.[42]

Though perhaps this might be revised to say Yiddish rather than Hebrew, follow Ariel Resnikoff's discussion of the pervasiveness of Yiddish in Jewish culture.[43]

The first archival footage we have of Caesar's mimicry is from *Tars and Spars*, a Coast Guard–produced war movie from 1946 in which the twenty-four-year-old Caesar does "Wings over Bombinschitzel," his "airplane-movie number," written with his brother Dave and created the year before for a "tabloid musical" recruitment revue for the Spars (the Coast Guard Women's Reserve).[44] Sid was billed as "Sydney Caesar." The first bit of

---

41. "Sid Caesar Performing in Four Different Languages": <writing.upenn.edu/ezurl/7>, date unknown. See also: "Sid Caesar Double-Talk Routine" (interview) <youtu.be/iL7efWcaVnk>; "Sid Caesar, Le Grande Amour" <youtu.be/JGHih5ISPhQ>, French doubletalk film satire; "Sid Caesar, The Russian Arthur Godfrey" <youtu.be/FHbscdj7OtU>, Russian doubletalk, ending with Carl Reiner doing movie star impressions in Russian doubletalk; and "Sid Caesar: Der Flying Ace" <youtu.be/GhXRZ7yw7Nw>. Caesar discusses "double-talk" in Sid Caesar with Eddy Friedfeld, *Caesar's Hours: My Life in Comedy, with Love and Laughter* (New York: Public Affairs, 2003), p. 58. "Sid Caesar's 80th Birthday Party" features a tour-de-force reprise, with Caesar, reading notes, doubletalking in French, German, Spanish, Italian, and Japanese <youtu.be/FETaKPtdaJM>.

42. Charles Reznikoff, "Joshua at Shechem," *Jerusalem the Golden* in *Complete Poems: Volume One* (Santa Barbara, CA: Black Sparrow Press, 1976), p. 126

43. Ariel Resnikoff, "Home Tongue Earthquake: The Radical Afterlives of Yiddishland" (PhD diss., University of Pennsylvania, 2019)

44. *Tars and Spars* (1946): <youtu.be/0HdD25USDV0> (among other places). Caesar's Russian double-talk begins around 48 minutes; his airplane routine begins at around 69 minutes. Caesar discusses the routine in *Caesar's Hours*, pp. 54–58. The show was written by Howard Dietz (who wrote the lyrics for "Dancing in the Dark" and "Alone Together") and Vernon Duke (born in 1903 as Vladimir Dukelsky, who wrote the music of "April in Paris" and "Taking a Chance on Love"). In addition to being a composer, Dukelsky, who to some extent discovered (and surely offered great support to) a very young

Caesar's multicultural "double-talk languages" is part of the ludicrous "I Love Eggs" number, where after doing a Mexican hat dance and playing a German cook, Caesar dives into a fake Russian song lyric, "Eggs Romanoff," after singing a few parodic verses in English set to what sounds like, that is to say, anticipates, the Russian folk song pastiche "To Life" from the 1964 musical *Fiddler on the Roof.*

In a video interview, Caesar says he didn't do mimicry but sound effects, an airplane taking off or the rain.[45] I take this to mean he viewed his foreign language and foreign accent mimicry as an extension of imitating mechanical or natural sounds. Indeed, in the movie he does *voices* and gestures and faces and pantomimed actions, moving from one to another to another as part of a rapid-fire collage of schticks, segueing from the sound of a plane taking off to the barked command of a pompous British military officer, with tones of Churchill (from some barked words Caesar moves in a low grumble—gewd luck my boyyyy, grrr, awwww—with no discernible words, a kind of proto sound poem). In the bit, Caesar notes how the American planes sound mellifluous while the Nazi planes sound ominous. He segues from the sound of a Nazi airplane motor right into German-Nazi doubletalk, together with a full sound opera of a machine gun battle between the two planes, followed by aerial bombardment of German targets. "I did all the sound effects with my mouth, including the starting of the airplane engines and the throttle" (*Caesar's Hours*, p. 54).

Caesar was the most important and influential comedy star of early American television, a key member of a generation that included Lenny Bruce (born Leonard Schneider in 1925), Jackie Gleason (born 1916), Ernie Kovacs (born 1919), and Jerry Lewis (born Joseph [or Jerome] Levitch in 1926). Isaac Sidney "Sid" Caesar was born in 1922 and died in 2014. His parents were Jewish immigrants, his father was from Poland and mother from Russia, both coming to New York as children, which means that Yiddish would have been their home language.

Yiddish is a nomadic language, not based in any nation but creating a common tongue for diasporic Jews in Poland, Hungary, Russia, and America, among other places. While sometimes thought to be a dialect of German, Yiddish is its own language, spoken by people who did not necessarily know German. As a consequence of the Systematic Extermination of the

---

Caesar, was a futurist-influenced Russian poet as well as translator of Frost, Stevens, Cummings, and Pound. Perhaps he is the "missing link" between Caesar and modernist poetry. See Elena Dubrovina, "'The Song of Time': Vladimir Dukelsky, Poet and Composer <gostinaya.net/?p=12060>.

45. "Sid Caesar Interview, part 2," with Dan Pasternack, March 14, 1997, Archive of American Television: <emmytvlegends.org/interviews/people/sid-caesar>

European Jews, compounded by Israel's turn against Yiddish by selecting Hebrew as its national language, Yiddish came to be a dead language, like Latin, though it persists, with vitality, in pockets.

In *Bridges of Words: Esperanto and the Dream of a Universal Language*, Esther Schor tells the story the invention of Esperanto by L. L. Zamenhof (1859–1917), an Eastern European Jew who grew up speaking Russian at home, Polish and German for business, Yiddish with other Jews, and Hebrew in synagogue. Zamenhof said that the hostility of one group of language speakers to another "made me feel that men did not exist, only Russians, Poles, Germans, Jews, and so on."[46] He conceived Esperanto as a way to overcome ethnic and national barriers, which echoes, while departing from, Khlebnikov's "single human conversation" (and given *zaum*'s "magical" derivations from Russian root words). Prior to his 1887 manifesto for Esperanto, Zamenhof had gone through a proto-Zionist period, where he advocated a Latin-scripted Yiddish. His vision for Esperanto's universality, in contrast, pushed back against antisemitic projections of a secret Jewish language. Then again in 1901, Zamenhof proposed Esperanto for an ethically (rather than ethnically) based Jewish language, an alternative to the liturgical Hebrew and the polyglot ("jargonized") Yiddish.

"Instead of being absorbed by the Christian world, we [Jews] shall absorb them," Zamenhof proclaimed in 1907 (pp. 82, 132). Schor comments that, in this context, Judaize means not to turn into Jews but to make justice and fraternity our foundation.

Sid Caesar was not likely to have known of Zamenhof or Esperanto. As a teenager, Caesar was a musician and comedian, if not quite sociable enough to be a *tummler* (MC/comic/entertainer-in-chief), in the Borscht Belt (the Jewish resort area in the Catskill mountains, just outside New York), where he absorbed classic burlesque sketch comedy (*Caesar's Hours*, p. 34). In 1942, he enlisted in the Coast Guard, where he ended up doing musical reviews. In 1948, live TV called, first through the invitation of Milton Berle. Caesar got in on the ground floor of the new medium. He was the star of the *Admiral Broadway Revue* in 1949. In 1950–1954 he starred in *Your Show of Shows*, the most watched television show of the time. He continued to do weekly TV from New York till 1958. In these shows, everything was performed live—though a team of comedy writers, including Mel Brooks, Woody Allen, Carl Reiner, and Neil Simon, wrote the sketches. But there were no cue cards or teleprompters.

In his autobiography, Caesar tells a story that brings Zamenhof to mind

---

46. Esther Schor, *Bridges of Words: Esperanto and the Dream of a Universal Language* (New York: Henry Holt, 2016), p. 63

(and ear). At his father's restaurant, where he worked, speakers of different language groups sat at different tables and Caesar would go from table to table mimicking the sounds of the customer's native tongues, much to their delight. The scene recalls lines by Hebrew poet Avot Yeshurun (born 1904) addressed to his mother, in which the poet expresses his sense of the loss of Yiddish, his mother/other tongue, while evoking a primal experience of doubletalk: "You who hear a language in seventy translations / at night in the garden of Dizengoff Square."[47]

> My love of music . . . led me to appreciate the melodies and rhymes of foreign language. I learned my signature double-talk, which was a fast-paced blend of different sounds and weds mimicking [different languages] from the customers at my father's restaurant. (*Caesar's Hours*, p. 15)

Key to Caesar's homophonic genius is that he was a professional jazz saxophone player before he became a comedian. The way some musicians can learn a song or a symphony by ear, Caesar learned languages, as if they were musical scores. One of his classic sketches involves his miming a pianist playing Grieg's *Piano Concerto in A Minor*. The music was being played offstage, but for all the world you'd think Caesar was playing it, hitting the notes *en plein air*, as if sound and gesture were totally indivisible. Think of Jerry Lewis's classic conducting sketch in *The Bellboy* (1960) or his Count Basie mime in *The Errand Boy* (1961). Caesar puts his gift for the homophonic succinctly: "To me it's song."[48]

Caesar's most famous opera sketch is "Gallipacci," a 1955 parody of *Pagliacci*.[49] Caesar, in the perfect role of the clown, sings in doubletalk Italian, mixed with some English, which allows him to cue plot points and adds a comic effect. His first number is, in effect, a homophonic version

47. Avot Yeshurun, "Got fun Avrohom," in *Kapella Kolot* (Tel Aviv: Siman Keriyah, 1977). Quoted by Neta Stahl in a review of Naomi Brenner's *Lingering Bilingualism: Modern Hebrew and Yiddish Literatures in Contact* in *Comparative Literature* 69:3 (2017), p. 350. The title of the poem means "God of Abraham" and refers to a Yiddish prayer for women (mothers), to protect Israel from harm; Dizengoff Square is in Tel Aviv. For homophonic plays between Hebrew and Yiddish see Roy Greenwald, "Homophony in Multilingual Jewish Cultures," *Dibur* 1 (2016): <arcade.stanford.edu/dibur/homophony-multilingual-jewish-cultures> (Greenwald discusses Yeshurun). I am grateful to Ariel Resnikoff for discussions about Yeshurun. See his essay, "Louis Zukofsky and Mikhl Likht, 'A Test of Jewish American Modernist Poetics,'" in *Jacket2* (2013): <jacket2.org/commentary/ariel-resnikoff-louis-zukofsky-and-mikhl-likht-test-jewish-american-modernist-poetics-p-0>.

48. Transcript, CNN: Larry King Live, "Hail Sid Caesar," September. 7, 2001 <transcripts.cnn.com/TRANSCRIPTS/0109/07/lkl.00.html>

49. "Sid Caesar, Gallipacci," *Caesar's Hour*, October 10, 1955. The cast included Nanette Fabray, Reiner, and Howard Morris: <youtu.be/5OW7GolI0T8>. The sketch was revived, in a watered-down version that undercuts the operatic doubletalk, on *The Sid Caesar, Imogene Coca, Carl Reiner, Howard Morris Reunion Special*, April 4, 1967: <youtu.be/ScqZW2NQwPY>.

of Leoncavallo's libretto sung to an *operaschmerz* pastiche of Leoncavallo's score (doubletalk music). But Caesar's next bit is an Italian doubletalk version of "Just One of Those Things," a 1935 Cole Porter song (with a whiff of Leoncavallo to boot), presented to resemble one of the most poignant scenes in Italian opera. Indeed, the whole cast sings (and speaks) in Italian doubletalk, occasionally mixed with stereotypical versions of ethnic Italian American speech. At one point Nanette Fabray sings (in Italian doubletalk à la Leoncavallo) the Fanny Brice standard, "My Man"; later Fabray and Carl Reiner throw in "Take Me Out to the Ball Game." The chorus opens with an Italian doubletalk operatic version of "Santa Claus (*Gallipacci*) is Coming to Town." The rousing final scene, the clown's tragic song after killing his wife, is set to the tune of "The Yellow Rose of Texas," with the cast singing in Italian doubletalk.

Caesar's doubletalk shtick was often used in elaborate parodies of foreign movies.[50] The best known is his version of Vittorio de Sica's 1948 neorealist film, *Ladri di biciclette* (*The Bicycle Thief*), which focused on the difficult life in Italy immediately following the war. Caesar and company would go to see foreign films at the Museum of Modern Art. "We did movies in Italian, French, German, and Japanese double-talk. We never wrote double-talk out word for word, just laid out the goals, the comic direction," he says in *Caesar's Hours* (p. 212).

"I've always considered doubletalk [*sic*] to be a form of music . . . with each language having its own rhythm," (*Caesar's Hours*, p. 211). For Caesar, the key to homophonic mimicry is "Lip movements and intonation" (*Caesar's Hours*, p. 15). At the Yonkers's 24-hour buffet and luncheonette, where he worked as a kid, the factory workers from Otis Elevator and other nearby factories and offices laughed heartily at his fluent ear: each table had a different language group and he moved from table to table, a multilectal collage epic poem in real time and space. Like Louis Zukofsky, though a generation younger, Caesar knew only Yiddish and English. But he realized his homophonic gift made people laugh.

> Nearly all [the customers] were young, single immigrants who would segregate into groups speaking Italian, Russian, Hungarian, Polish, French, Span-

50. Reiner takes the credit for suggesting the foreign film parodies, noting that he could also do "double talk" and sold the idea to Caesar by laying it on him. See his interview in *They'll Never Put That on the Air: An Oral History of Taboo-Breaking TV Comedy* by Allan Neuwirth (New York: Allsworth Press, 2006), pp. 5–6. Reiner gives a slightly different account in *Where Have I Been? An Autobiography* by Sid Caesar with Bill Davidson (New York: Crown Publishers, 1982), p. 109, which is the first and better of Caesar's two autobiographies, with its harrowing tale. In Adam Bernstein's Washington *Post* obituary for Reiner, Mel Brooks says, "Nobody could do *foreign gibberish* better than Sid Caesar, but this Reiner guy could keep up with him" (July 1, 2020, p. a10; italics added).

ish, Lithuanian, and even Bulgarian. I would go from table to table, listening to the sounds. I learned how to mimic them, sounding as if I were actually speaking their language. They weren't offended.[51]

In Yonkers in the 1930s, such parody was viewed as welcoming, not offensive. Difference was what was common in his father's restaurant. To bend Rimbaud, *Everyone is an other.*

> I would even do double-talk in synagogue. I wasn't doing it disrespectfully, but out of a desire to fit in and impress. There seemed to be a race to finish the prayers among the synagogue elders, which would end with the winner closing the prayer book shut while holding it up in the air. The double-talk made it seem like I was moving through the prayer book like a Torah scholar, as I would also slam the prayer book shut. The synagogue elders were in awe over my apparent expertise in the Scripture. (*Caesar's Hours*, p. 17)

The saying of Hebrew prayers quickly is often a matter of gesture and intonation, this is at the heart of davening, in which, like a Buddhist mantra, the sound carries the spirit. Indeed, for generations American Jews have learned to pronounce Hebrew without knowing what it means, bringing back to mind Zukofsky's homophonic translation of the Hebrew of *Job* in *"A"*-15.

In *Where Have I Been?*, Caesar gives another origin story for his homophonic practice. It seems baby Sid didn't start to talk till he was four, but he was already writing (40–41): "I'd sit at a table . . . for hours and make marks that *looked* exactly like writing. . . . It was like the beginning of the foreign-language double-talk I did later at the luncheonette." So there, Truman Capote!

Caesar's first cited (but not recorded) use of doubletalk was from *Six On, Twelve Off*, a Coast Guard review that he did with Vernon Duke in 1944 (*Where Have I Been?*, pp. 50–51). The doubletalk was part of a routine called "Conversation between Hitler and Donald Duck"—Caesar did both parts. The bit was likely inspired by the 1943 Walt Disney / RKO propaganda cartoon *Der Fuehrer's Face*, directed by Jack Kinney and originally titled *Donald Duck in Nutzi Land*, which won the Academy Award for Best Animated Short Film, though it was subsequently suppressed for fifty years. This sidesplitting short features the song Spike Jones made famous in 1942, "Der Fuehrer's Face," which was written by Oliver Wallace. *Donald Duck in Nutzi Land* bears a resemblance to *Ducktators*, directed by Norman

51. *Where Have I Been?*, p. 13. Caesar says that he was wanted to find a comedy that, unlike slapstick, did not "degrade another human being" (p. 30).

McCabe (WB / Looney Tunes, 1942) as well as to *Daffy Duck—the Commando*, directed by Fritz Freleng (WB / Looney Tunes, 1943). *Daffy–the Commando* features snippets of parodic Nazi-inflected doubletalk and ends with Hitler giving a doubletalk speech (that is, a homophonic version of Hitler oratory), which is stopped by Donald hitting him with giant mallet after which Hitler stutters and screams.[52]

But before Caesar or Looney Tunes did their German doubletalk, there was Charlie Chaplin's extended homophonic translation of a Hitler speech in *The Great Dictator* from 1940: doubletalk salted with English words. That speech is given by the dictator Adenoid Hynkel, whose double is Schultz, the Jewish barber. The film ends with a double of this speech, spoken by Schultz as Hynkel/Hitler. This rousing speech against tyranny, intolerance, and "national barriers," spoken in plain English and broadcast to the world, breaks the dictator's nightmarish spell. We can be sure Caesar, who idolized Chaplin, heard it. Just as he would have known Chaplin's Italian double-talking "nonsense" song in *Modern Times* (1936):

Se bella giu satore
Je notre so cafore
Je notre si cavore
Je la tu la ti la twah[53]

Homophonic works are usually funny, if not outright comic. They succeed because they have a sense of humor about the apparent absurdity of the idea. It's the humor, and the sense of identification with the other, that inflects the homophonics of Zukofsky and Caesar, who both grew up in a Yiddish-speaking household but for whom English was, if not the mother tongue, than the father tongue, the language they mastered. Ironically, for Caesar, doubletalk was not deceptive or artificial but a honing/homing into the language-spring of *mamaloshen*. Indeed, Caesar notes that some of his first jokes were based on translinguistic puns and mishearing between Yiddish and English, which greatly amused his audience, who were making their way to being American by moving from Yiddish to English. Caesar credits Yiddish dialect performers as precursors. He mentions Wil-

52. See Marc Shell's discussion of these cartoons, as well as *The Great Dictator* (and, at least in citation, *Modern Times*) in terms of the macaronic, in *Talking the Walk and Walking the Talk: A Rhetoric of Rhythm* (New York: Fordham University Press, 2015).

53. "Nonsense Song from Modern Times": <charliechaplin.com/en/lyrics/articles/114-Song-from-Modern-Times-Titine>

lie Howard, who sang Yiddish words to Mexican-themed skits (*Caesar's Hours*, p.16). Fanny Brice comes to mind.

Caesar's approach to all his performance art is that it "had to have a basis in reality. It had to be believable" (*Caesar's Hours*, p. xxi). It is this believability—what Zukofsky called "sincerity"—that undercuts parody and irony: it allows language to be reinhabited ("objectification" in Zukofsky's sense) rather than mocked.[54] This, in turn, brings back to mind Zukofsky's "An Foin Lass"—a translation that brings home the Cavalcanti, *makes it home* and a little bit homely. The doubleness in doubletalk is, then, not deception or evasion but double consciousness in W. E. B. Du Bois's sense—the consciousness of the dominant English but the echo of the *mamaloshen*. It's not about a return to an authentic original language, it's the dialectical relation of the two, the echopoetics, that is the ground. Doubletalk that foregrounds doubletalking as its own kind of poetry or verbal acrobatics. And just to bring this point ever more homeward: Caesar would intersperse Yiddish and English words into his doubletalk routines. As he boasts, a Yiddish word pronounced the right way can sound Japanese (*Caesar's Hours*, p. 214).

While all Caesar's doubletalk is done with good humor, his signature German doubletalk is also in effect proto-Nazi doubletalk and is laced with gentle, but devastating, mocking. The prime example is one of Caesar's best-known doubletalk skits, "The German General" from 1954, written with Mel Brooks.[55] With Howard Morris and Caesar both doing doubletalk, "The German General" is set in prewar Germany. The first of two scenes focuses on what appears to be the elaborate dressing of a patrician general (Caesar) by his servile underling, who polishes his chest medals and puffs his gold braids. The second scene involves a radical reversal, turning satire into pathos: the General walks from the dressing room through a hotel lobby filled with swankily dressed people. He heads to the hotel entrance, where we realize he is the doorman, his military dress is just a fancy uniform. By detouring the proto-Nazi figure, the entirely doubletalked performance explodes the master-slave dialectic—not by switching roles but by undermining mastery through recontextualization (a change of frame in Erving Goffman's sense). The Jewish parasites, in Nazi eyes, inhabit and

54. Louis Zukofsky, "An Objective," in *Prepositions +: The Collected Critical Essays*, ed. Mark Scroggins (Middletown, CT: Wesleyan University Press, 2000). My foreword is included in Act One of this book.

55. "Sid Caesar, The German General": <youtu.be/5m6Czgl1acU>, broadcast on *Caesar's Hour*, September 26, 1954. Caesar discusses the skit in *Caesar's Hours*, pp. 205ff, pp. 215–216. Mel Brooks takes the writing credit in a memorial tribute to Caesar on *Conan*, "Mel Brooks on Sid Caesar's Masterful Gibberish," February 19, 2014: <youtu.be/RUHemC_dvuU>.

make their own the German language. With their double voicing, Caesar and Brooks are tricksters, signifying on the German. The sketch is based on two foreign-language films unlikely to have been seen by most of the mass audience of the TV show: F. W. Murnau's 1925 *The Last Laugh* and Jean Renoir's 1937 *Grand Illusion* (with Walt Disney's 1937 *Snow White and the Seven Dwarfs* thrown in for good measure). This combination of high and low culture was an intentional part of Caesar's method. The method required that the skits would work even if the audience didn't know the sources of the parody. The performances had to be works in their own right, much as it is the goal of homophonic translations for autonomy from the source, free of secondary (or parasitic) status—not by reversing the power dynamic but reframing it. Brooks would come back to this theme thirteen years later with *The Producers*.[56]

Caesar's doubletalk uses the full prosodic resources of verbal language, foregrounding intonation, gesture, rhythm, syntax, and sound patterning rather than lexical identification. Doubletalk resembles sound poetry, but it is tied to the specific sounds and rhythms of the language being parodied. It is homophonic translation not of a specific text but, rather, of the texture of the source language.

Like doubletalk, homophonic translation, *zaum*, sound poetry, and scat singing are not against expression; they are hyper-communicative. Sound writing makes meaning by other means (*kio signifas per aliaj rimedoj* in Esperanto); other, that is, than lexical. This is meaning for those who feel at home in the world, or want to make the world more homely (*gemütlich*, *haimish*). "At home," according to theologian Ernst Fuchs, "one does not speak so that people will understand but because people understand."[57] Language at home is marked by the temporal, transient, always in-process "presence of a dialect": "Here language is emotional. Its understanding of time ranges between song and shout" (p. 126).

The presence of the word, that is, *verbing the word*, is antinomian: *the performance of language supersedes the law of language.*

> Only that which can become present as language is real. "For where meaning is, there also is language. And where language is, there is reality. Language

---

56. Brooks wanted Caesar to play the part of the Nazi in the 1968 movie, but the studio nixed the idea (*Where Have I Been?*, p. 189).

57. Ernst Fuchs, "The New Testament and the Hermeneutical Problem," in *New Frontiers in Theology: Volume Two, The New Hermeneutic*, tr. and ed. by James M. Robinson and John B. Cobb (New York: Harper and Row, 1964), p. 124 (italics removed). This quote, unsourced, comprises the 11th section of my "Three or Four Things I Know about Him," *Content's Dream: Essays 1975–1985* (Los Angeles: Sun and Moon Press, 1985), p. 30. Fuchs's first name is incorrectly cited as "Eduard."

belongs so closely to reality that it sets reality free for the first time: language *ex*-presses reality. . . . The word not merely conveys the concrete situation but creates it."[58]

In 1912, Franz Kafka gave an "Introductory Lecture on Jargon," a talk on Yiddish that he wrote as a prologue to a performance of Yiddish poetry. Yiddish represented for Kafka a "kind of immediacy of expression" in sharp contrast to the "endemic alienation of Western assimilated Jews" like himself.[59] Yiddish, for Kafka, is related to Fuchs's idea of a language of home. At the same time, Kafka saw Yiddish as *mißachtete*, a disregarded and stigmatized dialect, a language appropriated from other language, and a subculture argot (a "minor language" as Gilles Deleuze and Félix Guattari have it in *Kafka: Toward a Minor Literature*).

[Yiddish] consists solely of foreign words. But these words are not firmly rooted in it, they retain the speed and liveliness with which they were adopted. Great migrations move through Yiddish, from one end to the other. All this German, Hebrew, French, English, Slavonic, Dutch, Rumanian, and even Latin, is seized with curiosity and frivolity once it is contained within Yiddish, and it takes a good deal of strength to hold all these languages together in this state. . . . It is only thieves' cant [Gaunersprache, Klezmerloshen, argot] . . . because Yiddish was, after all, for a long time a despised [mißachtete] language. . . . And now the dialects enter into language's fabric of arbitration and law. Indeed, Yiddish as a whole consists only of dialect, even the written language [Schriftsprache, written speech].[60]

Doubletalk is akin to what David Antin calls a talk poem; as with jazz, the performance is live and improvised; both of these elements are essential. Caesar's doubletalk, while markedly American, is accessible to those who don't know English, and in that sense, it works like *zaum*, sound poetry, and scat singing: verbal works that do not require knowledge of a specific national language (call it *transnational*, to give that term a different spin). During, and in the immediate wake of, the systematic extermination of the European Jews, Caesar's doubletalk broke down the barrier of national

58. Gerald G. O'Collins, "Reality as Language: Ernst Fuchs's Theology of Revelation," *Theological Studies* 28:1 (1967), pp. 77–78. In internal quote, O'Collins translates Fuchs.

59. Richard T. Gray, Ruth V. Gross, Rolf J. Goebel, and Clayton Koelb, *A Franz Kafka Encyclopedia* (Westport, CT: Greenwood Press, 2005), p. 235. Eugene Ostashevsky pointed me to Kafka's talk.

60. Franz Kafka, "Einleitungsvortrag über Jargon": <www.kafka.org/index.php?jargon>. Translation by Ernst Kaiser and Eithne Wilkins, in *Dearest Father: Stories and Other Writings* (New York: Schocken Books, 1954), pp. 382–83. However, in the citation I have translated "*Sprachgebilde* [literally speechform] von Willkür und Gesetz" as "language's fabric of arbitration and law"; Kaiser and Wilkins's had "linguistic medley of whim and law."

languages by creating a sense of the delightful *comradery of difference* and by diffusing ethnic tension. Difference is elided through immediate accessibility. The Groucho Marxian comedy of puns and verbal wit may be difficult for nonnative speakers to fully understand; not so doubletalk. Doubletalk is verbal pantomime, as paradoxical as that sounds (or doesn't sound). It is words sublimed to music. In contrast, the American homophonic poem may have aspired to be non-English-bound but its reliance on puns and allusions may sometimes run counter to this.

Caesar's homophonics are all about accent, and accent is always a matter of class and ethnicity. In American culture, to have a marked accent is a stigma, a mark of your status as immigrant or ignorant. During Caesar's reign, people went to classes to lose their accent, or more accurate to say, learn the right accent. At the same time, in the years before the World War II, ethnic comedians had their audiences rolling in the aisles by performing their own and their audience's accents. This was the world of comedy Caesar came into. But it's one thing to make good fun with your own accent, another to mock the accents of others, which was also a staple of American ethnic comedy, which too often took an explicitly racist turn. Even if blackface performers identified with African Americans, it did not undercut the racism of the appropriation. Mimicry always risks being heard as ridicule or mockery.

Doubletalk is usually considered something bad, deceitful, fraudulent. Saying one thing and meaning another, a means of disguising the true meaning of something. It is connected with viral Jewish stereotypes, all repeatedly invoked in Pound's 1941–1943 Radio Rome speeches:[61] the uprooted, usurpers of a language not rightly one's own, destroyers of the plain sense of the word and authenticity, untrustworthy, "diabolically clever," as Joseph Litvak puts it. Litvak discusses the relation of Theodor Adorno's use of dialect to Jewish comedians, including Caesar, especially when they turn highfalutin language into gibberish, as, Litvak notes, Adorno does to Heideggerian lingo:

> How many of these jokes, that is, show the reversal as, precisely, an effect of gesture, where gesture is the part of language that, like a provincial accent or an unassimilated parent, embarrasses language? That the embarrassment should strike at the very moment when language is most concerned to make a good impression accounts, of course, for the particular sting with which the

---

61. See my 1984 "Pounding Fascism (Appropriating Ideology, Mystification, Aestheticization, and Authority in Pound's Poetic Practice)," collected in *A Poetics* (1992).

jokes themselves strike. Just when language thinks it has everything, espe-
cially itself, under control, it starts gesturing, or even gesticulating, thereby
hysterically displaying one of the classic signs of an always excessive Jewish
identity.[62]

Doubletalk is associated with gobbledygook, obfuscation, and
gibberish—fake or counterfeit language, what George Orwell famously
stigmatizes as doublespeak or bullshit, which gives "an appearance of solid-
ity to pure wind."[63] It's the talk of carnival barkers, crooked politicians and
kike lawyers, fascists and communists. It is nothing but bad faith. Double-
talk begins in the deliberately unintelligible and fragmented. Modernist
poetry has often been tarred with this brush. It's fast talking on theory
and chock full of elisions and evasions, obscure references, logical lapses,
emotional bankruptcy; in other words, *the kind of poetry I want*. Caesar saw
the poetry in these language textures, even if he would have figured them
as "material" not "poetry." In the immediate wake of the extermination
of the European Jews, he practiced a kind of shtick alchemy, turning the
Jewish stigmas of accent and shyster into song, in the process turning the
tools of intolerance and nationalism on their heads. Doubletalk is applied
nomadics (to use Pierre Joris's term for non-national language[64]): it pushes
back against blood and soil nativism.

Two American Jews—Caesar and Milton Berle—were among the most
popular TV entertainers in the United States in the years shortly following
the Khurbn.[65] In the context of popular entertainment of the time, paro-
dies of "foreign" languages and culture were common, ranging from racist
ethnic parody and blackface to self-parodies that actively mocked stereo-
types. It is a long way from Caesar to British Jewish comedian Sacha Baron
Cohen's accent-heavy Ali G and Borat. Caesar was unlikely to offend his
mass audience on grounds of cultural appropriation. Nonetheless, Jewish

---

62. Joseph Litvak, "Adorno Now," *Victorian Studies*, 44:1 (2001), p. 37

63. Orwell never uses the term *doublespeak* (or bullshit), though, in *1984*, he writes about "double-
think" and "new speak"; those two terms, combined, suggest *doublespeak*. In his 1946 essay against
the decay and corruption of language, "Politics and the English Language," Orwell argues for clear
language and against obfuscating writing styles, what he calls "swindles and perversions." In some
circumstance, his views offer practical advice; in others, they become a method of policing language
and enforcing normalization: <orwellfoundation.com/the-orwell-foundation/orwell/essays-and-other
-works/politics-and-the-english-language>.

64. Pierre Joris, *A Nomad Poetics* (Middletown, CT: Wesleyan University Press, 2003)

65. *Khurbn* is a Yiddish word for destruction and is synonymous with *Shoah*, which is the Hebrew
word for catastrophe.

comedians walked a fine line between their antic hysteria and antisemitic stereotypes related to rootlessness, parasitism, vulgarity, and impurity.

In the realm of High Modernism, the cultural supremacism of Pound and Eliot turned their cultural appropriations into a virtue, something Zukofsky targeted, at least in respect to *The Waste Land*, in his 1926 "Poem Beginning 'The.'" But virtue was not in the cards for the likes of Sid Caesar and his Jewish successors, from Jerry Lewis and Mel Brooks (born Melvin Kaminsky in 1926) to Don Rickles (1926), Jackie Mason (born Yacov Moshe Maza in 1931), Joan Rivers (born Joan Alexandra Molinsky in 1933), Larry David, and Sarah Silverman, nor his antic/anarchistic predecessors, the Marx Brothers and the Three Stooges. Much less for Rodney Dangerfield (born Jacob Cohen in 1921), who built his act around getting no respect.

If these outsider Jewish comedians risked mocking, albeit hilariously, conventional American sentimental norms, they often felt the need to show that in "real" life they were straight, well-adjusted Americans. The perfect realization of this is the split personality of Julius Kelp and Buddy Love in Jerry Lewis's 1963 film, *The Nutty Professor*. But it's there in the sycophantic sentimentality of Rickles when he stops his insult-shtick and gets personal with Johnny Carson (or, more accurately, launches into his ingratiation-shtick), just as it's there in Lewis's painfully sincere lounge singing and in his conspicuous philanthropy on his long-running, pity-inducing muscular dystrophy telethons. Significantly, Bruce had no "nice guy" alt. persona. In the age of reality TV, Rivers's "personal" side spins into yet more crazy parody with *Joan & Melissa: Joan Knows Best?*, the title mocking the classic American situation comedy of enforced normalcy, *Father Knows Best*. David, in his most commercially successful enterprise, *Seinfeld*, had the super nice Jerry Seinfeld as his foil; he turned his masterpiece, *Curb Your Enthusiasm*, into a celebration of misanthropy.

Caesar walked the line and the toll on him was enormous. He sputtered out of control midway in his life, falling prey to the drugs and drink he used to keep himself going at maximum speed and precarious abandon.[66] Bruce's fall was more severe, dying of a heroin overdose at forty in 1966, at the aesthetic height of his career. Bruce was just three years younger than Caesar. He was strictly downtown, nightclubs, intentionally offensive. In contrast,

---

66. Caesar suffered from violent manic outbursts, chronic anxiety, insecurity, and depression, with something like bulimia thrown in. It sounds bipolar. To curb his drinking, and for insomnia, his doctors prescribed pills, which he added to the booze. At various times, he was taking chloral hydrate, sodium amytal, amobarbital, Miltown, Placidyl, Equanil, and Seconal, all the while drinking heavily.—*Where Have I Been?*, pp. 135, 148, 184. Caesar depicts the toll of drink in the beautiful Chaplin/Keaton silent film pastiche, "A Drunk There Was," *Caesar's Hour*, January 16, 1956 <youtu.be/G76HrPTWj4I>.

Caesar was mainstream, TV, intentionally inoffensive. Caesar's best work was over by 1958, when he was thirty-six; after that, as he describes it, he was mostly on autopilot, with what he calls his "Dark Period" beginning in mid-6os.[67] Like Caesar, Bruce started as Borscht Belt entertainer, but he went on to create polyvocal long-form talking essays (call them talks or talk poems), before becoming a martyr, persecuted by the state as morally repugnant. A master of doing "the police in different voices,"[68] Bruce's counterculture genius has held up better than Caesar's commercial success.

Despite the essential sweetness of his on-screen performances, at the very height of his fame, Caesar felt a need to undercut the aesthetic and intellectual challenge of his work in order "humanize" himself, to show that the man behind the clown mask was not a vulgar, shrill, shtetl vaudevillian playing for easy laughs to the masses, not a queerly manic, doubletalking mongrel, not, that is, *too Jewish*, but rather someone who had "class." He needed to show he was a "real man" interested in guns, a devoted husband and father, and also to "couth up" and show he was refined connoisseur of high art to boot—mixed messages that go with the striving for assimilation.

There is tremendous pathos in watching Edward R. Murrow's live TV interview with Caesar in his upscale Park Avenue apartment in a 1954 segment of *Person to Person*.[69] Sid kisses his daughter goodnight for the benefit of the national audience (she stayed up late so she could be on TV, he tells us). Caesar then takes Murrow into his gun room, which is decked out with rifles on a rack and a mounted deer's head. "I used to do a lot of hunting," says Sid, and goes on to tell the story of his snagging the deer, the only animal he has ever killed, so he says. The room looks like it was installed by the prop people on his show.[70] As he points to the deer head, it falls off from the wall and he holds it up for the rest of the segment, keeping a straight face. The entire show gives the sense of Caesar as a deer caught in the headlights. It would take almost fifty years for this public flagellation of the Jewish comedian to be exorcised by Rivers on *Joan & Melissa*. In the

---

67. In *Caesar's Hour*, as well as various late video interviews, Caesar repeats the same stories with the same spin, sometimes in a mechanical way, with only flashes of the spark that made him great. After starting his career on the wild and crazy side, in the last decades of his life he did all he could keep his story, and himself, straight.

68. A draft title of Eliot's "The Waste Land" was "He Do the Police in Different Voices."

69. "Sid Caesar on *Person to Person* with Edward R. Murrow," October 1, 1954: <writing.upenn.edu /ezurl/8>. Caesar's apartment at 940 Park Ave. (81st Street) was in one of the most exclusive neighborhoods in the United States, in other words a WASP safe space. Such an apartment was the ultimate status symbol. My parents moved into a similarly decorated place around the same time, but on the less restricted Upper West Side.

70. Caesar was physically imposing, gun-obsessed, and had a violent temper. He blew off steam shooting at tin cans with the rifles he collected and kept in the apartment.—*Where Have I Been?*, pp. 132, 196.

final segment of the *Person to Person* interview, Sid proudly shows Murrow a painting he owns by Maurice de Vlaminck, his "favorite" work in a collection that was inspired, he says, by reading *Lust for Life*, the Van Gogh biography by Irving Stone. Sid is something of an Impressionist himself, he tells Murrow, suppressing the punch line: *I do impressions.*

"I have an interest in art," Sid Caesar tells Edward R. Murrow and the millions watching at home.[71]

—*You bet your life you do.*

4.

5. a jew / among the Indians

In America, we exiled the native peoples as part of a process of extermination, then endeavored to erase their languages from cultural memory. Early on Jerome Rothenberg, a Bronx native who came of age during the Khurbn, recognized himself as "a jew / among the Indians."[72] In 1968, he published *Technicians of the Sacred: A Range of Poetries from Africa, America, Asia, Europe, and Oceania.* Shortly after, with *The Horse Songs*, he introduced "total translation," which has close affinities with homophonic translation, carrying into the performance of the translation the "full" sound dynamic

71. *Your Show of Shows* (1950–1954) and *Caesar's Hour* (1954–1957) introduced many of genres that were later picked up by *SCTV*, *Monty Python*, and *Saturday Night Live*, among many other shows. Caesar's parodies of other TV shows qualify as postmodernism under most definitions of the term. Indeed, Caesar was one of the first artists to create "born TV" work.

72. "Jerome Rothenberg: Double Preface," *Pitch of Poetry* (Chicago: University of Chicago Press, 2016), p. 162

of the source text, including the vocables.[73] Rothenberg sought to bring the verbal art of analphabetic cultures into an active space of formally radical contemporary poetry. The question for him was not whether we have the right to translate the poetry of indigenous and non-alphabetic cultures but whether we have right not to. Up until that time, translations of this range of poetry focused more on plot than on sound, rhythm, and performance; this focus on content over form reflected the ideology of the translators and ethnologists and negated much of the culture they proposed to capture.[74] Rothenberg's commitment was to transcreation and transduction, sound writing and performance. He gathered midrashic translations for which process is commentary. The point was not to appropriate the source works but to enter into open-ended dialogs with them.

Ale modes fun iberzetsung, radikal nit mer vi kanvenshanal, fartrakhtn zikh di oryenteyshanz aun savs fun di transleyterz:[75] All modes of translation, radical no more than conventional, reflect the orientations and desires of the translators. And all translations are asymmetrical, both masking and revealing the discrepant cultural, economic, and political power of the translated and the translation. The ever-present danger is that the dominant party to the transaction is just toying with its object of affection and is aloof to, or incapable of, reciprocity. This is a pattern of supremacist exploitation that is repeated endless times. Yet, to refuse translation because too much is lost or distorted is to put purity above contamination and miscegenation. What or who gives the "right" to translate? If one translates works from within the Western canon, questions of appropriation do not arise. Except if you are viewed as a poacher or parasite, as Pound, Eliot, and legions of others, including Stalin, felt about rootless cosmopolitan Jews. As Eliot wrote, "Reasons of race and religion combine to make any large number of free-thinking Jews undesirable."[76] On the other side of the political spectrum, the Soviet campaign against Jews as "rootless cosmopolitans" (безродный космополит, bezrodnyi kosmopolit) began immediately after World War II. A crackdown on Yiddish writers and poets followed, culminating

---

73. Jerome Rothenberg, "Total Translation: An Experiment in the Translation of American Indian Poetry": <ubu.com/ethno/discourses/rothenberg_total.html>

74. See Dennis Tedlock, "On the Translation of Style in Oral Narrative," *The Spoken Word and the Work of Interpretation* (1983).

75. אלע מאָדעס פֿון איבערזעצונג, ראַדיקאַל ניט מער ווי קאָנווענשאַנאַל, פֿאַרטראַכטן זיך די אָריענטיישאַנז און סאָווס פֿון די טראַנסלייטערז.

76. T. S. Eliot, *After Strange Gods: A Primer of Modern Heresy* (London: Faber and Faber, 1933), p. 20. Also discussed in "Free Thinking," in the opening scene of Act Two of this collection. Translator's note: In the Esperanto original of this essay, the Eliot quote was translated as "Kialoj de raso kaj religio kombinas fari ajnan grandan nombron de libera-pensado judoj nedezirindaj."

in the state murder of leaders of the Jewish Anti-Fascist Committee on August 12, 1952, commemorated as the "Night of Murdered Poets." As Joseph Sherman puts it; "The trial of 1952 did more than wipe out some of the best Yiddish literary talents of the century; it completed the destruction of Yiddish in Europe."[77]

For fundamentalist Jews, the people of the book means *just one book* (and the commentaries on this one book). "Free-thinking" Jews are the ones who have broken with nativist orthodoxy, moving beyond their immediate culture to imagine themselves as part of a larger world, as did Zukofsky and Mandelstam, Caesar and Rothenberg. The break from the world of our parents is often traumatic. Zukofsky recounts his becoming other to his mother in "Poem Beginning 'The.'" In *Where Have I Been?*, Caesar recalls his father's silence when he sees him, near death, in a specially arranged screening of *Tars and Spars*: "You say you make five hundred dollars a week?" (p. 73). I remember my father, in the hospital in his last days in 1977, listening to a tape of a reading of mine, the only time he'd heard me, his disapproving silence melting, for a moment, into acknowledgment.

Cosmopolitan is a stigmatic code word for Jews as usurpers because it suggests global trafficking in cultural capital that doesn't belong to you, which only natives have the "right" to. Antinomian Jews are just one example of this phenomenon. African American poet Melvin Tolson ran up against just such a wall when he strayed from what was considered his rightful cultural materials by adopting a "high-modern" style related to Eliot's *The Waste Land* rather than sticking to what were assumed to be his own indigenous cultural styles.[78]

There is nothing so beautiful nor more essential for communication, nothing so sacred, as the inauthentic becoming aware of itself.

6. on wind, should be written, on running water

If Sid Caesar was the most popular Jewish comedian of the 1950s, Louis Zukofsky (born in 1904) was among the most unpopular Jewish poets, overshadowed by official verse culture favorites Delmore Schwartz and Karl Shapiro (both born in 1913). Zukofsky's son Paul reports that his family first got a TV around 1951–1953 and that he remembers his mother rec-

---

77. "Seven-fold Betrayal: The Murder of Soviet Yiddish," *Midstream* (2002): <www.thefreelibrary.com /"Seven-fold betrayal": the murder of Soviet Yiddish.-a090332016>

78. See Michael Berubé, *Marginal Forces / Cultural Centers: Tolson, Pynchon, and the Politics of the Canon* (Ithaca, NY: Cornell University Press, 1992).

ognizing a Yiddish word in one of Caesar's Japanese doubletalk routines, picking up on Caesar's boast.[79]

The most commonly cited origin for American homophonic translation is Louis and Celia Zukofsky's *Catullus*, written 1958–1966 and published in 1969. Like the Hebrew homophonics in *"A"*-15, *Catullus* is not pure— glosses of the non-homophonic lexical meaning poke through at times, for example, where Zukofsky has *wind* for the Latin *vento* in Catullus 70.[80] The fact that English and Latin allow so many cognates, and because of many specific choices and tweaks by the Zukofskys, *Catullus* abounds with semantic echoes, puns, and commentaries on the source poems, while at the same time bringing the listener closer to the sound and syntax of the Latin. Homophonic translations from languages with less in common with English, such as Hebrew, Finnish, Chinese, Tamil, or Basque, pose different problems and open up other possibilities but up the uncanniness factor for apparent synchronicities.

Nulli se dicit mulier mea nubere malle
quam mihi, non si se Iuppiter ipse petat.
dicit: sed mulier cupido quod dicit amanti,
in vento et rapida scribere oportet aqua.
         [Catullus 70]

Zukofskys:

Newly say dickered my love air my own would marry me all
    whom but me, none see say Jupiter if she petted.
Dickered: said my love air could be o could dickered a man too
    in wind o wet rapid a scribble reported in water.

Here's my translation:

None, says my woman, would she want to marry more
than me, not if Jupiter himself insisted.

---

79. Paul Zukofsky and Charles Bernstein, email exchange, November 9, 2016. Mixing Yiddish into the Japanese doubletalk is a perfect example of Caesar's macaronics.

80. For Latin versions of Catullus's poems see "The Poetry of Gaius Valerius Catullus": <en.wikibooks .org/wiki/The_Poetry_of_Gaius_Valerius_Catullus>. I included the Zukofskys' homophonic translation of 70 in the *Selected*, p. 158, along with my own translation of the poem, p. 172. The full set of the Zu- kofsky Catullus translations are collected in *Anew: Complete Shorter Poetry* (2011). Lawrence Venuti wrote about this work in his indispensable *The Translator's Invisibility* (1995).

says: but what a woman says to a smitten lover,
on wind, should be written, on running water.[81]

In their homophonic translation of Catullus 85, the Zukofskys have the
non-homophonic anchor words *hate* and *love* in their translation. Richard
Tuttle and I moved through several versions of this poem, before selecting
the last one.

Odi et amo. quare id faciam, fortasse requiris.
    nescio, sed fieri sentio et excrucior.

Zukofskys:

O th'hate I move love. Quarry it fact I am, for that's so re queries.
    Nescience, say th' fierry scent I owe whets crookeder.

Bernstein/Tuttle:

Odious and amorous: Query: why'd I do that?
Don't know, just feelings & excruciating

•

Hating & loving. Hey: why's that?
Beats me, just my feelings & I'm crucified

•

Hate and love. Why's that?, you'd ask
Don't know, I feel it and it's torture.[82]

Coming back to this I came up with another:

Odious & amorous. Query: id facts, foretaste requires
No sense, said fearing scent, it's excruciating.

"A"-15, was written in 1964. The second stanza begins with a homopho-
nic translation from The Book of Job. Without critical exegesis, it would
be unlikely most readers would get the source as The Book of Job, just

81. *Near/Miss* (Chicago: University of Chicago Press, 2018), p. 84

82. *Recalculating* (Chicago: University of Chicago Press, 2013), p. 136

as most of Caesar's viewers would probably not have recognized *The Last Laugh* as the source of "The German General." Both Zukofsky and Caesar insisted that their work could stand on its own. And yet knowing the source adds an uncanny dimension and marks the works as echopoetics ("low o loam echo"). Like Caesar's doubletalk ("coeval yammer"), Zukofsky's homophonics is not pure but part of the textual mixture. It's midrashic and antinomian, offering echoes of the sound of the Hebrew, but also a biting commentary on Job's "gall" in his whining neighing about the "cruel hire" that life has turned out to be. Jeff Twitchell-Waas tracked down the Hebrew source and transliteration (a.k.a. homophonic rendering), to which I added the King James translation:

He neigh ha lie low h'who y'he gall mood

[Job 3:7] הִנֵּה הַלַּיְלָה הַהוּא יְהִי גַלְמוּד אַל-תָּבוֹא רְנָנָה בוֹ

hine halaila hahu yehi galmud al-tavo renana vo

Lo, let that night be solitary, let no joyful voice come therein.

So roar cruel hire / Lo to achieve an eye leer rot off

[Job 7:7] זְכֹר כִּי-רוּחַ חַיָּי לֹא-תָשׁוּב עֵינִי לִרְאוֹת טוֹב

zekhor ki-ruakh khayai lo-tashuv eini lirot tov:

O remember that my life is wind: mine eye shall no more see good.

Mass th'lo low o loam echo / How deal me many coeval yammer

[Job 7:16] מָאַסְתִּי לֹא-לְעֹלָם אֶחְיֶה חֲדַל מִמֶּנִּי כִּי-הֶבֶל יָמָי

maasti lo-leolam ekhye khadal mimeni ki-hevel yamai

I loathe it; I would not live alway: let me alone; for my days are
　　vanity.[83]

The third stanza of "A-15" begins with an echo of God's answer to Job from out of a whirlwind (Zukofsky hears "wind" and "His roar" in the Hebrew). God answers, "Who is this that darkeneth counsel by words without knowledge?" (KJV, 38:2). (Zukofsky hears "milling bleat doubt.") Perhaps homophonic translation, like typing without writing, just scratches the surface: words without knowledge, blowin' in the wind, transient, a "cruel hire." Man up, says the big man to a despairing Job. But maybe Job knew what he was talking about. His words, even if they grind doubt, speak to

---

83. Zukofsky, *Selected*, p. 114. Interlinear notation from Jeff Twitchell-Waas: <z-site.net/notes-to-a/a-15>. Twitchell-Waas dates the poem October 3 to December 1, 1964.

diasporic peoples with more resonance than God's. Milling it into what? Poetry? Who is this, the Torah's God asks, who talks without accepting that the basis of knowledge must be grounded in God's nativism (in the "one" who "laid the foundations of the earth" [38:4])? Who is this who's got the "gall" to talk out of the top of the head and from all sides of the mouth.

—Let there be doubletalkers who "scribble" and "yammer" "in wind . . . reported in water"!

7. The Translation Is Father to the Poem

The most striking work of American homophonic translation after the Zukofskys' *Catullus* comes from another Jewish poet, and a close reader of Zukofsky, David Melnick (1938–2022). Melnick's 1975 *Pcoet* is a signal work of post-*zaum* sound writing. But it is Melnick's 1983 *Men in Aida* that is the breakthrough for homophonic translation. *Men in Aida* is a full-scale homophonic translation of the first two books of *The Iliad*, replete with echoes of contemporary San Francisco gay culture at the time of the AIDS catastrophe. *Homo* comes home. Here's the opening passage, Homer's Greek first, then a transliteration, then Melnick (in bold), and finally the standard (heterophonic) translation. Melnick's is a strict, rather than loose, homophonic translation:

μῆνιν ἄειδε θεὰ Πηληϊάδεω Ἀχιλῆος
mênin aeide thea Pêlêïadeô Achilêos
Men in Aïda, they appeal, eh? A day, O Achilles!
SING, goddess, the anger of Peleus' son Achilleus

οὐλομένην, ἣ μυρί᾽ Ἀχαιοῖς ἄλγε᾽ ἔθηκε,
oulomenên, hê muri᾽ Achaiois alge᾽ ethêke,
Allow men in, emery Achaians. All gay ethic, eh?
and its devastation, which put pains thousandfold upon the
    Achaians,

πολλὰς δ᾽ ἰφθίμους ψυχὰς Ἄϊδι προΐαψεν
pollas d᾽ iphthimous psuchas Aïdi proïapsen
Paul asked if teach mousse suck, as Aïda, pro, yaps in.
hurled in their multitudes to the house of Hades strong souls

ἡρώων, αὐτοὺς δὲ ἑλώρια τεῦχε κύνεσσιν
hêrôôn, autous de helôria teuche kunessin
Here on a Tuesday. 'Hello,' Rhea to cake Eunice in.
of heroes, but gave their bodies to be the delicate feasting

οἰωνοῖσί τε πᾶσι, Διὸς δ' ἐτελείετο7 βουλή,
oiônoisi te pasi, Dios d' eteleieto boulê,
'Hojo' noisy tap as hideous debt to lay at a bully.
of dogs, of all birds, and the will of Zeus was accomplished

ἐξ οὗ δὴ τὰ πρῶτα διαστήτην ἐρίσαντε
ex hou dê ta prôta diastêtên erisante
Ex you, day. Tap write a 'D,' a stay. Tenor is Sunday.
since that time when first there stood in division of conflict

Ἀτρεΐδης τε ἄναξ ἀνδρῶν καὶ δῖος Ἀχιλλεύς.
Atreïdês te anax andrôn kai dios Achilleus.
Atriedes stain axe and Ron ideas 'll kill you.
Atreus' son the lord of men and brilliant Achilleus.[84]

Ron Silliman, a great proponent of Melnick, published his one and only homophonic translation in 1978, with Rilke's title "Duino Elegies" transformed into Silliman's "Do We Know Ella Cheese?," and the opening of the first elegy, "Wer, wenn ich schriee, hörte mich denn aus der Engel / Ordnungen?" becoming "Where / when itch scree / hurt as much / Then how's their angle / or known gun?"[85]

Any overview of postwar North American radical translation practices also needs to give a place of honor to bpNichol's 1979 *Translating Translating Apollinaire.*[86] Nichol and a few friends, including Steve McCaffery and

84. David Melnick, *Men in Aida*, Book One (Berkeley: Tuumba Press, 1983) and Book Two (Editions Eclipse, 2002), online at <eclipsearchive.org> and, for the Greek text and standard translation, *The Chicago Homer* <homer.library.northwestern.edu>. Listen to the Greek recited by Stephen G. Daitz at <writing.upenn.edu/ezurl/9>, excerpted from The Society for the Oral Reading of Greek and Latin: <rhapsodes.fll.vt.edu/Greek.htm>. Transliterations from <tlg.uci.edu/help/TranslitTest.php>. "Ron" in the final cited line of Melnick's is presumably his friend Ron Silliman.

85. Ron Silliman, notes on homophonic translation from his blog, August 30 and 31, 2003: <writing .upenn.edu/epc/authors/bernstein/syllabi/readings/silliman.html>

86. bpNichol, *Translating Translating Apollinaire: A Preliminary Report* (1979), on-line at <bpnichol .ca/sites/default/files/archives/document/Translating%20Translating.pdf>. Also of note: *Six Fillious,*

Dick Higgins, devised over fifty approaches to translating the first poem
Nichol published, a 1964 impressionistic, sampled version of Apollinaire's
iconic 1913 poem "Zone." There is one French phrase that runs throughout
the versions, "soleil cou coupé" (sun throat cut; sun a cut neck; cutthroat
sun; so lay, cool, coupé), the famous last line of "Zone," as well as two of
the proper names from Apollinaire's poem—Simon and Icarus. The "sound
translation" in Nichol's book (his phrase) is not of the Apollinaire poem but
Nichol's early translation of that poem. This is the first instance I know of
an English-to-English homophonic translation, though related forms of
echopoetics are hardly new in the long history of poetry. That one French
phrase becomes "soil hay coo coup hay" and Nichol's whole poem has a
sound typical of homophonic translation.

First stanzas of Nichol's echoing of "Zone":

Icharrus   winging   up
Simon the   Magician   from Judas   high in a tree,
everyone   reaching for the sun

                          great towers of stone
built by the Aztec, tearing their hearts out
to offer them, wet and beating

Nichol's "sound translation" of his "Zone" poem:

hick or ass   was king cup
Samantha   my chess yen   front   chew   deo   hyena tory,
heavy Juan   Gris   chin   guffaw   earth son

                     Greta hours office tone
bill to buy Thea's texts, terrier hard stout
two hover then, whet tongue bee sting

    In "Acoustic Room" (2000), Chris Tysh does a homophonic translation
from the second of Lautréamont's *Les Chants de Maldoror*: "Allons, Sultan,

---

by bpNichol, Robert Filliou, McCaffery, George Brecht, Higgins, and Dieter Roth (1978), in which a
poem by Filliou is the seed for a chain of translations, none of which are homophonic; and *Rational
Geomancy: The Kids of the Book-machine: The Collected Research Reports of the Toronto Research
Group, 1973–82* by Nichol and McCaffery (1992), which includes far-ranging discussions of radical
approaches to translation.

avec ta langue, débarrasse-moi de ce sang qui salit le parquet. Le bandage est fini: mon front étanché a été lavé avec de l'eau salée, et j'ai croisé des bandelettes à travers mon visage" becoming "All on, Sultan, evoke two languages, debar us, my dizzy song key, sail / it o'er the parquet. The bandage is fine: man, front attention, hate / to lovey away; deal o Sally, edgy crossy, this bandolier, a travesty / of my visage."[87]

There is a comic dimension to these sound translations. Humor is a fundamental structure of homophonic translation, even if done with a straight face. In contrast, my homophonic translations of Georg, and Celan, and my quasi-homophonic Royet-Journoud and Albiach, avert comedy. From 2002 to 2007, Robert Kelly wrote a series of non-comic "homeophonic" (as he terms them) translations of Paul Celan called "Earish."[88] In 2011, he published a homeophonic, and non-comic, translation of Friedrich Hölderlin called *Unquell the Dawn Now*.

Jean Donnelly's *Green Oil* is a homophonic, and non-comic, translation of Francis Ponge's *Pièces*. *Green Oil* is an elegant long poem made up of short lines (eight sections of unrhymed couplets with no punctuation).[89] The work has the sharp torquing rhythm of Robert Creeley or George Oppen, but it is more semantically labyrinthine, bouncing off word associations and evocative enjambments. *Green Oil* would be unrecognizable as a homophonic translation since it has only slight traces of specifically French syntax or idiom. Donnelly provides few keys to specific sound associations between her poem and Ponge's:

we lash a trop
to meaning

on it quells
our touching

docks of
ravishing

87. *Continuity Girl* (New York: United Artists, 2000). See Silliman's notes on homophonic translation, cited above. In later work, Tysh has done transcreations of Beckett and Genet.

88. Robert Kelly, "Earish" <writing.upenn.edu/library/Kelly-Robert_Earish.html> and <rk-ology.com /book/earish-2/>; collected, for the first time including Celan's source poems, as *Earish: Thirty Poems of Paul Celan* (Toronto: Beautiful Outlaw, 2022). "Celan" is a partial anagram of the poet's birth name, Antschel.

89. Jean Donnelly, *Green Oil* (Colorado Springs: Further Other Book Works, 2014). The poems, she says, "began in the process of liberal homophonic readings and orthographical transcriptions" (p. 9).

moments with
magnificent

characters
like loons

that enter
water

in sight of
every word

despite
every word (47)

As Maureen Thorsen points out in a review of the book, Donnelly's title "Green Oil" plays off Ponge's "La Grenouille" ("The Frog"):[90]

Lorsque la pluie en courtes aiguillettes
lords do squalls ply a court of aging
rebondit aux prés
that rebounds our praise

saturés, une naine amphibie,
& saturates our *amphibian* impulse
une Ophélie
one Ophelia version

manchote, grosse à peine comme le poing,
mangled gross & pained with being
. . . poète et se jette . . .
poets & suggestions[91]

90. Maureen Thorson, "I Think We Are Alone Now," in *Open Letters Monthly* (November 1, 2015): <openlettersmonthly.com/i-think-were-alone-now/>

91. "Green Oil," *Green Oil*, p. 49. I have braided the first lines of the poem with the source, Francis Ponge, "La Grenouille," in *Le Grand Recueil-Pièces* (Paris: Gallimard, 1961), p. 59.

Jonathan Stallings's 2011 work, *Yingelishi* 吟歌丽诗 *(Chanted Songs Beautiful Poetry): Sinophonic English Poetry and Poetics*, takes stock English phrases from a travel guide for Chinese speakers and provides homophonic Chinese versions. Stallings then uses the isophones for an opera libretto.[92] In the process, simple English phrases are transformed into a narrative in Chinese: the quotidian English is transformed into lyrically fanciful Chinese. The stock phrase "Close your eyes" is homophonically rendered as Chinese; the Chinese isophone is, in turn, translated into English as "Jade dew appears as mourning memories." *English* becomes *Yingelishi*, which translates as "chanted beautiful poetry." The opera can be heard simultaneously as English or Chinese. For English speakers, the work creates a Chinese-sounding accent that is solemn and lyric, which for Stallings is meant to counter "yellow-face minstrelsy" (stereotyped Chinese accent in English, often used in racist ethnic comedy routines). If the English sinophonics are intentionally not comic, the Chinese homophonic translation is, since it produces, for Chinese listeners, a doubletalk mishmashed from "real" linguistic elements, perhaps a macaronic cousin to Caesar's doubletalk.

Cousins to the homophonic are the *homeographic* and *homeomorphic* (which might more broadly be called *parallelism*). "The 85 Project" by Robert Majzels, Claire Huot, and Nathan Tremblay consists of transcreations of Chinese poems into 85-character English visual poems.[93] Majzels also has transcreations from the Hebrew of *The Song of Songs*. The "85" poems begin by translating each Chinese character into an English word, echoing Xu Bing's homeographic "Art for the People" (1999) and "Square Word" calligraphy, which designs English words as Chinese characters (block constellations of several letters). Yunte Huang's homeomorphic (word-for-word) *SHI: A Radical Reading of Chinese Poetry* provides literal, character-for-character, translation of classic Chinese poems.

Red, Green, and Black, my 1990 translation, with Olivier Cadiot, of a work of his, is an example of what I mean by homeomorphic.

Dirk Weissmann, the co-organizer of the "Sound / Writing" confer-

---

92. Jonathan Stalling, *Yingelishi* (Boulder, CO: Counterpath Press, 2011) and the website for the work: <jstalling.com/yingelishi.html>. See Jacob Edmund, "English and Yíngēlìshī: Jonathan Stalling's Homophonic Translations" <jacket2.org/commentary/english-and-yingelishi> and <quarterlyconversation .com/yingelishi-and-grotto-heaven-by-jonathan-stalling>. Stallings talked about his work at the fifth Chinese/American Association for Poetry and Poetics Conference, at California State University, Los Angeles, November 14, 2016. He has gone on to use the sinophonic written characters as a way to teach both English and Chinese.

93. "The 85 Project": <85bawu.com>

ence, points to Ernst Jandl's early 1960s "oberflächenübersetzung" ("surface translation") as another early example of homophonic translation, in this case from English to German.[94] Jandl turns Wordsworth's "My heart leaps up when I behold / A rainbow in the sky" into "mai hart lieb zapfen eibe hold / er renn bohr in sees kai" and "The Child is father of the Man" into "seht steil dies fader rosse mähen." Perhaps we could translate this famous line back into the American as "see this upright, faded horse mowing," which is uncannily close to Wordsworth's meaning. The translation is father to the poem.

For *Shadowtime*, I made a homophonic translation of Jandl's "der und die" (1964).[95] Here are the first two lines, braided (the work is both homophonic and homeographic):

can dew and die can and die can tie his sin tap and
kam der und die kam und die kam vor ihm ins tal und
the war dew hoe and die has him and her and tar the
das war der ort und die sah hin und her und tat das

Voice recognition software brings another dimension to the homophonic. In *Hearing Things*, British deaf poet Aaron Williamson used voice recognition software to dictate/transcreate poems. Williamson speaks but can't hear his own voice. He describes the results as "deaf gain" in contrast to "hearing loss": "Why had all the doctors told me that I was losing my hearing, and not a single one told me that I was gaining my deafness?"[96] Within the larger context of the poetics of disability, I call this *deficit gain*, which might be a useful frame for the poetics of homophony and sound-alikeness. The title of one of Williamson's poems is "Geomancy," suggesting reading meaning into verbal scatter. Geomancy and deficit gain both resonate with homophonics, though it's essential to remain chary about eliding the circumstances of disabled people with terms for poetics.

94. Dirk Weissmann, "Übersetzung als kritisches Spiel: Zu Ernst Jandl's *oberflächenübersetzung*," *Das Spiel in der Literatur*, ed. Philipp Wellnitz (Berlin: Frank und Timme, 2013)

95. First published, with Jandl's original, in *Reft and Light: Poems by Ernst Jandl with Multiple Versions by American Poets* (2000). Juliette Valery did a French translation that begins—"pût eau tel tué pût tel tué pût lie son mal bat tel." For an informative study of my translation of Jandl, see Katja Stuckatz, *Ernst Jandl und Die Internationale Avantgarde: Über Einen Beitrag Zur Modernen Weltdichtung* (Berlin: Walter de Gruyter GmbH, 2016), pp. 320–26.

96. Introduction," in H-Dirksen L. Bauman and Joseph J. Murray, eds., *"Deaf Gain: Raising the Stakes for Human Diversity* (Minneapolis: University of Minnesota Press, 2014), p. xv

You need to bend to listen, further to hear. . . . Feeble configurations skid out of forced swoons and dives, frail transport for the ear to zoom in and make something at will. Marks to the paper arc your prostrate conclusions yet your veiled head dullens design against any end at all.[97]

Pierre Joris tested the possibilities of voice recognition software in a different way. He emailed me about it while I was in Paris for the "Sound / Writing" conference and staying at Hotel Des Grandes Hommes, where André Breton and Philippe Soupault employed "automatic writing" to compose *Magnetic Fields* in 1919. Joris read the French poem aloud into his computer's "MacSpeech Dictate" application, which was set to transcribe from English. Here is a bit of what he got (what was dictated followed by the computer transcription), with its wry evocation of the bad student of French (such as I was) taking dictation during class:

LA GLACE SANS TAIN
Prisonniers des gouttes d'eau, nous ne sommes que des animaux perpétuels. Nous courons dans les villes sans bruits et les affiches enchantées ne nous touchent plus. À quoi bon ces grands enthousiasmes fragiles, ces sauts de joie desséchés ? Nous ne savons plus rien que les astres; nous regardons les visages; et nous soupirons de plaisirs. Notre bouche est plus sèche que les pages perdues; nos yeux tournent sans but, sans espoir. Il n'y a plus que ces cafés où nous nous réunissons pour boire ces boissons fraîches, ces alcools délayés et les tables sont plus poisseuses que ces trottoirs où sont tombées nos ombres mortes de la veille.[98]

LAG SOL TIME
Please are the big good door, no one is so did it anymore will be to period. No: only if he'd sown wheat in a set fiche are shown being and pushed crude. Aqua balls into all on Tuesday I submit IG unit, six cylinders what do I think? Knew several people he and Kerry Seth Amo; no load up on a recession; in whose appeal to pity he. Not put Bush at 2/good/bad dude; knows you ~ Psalm bitch, saws as well. The reactor due to think deftly when will they be so bold whilst they were so fresh, since I go in the 8880 tablets and replaced it is ethical to our slumped on being a zone while not that EA period.

In 1999, Richard Caddel did a "loose phonic version" of the early medieval Welsh poem "Y Gododin" by Neirin (or Aneurin). Here is #75, braided

97. From Aaron Williamson, "Geomancy," in *Hearing Things* (London: Bookworks, 2001), p. 22. Michael Davidson discusses Williamson's work in *Concerto for Left Hand: Disability and the Defamiliar Body* (Ann Arbor: University of Michigan Press, 2008), pp. 87–93.

98. André Breton, *Oeuvres complètes* I (Paris: Gallimard, 1966), p. 106

with the Welsh poem of that same number, which, however, is not neces-
sarily the source:

earthly songs with common refrains
Ardyledawc canu kenian kywreint
loud lodger-bird by dizzy want
Llawen llogell byt bu didichwant
how many in hill bird idle amount
Hu mynnei engkylch byt eidol anant
every great march a mead feathering
Yr eur a meirch mawr a med medweint
forgetting the airing when fainting
Namen ene delei o vyt hoffeint / Kyndilic aeron wyr enouant[99]

Andrew Duncan, in his "Note" on Caddel's "phonic version," suggests that
the text of *Y Gododin* comes to us as sound echoes of a possible original rather
than as a lexically accurate version—"Ifor Williams' introduction to his
edition [of *Y Gododin*] points out the nature of the text as we have it, where
phonetic drift and association have taken over parts of the original text."[100]
    In more recent years, there has been a proliferation of novel transla-
tion practices, multilectical poetry, and poetry written by second-language
speakers of English who live in non-English speaking places. Caroline
Bergvall—a British/French/Norwegian poet—has been creating a mixed
language or loose or macaronic homophonic poetry: doubletalking in
Middle and Old English. *Meddle English* is Bergvall's remarkable Chau-
cerian vocal insinuations and extensions. In these layered excavations of
Middle English, the old literally melts into the new, dwelling in the space
between languages, which for her is not an abstraction but an embodying/
enveloping ground. Moving from but burrowing into ESL/PSL (English/
poetry as a second language), Bergvall's bravura performances move toward
a fluid third term, not bilingual but n-lingual, as in the final section of "Crop,"
woven with permutations of an English phrase in Norwegian and French.

99. Richard Caddel, "For the Fallen," *Angel August* 16 (January 1999): <poetrymagazines.org.uk
/magazine/record9ed3.html?id=13867>; *Y Gododin: A Poem on the Battle of Cattraeth* (1852 edition):
<gutenberg.org/files/9842/9842-h/9842-h.htm>

100. <poetrymagazines.org.uk/magazine/record82c5.html?id=13917>. In Wild Honey Press's chapbook
of the complete series (Dublin, 2000), which is presented as an elegy for his son, Caddel offers various
approaches to *Y Gododin*.

Some never had a body to call their own before it was taken away
som aldri hadde en kropp de kunne kalle sin egen før den ble
    revet bort
ceux dont le corps d'emblée leur est arraché

Some never had a chance to feel a body as their own before it was
    taken away
som aldri fikk oppleve en kropp som sin egen før den ble revet bort
ceux dont le corps d'emblée leur est arraché

Some never had a chance to know their body before it was
    taken away
som aldri fikk kjenne sin kropp før den ble revet bort
ceux dont le corps méconnu d'être arraché

Some were never free to speak their body before it was taken up
    and taken away
som var aldri frie til å si sin kropp før den ble løftet opp og
    revet bort
ceux dont le corps est arraché

Some tried their body on to pleasure in it before it was taken up
    beaten violated taken away
som tok sin kropp på for å nyte den før den ble løftet opp slått
    krenket revet bort
sont ceux au corps choppé violé arraché[101]

Bergvall's is an echopoetics of the "nomadic" and "disfluency," where
blockages, stuttering, error, code-switching, and skips are not fragments of
a lost whole but stitches that make up a fabric. In *Meddle English* the frogs
in our throats become catnip. This work continues with *Drift* (Nightboat,
2014) with its extensions, samplings, warpings, and deformations of the
Old English of "The Seafarer," connecting the work of sound writing to
migrancy and to the fate of refugees.

101. "Caroline Bergvall, "Crop" in "Cropper," *Meddle English* (New York: Nightboat, 2011), pp. 147–48.
There is a recording of Bergvall reading this passage on her PennSound page.

8. Wee Da Sign

Benny Lava is a YouTube video from 2007 that has clocked seven million views.[102] Like Caesar's doubletalk, it is an example of a wildly popular work, not identified with poetry, that nonetheless has striking similarities to the mostly unpopular, if not to say deeply obscure, homophonic transcreations of the Zukofskys, Melnick, Bergvall, and others.

Benny Lava is based on a music video for the Tamil song "Kalluri Vaanil" from the 2000 Indian Tamil movie *Pennin Manathai Thottu*, with homophonic subtitles added by Mike Sutton (Buffalax). "The name Benny Lava comes from Sutton's homophonic translation of the Tamil lead line 'Kalluri vaanil kaayndha nilaavo?' as 'My loony bun is fine, Benny Lava!'"[103]

This is the beginning of the full text of homophonic subtitles, which is provided, in full, on the YouTube page:

My loony bun is fine Benny Lava!
Minor bun engine made Benny Lava!
Anybody need this sign? Benny Lava!
You need a bun to bite Benny Lava!
Have you been high today?
I see the nuns are gay!

This comic video is considered an example of a genre called Soramimi (from the Japanese 空耳, mishearing, literally "air ear") or *soramimi kashi* (空耳歌詞, mishearing lyrics). The homophonic process foments a proliferation of puns, double entendres, and off references and brings to mind Sid Caesar's comment that one of the sources of his verbal acrobatics, from when he worked in the Borscht Belt, was the jokes he and his friends made with misunderstandings between Yiddish and English. Kenneth Goldsmith's 2002 "Head Citations"—his comic compilation of misheard song lyrics—come to mind as another work based on mishearing, or let's just say where mishearing becomes rehearings becomes new hearings.[104]

There are other examples of popular homophonic videos.

Skwerl ("How English sounds to non-English speakers") is a 2011 short

102. "Benny Lava": <youtu.be/sdyC1BrQd6g>

103. "Pennin Manathai Thottu," *Wikipedia* <en.wikipedia.org/wiki/Pennin_Manathai_Thottu>

104. Kenneth Goldsmith, "Head Citations": <writing.upenn.edu/epc/authors/goldsmith/works/head _citations.html>

video by Karl Eccleston and Brian Fairbairn in which the dialogue is done in English doublespeak.[105]

There is a related genre, where singers make up lyrics to pop songs without knowing the actual words or language.[106] In French, this is called *chanter en yaourt* and *yaourter*. The best-known example of this is Italian superstar Adriano Celentano's 1972 comic and delightfully pulsing song (and later TV clip), "Prisencolinensinainciusol," which is in English doublespeak. When you first hear it, it sounds like an American post-Elvis, pop song, punctuated by "all right!" The rollicking video has Celentano (born in 1938) as swinging, hip professor, giving a lesson, perhaps on global asymmetries to a class of schoolgirls seated as desks (the one prop is a globe).[107] Gramsci's "Some Aspects of the Southern Question" this is not. But it does express the global desire to be an American pop icon and Celentano plays the role, and has the sound down, better than most American pop stars.

YouTube user "orangebroomhead" has done a transcription of the song as if it were in English:

You're the call may the say one
Prisencolinensinainciusol ol all right

Wee da sign nah shoes now da whole baby scene
then a whole rate maybe give de collar bus die
Brrrr, chance in my head begin the coal-hold
Baby just teh-yeh bush joe hoe[108]

LyricWiki offers a quite different transcription, which makes no attempt to hear it as English. Indeed, it reads something like sound poetry or *zaum*:

In de col men seivuan
prisencolinensinainciusol all right

105. Brian and Karl, *Skwerl*: <brianandkarl.com/SKWERL>. The shooting script is at <brianandkarl .tumblr.com/post/110560981278/we-get-a-lot-of-emails-asking-for-the-skwerl>.

106. Caesar, Reiner, and Morris do something like this in 1956 and 1957 with their recurring rock band parody group "The Haircuts," making up "nonsense" lyrics, as Caesar calls them in *Where Have I Been?*, p. 160.

107. Adriano Celentano, "Prisencolinensinainciuso": <youtu.be/-VsmF9m_Nt8>

108. "Prisencolinensinainciusol (Lyrics) (English translation)": <youtu.be/6bc7BuLi1kw>. Line breaks follow the LyricWiki transcription.

Uis de seim cius nau op de seim
Ol uait men in de colobos dai
Trrr—ciak is e maind beghin de col
Bebi stei ye push yo oh[109]

Benny Lava is either funny or offensive, maybe both. Does it appropriate and caricature, mocking the original language in a proud display of ignorance and condescension, is it a new kind of ethnically demeaning humor? Or does it use a homophonic procedure to create a virtual space of lingua franca, a non-national overlay of languages? In other words, who is the joke on? Stalling's sinophonic translations are meant, he says, to counter the stereotyping of Chinese accents in English, though for Chinese speakers he has created a kind of whiteface. Caesar's good humor manages to make his doubletalking *laughing with* not *at*, except, and this exception is the rule, with Nazi doubletalk, where there is, still, plenty of good humor, an (un)leavening humor. But as a Jewish commercial entertainer, Caesar's approach has to lead to ingratiation, bathos, and charm: the clown telling jokes. And that's a lead hard to turn into gold.

Zukofsky remains rebarbative, inaccessible, and decidedly not ingratiating: difficulty that stays difficult. In this light, Zukofsky's poetry is a kind of doubletalk—an act on, as well in, English, kissing cousin to the poetry of Paul Celan (1920–1970).

For Caesar, homophonic translation begins in bad faith and ends in the communal song of laughter. For Zukofsky, the sincerity and objectification of homophonic translation offers a way to reveal the truth in the materials of language, to make a deeper connection or fraternity between translated and translation. That is, not to begin with an original and then make a faithful copy, which is always a betrayal; but rather, to begin with an original and then make a cousin or clone or, indeed, *an* 'other' original. Homophonic translation becomes a way to counter the bad faith inherent in conventional (*heterophonic*/ hegemonic), translation; that is to say, the replacement of one meaning complex with another, a replacement that often entails erasing the mark or stigmata of translation in an attempt to make the translation feel seamless or fluent.

In *Meddle English*, Bergvall puts it this way:

109. "Adriano Celentano: Prisencolinensinainciusol Lyrics," LyricWiki: <lyrics.wikia.com/wiki/Adriano _Celentano:Prisencolinensinainciusol>. Mark Liberman's Language Log alerted me to this song: <languagelog.ldc.upenn.edu/nll/?p=1838>.

I repeat what many have said, that poetic or art language must not implicitly be held to account of identities and national language, the seductions of literary history, or the frequently fetishistic methodologies of art movements, but rather seek, far and close, the indicators and practices of language in flux, of thought in making: pleasured language, pressured language, language in heated use, harangued language, forms of language revolutionized by action, polemical language structures that propose an intense deliberate reappraisal of the given world and its given forms.[110]

Zukofsky and Melnick are not likely to offend classical Greeks or Latins or Rome-anians (as Caesar puns in a 1964 sketch). But this is perhaps what separates unpopular poetry with mass-market comedy and commercial entertainment.

The dialectal power relation in translation, who's on top or what's dominant, source or target, cannot be abolished by poetic fiat. The promise of the homophonic sublime is always imaginary, or, perhaps to say, a fantasy of the imaginary.

[2016–2019: First presented on November 17, 2016, at École Normale Supérieure, Paris, as the keynote for "Sound / Writing: On Homophonic Translation," an international trilingual colloquium, organized by Vincent Broqua and Dirk Weissmann. An audio-visual supplement (ppt), including easy links to some of the works discussed, can be downloaded at <writing.upenn.edu/ezurl/10/>. *Sound / Writing: On Homophonic Translation*, ed. Vincent Broqua and Dirk Weissmann (Paris: Éditions des archives contemporaines, 2019)]

110. Caroline Bergvall, "the meddle," from *Meddle English*, p. 17. Excerpt in *Sybil* (May 30, 2011) <sibila .com.br/english/caroline-bergvall/4785>.

INDEX OF NAMES

INDEX OF MOTIFS

democracy, 3, 248, 255, 286
despair, 5, 12, 32, 152, 193
dialect, 21, 35, 49, 138, 362–63, 365–66, 370, 372–74
dialectical, 13, 129, 131–32, 140–42, 167, 169, 371
diaspora, 5, 17, 42, 45, 195, 249–51, 298, 335, 364–65, 384
difficulty, 6, 12, 33, 80, 90, 93, 177, 239–40, 269–70, 296, 334, 396
digression, 63–65, 292, 331
disability, 160, 192–94, 229, 390–91
discourse, 33, 41, 93, 110, 124–26, 129, 139, 191–94, 229, 315, 330–31, 361
dyspraxia, 21–22, 81, 133, 152, 234

echopoetics, 41–42, 133, 227, 255–61, 265–70, 276–78, 336–37, 393
ecstasy, 12, 33, 92, 360
education, 15, 41, 49–50, 124, 141, 164–65, 167–68, 171–72, 227–28, 239–40, 269–70, 304–5, 322
emotion, 21–22, 36, 39, 47, 126–30, 152, 161, 168, 170. *See also* affect
epic, 21, 149, 368. *See also* lyric
erasure, 50, 304, 317–19, 330–31, 333, 344–46, 378, 396
Esperanto, 356, 366–67, 372, 379n76
ethnicity, 105–6, 139n35, 157, 160, 167, 194–95, 253, 261, 297, 303, 305, 366–68, 374–75, 389, 396. *See also* race
exaggeration, 33, 55, 61, 71, 133, 263–64, 315–16, 360
experiment, 16, 39, 63–64, 70, 122, 143, 260, 269, 272, 288n5, 315
expository writing, 17, 120, 122, 125–26, 146

falsity, 18, 125–27, 149, 158, 205, 241–42, 263, 315–16, 328, 333. *See also* lies; truth
fascism, 93, 246–49, 310–11, 313, 318, 322, 369–72
fear, 111, 124, 126, 157–58, 213, 255, 299
feminism, 134–40, 159–60, 163–64, 167–68, 177, 180, 194–95, 212, 229, 240–41, 247–48, 276, 279, 287–88, 335n12, 381–82
figuration, 21, 60, 105, 190, 230, 232, 245, 258, 278

fragmentation, 16, 23, 60, 152, 209, 214, 234, 261, 304, 315, 330–32, 375, 393
freedom, 25–27, 34–35, 42, 46, 81, 90–91, 144, 155–56, 217–18, 234, 299–301, 311, 380

gender, 128, 167–68, 170–71, 177, 179–80, 240, 289, 335n12
God, 26–27, 157–58, 163–64, 171, 193, 224–25, 253, 274, 383–84
grief, 12, 151, 256

happiness, 13–14, 35, 46, 76, 92, 217, 277, 311
hatred, 22, 80, 106, 157, 202, 239, 255, 279, 382, 387
hegemony, 21, 34, 82, 167, 335
Holocaust, 13, 63, 158, 243, 296–97, 313, 365–66, 373–75
humor, 44–45, 61, 63, 89–90, 130, 233–34, 349–50. *See also* comedy; jokes
hypotaxis, 94, 124–25

identity, 11, 17, 25–26, 39, 54, 56–61, 87, 93, 107, 136–39, 156–57, 160–61, 167–68, 170–71, 191, 217–18, 303, 334–35
idiolect, 35, 49, 336–37, 336n15
ideology, 16, 32, 89, 105, 129, 131–36, 146, 184, 226, 261, 280–81, 304, 316–17, 379–80. *See also* Romantic ideology
imaginary, 27, 39, 46, 53, 105, 167–69, 179–83, 193, 216, 221, 236, 259–63, 270, 298, 333, 351, 397
improvisation, 64, 72–73, 97–98, 172, 196–97, 331–32, 335, 363, 373. *See also* performance
incommensurability, 8, 34, 46, 130–31, 177, 197, 264, 280, 332, 335
inconsistency, 28, 30, 233, 262
innovation, 38, 62, 68, 83, 99, 139, 168, 171, 191–96, 305, 310, 313, 334–35, 363
intellect, 47, 70, 73, 90, 153, 170, 179, 189, 299, 334, 355, 377
interpretation, 7–8, 16, 43, 67, 71, 133, 159, 165, 188, 202–3, 227–30, 237–38, 270, 273, 299–300, 337
interruption, 152, 181, 191, 207, 291, 327, 329
invention, 38–40, 49, 68–70, 82–83, 94, 136–37, 139–40, 157–58, 167, 171, 179,